TWICE THROUGH
THE LINES

TWICE THROUGH THE LINES

The Autobiography of
OTTO JOHN

TRANSLATED FROM THE GERMAN BY
Richard Barry

WITH AN INTRODUCTION BY
H. R. Trevor-Roper

*How narrow is the line which separates
an adventure from an ordeal and escape
from exile.* HAROLD NICOLSON

HARPER & ROW, PUBLISHERS
NEW YORK, EVANSTON, SAN FRANCISCO, LONDON

First published in Germany under the title *Zweimal kam ich heim* © 1969 by Econ Verlag Gmbh

FIRST U.S. EDITION

STANDARD BOOK NUMBER: 06-012199-8

LIBRARY OF CONGRESS CATALOG CARD NUMBER: 72-9127

Contents

List of Illustrations

DAIMON

Wie an dem Tag, der dich der Welt verliehen,
Die Sonne stand zum Grusse der Planeten,
Bist alsobald und fort und fort gediehen
Nach dem Gesetz, wonach du angetreten.
So musst du sein, dir kannst du nicht entfliehen,
So sagten schon Sibyllen, so Propheten;
Und keine Zeit und keine Macht zerstückelt
Geprägte Form, die lebend sich entwickelt.

Johann Wolfgang von Goethe, *Urworte Orphisch*

As, on the day when you first saw the world,
The sun stood aloft holding court to the planets,
So from birth you grew and went on growing
In accordance with the law under which you set forth.
Thus you must be; you cannot flee from yourself,
As sibyls and prophets have long ago said.
No flight of time, no power can break
The minted mould which forms as life proceeds.

Introduction

DR OTTO JOHN'S book is a moving record. In form, it is his memoirs, the record of a life of conspiracy, danger, frustration and failure. In substance it is his *Apologia pro Vita sua*: the apologia of a German liberal who not only hated Nazism but was resolved to act effectively against it. His resolution sprang not out of expediency, nor out of objection to this or that policy, but out of conviction: both as a liberal and as a lawyer, he believed that there was no political salvation outside the *Rechtsstaat*, the state that is bound by law. In this conviction he refused to serve Hitler. He gave up an early plan to emigrate abroad, to South America. He would not consider 'internal emigration'. He was determined to act. So, during the war, he conspired against the rule of Hitler, and failed – as all the internal enemies of Hitler failed. After the war, he stood out against certain tendencies in the rule of Dr Adenauer, and failed again. His failure has cost him dear. He has seen his fellow-conspirators against Hitler, including his brother, sent one by one to the gallows or the firing-squad. He has been deprived of his position in the Federal Republic of Germany. He has been in prison or internment in Portugal, in England, in Russia, in Germany. He has broadcast to Hitler's Germany from the enemy capital of London and, more reluctantly, to Adenauer's Germany from the hostile capital of East Berlin. Inevitably, he has been widely misrepresented, even slandered. It is fair that he should now represent himself.

I first heard the name of Otto John in 1944. He was then in Madrid, and gave information to the British Intelligence Service, with which he had been in touch since 1942, of the plots being prepared against Hitler. In July 1944 he returned to Germany and was in Berlin, and in the War Office building in the Bendlerstrasse, on the crucial 20 July when Count Claus Schenck von Stauffenberg, convinced that he had killed Hitler at Rastenburg, sought, with his friends, to seize power in the state. Four days later, while Himmler's Gestapo were rounding up the survivors of that abortive conspiracy,

Dr John (whose position as an official of the German airline Lufthansa gave him a useful mobility) escaped back to Madrid, and thence, for greater security, to Lisbon. Even in Lisbon he was not safe. The long arm of Himmler reached out even there, and a local officer of the *Abwehr*, or German Secret Service, was sent to Berlin, dead, in a trunk. Dr John may well have owed his life to his incarceration by the Portuguese authorities in the uncomfortable Aljube prison. Later he was conveyed to Britain. There, naturally enough, he hoped to be able to tell the Allies of that 'other Germany' which, by then, was more than ever distracted and impotent. He was employed, naturally enough, in less independent work. He advised the B.B.C. on its broadcast programmes for the German troops and interviewed high-ranking German prisoners to determine the order of their release. Later he acted as legal assistant and interpreter in the prosecution of Field Marshal von Manstein at Hamburg. Equally naturally, these activities did not commend him to those whose ideas about Nazism were more tolerant than his, and of whom Dr Adenauer, as Chancellor of the Federal Republic, would be far more tolerant than he.

Fortunately, he also had friends from the days of resistance, and through them, he ultimately achieved office in Germany. In 1950 the post of *Bundesamt für Verfassungsschütz*, 'Federal Office for the protection of the constitution', was created. It was designed to secure the new government against internal enemies, and particularly against communists and neo-Nazis. The old opponents of Nazism were naturally anxious to ensure that this important post should not fall into sinister hands, and who, in their eyes, could be more appropriate, as its first head, than one of the few survivors of the active opposition to Hitler who was also a lawyer and a convinced devotee of the rule of law? Dr Adenauer did not relish the appointment of Dr John as head of the *BfV*, but he had to accept it. It was even less relished by the survivors of the old Nazis and pro-Nazis. It was particularly distasteful to the most famous and most successful of such survivors. This was General Reinhard Gehlen, who was now seeking, with American support, to become the head of a new German secret service, and who would not scruple to incorporate into it his old associates in the Nazi Party and old members of the S.S.

Gehlen disliked John on several counts. The general disliked the civilian, the Nazi the anti-Nazi; there was also the inevitable dislike of a competitor. Moreover, all these general dislikes were inflamed by a particular incident: for John had advised the prosecution in the damaging trial of Gehlen's hero, Field Marshal von Manstein. In the three-year duel which followed John's appointment, Gehlen had the advantage, for the Chancellor clearly preferred him to his rival. But the completeness of Gehlen's victory was ensured by an extraordinary episode which no one could have forecast: an episode which forms the second part of this book, the second 'crossing of the lines'.

In July 1954 Dr John went to Berlin to take part in the celebration of the tenth anniversary of the plot against Hitler. After the celebration, he left his hotel in West Berlin and did not return. The Bonn government was alarmed: both defections and kidnappings had happened lately in that still unwalled city. The disappearance of an important Federal official, the head of its internal secret service, was therefore very sinister. Only one official of that government could derive any satisfaction from it. That happy officer was General Gehlen. Asked for his opinion about it, Gehlen spoke clearly. 'Once a traitor, always a traitor,' he replied. To him, opposition to Hitler was still treason, although, as Dr John drily retorts, 'I had never been pledged to Hitler, either ideologically or by personal oath – as he had been.' A few days later Gehlen's happiness was increased when John held a press conference in East Berlin at which he made statements satisfactory to the Russians. That seemed to settle the matter. From that moment, John was written off as a defector, and this second defection was held to prove a constitutional instability of character which discredited, in retrospect, even his earlier anti-Nazi record. Eighteen months later, when he suddenly reappeared in the Federal Republic, he was arrested, tried and sentenced, without right of appeal, to four years' hard labour. The reasons given for this verdict are not convincing in law or in logic; but to Dr John there was a certain ironical consistency in his fate: 'each time I had succeeded in escaping to the freedom of the West, I had ended in prison'.

For Dr John had not, in fact, 'defected' to the East. In this book he gives the full story of his kidnapping in Berlin, his abduction to Russia, the pressure put upon him, the questions asked, and of his own policy of 'playing along' with the Russians in order ultimately to escape, as he did. I do not doubt that his account is true. Whether his policy was the best in the circumstances may be questioned, but it would be presumptuous in those who have never faced such problems to pronounce the answers to them. The question on which we may legitimately speculate concerns the motives of the Russian Secret Service in abducting him.

Possibly, as Dr John suggests, the Russians were eager to find a 'cover' for their own mass arrest of Gehlen's agents in East Germany. Having kidnapped the head of the *BfV*, they could let it be believed that it was he who had revealed the identity of these agents, and thus divert attention from their real informant. This was Heinz Felfe, a former S.S. officer whom, in 1950, they had inserted into Gehlen's organisation, and who, for the next ten years, systematically betrayed Federal secrets to the Russians. Thus John's abduction not only confirmed Gehlen's authority with Adenauer, it also ensured that Gehlen's intelligence service continued to be penetrated by the Russians. But though this may well have been one reason for the abduction, there were probably others too, and they may well have lain outside the Federal Republic. It seems certain that, because of his previous work in Britain, the Russians (like some Germans) regarded John as a British agent, and it may be that it was for obscurer and more indirect purposes that they now went to such lengths. On this subject Dr John himself offers some interesting speculations, which I shall not here anticipate. They may well be true.

Dr John served his full legal term in prison in West Germany, all of it in solitary confinement. He has never been rehabilitated there. He has written this book in order to rehabilitate himself in the eyes of the world. It should certainly do so. But it also does more than this. Not only is it an important historical record, both of anti-Nazi conspiracy and of post-war German affairs: it also, like any autobiography, reveals the personality of the author. That personality has aroused much speculation in the past: here it emerges clearly. Dr John reveals himself as a liberal, honourable man, a good European, whose misfortune it has been to live in a disjointed time, and whose virtue it is that, though often discouraged, he has never flinched from the impossible duty of setting them right.

The discouragement is clear enough. Dr John does not write for Germans, at least of his own generation. He is indeed impatient of that generation. He despises the docility, the vacillation, the blind stupidity of those classes who, in Germany, held power – power to rule and make war, power (if they would use it) to destroy Hitler, power to create a new Germany after the war. He is particularly impatient of the war-time generals who were such bold conspirators in talk, so pusillanimous in action. He has little respect for the German people or their comfortable myths. He does not allow that it was the demand for 'unconditional surrender' that prolonged the war: the war, he insists, was prolonged by the faults, not the virtues of the Germans, by their stupidity and lack of civil courage, not their patriotic solidarity. He does not agree that the war crimes of the Nazi leaders should have been tried by German courts: the German people, he believes, had forfeited the right to sit in judgment on those criminals whom they had elected into power over them and whom, thereafter, they had not had the courage to overthrow. And anyway, he might add, after his own experience, what justice could have been expected from German courts in 1945, or even in the Adenauer era? But, if there are traces of bitterness in this book, they are easily excused. They are excused by the authority which Dr John, by his own civil courage, is entitled to claim. His is the voice of a European who refused to minister to his own comfort by despairing of Europe.

H. R. Trevor-Roper

TWICE THROUGH
THE LINES

1

Political Awakening

My whole life has been coloured by the events leading from the outbreak of the First World War to the German catastrophe of 1945. When the First World War began I was aged five and a half. Even in my little home town, Treysa in Hesse, there was great patriotic fervour, and, like all other youngsters, I was fired with enthusiasm for our soldiers and the war. My father, a senior civil servant, was a captain in the Reserve; early in the war he was awarded the Iron Cross and his picture appeared in the illustrated paper *Die Woche*. I was immensely proud, and equally proud of the victories of our armies. My warlike ardour vanished, however, when my uncle, who was a chemist by profession and was working with the Red Cross at the railway station of our little town, took me along with him one day to a hospital train. I did not follow him closely enough through the train and was 'lost'. Searching for my uncle, I wandered through the train alone. At first I saw only the slightly wounded; they laughed gaily at my Bavarian leather shorts. Then, however, I reached the compartments of the severely wounded; the repellent penetrating smell of carbolic half-choked me; ashen faces stared at me; I was aghast at the blood-soaked bandages; I heard pitiful groanings. It was all most sinister and I could not leave that train quickly enough. On the last stretcher which I had to pass lay a soldier gazing at me with blazing eyes. For the first time I had been in contact with death.

My uncle was standing beside the train talking to a white-coated medical orderly. A badly wounded man, moaning softly, was carried off the train and taken away to be operated on in the local hospital. As we passed, Red Cross sisters were handing out refreshments through the train windows. At the end of the train was a goods wagon, in the open door of which sat a bearded German soldier with his rifle over his arm. Inside the wagon French soldiers in their blue tunics and red trousers, wearing dirty bandages, were crouching or lying on straw. They wailed and gesticulated, trying to get out on to the platform to fetch water from the pump – or so it seemed to me. But they were not allowed out. I was very sorry for them but at the same time sensed that sympathy was against the rules because these Frenchmen were our 'enemies'. Before the war we had always said 'Adieu', but children were forbidden to say that now.

So for the first time I found myself faced with a conflict between my true feelings or thoughts and the political forces, of which I had as yet no very concrete idea but which I nevertheless sensed had authority over me. It was a long time before I could rid myself of the impressions of that hospital train. I could no longer raise any enthusiasm for the war and I no longer wanted ever to be a soldier. The more I heard of the war, the more sinister it seemed to me. Outside our little town a young officer shot himself in his own garden because he did not want to go back to the front. I began to be afraid of being turned into a soldier; all my illusions about our 'heroic' soldiery vanished. But I did not dare say so out loud, for I knew that this fear was not compatible with the behaviour expected of me as a member of 'German youth'. I was relieved when the war ended and its impressions melted into the realm of the subconscious. They faded before new experiences born of the political upheavals in post-war Germany, revolution and inflation.

During these formative years I could not remain insulated from the political developments of the time. The repercussions of high-level politics on day-to-day matters exerted a more lasting influence on the formation of my views than did my education at school. While at school I, in common with the whole of German bourgeois society, was torn between revolution and counter-revolution. At High School we were brought up as strict German nationalists and were taught to despise the flag of the Republic, the 'black-red-mustard'. Almost without exception our masters had been wartime officers and they indoctrinated us into the 'stab-in-the-back' legend. I sensed the discrepancy between official public opinion and what I heard people saying. I did not yet realise, however, that the Weimar Republic had been a great illusion of the republican minority and was a bare-faced imposture in the eyes of the monarchically minded majority. In the room which I shared with my younger brother Hans was a life-size picture of the Kaiser and one of Hindenburg in uniform. For a long time Hindenburg, the national hero, was my idol; like the mass of the people I regarded his election to the Presidency in 1925 as a great national event.

I began to learn to think for myself when my father was transferred to Wiesbaden in 1922. For me our move from the little country town in Hesse to this sophisticated international spa resembled the transplantation of a seedling from the open air into a hothouse. Wiesbaden was occupied by the French Army, primarily Moroccans and other coloured troops. Outside the Rhineland the occupation was referred to as 'The Black Stain on the Rhine'. Like everyone else I thought it the self-evident duty of any patriot to register permanent indignation on the subject. I was surprised to find, therefore, on our arrival in Wiesbaden that the sight of the 'Black Stain' aroused no feelings of hatred in me whatsoever. The elegant French women fascinated me and secretly I found them exciting. I had no difficulty in adapting myself to the presence of French soldiers, whether white or coloured. Only once was this peaceful coexistence disturbed – during the so-called 'passive resistance' to the French occupation of the Ruhr early in 1923.

At this time the German government was in default on its reparations deliveries and, as surety, France occupied the Ruhr area. In answer the Reich government called for 'passive resistance'. The railways and post office went on strike, owners and workers in the Ruhr stopped production of coal, iron and steel. The result was complete ruination of the German economy and bankruptcy for the German Reich – early in 1923 one American dollar cost 4,200,000,000 marks in Germany! Parallel with this economic collapse came political chaos, exploited by the Rhineland 'separatists' in an attempt to set up, with French support, a 'Rhineland republic' independent of the rest of Germany. The separatist leader was Dr Dorten, a Wiesbaden lawyer; his Minister of Culture designate, a schoolteacher named Dr Krehmer, lived opposite us. Dr Konrad Adenauer, the Burgomaster of Cologne, played a not insignificant role in all this.

I was a witness of the separatist rising in the streets of Wiesbaden. It was suppressed by the hoses of the Fire Brigade and in scuffles during which the loyal population gave vent to their fury against the separatists. Dr Dorten was thrown down a staircase and Dr Krehmer spat upon in the street by his ex-pupils. The separatist rising was over. Its effect on me, as on many other schoolboys, particularly my friend Fritz Göring, a nephew of the future Reich Marshal Hermann Göring, was to produce an upsurge of patriotic sentiment, which our schoolmasters took care to encourage. We felt the urge to do something patriotic. Some of my elder sister's friends were members of the 'German National Youth League' and had been expelled from the occupied area by the French Military Government for passive resistance activities. It occurred to me that I might take money and letters from their relatives to them in their hide-out in Frankfurt am Main.

I set forth on my bicycle – it would have been most unpatriotic to use the railway which was being run by the French. On the way I was stopped at a level crossing by a Moroccan sentry. I showed ill humour – that was, after all, active resistance against the French Military Government. With fixed bayonet the Moroccan drove me into a temporary guard-room near by and talked to the others in a language I could not understand. In view of the money and letters which I was carrying in a bag underneath my shirt I was afraid that I might be searched. I was even more afraid of a pock-marked Moroccan who, with an impudent leer, tried to make advances to me – a number of fair-haired boys had already been raped by Moroccans. It was a highly uncomfortable situation but eventually a French sergeant appeared. He accepted my statement that I was on a bicycling tour, looked at the sandwiches in my rucksack and let me ride on.

Leaving the main road, I took to the lanes in the direction of Frankfurt until stopped by a farmer who told me that there was a forbidden zone between the next village and the frontier; the French had banned all bicycling to ensure that no one slipped through their patrols; if they caught me on a bicycle I would be put inside. So I left my bicycle in the village and plodded on towards Frankfurt on foot. It was hot and I was thirsty; for the first time, for purely personal reasons, I cursed the Treaty of Versailles and the French occupation régime which had the impertinence to curtail our rights and stop me riding my bicycle. After an exhausting tramp across the fields I slunk into Frankfurt through the allotment gardens and fulfilled my patriotic mission. I was thanked and congratulated by the young passive resistance heroes-in-exile and was proud to be accepted as a sworn member of this secret youthful resistance group. Ten years later one of them named Theo Habicht was to become notorious for subversive Nazi activity in Austria and the murder of the Austrian Chancellor, Engelbert Dollfuss.

2
Meeting of Minds

WHY could I not become a Nazi? How did it happen that I joined the anti-Hitler conspiracy? I was not politically minded. I was certainly no born conspirator. I could well have had a quite different career. After graduating from college I had first been apprenticed to a chemical and pharmaceutical firm in Mainz, but the prospect of earning a great deal of money or even of becoming managing director of a big chemical firm held no attractions for me. I thought of studying medicine but gave that up because I did not think I had the ability to diagnose with absolute certainty. If psychology had been a field of its own at the time, I would have plunged into that, for I have always been fascinated by human problems which can now be dealt with by the resources and methods of modern psychology. So I studied law without any very definite ideas on a career.

Hitler came to power as my last term at Frankfurt University was ending, and as a result my life assumed a completely new pattern. I anticipated from Hitler's tyranny no more and no less than what he gave us. Such perspicacity required no great political acumen, merely sober consideration of the behaviour of Hitler and his S.A. [Sturmabteilung – Storm Troopers] from the moment of their appearance. It was always incomprehensible to me how men, who in other respects were perfectly sensible, could fall victim to belief in Hitler as the political saviour. From the outset this 'Germany awake!' movement was repugnant to me and totally lacking in credibility. I found the Communist gospel equally implausible. Ever since I became capable of independent thought I have been, and still am, basically a liberal but an adherent of no particular political party. While still a student the German national heroes lost their attraction for me, and Albert Schweitzer became my model.

Nevertheless, I had opportunities of a career in the Nazi state. Early in April 1933 my school-friend Fritz Göring offered me a post on the staff of his uncle Hermann, who had already become the heir-apparent to Hitler in the German Reich. But I was not even tempted. Fritz Göring was a decent fellow and remained so, even though he had every opportunity to follow in his uncle's footsteps. After the war his mother said to a friend, mother-in-law to my sister Erika: 'We were not surprised that Otto and Hans John were in the 20 July plot. We knew their views. But we would never have denounced them to the Gestapo – they were such nice boys.'

And there were nice young people. There were quite a few faithful Nazis who were perfectly decent human beings and remained so. For them, in some cases soon and in some later, came a fearful eye-opening when they realised how Hitler had misused his position as Reich Chancellor and how, by political intrigue, riding roughshod over the constitution, inhuman outrage and common crime, he had made himself dictator of the German people until he finally let loose a war for world conquest. 'Let Hitler come to power and he will be the first to ruin himself.' These were the words of innumerable democratic opponents of Hitler before the senile Field Marshal von Hindenburg had appointed him Reich Chancellor. But it took twelve years for Hitler to ruin himself, and he plunged millions upon millions of men into catastrophe in the process.

This catastrophe was not an act of God. It was brought about by men, German men seduced by Hitler. Ever since 1933 I was certain that this 'Führer' would plunge us and all Europe into war. Politically, economically and even intellectually, in so far as intellectual life was not stifled altogether, the nation voluntarily submitted itself to regimentation or *Gleichschaltung* and geared its efforts with enthusiasm to increasing the war potential; the rearmament motto was 'Guns before butter'. But this militarism was not restricted to the expansion and re-equipment of the military forces. Germany's entire life was organised and regimented on military lines. As law graduates the President of our provincial court urged us with promises of specially favourable prospects for promotion, to join the Wehrmacht and become officers. A member of the Frankfurt Bench, Dr Schäfer, was in charge of our political education. He took every opportunity to emphasise the imminence of war and tried to explain to us that in an emergency every house and every lamp-post would have some military value.

The State was thus organised to sweep up everybody into the service of 'Führer and People'. It was not possible to stand aside and watch. One had to decide whether to be for or against. The upper and lower middle classes and the mass of the people, whether of right- or left-wing tendencies, rallied to Hitler because they were profiting from what Goebbels was already calling the 'German economic miracle', in other words the expansion of the German economy resulting from a large-scale rearmament programme. I neither could nor would have anything to do with it. Why? It was all repugnant to me – the figure of the Führer with his deceptive ideology and demagogic speeches, the false jargon of the crowd of lower-level leaders, the boorish behaviour of the brown-shirts, the parades of semi-militarised organisations, the people's complacency in face of official crime and acts of violence, the cowardly submission of all those who feared for their business or their career.

My indignation at all this grew daily. It was incompatible with everything I thought or felt. For me it literally removed all pleasure from life. In addition the profession I had studied was turned into a farce. As lawyers we were raised to the status of 'guardians of the law'. But the law was laid down by the Nazi ideology or rather by Hitler himself; after his great reckoning with the S.A. on 30 June 1934 with all its associated murders including that of Röhm, the S.A. Chief of Staff, he had proclaimed himself the 'Supreme Judge of the German People'. When he took over the powers of Reich President together with supreme command of the Reichswehr shortly after the death of Hindenburg and ordered officers and men to take an oath to him personally, he had become the unbridled dictator of Germany. From now on – as we were told – 'his will was a command'. He alone could decide on peace or war – and he wanted war, which he let loose with the attack on Poland.

One could hardly be expected to realise all this at the time, people will say. I do not regard myself as particularly clever but the fact remains that I realised it. Millions of others could have realised it too, had they read *Mein Kampf* and had they not been blinded by Hitler's 'successes'. I had no wish to fight for Hitler and so I wanted to get out of Germany, but I had neither the money nor the contacts to enable me to set myself up abroad. I happened to meet a friend from my early school-days in Treysa, Horst von Baumbach; he was working as a Lufthansa pilot and this gave me the idea of applying for a Lufthansa job and so getting abroad to South America or China, as far away from Germany as possible. In the spring of 1936 I started as an unpaid worker at the old Frankfurt airport of Rebstock. I preferred to hump luggage rather than kow-tow to the Nazis.

Lufthansa, in co-operation with Air France, was at the time in the process of establishing the first intercontinental airmail service from Frankfurt to South America. Once a week I was on night duty preparing the South American mail bags. When Carl August Freiherr von Gablenz, the head of Lufthansa, left from Frankfurt on an inspection trip to South America he talked to me about my plans for a career and asked why I did not wish to take my law finals. I felt that he was a man to whom I could speak frankly and openly and so I said that the law no longer ruled in Germany and working as a 'guardian of the law' was therefore meaningless; for this reason I wished to get abroad.

Gablenz asked about my language capabilities. During my studies I had learnt English, French and Spanish, intending possibly to apply for a post with the Foreign Ministry after my law examination. I would not, however, consider any official position under Hitler, and I told Gablenz so. A few weeks later he passed me word that he would consider me for a post of Lufthansa representative abroad but only on condition that I passed my law finals.

Grudgingly I completed my final period of legal training with the Frankfurt Provincial Court of Appeal and at the same time worked as expert assistant on aeronautical law with Professor Adalbert von Unruh at Frankfurt University. My only acquaintance at the University was a Spaniard, Angel Ferrari-Nunez, now Professor of Medieval History in Spain. Apart from this I lived a lonely life. It was clear to me that, in view of my attitude to the Nazi state, my rights were no greater than those of a helot in Sparta. I was merely a distant onlooker of events in Germany, a position which I found all the more tolerable since I thought that it was only a question of time before I could turn my back on the country and go overseas for Lufthansa.

What else could I have done? Resist? I felt no urge to provide a lone heroic example and become a political martyr. In any case the political effect would have been nil. There was no resistance movement. Most of the former leading anti-Nazi politicians had either fled abroad, were incarcerated in concentration camps or had otherwise been rendered 'harmless' by the Gestapo. Individual groups of uncompromising opponents drawn from the most diverse political backgrounds still existed, but their resistance activity was in effect confined to secret discussions.

There were certain acts of open and heroic resistance such as the distribution of secret leaflets and acts of sabotage, but the resulting casualties bore no relation to results achieved. The only effective form of resistance was the spiritual, led primarily by the churches. Organisation of a resistance movement among the people was impossible. With the murder of Röhm, Hitler's one-time crony and rival, S.A. atrocities had been stopped; but since then the people had been held in check by the sinister terror of the S.S. [Schutzstaffel – the Nazi elite], primarily the Gestapo and S.D. [Sicherheitsdienst – the S.S. Security Service]. Resistance even by the most irreconcilable opponents of the régime was inevitably reduced to a wait-and-see movement.

Even at this time I felt that the only possibility of liberating Germany from Hitler's dictatorship lay in total military defeat in the war which, I was convinced, Hitler would let loose in time. When that time would be was difficult to estimate, if only because it was impossible to foresee how long the Western Powers would continue with the criminally stupid policy of appeasement, of which Neville Chamberlain had become the symbol. After the reoccupation of the Rhineland by German troops in March 1936 Eden had said in the Commons: 'There is no reason to suppose that the present German action implies a threat of hostilities.' From that moment I was clear that the Western Powers would swallow much from Hitler before we could expect any intervention from them.

3

Peace Slips Away

ON 1 November 1937 I was summoned to the Lufthansa head office, having passed my law finals and concluded a period of training as flight controller at Rhine-Main airfield. I was to be introduced into headquarters administration in Berlin and then, as I was still longing to do, go overseas for Lufthansa. I arrived determined to learn all I could as quickly as I could and so fit myself for a Lufthansa post abroad enabling me to get as far and as quickly away from Germany as might be. In view of my previous legal experience I started in the legal department.

Head of the department was Klaus Bonhoeffer, then thirty-six years old, son of the well-known psychiatrist Karl Bonhoeffer; he was married to the daughter of Hans Delbrück, the historian, and through her related to the family of the famous theologian Adolf von Harnack. The Bonhoeffer, Delbrück and Harnack families were typical of the best traditions of the educated German bourgeoisie. They suffered severely as a result of their resistance to Hitler. Through Klaus Bonhoeffer I, and later my brother Hans, were introduced into the anti-Hitler conspiracy. His first question to me was whether I was a member of the Nazi Party. I replied 'No', adding that I had no intention of joining this 'curious association'. He wished to know the colour of my political thinking from the outset and I felt that he should.

Klaus Bonhoeffer was a sturdy thick-set figure, a passionate opponent of the régime. With his thick black hair, brown eyes and dark skin he seemed to me the very prototype of his Swabian forebears, whose sense of democracy and dogged self-will he had inherited. He was extremely versatile and a good musician. He had studied international law in Geneva, had then been apprenticed to an Amsterdam bank and had given up his practice as an international lawyer in Berlin because after the murders of 30 June 1934 he had realised that there was no future for a freelance 'guardian of the law'.

Every day there was some reason to talk politics and I noticed that Klaus Bonhoeffer was invariably well informed particularly on developments happening in backstage Berlin politics. One day, for instance, he arrived with the news that Schacht was to resign owing to a clash with Hitler. That meant complete economic ruin and the end of the régime, he thought, since Schacht was 'indispensable'. To expect that Hitler would fall as the result of some economic collapse, however, was mere wishful thinking. 'We must put an end to the fellow,' I said.

Klaus Bonhoeffer leapt from his chair, pointed in consternation at the telephone and whispered: 'If I am to be hauled in by the Gestapo, then I would at least like first to have done something worth losing one's head for! Any washerwoman can gabble away but there's more than that to be done.' 'What?' I asked. 'We'll talk about that some other time – best during a walk in the Grunewald.' Having spoken my mind so clearly, Klaus Bonhoeffer invited me to his house where I made the acquaintance of his parents, brothers and sisters, and subsequently also of the Delbrück and Harnack families.

I was soon on terms of confidence and friendship with these families. My relationship with them and their friends opened a new world to me and remains one of my most treasured memories of the last two pre-war years in Berlin. Nevertheless, I was still trying to get out of Germany. Klaus Bonhoeffer knew it and did what he could to dissuade me, for he found that we complemented each other perfectly – to our mutual advantage. He held out great hopes of a career to me if only I would cling on in Berlin until the régime collapsed. But I did not want to.

My permanent nightmare was that I might have to fight for Hitler in the forthcoming war, and that this was no illusion was confirmed to me for the first time by Klaus Bonhoeffer himself. Hans von Dohnanyi, his brother-in-law, was at the time personal assistant (official title Senior Aide) to Dr Gürtner, the Reich Minister of Justice, and was on intimate terms with ex-Captain Wiedemann who had been Hitler's Company Commander during the First World War. In the summer of 1937 he told Dohnanyi that he had actually heard Hitler say to some of his cronies: 'Every generation needs its war and I shall take care that this generation gets its war.'

From his brother-in-law Dohnanyi Klaus Bonhoeffer got what he called his 'first-hand information'. Unknown to me Dohnanyi was even then plotting a *coup d'état* against Hitler. He had the complete confidence of the Minister of Justice and so knew of all the internal goings-on within the Reich government; he heard much of what went on in Hitler's immediate entourage both in the Berlin Chancellery and at Berchtesgaden, where he had met Hitler in person. In late November 1937 Klaus Bonhoeffer received from him information which subsequently led to serious errors; it gave Dohnanyi's friends the false impression that the Western Powers would intervene far earlier than they ultimately did in order to stop Hitler's policy of conquest in the East.

Klaus Bonhoeffer said that Hitler's reaction to his talk with Lord Halifax in Berchtesgaden had been an outburst of rage because he had 'broken his teeth on a rock'. If Hitler allowed himself to think that he could acquire *Lebensraum* in the East by force, the Western Powers, led by Britain, would intervene militarily. This false impression led Klaus Bonhoeffer to hint to me during our first walk in the Grunewald that there was a faction among the generals and senior officers ready to overthrow Hitler whenever he first attempted to engineer a war. I therefore had no reason to fear, he said, that I should have to fight for Hitler; I should remain in Berlin since I should be needed there.

At the time there was considerable private talk in various German opposition circles, both right-wing and left-wing, of Colonel-General von Fritsch, the Commander-in-Chief of the Army, as a resolute opponent of the régime. He was said merely to be waiting for the right psychological moment and a suitable opportunity to 'strike against the Nazis and lay the brown-shirted ghost'. I asked Klaus Bonhoeffer about this. He thought that there were other and better people than Fritsch but mentioned no names, although he knew that a military faction had formed round General Ludwig Beck, the Chief of Staff of the Army. He indicated that he would tell me more about this if I could make up my mind to stay in Berlin.

It was soon to become clear that Fritsch had never even thought of doing anything against Hitler's dictatorship. In fact, those who looked to him to do so and hoped that he would be the man to liberate Germany from the dictator were suffering from a fearful delusion. They believed that Hitler would be brought down by a conspiracy of generals because that was what they wished to believe. A year later I myself fell victim to this illusion, but I did not realise why until I was in a British internment camp when I read in English the history of British pre-war policy and then thought over my Berlin experiences afresh.

Lord Halifax's visit to Hitler in Berchtesgaden was a source of complete puzzlement to all those, both in Britain and Germany, who were striving to preserve the peace. As his statements in his book *The Fullness of Days* show, he never grasped what he had done. He was highly respected both in Britain and by the Germans for whom he personified many of the established virtues. In November 1937 he arrived in Berlin ostensibly at Göring's invitation to visit the hunting exhibition organised by the latter in his capacity as Reichsjäger-meister [Reich Hunt Master]. Actually he came on behalf of Chamberlain to initiate the appeasement policy which enabled Hitler to gobble up one piece of *Lebensraum* after another, first Austria and then Czechoslovakia. Hitler had retired to Berchtesgaden in order to lend verisimilitude to the 'spontaneity' of his invitation to Lord Halifax.

Halifax allowed himself to be highly impressed by Hitler and his demagogue arguments; Chamberlain noted in his diary that the visit to Germany had been 'a great success' and that Halifax had 'created an atmosphere in which we can discuss with Germany all questions concerning a European settlement'. From this time Chamberlain believed that he could clear up all outstanding questions round the table. Meanwhile in Germany the anti-Hitler conspirators were convinced by Halifax's visit to Berchtesgaden that any military adventure by Hitler outside the German frontiers would be the signal for war with Britain and France. After all, had not Hitler 'broken his teeth on a rock'? For me, however, this 'first-hand information' merely confirmed my view that war must come.

This conviction was reinforced by the backstairs intrigues among the German leaders early in 1938. I should have known as little about all this as did the rest of the German people, had not Klaus Bon-hoeffer continued to try to convince me with his 'first-hand informa-tion' that the generals in the conspiracy were setting out to assert themselves and bring Hitler down. One day early in January 1938 he told me that 'the hour of the decent generals has now struck' and confided to me as a state secret that Field Marshal von Blomberg, the War Minister, had been unseated by Göring because the latter wished to become War Minister himself. Only after the war, when a prisoner of the Allies, did Blomberg pluck up courage to admit that he had been 'the victim of skulduggery by Göring'. He had always been 'afraid of Göring's vengeance', he said. This I read in 1948 in the record of Blomberg's interrogation by American officers which General Telford Taylor made available to me.

According to the established rules of the officer corps, as Commander-in-Chief of the Army von Fritsch would have been the natural successor to Blomberg in the office of War Minister. Himmler and Heydrich, the head of the S.S. Secret Service, however, were naturally well aware of the talk about Fritsch in opposition circles. They regarded Fritsch as the leader of reactionary monarchist generals and officers whose purpose was to bring down Hitler and restore the monarchy. In order to make his appointment as War Minister impossible they fabricated a file containing false evidence accusing Fritsch of homosexual practices. Hitler passed the papers to Dr Gürtner, the Reich Minister of Justice, and the latter commissioned Dohnanyi to prepare a legal opinion on the case. Dohnanyi quickly realised that the whole matter was an intrigue and he consulted Colonel Hans Oster, a fellow-officer of Fritsch's regiment. Oster was head of the Abwehr [Military Intelligence] co-ordinating office under Admiral Canaris and a passionate uncompromising opponent of the régime. With the assistance of Dr Sack, a military judge advocate who thought the same way, Dohnanyi and Oster managed to shake the credibility of the Gestapo's evidence; they did this so effectively that, urged by Beck, his Chief of Staff, von Brauchitsch, the newly appointed Commander-in-Chief of the Army, extracted from Hitler agreement to the convention of a court martial under Göring's presidency to examine the accusations against Fritsch. The court found Fritsch's innocence proved and acquitted him. The Gestapo's witness for the prosecution had mistaken him for an ex-captain named 'von Frisch'. Hitler had the witness shot for his pains.

This whole affair was treated as 'Top Secret' and concealed from the German people. Through his brother-in-law Dohnanyi, however, Klaus Bonhoeffer received continuous 'first-hand information' and he hinted to me that the discontented generals would now strike. But nothing whatsoever happened. Urged by Beck and Oster, Fritsch did challenge Himmler to a duel with pistols 'because of the serious wrong done to him by the S.S.' Oster and Dohnanyi thought that this would bring about the decisive confrontation between Army and S.S. and lead to the fall of the régime. As the

Army's most senior officer Colonel-General von Rundstedt undertook to deliver the challenge to Himmler; but not until 1947, when talking to von Rundstedt in the prisoner-of-war camp at Bridgend in Wales, did I discover why this had never happened. Von Rundstedt said: 'I carried the challenge around with me for a long time. At my request, however, Fritsch then let the matter drop. On Hitler's instructions Himmler would never have accepted a duel and the affair would only have stirred up a lot of mud against the Army.'

The post-war build-up of this so-called 'Fritsch crisis' has placed a resistance halo around Fritsch's head; and in fact, as Walter Schellenberg records in his memoirs, the S.S. leaders did fear that 'the officers in Potsdam might resort to force against the political leadership'. Such fears, however, were totally unfounded, as unfounded as the hopes of those on the other side who had confidently expected that Fritsch would now 'strike'. To the bitter disappointment of all those who had placed their hopes in Fritsch as the potential liberator of the German people from Hitler's tyranny, in the hour of decision he showed himself incapable of any such patriotic action; he did not even feel it his duty to do anything. Himmler and the S.S. were wrong in suspecting him as an opponent of the régime. He was no Nazi in the ideological sense; he was not even a member of the Nazi Party, because as an officer he could not be. But to his dying day he was a faithful servant to Hitler.

Though initially engineered by Göring, the result of the 'Fritsch crisis' was a considerable increase in the power of Hitler. Göring did not become War Minister because in Hitler's view he was 'too idle', and he had to content himself with promotion to field marshal. This also Rundstedt told me during the Bridgend Camp conversation already mentioned. He (Rundstedt) had been consulted by Hitler about the appointment of Fritsch's successor and had proposed Göring. The *volte-face* which turned Hitler into the complete autocrat over both the state and the armed forces had disastrous effects. Hitler himself took over supreme command of the Wehrmacht with Keitel as Chief of O.K.W. [Oberkommando der Wehrmacht – High Command of the Armed Forces], and Keitel ensured that the 'decent' generals who were not subservient to Hitler were removed from all important commands. Ribbentrop became Foreign Minister and Funk Reich Minister of Economics. Hitler now had as the men in charge both of the political and military machines the blindly obedient disciples whom he required for the conquest of his *Lebensraum*.

Hitler's first use of force as Supreme Commander of the Wehrmacht was on the occasion of the occupation of Austria. This bloodless victory fired people with enthusiasm for the concept of Greater Germany and new adherents flocked to Hitler. Those who had feared military intervention by Mussolini or the Western Powers were made to look foolish. 'It was a walk-over war,' General Elfeldt said to me later. Cardinal Innitzer and the Head [Oberkirchenrat] of the Austrian Evangelical Church publicly and spontaneously paid allegiance to Hitler and called the people to a 'plebiscite on the *Anschluss*'. They made no public plea for those who, since the invasion of Austria by German troops, were being persecuted, arrested and tortured by the Gestapo. The Austrians voted 99·75 per cent for Hitler. They thought that they had reunited with Germany and only realised too late that they had been demoted to the status of the Nazi *Ostmark* [eastern province].

Hitler and his followers were now intoxicated by the 'Greater Germany' idea. Three and a half million Sudeten Germans were incited to revolt against their legal democratic government with the slogan 'Home to the Reich'. Early in June 1938 Klaus Bonhoeffer reported that Hitler had ordered military preparations for the 'destruction of Czechoslovakia'. Dohnanyi told me only a few days after I met him that this meant war. It seemed to me high time to get out of Germany. Von Gablenz had proposed me as Director of the 'German Civil Airline Pilots School' which had been neglected owing to the expansion of the Luftwaffe and required reorganisation. I could hardly resign from this post at a moment's notice without spoiling my chances with Gablenz, who wished to promote me.

In the frenzied enthusiasm over the creation of the 'Great German Reich' opposition in Germany shrank but, though I did not know it until a year later, Oster and Dohnanyi continued with their plans for a rising. During the 'Fritsch crisis' the two had recognised each other as uncompromising opponents of the régime and had become close friends. After the failure of their plan to provoke an anti-Hitler rising through Fritsch's challenge to Himmler they both felt themselves faced with the decision whether to resign and refuse to serve the régime further or whether to make use of the unique opportunities afforded by their key official positions to make proper preparations for a *coup d'état* against Hitler. In agreement with

General Ludwig Beck, the Army Chief of Staff, they opted for the latter. Fritsch having dashed all the hopes of the military conspirators, Beck became their undisputed leader until his suicide after the failure of the 20 July 1944 *coup*.

As Chief of Staff, Beck held a position which, by German Army tradition, was highly respected. He was the authoritative adviser of the Commander-in-Chief but himself held no power of command. His only weapons in the struggle against Hitler, therefore, were his intellect and his moral ascendancy. Unfortunately, they did not enable him to assert himself over the majority of the generals who were now disciples of Hitler. When Hitler engineered the 'Sudeten crisis' as psychological preparation for his real aim, the 'destruction of Czechoslovakia', Beck showed unique moral courage in raising a lone voice urging an end to Hitler. Both by memoranda and in conversation he pointed out to the senior army generals – Brauchitsch the Commander-in-Chief, army group commanders and corps commanders – that military action against Czechoslovakia, preparations for which had been ordered by Hitler, would bring about the outbreak of world war and that this could only end in total defeat and catastrophe for Germany. Passionately though he argued, however, he could not persuade Brauchitsch and the senior generals to fulfil the duty to the country which he demanded of them – an approach to Hitler to force him to halt his war preparations.

People in other countries have protested to me that, before he turned against Hitler, Beck was not entirely immune to Nazi ideology. He became the mentor of the anti-Hitler conspiracy, they say, for military rather than moral reasons; in any case he was no pacifist. During Hitler's struggle for power Beck had supported him in that in September 1930 he had made representations on behalf of three young officers of 5 Artillery Regiment which he was commanding, when they were accused of treason for spreading Nazi subversion in the Reichswehr. His opposition to Hitler's war preparations, people say, was based on military considerations. He had tried to prevent Hitler going to war against Czechoslovakia merely because 'at the time the Wehrmacht was not adequately equipped'. I first saw this theory in print in an unsigned article in the *Times Literary Supplement* of 1946.

When I first met Beck, which I did through Dohnanyi, he was already retired; later I knew him well in the resistance. I do not feel qualified to pass historical judgement upon him, but I can testify to the fact that throughout my acquaintance with him and up to the time of his death he was conducting his battle against Hitler out of profound moral indignation at the criminal nature of the régime; naturally, when dealing with generals subservient to Hitler, he used military and politico-military arguments, since such men were deaf to political considerations or argument. Beck was certainly not the type of pacifist who refuses to bear arms and preaches the brotherhood of man, but there is no need to try to excuse him for that. He did everything in his power to avert Hitler's war and its resulting catastrophe. In this wider sense he was a pacifist, a champion of peace.

Beck could not bring himself to sanction tyrannicide until after the outbreak of war. Until then he had striven to persuade Brauchitsch, the senior army generals and via them O.K.W. as a whole to threaten resignation in a body and so compel Hitler to abandon his policy of violence and ultimately war. The project was democratic but totally illusory. After the war Brauchitsch said to me: 'Beck and I had extremely violent discussions and disagreements on the subject. Beck's proposals amounted to incitement of all the generals to mutiny.' He had passed Beck's memorandum to Hitler who had 'once and for all' forbidden any interference in his policy by generals and had demanded 'unconditional obedience' even from the Chief of the General Staff. Beck had thereupon offered his resignation. Yet even this last demonstrative step by Beck, intended as a final appeal to the generals and officers of the Wehrmacht, remained without effect. On Hitler's orders the retirement of the Chief of the General Staff was kept secret.

Beck was certainly not one of Hitler's opportunist generals who only turned against him when the war could no longer be won.

The 'pre-war generals' missed their opportunity of saving the world from war and Germany from its consequences. Nevertheless a plan to do just this existed, thought up primarily by Oster and Dohnanyi. It was based upon the near-certainty that early in the autumn of 1938, as soon as the harvest was in, Hitler would issue the Wehrmacht with an order to invade Czechoslovakia. As soon as he had thus provoked war, he was to be arrested, arraigned before a People's Court and his mental health examined by a board of psychiatrists under the chairmanship of Professor Karl Bonhoeffer. To judge from his medical history, of which Dohnanyi possessed a copy, it was to be assumed that Hitler would be declared insane and confined to a lunatic asylum. If the psychiatrists' opinion did not justify this, he was to be condemned as 'injurious to the people' [*Volksschädling*] for irresponsible conduct of official business and declared to have forfeited all his offices. General (later Field Marshal) Erwin von Witzleben, later condemned to death and hanged for his part in the rising against Hitler, had undertaken to arrest Hitler, Himmler and certain other notorious S.S. leaders, using the troops under his command. The project never got beyond the planning stage, although it later became a resistance legend. Under interrogation before the International Military Tribunal in Nuremberg after the war General Franz Halder, Beck's successor as Chief of the General Staff, stated in evidence that, when Hitler had brought the Sudeten crisis to its height, he would, in agreement with Brauchitsch, have issued the code-word leading to Hitler's arrest, had not Chamberlain come to Germany to hand the Sudetenland over to Hitler under the Munich Agreement. In the interests of historical accuracy I asked von Brauchitsch about this in Bridgend Camp after the war and he gave me a very frank answer. He assured me that at the time nobody had approached him with any plan to overthrow Hitler. Nothing was farther from his thoughts than the issue of an order for a rising against Hitler and even subsequently he had no intention of allowing himself to become a tool of an anti-Hitler conspiracy. He said emphatically but with noticeable irritation and emotion: 'For God's sake, Doctor John, why should I, of all people, have undertaken some action against Hitler? The German people had elected him and was extremely content with his political successes. Those who were so intelligent at the time and thought it necessary to eliminate Hitler should have done it themselves.'

Brauchitsch did not know that during the 'Fritsch crisis' which had led to his appointment as Commander-in-Chief of the Army, Fritsch's challenge to Himmler had been intended to lead to a showdown between Army and S.S. which would bring about the fall of Hitler. Equally he had not realised that with what he called 'incitement to mutiny' Beck had been working for the fall of Hitler even before the war. 'I would not have gone along with it,' he said. Before the war neither he nor any other general would have had any support from the troops in an attempt to bring Hitler down.

On Brauchitsch's proposal Halder was nominated to succeed Beck as Chief of the General Staff. He had previously been Deputy Chief of Staff under Beck. He had promised Beck that he would only accept the office of Chief of Staff in order to restrain Hitler from war. His first action in office, however, was the issue of a most peculiar order. When Hitler had blown the 'Sudeten question' up into a world crisis, he commissioned General Max von Viebahn to 'dig out the files containing the regulations for offensive war'. They had been mouldering in the General Staff archives ever since 1923. When Viebahn expressed surprise, Halder, who had sworn to Beck that he would oppose Hitler's war policy, said: 'But we must prepare ourselves for war anyway.' All the time until his dismissal by Hitler in September 1942 Halder wavered between fulfilment of his duty as Chief of Staff and his self-appointed mission to protect the German people from the catastrophe of war by overthrowing Hitler.

In addition to this military faction a political opposition to Hitler existed before the war. It included the original opponents of the régime from the political Left, members of the bourgeoisie and aristocracy who believed in a state based on the rule of law, nonconformists from all sections of the population who had grasped the realities of this criminal régime, those persecuted on political, religious or racial grounds and last but not least the churches. But faced with Hitler's complete authority over the Wehrmacht, the police and the armed Party organisations, this opposition was totally ineffective. It could have done something only in co-operation with the military faction – and the latter was not organised; it was no more than a consensus of conservative views on the part of officers of the old school who refused to renounce the principles of law and morality in which they had been brought up. Nevertheless, the non-military opposition from the most varied professional and political circles made common cause with these officers in secret criticism of the régime. Thus before the war various opposition groups and circles formed in Germany; their existence only became known after the war.

In Berlin a variety of personal contacts, private friendships or official dealings had led to the formation of a civilian opposition before the war; it was in contact with the military faction and, like the latter, regarded prevention of war as its most vital political objective. It was composed of men of primarily conservative background who were or had been employed in senior positions in the economy, the administration, the diplomatic service, the sciences,

the churches or the land-owning aristocracy; many had initially failed
to recognise the criminal nature of the régime but had been turned
against it by bitter experience. The Wednesday Society [Mittwoch-
Gesellschaft] acted both as catalyst and as cover for this leading
opposition group. It had originally been formed by Wilhelm von
Humboldt as a forum for the exchange of views between men who
had distinguished themselves in their various fields. It met every
other Wednesday for lectures and discussions on the widest range of
subjects.

Beck was introduced into this club by Professor Johannes Popitz.
He was a highly respected financial and administrative expert who
had become Finance Minister of Prussia. As such he ranked as a
Reich Minister and he continued to administer the public properties
of Prussia until executed following the abortive rising against Hitler.
He had introduced Beck to Dr Carl Goerdeler, the ex-Burgomaster
of Leipzig and the most energetic advocate of an anti-Hitler *coup
d'état*. In this circle Beck had also met Dr Erwin Planck, son of the
famous physicist and ex-State Secretary to Chancellor Brüning, Dr
Carl Langbehn the lawyer, Albrecht Haushofer, a professor of
geopolitics and son of General (retd) Karl Haushofer, the geo-
politician who was friendly with Hess, Ambassador (retd) Ulrich
von Hassell and a number of other well-known people who later
paid with their lives for their opposition to Hitler. These were the
opposition leaders or 'dignitaries'.

Thanks to their widespread contacts with other opposition circles
all over Germany they were able to plan the introduction of honest
and capable men to take over from the régime in the event of a
military rising against Hitler. But, apart from this, they could do
nothing to deprive Hitler of his power. This could only be done by
the military faction, upon whom they urged action with passionate
eloquence. Throughout the Army, primarily among officers of the
older school, far less so in the Luftwaffe and the Navy, were to be
found men who despised and hated the régime and its upstart Party
functionaries and who did not rejoice over Hitler's political victories
because they detested his political methods. It was impossible to
estimate the potential strength of this movement. In addition to
Beck the activists among them were Colonel-General (retd) von
Hammerstein-Equord, the ex-Commander-in-Chief of the Army
and therefore Beck's late master, Generals Karl Heinrich von
Stülpnagel, Eduard Wagner, Erwin von Witzleben, Erich Hoepner,

Friedrich Olbricht, Georg Thomas and Admiral Canaris – to name only a few of those whom I came to know in the resistance after the outbreak of war.

In the summer of 1938 the leaders both of the military faction and the civilian opposition knew that Hitler wished to provoke war in the autumn in order to solve 'the Czech question' by force. They were convinced that the result would be world war with catastrophic consequences for Germany since, after Lord Halifax's visit to Hitler in Berchtesgaden, they believed that the British and French would fight for the preservation of Czechoslovakia. Nevertheless, they thought it wise to send secret emissaries to London to warn the British government once more and in explicit terms of Hitler's 'unalterable' warlike intentions and to urge the British to remain firm in face of Hitler's demands. The British government was therefore supposed to restrain Hitler from war by threat of military intervention!

I long found this preposterous notion incomprehensible and the background was only made clear to me in conversation with Lord Vansittart after the war. After his appointment as Foreign Minister Ribbentrop, basing himself upon his experience as German Ambassador in London, had not ceased to urge upon Hitler, his entourage and the Foreign Ministry his personal view that the British would not fight. This was known to von Weizsäcker, Ribbentrop's State Secretary, who was confidentially in touch with the leaders both of the military faction and the civilian opposition. The latter, therefore, began seriously to fear that the British government might yet give way to Hitler. To give them a warning Goerdeler, Ewald von Kleist-Schmenzin a large landowner, ex-Lieutenant-Colonel Hans Böhm-Tettelbach and a number of others with personal contacts in London went over to England.

They passed their warnings to Vansittart (then Sir Robert) who was Senior Diplomatic Adviser to the British government, also to Churchill and via him to the British government and opposition. They were outwitted, however, by Chamberlain, Halifax and Henderson who had long since decided to sacrifice Czechoslovakia rather than risk war with Germany. Vansittart described Goerdeler to me as a 'most estimable man', saying that well before the war he had credited him with the determination to eliminate Hitler in order to avert war. Goerdeler had been under an illusion, however, he said, in thinking that he could persuade German generals to carry out a *coup d'état* against Hitler. Theodor Kordt, the German Chargé d'Affaires in London who had tried to persuade the British government not to give way to Hitler over the Sudeten crisis, was fooled by Lord Halifax. Chamberlain, who relied on the advice, not of Vansittart but of Sir Horace Wilson who was his closest confidant as 'Senior Industrial Adviser' to the government, had long since decided to allow the Sudeten Germans to go 'home to the Reich'. This Kordt only realised as a result of Chamberlain's negotiations with Hitler which led to the Munich Agreement.

The world breathed again because peace had been preserved by the Munich Agreement. Hitler, however, was furious because, as Albrecht Haushofer told me later, with the Agreement Chamberlain had 'struck the sword of war from his hand'. At first I was glad to have been granted a further breathing space to get out of Germany before the outbreak of war. Then on the night of 9 November 1938 the world was shown what it might expect from Hitler's régime. An anti-Jewish pogrom began, more barbaric than anything previously suffered by the Jews in a Christian country of the West. During the military activities connected with the foundation of the 'Great German Reich' Goebbels had been driven into the background politically. He seized upon the murder of vom Rath, a young German diplomat in Paris, by Herschel Grünspan, a young Jew from Poland, as an excuse to remind the 'boiling soul of the people' of his existence.

On this so-called 'Kristallnacht' ['Plate-glass Night'] thousands of Jews, men, women and children, were hunted from their beds on Goebbels' orders, synagogues were set on fire, Jewish houses, flats and businesses destroyed, laid waste and looted. Jewish men, women and children were tortured and dragged off to concentration camps. Everywhere the police, acting under orders, remained passive onlookers of this savage display. On the next day, in every town in Germany, it was plain for all to see that the synagogues were in flames, Jewish businesses and houses in ruins and that innocent people were suffering. This could not go unnoticed by anyone who wished to see.

As long as my dislike of the régime was not discovered, I had no need to fear persecution. But life in Germany seemed to me increasingly sinister. Klaus Bonhoeffer's 'first-hand information' was becoming more spasmodic. Even before 'Kristallnacht', Dohnanyi, his brother-in-law, had been transferred to Leipzig as Judge of the

Reich Court [Reichsgerichtsrat]. There were no signs of resistance to be seen. Rearmament for war, however, was going full steam ahead. Even garden railings were dismantled and melted down. The propaganda on the grapevine was fantastic – we had 'death rays' and other secret weapons and so were militarily superior to all other peoples, unconquerable in fact! The Hitler Youth enthusiasts were not the only ones to take such stuff seriously.

As Director of Studies in the 'German Civil Airline Pilots School' I was entitled to free training as a civil pilot but I avoided taking the examination, continually pleading pressure of work – as a civil pilot I should automatically have been placed on the Luftwaffe reserve.

Early in 1939 I took the first steps preparatory to emigration. A Lufthansa affiliated company, 'Sedta' in Ecuador, was setting up an air line between Quito and Guayaquil, and in discussion with Gablenz he told me that the stage would soon be reached when I 'should have to go over there'. He ordered that my friend Horst von Baumbach be seconded to Sedta in advance with a Junkers 52, an arrangement suggested by me not without ulterior motives. Baumbach and I hoped to buy a farm together in Ecuador to which we could withdraw before war broke out. Owing to the currency restrictions I had arranged to finance the purchase with gold and platinum which Baumbach took to Ecuador in the form of jewellery. I ordered collections of plants for our farm to be dispatched to Ecuador from one of the world-famous nursery gardens in Erfurt. There, I thought, we would survive as country folk while Germany was reduced to ruins by the bombers of the Western Powers.

One of Hitler's more crazy ideas was the 'rebuilding of the Reich capital'. As a result of 'the Führer's building urge' I tumbled into a curious situation whereby I learnt of Hitler's order for the invasion of the 'rump of Czechoslovakia' even before the generals who were due to carry it out.

Construction of a new university quarter for Berlin entailed demolition of a house on the edge of Charlottenburg built by Flight Captain Hannes Rathje out of his savings. To avoid having his children brought up as Nazis he had gone to China where he was flying for Eurasia, a subsidiary of Lufthansa. I represented him against Berlin City in the matter of compensation for the demolition of his house. In support of his claim I arranged to contact Flight Captain Hansl Baur who had been a crew-member with Rathje and was now Hitler's pilot.

When in Berlin Baur and Hitler's minions had a communal lodging at their disposal, in the Kanonierstrasse near the Reich Chancellery. Baur was frequently present with Hitler's closest cronies at the nocturnal talks in the Chancellery. General Röhricht told me that the most vital decisions regarding the fate of the German people were frequently taken in this 'Midnight Round-the-fire Club'. It was a club into which no general would ever have fitted.

One morning at about ten o'clock, having previously made an appointment by telephone, I went to see Baur in the pilots' and chauffeurs' lodging. A friendly Bavarian housekeeper led me into a large room where a dozen or so men, some in civilian clothes, some in S.S. uniform, were sitting round a long well-stocked table having breakfast. They summed me up with long piercing glances, but the Lufthansa badge in my buttonhole gave me adequate entrée to this circle. Baur was summoned. He arrived in a dressing-gown. 'Excuse me, Doctor,' he said, 'but we were very late last night. I was with the Führer in the Chancellery until 4 a.m. I have talked to him about Rathje. I'm just going to have a bath. Sit yourself down here and have a good breakfast meanwhile.'

I sat down away from the table and took a cigarette out of my pocket. At once a couple of obliging hands were stretched out to me with lighted matches. While I smoked I listened to the conversation at the breakfast table which had clearly been interrupted by my arrival and was now continued. One of them said: 'The Chief has said it; Czechoslovakia will now be destroyed. The balloon goes up first thing Thursday of next week. We're flying down to Eiring on Wednesday.' I could hardly believe my ears. The men round the table took note of what was said as if it had been an invitation to a day's hunting. The speaker continued, stretching himself contentedly: 'Yes, old chap, it's spring. The eagle is stretching his wings.'

Such were my initial first-hand impressions of the most senior levels of our government, of Hitler's much-trumpeted leadership of the state and of his 'sleep-walker's surefootedness'. I drove into the Tiergarten, parked my car and sat down on a bench to think over what I had heard that morning. The invasion of the 'rump of Czechoslovakia' was by no means news to me, but it had now been ordered by Hitler for Thursday of next week. I visualised German bombs raining down on Prague and retaliatory attacks on the Ruhr by British and French bombers. It seemed certain to me that this time the Western Powers would intervene. I had a friend in Prague, Coelestin Rypl the pianist. He had composed a hymn to Masaryk and was a friend of Jan Masaryk. Ought I to fly to Prague to warn the Czech government through Coelestin Rypl? I still had more than a week's time.

I discussed the matter with Klaus Bonhoeffer. He asked me to do nothing but to wait and do whatever Dohnanyi might advise. The latter came to Berlin frequently and regularly from Leipzig to keep himself informed and maintain his political contacts. Klaus Bonhoeffer now summoned him to Berlin and late that evening told him what I had heard. Dohnanyi informed Colonel Oster who, like his chief Admiral Canaris, had no inkling that Hitler had already laid down the timing of the attack on Czechoslovakia and issued the necessary order to Keitel. Like Klaus Bonhoeffer and me, Oster and Dohnanyi were convinced that the Western Powers would act this time and that a new world war was unavoidable. They sent word to me to make no attempt to contact my friend Rypl in Prague. Prague would be warned in any case.

On 15 March the world was told that 'President Hacha has confidently placed the fate of the Czech people in the hands of the Führer' and that Czechoslovakia would be taken 'under the protection' of the Wehrmacht. Sirovadka, the head of the Czech Civil Aviation authority, told me shortly afterwards why Hacha had submitted himself and his people to Hitler. Hacha and Chvalkovsky, his Foreign Minister, had hastened to Berlin because a mutual friend of Sirovadka and Chvalkovsky had obtained completely reliable information that the Wehrmacht was massing against Czechoslovakia with explicit orders to invade. He knew that, even had they wished to, Britain and France were in no position to prevent the destruction of Prague by dive-bombers. He wished to spare his people hopeless and senseless resistance to a *blitzkrieg*. Shortly thereafter Sirovadka was murdered by the S.S.

I was infuriated that the Czechs should have been left in the lurch by their allies, the French and British. It looked as if, by a series of bloodless victories, Hitler could now lay hands on one piece of *lebensraum* after another without having to fear military intervention by the Western Powers. Obviously it would now be the turn of Danzig and the Polish Corridor to be brought 'home to the Reich'. Who could or would stop Hitler from raping the Poles just as he had the Czechs or from laying Warsaw in ruins by dive-bombers if they did not comply? The war which for years I had regarded as unavoidable, which indeed I had hoped for as the only way of removing Hitler, now seemed postponed, if not for ever, at least for a long period. I had not realised that, with the invasion of Czechoslovakia, Hitler had finally destroyed all the illusions of the British appeasement politicians, that influential politicians in Britain and the British people as a whole were now incensed and on the move to put a final end by military means to Hitler's policy of violence.

4

Chance Encounters

KLAUS BONHOEFFER once said that he was afraid for me because I seemed to be one of those people for whom everything went too easily. What he meant was that, before he is fully matured, a man must have been tested. Next morning I was summoned from my office by the Gestapo. One of my oldest school-friends had been denounced for non-conformist tendencies and inquiries were being made among his friends and acquaintances. I was quickly released since there was no shadow of suspicion against me, but I now knew what it felt like to be carted away by the Gestapo. Outwardly I was unchanged, Klaus Bonhoeffer said. From his desk he had seen me arrested and it had shaken him severely. He was afraid that I might be 'squeezed' and he had a bad time until I returned. Simply because of what I knew, he said, I was now so involved in the anti-Hitler plans that I was committed and no longer so free to go abroad.

I thereupon decided to stay in Germany. Contributory factors were certain incidents which I regarded as purely fortuitous but which proved to be turning-points in my life. Very late one evening I went into the Savarin bar, an habitual meeting-place of civil aviation people. The waiter was already adding up his bills and Herr Martius, the proprietor, was talking to a lone remaining visitor. I sat down at a nearby table. Herr Martius retailed a joke so loud that I could not fail to overhear it and I burst out laughing. This seemed to please the other man and he ordered drinks all round. We started talking, drinking and being generally merry.

The stranger took up an accordion lying near the piano and tried it out with a few expert touches while Herr Martius locked the door. The man obviously realised that I liked listening to him and struck up a tuneful improvisation. He was clearly a maestro with the accordion, playing as if his thoughts were elsewhere – absorbed. I raised my glass to him. 'Let's sing,' he said. He struck up and I followed. We sang one or two songs, as they came into his head.

Then we drank another round and he departed with 'Auf Wiedersehen'. I asked Herr Martius who he was. He was astounded that I did not know and whispered, 'Kannenberg.' The name meant nothing to me. 'Hitler's chef and major-domo,' Martius whispered. 'He comes here off and on after a late evening. I thought you must know because he seemed so pleased to see you.' I replied that I had not yet had the honour of being invited to Hitler's table.

When I told Klaus Bonhoeffer and his brother-in-law Justus Delbrück of my encounter with Kannenberg, Bonhoeffer said: 'There is more than just chance to this.' 'What should he do about it?' Justus Delbrück asked; 'he certainly can't persuade Kannenberg to put poison in Hitler's soup.' 'John must do a good deal of drinking with Kannenberg,' Klaus Bonhoeffer said. 'This is an important contact for us. We will see what we can make of it.'

I continued to frequent the Savarin, though without any particular intention of meeting Kannenberg again. One evening, again by chance, I met there Prince Louis Ferdinand and the Grand Duchess Kira of Russia whom he had married a year earlier; for us this chance encounter was to be of fateful significance. The Prince was now head of the House of Hohenzollern; for many years he had lived as a private citizen in North and South America but had been ordered back to Germany by the Kaiser since, after the morganatic marriage of his brother Wilhelm, he had become first in line of succession. Thereafter, until his marriage in May 1938, he had worked in the Political Communications Division of Lufthansa. When going round the head office introducing myself, I had knocked on the Prince's door – a small backroom office. He had a cup of coffee on his desk and was spreading goose-dripping on a roll. He invited me to share his breakfast.

My intention had been to say a few polite words to the Prince, purely as a matter of form. The impression he made upon me, however, was so totally different from my picture of 'a Hohenzollern' that I decided on the spot that here was a man to whom I could talk seriously. When he asked me whether I liked it in Berlin, I replied flatly, 'Not at all,' adding that I intended to go abroad as soon as I could. 'What is going on in Germany can't be right,' I said, 'otherwise everything that is considered right and decent in the rest of the civilised world is wrong.' He remained silent. 'In any case,' I said, 'the words are not mine. This was precisely what was said to me in Frankfurt last summer by Hopkins, the American Minister of

Commerce, when I accompanied him on a visit to the airport and the Zeppelin.' I realised that the Prince did not wish to become involved with my political views. With one or two commonplaces I took my leave.

Later the Prince told me that he had been somewhat taken aback at this first conversation and had even wondered whether I was acting as a political *provocateur*. Although we continued to meet officially, we should certainly never have known each other better, had not chance intervened once more: Thekla Hauschild, wife of Rudolf Hauschild the pianist with whom the Prince played, taught the Bonhoeffer and Dohnanyi children the piano, and via the Hauschilds the Prince learnt that he could talk quite openly with me.

Before he resigned from Lufthansa in May 1938 I had another conversation with the Prince, when I told him what I thought about the situation in Germany and indicated that there was a faction centred on Beck which was working for the downfall of the régime in co-operation with Popitz, Goerdeler and others. I had previously discussed with Bonhoeffer and Dohnanyi how much I should disclose. The object, of course, was to gain the Prince's confidence, by which Oster in particular set much store. From the outset he and Beck had planned to set up a constitutional monarchy sooner or later after the overthrow of the régime. He would not even consider anyone other than a Hohenzollern, and Louis Ferdinand seemed the obvious choice since he had always been an uncompromising opponent of the régime, was the legitimate successor of the last German Kaiser and potentially had great political influence abroad, being a personal friend of President Roosevelt.

Dohnanyi and Oster considered that I had scored a considerable diplomatic victory when I was able to report to Beck that the Prince was on our side and was in principle prepared to make himself available. A meeting between him and Beck was contemplated but never took place because the Prince and his wife departed on a honeymoon trip round the world. Klaus Bonhoeffer did not like this at all. The Prince should have stayed in Germany or at least in Europe where he would have been accessible, he said, adding: 'He should have stayed here where his opportunities are. When he gets back it may well be too late and we shan't need him any more.' This was also aimed at me since I was still wanting to leave Germany. I ignored it, however, and said: 'Princes and peasants think in generations. They have to think of their descendants.'

When I next met the Prince and Princess in the Savarin, their little Crown Prince was already two months old. They were in a modest villa in the Grunewald, living a happy family life. The Prince was far more of a musician than a politician; his main occupation was music, like his great ancestor who had fallen in battle against Napoleon at Saalfeld and who also, out of sheer humanity, had been the enemy of violence and tyranny. 'How is it going? What are our friends doing?' the Prince asked. All eyes in the bar were on us and he realised that we could not talk there. 'Prosit!' he said. 'I think we'll drink up and go home. Our champagne is no worse than this and it's cheaper.'

On arrival at the Prince's villa Princess Kira made us a sausage salad and went upstairs to her baby. We began discussing the situation at once. The Prince was quite clear that war and catastrophe for Germany and the world could only be avoided by overthrowing the régime. His round-the-world honeymoon trip had swept away his last scruples; he had talked to statesmen, monarchs and politicians in many countries, including Roosevelt who had invited both him and the Princess to the White House and to his private estate. During the voyage from Port Said to Genoa on the return journey Captain Prehn of the *Potsdam* had told him privately of the horrors of the Jewish pogrom. 'The most awful disgrace for Germany,' the Prince said.

I made no bones about my view that the régime could only be overthrown through the elimination of Hitler and that this could only be done by monarchist officers on orders from Beck. The two of us could do nothing towards it. He was no longer alone, the Prince said, and was responsible for a family. He went on: 'There are no secrets between me and my wife. I have told her about you. She thinks as we do and has confidence in you. I shall talk over everything you tell me with my wife – or not at all. I would like you to be clear on that.'

I was somewhat embarrassed. I had never divulged the conspiracy's plans to any woman. But I was, of course, a bachelor. Meanwhile I was certain, however, that the Prince had no political ambitions in talking to me; his sense of humanity and responsibility was driving him to play his part in averting war and the resulting threatened catastrophe. I said: 'Certainly' or 'Yes, Your Royal Highness'. Everything between us was therefore clear, he said, adding: 'Now, let's first drink to brotherhood.' We did so without formality but all the while I was thinking that one day this Prince might be head of our state. I said: 'I regard our friendship as giving me both the duty and the right invariably to say what I think to you.' 'Good,' he replied at once, 'to me and Kira.'

Louis Ferdinand confided to me that he and Roosevelt had made one final attempt to bring Hitler to reason through discussion. When he visited the White House Roosevelt had asked the Prince to sound out Ribbentrop as to whether Hitler would be willing to meet him (Roosevelt), Chamberlain and Mussolini in the Azores. Louis Ferdinand had sent Ribbentrop a letter to this effect but he had not even acknowledged it.

Louis Ferdinand had already been threatened by Göring because of his friendship with Roosevelt. Kira and he had sent the Roosevelt family a Christmas telegram. Thereupon Göring dispatched an officer to inquire how it came about that he had sent a goodwill telegram 'to the Führer's greatest enemy'. He must produce an explanation or he would be expelled from the Luftwaffe; something worse might happen to him too! Louis Ferdinand replied that he had sent Christmas telegrams to all the heads of state whom he had visited during his honeymoon trip. 'Since then,' he said, 'I have heard no more from Göring.'

Via Dohnanyi Beck was told of my talk with Louis Ferdinand. He sent word that I should exercise the greatest caution in my dealings with the Prince but keep up the relationship so that Beck could contact him at any time through me. I had therefore now acquired a secret function which could hardly be passed on to anyone else. 'If only for this reason,' Klaus Bonhoeffer urged, 'you must remain here in Berlin.'

Among my political friends I made the acquaintance of Adam von Trott zu Solz. He had just returned from China where he had been studying sinology. He told me that he had come 'in order to be in Germany when the balloon goes up'.

By training and inclination Adam von Trott was designed for the foreign service, but he was reluctant to join the Foreign Ministry under Ribbentrop and asked me to find out whether Lufthansa would have a job for him. The Political Communications Division, however, under Hans Karl von Winterfeld, Louis Ferdinand's ex-master and a mutual friend, was fully staffed. Gablenz thought that von Trott should go to the Foreign Ministry because there were far too few decent and sensible men there. Ribbentrop would not remain

Foreign Minister for ever, after all. Trott did go to the Foreign Ministry where he was able to do most effective work for the Resistance. He was hanged after the *coup* against Hitler. His name has been much misused since the war by many of his foreign service colleagues who alleged that they were working with him in the Resistance.

In the last six months of peace when the psychological build-up for war against Poland was under way, I mostly went about with people who were considering plans for the overthrow of the régime. In the spring of 1939 they had concluded that Hitler should be allowed to have his war so that, under the shock effect both on the armed forces and the people of some military defeat, they could overturn Hitler and his régime. My assistance in these plans was now counted upon, particularly by Colonel Oster. He was still impressed by the fact that I had heard of Hitler's order for the invasion of the rump of Czechoslovakia before the Head of the Abwehr.

The time of decision was drawing nearer. In the summer Gablenz made a round-the-world tour with the intention of reorganising Lufthansa's overseas representation on his return. He had picked me for South America. I still regarded the prospect of having to fight for Hitler with horror. Having no military training, I was earmarked in the Lufthansa mobilisation plan for call-up to a transport squadron. On the other hand I felt myself obligated towards the circle of men who had placed their confidence in me and I felt that to clear off just now would be a dirty trick.

I talked all this over with my brother Hans. He was at this time working as legal assistant in Leipzig University, but frequently came to Berlin to get the latest news from me. Politically he was more extreme than I and as a student had collected a circle of left-wing intellectuals around him; to my parent's consternation he had even been prominent in anti-Nazi demonstrations by various left-wing organisations. Since the Left failed to produce any real resistance to the régime, however, he lost all interest in political activity and devoted himself exclusively and intensively to his professional studies. Discussing the pros and cons of staying in Berlin with him, I came to the decision to remain.

Gablenz returned from his world tour and gave senior personnel of Lufthansa a talk on the information he had acquired about air traffic. In this he said, looking at me: 'There are many interesting jobs for us in South America. This is a field for determined young men who have the necessary spirit of enterprise to do a real pioneering job.' Hans Hickmann, a friend of Klaus Bonhoeffer and myself who ran the 'Fuel' Division, noticed this together with the fact that Gablenz had looked at me at this point and he congratulated me on my luck. Unfortunately I had to tell him that I had decided to remain in Berlin. I now had to tell Gablenz also quite frankly that I had changed my mind about going abroad. He listened to me thoughtfully – not at all his habit – and finally said: 'For God's sake don't produce another Kapp *putsch* or things will get even worse here.'

In mid-July Dietrich Bonhoeffer (brother of Klaus – five years younger) returned via London from a trip to America. I had met him and his friend Pastor Eberhard Bethge in the Bonhoeffer house but only in passing. Both later became well known as activists in the 'Confessional Church' resistance movement. Dietrich Bonhoeffer could well have dodged the war by remaining in America as many of his friends advised him to do, but he insisted on sharing such sufferings as our people might have to undergo in the war which had now become inevitable. He was martyred as a result of his battle against Hitlerian barbarity, being hanged in Flossenbürg concentration camp shortly before the end of the war. His example was often an encouragement to me. His return from America before the outbreak of war was a special source of strength to me since I had taken a similar decision myself.

Ever since the spring of 1939 we had known that Hitler had issued his orders to the Wehrmacht for the invasion of Poland. To me this meant that Poland was doomed. Thekla Hauschild, who was Polish by birth, said: 'Our people will fight to the last man,' but I was sure that dive-bomber attacks on Polish cities and communication centres would soon reduce both the country and the people to paralysis. Klaus Bonhoeffer and others had no conception of the striking power of the Luftwaffe and most of the army officers in the anti-Hitler movement thought only in terms of land warfare; they were all convinced that the Poles would hold out until the British and French came to their assistance. This seemed to me more than questionable. I saw no hope of saving Poland from invasion by the Wehrmacht until negotiations were opened between London and Moscow to encircle Hitler.

An alliance between the Western Powers and Stalin would

certainly not have prevented Hitler attacking Poland because he was bent on war. If, however, he was strategically surrounded, we could count upon an early military defeat and this would have created the psychological conditions for an anti-Hitler military rising. We had no inkling, of course, that Hitler would succeed in outwitting Chamberlain once more and concluding a non-aggression pact with Stalin.

In Moscow the British and French delegations had had dust thrown in their eyes by Stalin exactly as had Theodor Kordt, the German Chargé d'Affaires, by Lord Halifax during the 'Sudeten crisis'. Meanwhile Kordt and his brother Erich, who was head of Ribbentrop's personal staff, had made a further, somewhat peculiar, attempt to act as advisers to the British government and so save the peace. They had a friend, Philip Conwell-Evans, who had developed Nazi leanings when a lecturer in Königsberg University and who had played a not inconsiderable role on his return to England as a source of information for people close to Chamberlain. 'This silly little man,' as his British secret service watchdog described him to me after the war, was bent on maintaining peace and friendship with the Nazi Germany which he admired so much. During the Polish crisis Conwell-Evans invited the Kordt brothers, at their request, to his private apartment to meet Vansittart for a last-minute secret discussion. In a final attempt to avert war the Kordt brothers urged upon Vansittart the conclusion by the British government of a 'heterogeneous coalition' with Moscow. Once again, as during the Sudeten crisis, the British government was supposed to avert war by threatening Hitler with military measures, this time based on a British–Soviet alliance. At the time Vansittart thought that the Kordt brothers were unnecessarily anxious. The British government would definitely conclude an agreement with the Soviet Union, he said.

Vansittart was wrong. He may at the time have had the sonorous title of 'Senior Diplomatic Adviser to His Britannic Majesty's Government', but, as he said to me after the war, he had in fact been kicked upstairs by Chamberlain because from the outset he had opposed the latter's catastrophic appeasement policy. Important political dispatches were withheld from him and his advice was not listened to. Chamberlain did not want a pact with the Russians; he thought that he could come to some understanding with Hitler against the bolsheviks. Accordingly he ignored the advice of the

Kordt brothers, whose secret talks – diplomatically unauthorised, of course – only became known to me after the war. Although in the post-war period much was made of this secret diplomacy as a remarkable aspect of resistance, I have never been able to see much sense in it, perhaps because I lacked the sapience conferred by diplomatic training. A British–Soviet alliance never had any prospect of restraining Hitler from war because neither Chamberlain nor Stalin wanted an alliance.

With the announcement of the Hitler–Stalin pact war became only a matter of days. Halder, the Chief of Staff, who on assuming his office had undertaken to do all in his power to avert war, waved Colonel Oster away when the latter made a last attempt to hold him to his allegiance to the plans for a *coup*. Halder said after the war: 'With the conclusion of the non-aggression pact with Russia, Germany's military situation was such that a breach of my oath could not be justified.' After the war he nevertheless presented himself as the 'foremost resistance fighter among the generals', although in a monograph he also pointed out to the German people that the war against Russia would have been won, had Hitler taken his military advice!

Until the final failure of all our efforts I was in a position to observe from the closest of quarters what resistance by this type of general meant. Frequently I was in despair. Sometimes I thought of dropping everything, getting into a Lufthansa aircraft and taking refuge in London so that I might do my best to put a quicker end to Hitler's rule of terror. I never did so, not even in the spring of 1944 when, during the final months before our *coup*, the Gestapo was hard on my heels. I was already too deeply involved in the anti-Hitler conspiracy.

5

The Secret Front against Hitler

ON the day after the invasion of Poland Gablenz invited me and some others of his immediate staff to a farewell lunch in the Kaiserhof Hotel. He was now entitled 'Air Transport Commander' and had assumed command of a transport wing formed from Lufthansa; he was stationed in Berlin, however, and contined to act as manager of Lufthansa civil operations. He asked Hans Lyncke, head of the Personnel Department, what wartime post I was earmarked for. Being totally untrained militarily, I belonged initially to Supplementary Reserve [Ersatzreserve] Class 2, but, as Lyncke said, I could be called up at any time to be 'turned into an officer as soon as possible'. Knowing my private feelings, Gablenz said that he had a more important job for me as a lawyer – supervision of our subsidiary companies overseas to ensure that they were not severed from us during the war by 'some legal dodge'. He ordered my occupation to be classified 'reserved', thus giving me a well-camouflaged position as legal adviser to Lufthansa in which I continued to work for the overthrow of Hitler until our *coup* took place.

In agreement with Admiral Canaris, Oster and Dohnanyi had made preparations to organise the military faction and the political opposition into a proper conspiracy in the event of war. A few days after the outbreak of war Dohnanyi was recalled from Leipzig and appointed to O.K.W. Ausland/Abwehr [Military Intelligence] with the rank of Major; he was in charge of the 'Policy' desk in the 'Central Directorate'. As such and with his remarkable capabilities, which had already earned him an exceptional career as a lawyer, he became Admiral Canaris' closest confidant and adviser. Canaris left him and Colonel Oster, his Chief of Staff, a completely free hand to organise the *coup*. Oster co-ordinated the military faction in agreement with Beck, Dohnanyi the political plans of the civilian opposition groups. The latter had available a secret list which he himself had compiled from 1933 onwards for the benefit of Dr Gürtner, the Reich Minister of Justice, recording the crimes of every sort committed by the most senior functionaries in Party and State who were to be dismissed. This list was found by the Gestapo after 20 July 1944; its whereabouts are not now known.

Oster had his informers and helpers in various military headquarters; in Berlin they were mostly in the War Ministry which was under command of Colonel-General Fromm, Commander-in-Chief of the Replacement Army. His Deputy, General Friedrich Olbricht, head of the General Army Office [Allgemeines Heeresamt] was a vehement opponent of the régime; he, in agreement with Beck, directed the General Staff planning for a military rising. As his personal and immediate staff officer Dohnanyi summoned Justus Delbrück, a close friend since boyhood; he also found a post in his section for Karl Ludwig Freiherr von Guttenberg, editor of the *White Papers* [*Weisse Blätter*]. Of the Abwehr officers these two were in closest touch with Captain Ludwig Gehre who, through Justus Delbrück, became my closest personal friend among the movement's officers.

Thus by the outbreak of war Oster and Dohnanyi had assembled a nucleus from which grew a widespread conspiracy to overthrow the régime; despite the failure of numerous assassination attempts it remained undiscovered until 20 July 1944. We did all we could to persuade one of the great commanders who stood high in the esteem both of the Wehrmacht and the people to lead a patriotic rising against Hitler and his régime of tyranny, and in the early days of the war, while the Stukas were descending on Warsaw and the panzers rolling into Poland, we had very real hopes.

Colonel-General von Hammerstein-Equord, the former Commander-in-Chief of the Army, had assumed command of one of the armies stationed along the Rhine. He was determined to eliminate Hitler 'like a wolf which has broken into the flock'. This he felt it his duty to do primarily because, before his resignation as Commander-in-Chief in January 1934, he had failed to bring himself to put an end to Hitler and the arbitrary tyranny of his S.A. Now, after the outbreak of war, he proposed to Hitler a visit of inspection to his sector of the front, intending on this occasion, as he said to me later, 'to eliminate Hitler once and for all – no question of judicial proceedings'. But Hitler did not come. Moreover, he relieved Hammerstein of his command – he had always feared him as a resolute opponent ever since the Nazi seizure of power. After his farewell dinner Hammerstein said to his officers: 'I am a victim of the inflation among senior commanders.' This sounded as if Hammerstein had resigned himself to his fate, but he had not. He remained actively in touch with the military faction, but, as a retired officer without a command, he was powerless. I myself only made Hammerstein's acquaintance through Jakob Kaiser after the outbreak of war.

Our hopes of Hammerstein were not based on mere wishful thinking. After his departure many other senior commanders on the active list gave vent to derogatory or even treasonable criticism of Hitler and his régime; after Stalingrad they raised wails of defeatism and acted as though they were prepared to do something against Hitler. But all proved to be failures. Though they raged against the incompetence of 'Corporal Hitler', on his orders they repeatedly sent more and more soldiers to their death. A particular case was Field Marshal Günther von Kluge. He took part in conspiratorial discussions and plans for Hitler's overthrow; he declared himself ready to assume supreme command of the Wehrmacht in place of Hitler after a successful *coup d'état* – but he refused to lead the rising against Hitler himself. After the failure of the *coup* on 20 July 1944 he did nothing. Since the fact that for years he had been involved in the conspiracy could not remain a secret in the long run, he eventually committed suicide, but not before he had written a farewell letter to Hitler:

> My Führer, I have always admired your greatness . . . and your iron determination to maintain your own position and that of National-Socialism. . . . You have fought a great and honourable fight. . . . May you now prove yourself great enough to put an end to this hopeless struggle, should that prove necessary. . . . I take leave of you, my Führer, as one who, conscious of having done his duty to the utmost, has stood closer to you than you perhaps realised.

As a result of the false hopes placed in these 'great commanders' the retired generals of the military faction and the dignitaries of the civilian resistance groups held their hands for years until eventually Stauffenberg acted on his own initiative.

The blitz victory over Poland had, in Beck's words, 'no significance for the outcome of the war'. Decision could only be reached on the Western Front. Generals, officers and civilians of the opposition who had lived through the First World War, all the leading figures of the opposition in other words, regarded the prospect with the utmost anxiety. They were still under the spell of the trauma of the 1918 defeat. In addition, as Gehre told me, people in the Army General Staff were convinced that an attack on the Maginot Line would result in enormous casualties – at least two million dead! In the Luftwaffe there was no sign of this defeatism since the French Air Force was hardly to be seen and the R.A.F.'s nightly harassing attacks made little impression.

Beck, his associates in the military faction and the civilian resistance leaders considered that the defeatist apprehensions of those officers who had fought in the trenches of the First World War and were now in senior positions offered a possibility of winning over Brauchitsch to the idea of a *coup d'état* against Hitler; he was to be approached through Halder – who unfortunately proved to be a heroic conspirator in word but not in deed. The plan for the Western Front offensive provided for the dreaded Maginot Line to be out-flanked by surprise attack on the neutral countries of Holland and Belgium and the capture of Paris along the lines of the Schlieffen Plan in the First World War. The idea was that Brauchitsch should contest Hitler's order for an attack on neutral countries on the grounds of international law and so set a *coup d'état* against Hitler in motion.

Meanwhile the civilian leaders, primarily the indefatigable Dr Goerdeler but also Dr Schacht, Professor Popitz and von Hassell the former Ambassador, had been secretly active, using their varied and widespread connections to recruit men who could take over the administration of the State on the overthrow of the régime. During discussion of this subject with Klaus Bonhoeffer and me, Ernst von Harnack urged that the underground leaders of the proscribed workers' organisations be approached and included. The Kapp *putsch*, he said, had failed because of a general strike. If the generals could agree with the workers and co-operate with them, the *coup d'état* was bound to succeed. After the collapse of 1918 Harnack had joined the Socialist Party and was still in touch with some of his Party friends in the underground. He introduced Klaus Bonhoeffer and myself to Julius Leber, the former socialist Reichstag deputy; I remember him as one of the best political brains in the anti-Hitler conspiracy.

As cover for his illegal activities Ernst von Harnack had set himself up in a backroom office in the Mohrenstrasse in the centre of Berlin, where he masqueraded as 'Representative of the Sommerfeld Cloth Factory' owned by his cousin, Justus Delbrück. As an alibi to provide him with the entrée to official agencies he had undertaken, in connection with the reconstruction of Berlin, to search for graves of special historical interest which were to be transferred to an 'Historic Cemetery'. His official title in this post was 'Graves Commissar attached to the Reich Commissar for the Reconstruction of the Reich Capital'. His expert on historic military graves was Colonel-General (retd) Ludwig Beck; the two, therefore, had a perfectly innocent pretext for meeting – when they could discuss conspiratorial matters. The first time Klaus Bonhoeffer and I met Dr Goerdeler was in Harnack's backroom office in the Mohrenstrasse. He was passing through on his way to secret talks in the country and was disguised as a hiker, carrying a rucksack.

Through Adam von Trott I made the acquaintance of Dr Curt Bley. He was still in contact with a number of former socialist students whom he had known before the Nazi seizure of power. I was able to arrange some financial support for their illegal activity through Dr Walter Bauer who, as an industrialist, was a real Croesus to the conspiracy and frequently provided money. In these and similar ways we forged many new contacts. Colonel-General von Hammerstein (he was known as 'the red general' because, before the seizure of power, he had discussed Hitler with socialists and trade-union leaders and had little time for the German Nationals) was in touch with Jakob Kaiser, leader of the Christian Trades Unions, and through him with Wilhelm Leuschner, leader of the banned Socialist Trades Unions. Klaus Bonhoeffer and I frequently met the latter in Ernst von Harnack's office.

In the house of Dr Elfriede Nebgen (she later married Jakob Kaiser) I met Bernhard Letterhaus, secretary of the Catholic Workers Union, also Dr Josef Wirmer whom Klaus Bonhoeffer had known when they were junior barristers together. This brought us into contact with a network of catholic resisters spreading far outside Berlin and all across Germany. From Cologne came the Dominican Father Laurentius Siemer seeking information on the *coup d'état* position for his friends in West Germany. Discussing this subject in Klaus Bonhoeffer's house in the autumn of 1939, we drew up the first balance sheet of our resistance activity. It was encouraging but also showed us where the gaps still were. It did not take account of the military preparations for the *coup d'état*. They were not our business and we could do nothing to further them. We relied upon Halder's ability to play upon Brauchitsch's serious anxieties over the Western offensive and persuade him to take action against Hitler.

Though ideological and political divergencies had existed between the various resistance groups forming the civilian opposition, they had been ironed out through discussion and by bitter experience. However divergent their earlier political opinions, all were now at one in regarding co-operation with the military faction as offering the only possibility for an overthrow of the régime. In Berlin, for instance, the conservative leaders and Christian resisters of both denominations combined with socialists and trade unionists to form a steering group, the object of which was to create a common basis for political reconstruction after a successful *coup d'état*. Before the Nazi seizure of power differences between the political leaders of these groups had prevented the formation of a united front against Hitler; now their alliance was finally cemented during a discussion between Beck and Leuschner arranged by Harnack and myself.

Obviously, in the event of a successful *coup d'état*, the régime could not be transformed in twenty-four hours into a parliamentary republic on the lines of the Weimar constitution nor could the state of war be ended overnight. Within the civil resistance steering group, therefore, it was agreed that on the fall of Hitler the régime should be replaced by a military state of emergency under the over-all authority of General Beck; this state of emergency should be abolished as soon as possible and replaced by a provisional civil government nominated by Beck, pending fresh elections to the Reichstag. Goerdeler held ready a ministerial list for the provisional government together with memoranda containing suggestions and proposals for peace negotiations. Not being privy to these, Leuschner and some of his friends became sceptical and were afraid that they might be outwitted by the conservative leaders. They sent word to Beck through Harnack that they reserved complete freedom of action unless they were included in all planning for the post-revolutionary political régime and had knowledge of the latest political aims and intentions.

Ernst von Harnack was held in high regard by the socialists and trade unionists for his courageous intervention with the Gestapo on behalf of people persecuted on political or religious grounds. Beck accordingly asked him to pacify Leuschner and his friends who had been upset by Goerdeler. With his remarkable negotiating ability Harnack produced a plan which Beck approved. On proclamation of the state of emergency Leuschner was to become Reich Commissar in charge of the German Labour Front with all its subordinate organisations and very considerable assets pending re-establishment of freedom of association and the reconstitution of free trade unions by means of free elections. As a result Beck guaranteed to Leuschner the political authority to fulfil the aim for which he strove so passionately: re-establishment of a General German Trade Union League as an independent political organ of the State to promote the economic and cultural interests of the working class. The new feature of the plan, suggested by Carlo Mierendorff, Leuschner's brilliant fellow-countryman and political friend, was a guarantee of working-class cultural requirements, for instance the raising of the school-leaving age by at least a year. Beck having thus given Leuschner the widest possible opening for action on behalf of the working class, Harnack found it all the easier to convince him that the form of state visualised by Beck and the leaders of the conspiracy, in other words a constitutional monarchy, was that best suited to the German people and would be the best possible guarantee of the fundamental political rights of all classes. Leuschner eventually agreed when Beck gave his word of honour that final decision on the future form of state would be taken by referendum.

Until the spring of 1942 I was occupied, as far as the conspiracy was concerned, primarily with internal political problems connected with the new régime to be set up after the overthrow of Hitler. As for external political problems, I did no more than take note of what was obvious or what I heard during discussions within the conspiracy. Nevertheless, from the outset I was sceptical about the ideas of the 'peace hopes experts' after the outbreak of war. Early in October 1939 Hitler made patent efforts by speeches to the Reichstag and in the *Sportspalast* to persuade the Western Powers to recognise his conquests in Poland and Czechoslovakia and make peace. Chamberlain's and Daladier's refusals were categoric. Nevertheless, some of the opposition leaders believed that they could negotiate a peace without having first achieved the overthrow of the German régime. Even the fantastic idea of taking Göring into our confidence was discussed. He was known as a sybarite and had once been heard to say in Karinhall 'how terrible it was to him to think that all this might be destroyed'; so it was thought that he could be divorced from Hitler! Goerdeler, Schacht, von Hassell and even Adam von Trott used their personal contacts in Switzerland and the United States to explore the ground for peace conditions, if possible to persuade Roosevelt to mediate. Our professional diplomats showed particular ineptitude in underground diplomacy. Weizsäcker, Ribbentrop's State Secretary, had transferred Theodor Kordt, the last Chargé d'Affaires in London and one of his protégés, to Berne where he could still keep in touch with his London informant, Philip Conwell-Evans. As his contact confided to me after the war, however, on the outbreak of war Evans had been taken on by the British Secret Service. He came once or twice to Berne for confidential talks with Kordt, the real object of which was to gain information – a fact which Kordt did not perceive. At the end of October he handed over as 'material' the conditions which Chamberlain would supposedly guarantee if the Nazi régime were replaced by a trustworthy German government. These 'secret peace terms', however, differed in no way from what Chamberlain had already publicly said in a speech. Yet Erich Kordt passed them via Oster to the conspirators as a sort of 'Open Sesame' to peace.

Everyone's terror was that an offensive by the Wehrmacht on the Western Front might end in position warfare of the First World War type; it was this which caused Brauchitsch, Halder and the generals the greatest anxiety. In addition there were serious doubts about the ability of the German war potential to sustain prolonged position warfare in the West, particularly since Roosevelt's unequivocal antagonism to 'the aggressors' left no doubt that he would come to the aid of Britain and France with America's inexhaustible arsenal. General Thomas, head of the War Economy and Armaments Office, pointed this out to the German generals in words of one syllable. In addition Brauchitsch, Halder and the Western Front army commanders had their own political and moral scruples about Hitler's planned offensive; the First World War had taught them that, in the event of defeat, invasion of the neutral countries of Belgium and Holland would be laid at their door personally as a crime against both international law and the laws of war. All these doubts and problems, however, were not enough to bring Brauchitsch over to our side. He countered Halder and General Thomas by saying that after the victory over Poland the majority of the soldiery and of the people were more pro-Hitler than ever; any act of violence against Hitler, therefore, would find no support and would merely lead to internal political chaos. To counter this argument, which had much to be said for it, in October Ernst von Harnack and I drafted a memorandum to explain to the generals, in words which they could understand, what the real mood of the people was.

This memorandum of just under four pages was in effect a manifesto proclaiming that all the main pre-1933 political parties had now united to form a single anti-régime opposition front. Professor Popitz and Dr Goerdeler for the conservative Right, Josef Wirmer and Jakob Kaiser for the Catholic bourgeoisie, Bernhard Letterhaus for the Catholic working class, Ernst von Harnack and Julius Leber for the underground socialist party and Wilhelm Leuschner for the trade unionists all went on record in declaring that they stood inflexibly shoulder to shoulder behind General Beck in order to overthrow the régime and so save the German people from a catastrophe from which the working class would be the principal sufferers as in the First World War. Special emphasis was laid on this last point in order to counter Brauchitsch's argument about the working-class attitude to Hitler. The memorandum also stressed the criminal nature of the régime and the misuse made of German soldiers. At Oster's and Dohnanyi's suggestion I handed to Beck a letter from Prince Louis Ferdinand in which he said: 'If I am called upon, I am ready.'

In his usual way Brauchitsch refuted these arguments by adroitly turning the tables. If the people and the working class were really so anti-Hitler,' he said to General Thomas, then they could overthrow him quite simply by means of a general strike. They had proved their strength, after all, during the Kapp *putsch*. If the working class would initiate a general strike, he would line up the Army behind them. Dohnanyi told Leuschner of this – not without some ulterior motive, since he wished to test the working-class attitude, on which Harnack had laid so much emphasis. He did not always agree with Harnack and, though outwardly friendly, never really got on well with him. Leuschner was furious with Brauchitsch, saying to Dohnanyi that his remarks showed that these gentlemen, the officers, still had not grasped the realities. The working class did not exist simply to pull their chestnuts out of the fire. He was sure that the officers would open fire on the workers – they had always fired on the Left but never on the Right.

Equally unavailing were the efforts made by the military faction to persuade Brauchitsch to support a *coup* by extracting concessions from the British government. Ever since 1933 Dr Josef Müller ('Cowboy Joe'), a Munich lawyer, and a member of the Catholic resistance, had been a confidant of Cardinal Faulhaber and his political adviser, Canon Johannes Neuhäusler. As adviser to Catholic bishops and priestly orders he was in close touch with the Vatican. Colonel Oster had recruited him into the movement and, since he had been a First World War Lieutenant, had no difficulty in getting him appointed to the Abwehr office in Munich. Using his Vatican connections he was to find out what peace terms would be granted to a Reich government purged of National Socialism. Dr Müller was well known to Pius XII from the time when the latter had been Papal Nuncio. Father Leiber, his Political Secretary, offered to act as intermediary. Through D'Arcy Osborne, the British Minister to the Vatican, Lord Halifax sent word that the British government would in principle be prepared to grant Germany an honourable peace on the basis of the Munich Agreement, if the present régime were replaced by a government whose word could be trusted and who would abide by treaties.

Brauchitsch, Halder and other generals raised fresh objections to this also, when told about it. If they made a *putsch*, they said, the Western Front could not be held against sudden attack by the Western Powers. We should then get another peace *diktat* like Versailles but this time the 'stab-in-the-back' would have come from the generals. In any case 'blind obedience was a soldier's duty in war' and 'one could not change horses in midstream'. There were generals who loathed the régime but even they thought that 'the war must first be won and then the pigsty could be cleaned out'. To cut the ground from under the feet of these arguments the energetic and indefatigable Josef Müller continued his probings in order to provide the generals with some guarantee that the Vatican peace terms were no mere empty words nor some clever trap.

At this point Müller ran into danger. Father Keller, a Benedictine monk who had adopted the Nazi ideology, was spying for the S.D. and therefore on Müller. Keller hinted that Müller was carrying out some high-level political mission to the Vatican, but fortunately he did so to a Berlin lawyer whom Halder had recommended to Dohnanyi as a safe channel for the occasional transmission of information and intelligence. Father Keller proved to have discovered nothing and so Canaris had no difficulty in persuading Himmler and Heydrich that Müller had been in Rome for some perfectly ordinary information-collecting job on behalf of the Abwehr. On the other hand Müller now became suspect to Halifax as an *agent provocateur*, particularly since just at this time two British Secret Service agents, Stevens and Best, had fallen into a trap laid by Himmler's secret service masquerading as a Wehrmacht resistance organisation. Müller would have had to bring his activities in Rome to an end had not the Pope assured Lord Halifax that he was completely trustworthy.

Hitler had laid down 12 November 1939 as the date for the Western Front offensive. Brauchitsch, Halder, the Western Front army commanders and the Luftwaffe generals, including even Göring himself, had objected, pointing out that an attack was too risky with the uncertain weather conditions at the beginning of winter. Tanks could only advance slowly through the mud or might even be bogged down. Land and air forces could not co-operate properly in bad weather, and the operation of Stukas might even be impossible, Göring thought. But Hitler refused to accept these technical military objections. Nevertheless, on 5 November Brauchitsch urged them upon him once more. Hitler replied sarcastically: 'Neither is the French army equipped with umbrellas against bad weather.' This and the subsequent private interview with Hitler was retailed to me by Brauchitsch after the war in the Bridgend prisoner-of-war camp. To dissuade Hitler from his offensive in the West Brauchitsch had told him that the morale of the troops was not such as to guarantee victory; an attack on the Maginot Line demanded an offensive spirit which the troops did not possess; cases of indiscipline had consequently occurred. During the argument Hitler completely lost his temper. He dressed down Brauchitsch and 'the generals' 'as one would not do even to the stupidest recruit', Brauchitsch said. He had thereupon offered his resignation. This Hitler had refused, screaming louder all the time and cursing the cowardice of 'his' generals in the filthiest language until eventually he ran out of breath. Then he had left Brauchitsch standing and stormed out of the room.

Brauchitsch said: 'I tried to dissuade Hitler from this offensive primarily on political grounds. I was convinced that the war would have to be fought out to the bitter end once it had really been set in motion with an offensive against France on First World War lines. And this was precisely what I wished to avoid – catastrophe. I hoped to gain time, that the politicians would meanwhile get together and negotiate in order to reach some understanding. Of course, I had not realised at the time that Chamberlain would never negotiate with Hitler.' In addition, when arguing with Hitler early in November, Brauchitsch can have had no inkling that, via Dr Müller's links with the Vatican, possibilities existed that an anti-Nazi government might be able to negotiate with Britain. He was not told of these potentialities until the spring of 1940.

My talks with Brauchitsch after the war, therefore, showed me that before the Western offensive there was never a chance of persuading him to initiate a *coup d'état*, as I and my political friends confidently believed. Goerdeler was persistently urging action, and Beck seriously considered appearing at headquarters in uniform to seize Brauchitsch's command authority and initiate a *coup* that way. Unfortunately, though honest and unselfish patriots, these men were utopians. They lived under the illusion that Brauchitsch and Halder would refuse to issue the orders for the Western offensive and so start the revolt.

While we waited tensely for the day I, like the rest of the world, was astonished to hear over the radio on the morning of 9 November that the previous evening an abortive attempt to assassinate Hitler had been made in the Bürgerbräukeller, Munich, during the commemorative festival for the ill-fated Hitler *putsch* of 1923. To this day no one knows who was behind the would-be assassin, a cabinet-maker named Georg Elser, or whether he was really making a lone-wolf effort to rid the world of Hitler. From the outset we suspected that the affair had been engineered by Heydrich with Himmler's and Hitler's knowledge. Hitler had ended his speech prematurely and left the room before the infernal machine, which was built into a pillar, exploded. Professor de Crinis, the psychiatrist, gave his young friend Walter Schellenberg, the S.S. leader, the idea of laying the attempt at the door of Stevens and Best, the British Secret Service agents who had been kidnapped in Venlo shortly before. De Crinis was awarded the Iron Cross for his pains!

To ensure that his 'miraculous deliverance by Providence' had the maximum psychological effect on the soldiery and the people, Hitler cancelled his order for the Western offensive. Thereafter he repeatedly postponed it, accepting the generals' arguments about increasingly unfavourable weather. Early in January he put it off indefinitely because the General Staff's plans for the offensive had fallen into the hands of the Western Powers when a Luftwaffe courier aircraft made a forced landing near Mechelen in Belgium. Meanwhile Dr Müller in Rome had achieved more for the re-establishment and assurance of peace in Europe after the collapse of Nazism than we had dreamed was possible.

Müller discussed the results of his soundings in the Vatican exhaustively with Beck, Oster and Dohnanyi and they were ultimately summarised by Dohnanyi in a report known as the 'X Report'. I have never read it but I discussed it with Dohnanyi on several occasions, including one in the winter of 1943 when he had taken refuge in Professor Sauerbruch's clinic after his arrest and was secretly briefing me for a journey to Rome, where I was to discuss with Father Leiber destruction of all 'X Report' material. The report recorded that on replacement of the Nazi régime by a new trustworthy Reich government and provided that no hostilities had broken out on the Western Front in the meantime, the British government would negotiate on the problem of the Eastern frontiers in a spirit favourable to Germany. The Pope had guaranteed the sincerity of the British offer of negotiations. After the war all manner of speculation took place over the contents of the 'X Report'; General Halder maintained that it had referred to 're-establishment of the 1914 Western frontiers'. In fact, Dohnanyi never set out such utopian terms.

The report was long withheld because both the military faction and the civilian resistance dignitaries interpreted the continual postponement of the Western offensive to mean that Brauchitsch was at last coming to the realisation that he must do something to prevent expansion of the conflict into world war. In March, however, after the unusually hard and snowy winter, Hitler began once more to press for the Western offensive; General Thomas then gave the report to Halder and the latter passed it on to Brauchitsch. The next day Brauchitsch asked Halder who had drafted the report; he would have him arrested; its contents amounted to treason. Brauchitsch told me in Bridgend camp that Halder's reply was: 'If you want to arrest someone, then arrest me.'

When we discussed the 'X Report' in Bridgend camp Brauchitsch said: 'The whole thing was treason – as a lawyer you must admit that. Nevertheless, I took no action against your friends at the time. Naturally I read the report – with great care. But I could do nothing with it. Of course, I could have had Hitler arrested and even imprisoned him. Easily! I had enough officers loyal to me who would have carried out even that order if given by me. But that was not the problem. Why should I have initiated action against Hitler – tell me that. It would have been action against the German people. Let's be honest. I was well informed at the time about the people's mood – well informed through my son and others. The German people were pro-Hitler.'

6

The Scourge of Victory

GERMANS, British and French sat on either side of the Rhine and waited for the war. This was the period known as the 'phoney war'. For the ordinary people of both sides this type of war was still tolerable, but not for those who realised that the opening of hostilities in the West would let loose a hurricane before which Germany must collapse sooner or later. Beck, who as an ex-Chief of Staff knew what he was talking about, had foretold it during the Sudeten crisis and this was how I imagined the war ending for Germany. As I had done when Hitler came to power, I often quoted to my friends Heinrich Heine's prophecy:

. . . and finally Thor arises with his giant hammer and destroys the Gothic cathedrals. . . . The German is indeed also a German man. . . . But it will come and if at any time you, the French, hear it roar as it has never roared before in the history of the world, then know that the German thunder has ultimately reached its goal. At its clamour eagles will fall dead from the sky and the lions in the furthest deserts of Africa will crawl into their lairs with their tails down.

I had my own ideas. Whenever we were discussing the Western Front offensive and people said that it would end in position warfare, I was reminded of Oswald Spengler. Somewhere I had read him saying that 'in the next war the French Army will simply be swept away'. I quoted this to my brother and also to our officer 'experts' such as Ludwig Gehre and his friend Colonel Jaeger, who had fought in the First World War. Their reply was that Spengler did not know of the Maginot Line. As it turned out, Spengler, the 'pedagogue', of whom Albert Schweitzer had said that he 'stumbled through history in seven-league boots', was right. The French Army was 'swept away' and the British driven back across the Channel;

Beck and the General Staff 'experts' were apparently made to look foolish, though they had not yet been proved wrong. These lightning victories meant that the war would be a long one, but they were not decisive. With the expansion of the war into the Second World War the politico-military situation developed precisely as Beck had forecast in his memoranda.

But first we had to suffer setbacks greater than anything which little Karl Miessnick, the famous third-former so often quoted by Goerdeler, could have expected even from his 'greatest warlord of all time'. Against the Army's 'expert' advice, in other words that of Brauchitsch and Halder, Hitler ordered Germany's first amphibious operation to drive the Franco-British expeditionary force from Norway. It succeeded. Within three weeks in April 1940 Denmark and Norway had been occupied by the Wehrmacht. Hitler and O.K.W. had triumphed over the General Staff sceptics who had described this first amphibious operation as 'militarily irresponsible' and had foretold a catastrophic end to it. Dohnanyi was bitter and said sarcastically that the British still had not realised what sort of man they were dealing with.

My friends and I were as dumbfounded by Hitler's victory over the Western Powers in Denmark and Norway as were the General Staff experts. We comforted ourselves by saying that the casualties were out of all proportion to results achieved, but, apart from the families concerned, who among the German people cared? Meanwhile nobody could suspect that Hitler would shortly present the German people with the greatest possible political temptation by his victory over France.

During the spring of 1940 Prince Louis Ferdinand was serving as instrument-flying instructor at an airfield near Danzig; he frequently came to Berlin since Princess Kira had given birth to a second son on 22 March. While on training flights over Poland he had seen the ruins of Warsaw and other war devastation and had been profoundly shaken. Dohnanyi was saying that someone must bring the generals to a sense of their responsibilities and wondered whether the Prince could not do it. He declared himself ready at once and of his own accord wrote a letter to Beck which Dohnanyi handed over. Beck was most impressed by the Prince's readiness to take a personal initiative, but sent word to say that it was too late; the Western offensive had been ordered and could no longer be stopped – who would survive? In the light of this the Prince wrote a political testament for the benefit of his sons, in which he recognised his moral obligation to liberate the German people from the régime and protect the peoples of Europe from a life of slavery under Hitler.

On the day before the Western offensive Prince Michael was baptised. While I was changing for Prince Louis' reception in the evening, Ernst von Harnack appeared and implored me to arrange an interview for him with the Crown Prince. He had just heard from Klaus Bonhoeffer that I was going to the Hohenzollern family party, where the Crown Prince would be. Harnack wished to appeal to him to place himself at the head of the generals in order to save Germany. This idea had frequently been considered and discussed, Harnack's father, the famous theologian, being a close friend of the Kaiser. Nothing of this sort could be done, however, without prior agreement from Beck, to whom I felt myself pledged, as I told Harnack. He accompanied me to the Prince's villa in the Grunewald, all the time urging me to arrange an audience for him with the Crown Prince even without Beck's agreement.

It was a modest occasion with merely a cold buffet, but nevertheless memorable as a reflection of the old world – the women simply but elegantly dressed and the men in black, the Crown Prince among them resplendent in the uniform of the Death's Head Hussars, an impressive figure with his snow-white hair. He was full of grandfatherly *bonhomie*. He seemed to radiate something which made me wonder whether Harnack's idea was not a sensible one. Perhaps he was really the man who could carry the soldiers and officers along with him. Perhaps all the generals who had fought with him in the First World War would now follow him against Hitler. In fact there was never a possibility of winning the Crown Prince over to a *coup d'état* against Hitler. This Louis Ferdinand told me after a talk with his father after the Stalingrad catastrophe.

The lightning victory over France was a severe shock to my circle of friends. Psychologically we were in no way prepared for it. The General Staff 'experts' had been fatally wrong and had given us completely erroneous ideas about the course of the war. In their dejection and impotent rage many gave way to ill-humour – my brother Hans for instance. I reminded him that I had often quoted Spengler's forecast that in the next, now the present, war the French Army would simply be swept away. This somewhat smug remark infuriated him. When I then said that victory over France merely meant 'prolongation of the war – nothing else', he lost his temper and shouted at me: '*Will* you stop your blather! Everything that you and your friends have said since the outbreak of war has proved to be total nonsense. Surely you must at last realise that every forecast of Beck's has been disproved by the facts. The Nazis are winning the war.'

This was his fear, but it made no difference to his attitude to the régime. Not a single one of our conspiracy wavered after the victory over France; very many others in Germany, however, abandoned their last 'scruples' about the régime and the outcome of the war. They simply lined up behind the big battalions and made the most of the loot – after all, lobster and silver-fox furs were coming from Norway and brandy and champagne from France.

Those who no longer wished to win the war either on their own account or that of Hitler were few indeed. We had a difficult time until it finally began to dawn even on the opportunists that the 'final victory', for which men were still fighting and dying, was a will-o'-the-wisp. On the tactical level, I used to say among our friends that we must now wait, since something could be done against Hitler only when Germany had been bombed into ruins, when war had really been brought home to the people and when their attitude towards Hitler had changed. Dietrich Bonhoeffer emphasised to me that we should not take it upon ourselves to 'play the part of God and act as mentor to our people'. That was not our business. 'But because we are convinced,' he said, 'that Hitler is anti-Christ and the perverter of our people, we must fight him relentlessly and attempt to eliminate him entirely irrespective of whether he is gaining political successes and winning military victories for the German people.'

Shortly after the armistice with France Prince Wilhelm of Prussia, Louis Ferdinand's elder brother, died in hospital; he had been happy as a soldier and was highly popular with both officers and men in his regiment. His funeral in Potsdam was the occasion for a vast demonstration of loyalty to the House of Hohenzollern by all sections of the German people. The Hohenzollerns consequently became an object of suspicion to Heydrich's S.D. Oster and Dohnanyi warned me, and through me Louis Ferdinand, to be more watchful than ever for S.D. drawing-room spies and for Gestapo agents. Matters became easier when Princess Kira and her two sons moved to Zoppot near the airfield where Louis Ferdinand was on duty.

Intellectually and psychologically my friends and I lived in a curious sort of isolation from our fellow-men; since Hitler's lightning victories ordinary folk had increasingly abandoned all scruple about the oppression of Europe by his régime of violence. Despite the misjudgement by the General Staff of the prospects of success of certain individual operations, no doubt existed in our circle that the outcome of the war must be catastrophe for Germany. For the moment, however, we could do no more than wait until the trumpetings of victory had died away and the Wehrmacht had turned back before Moscow.

Even in the early days of the Second World War the lesson of the First held good – that the commitment of the American war potential would be decisive, and with Roosevelt's re-election in November 1940 the British were assured of the support of 'the most powerful man on earth'. In August 1941, when Hitler's last great victory in the Battle of Kiev was under way, Churchill and Roosevelt met to discuss the war situation and they signed the Atlantic Charter. Despite its involved diplomatic language it was unmistakably a pact for the overthrow and disarmament of Germany, all the more remarkable since theoretically the United States was still neutral. In the general jubilation over the Kiev victory and because Hitler announced to the world through Goebbels that the war in Russia had been won, little notice was taken of the Atlantic Charter in Germany. For us, however, there was now no longer any doubt that, whether the United States was involved in the war or not, Roosevelt's voice would be heard on all vital decisions, not least in the event of a change of régime in Germany. Our hopes revived, particularly after the invasion of Russia.

As a preparatory step on the psychological side it seemed to me of value to put the friendship between Prince Louis Ferdinand and Roosevelt in the right light and show that this was no mere high-level social contact but a true friendship based on serious and repeated discussion of political and other contemporary problems. I therefore asked Louis Lochner, head of the Associated Press in Berlin whom both Louis Ferdinand and I knew well, to interview the Prince in American fashion about his relationships with Roosevelt, so that any reader of the interview might get a true picture. Louis Lochner and I accordingly met Louis Ferdinand in Schildberg, a Hohenzollern estate in Brandenburg where Princess Kira and the children were living at the time.

Copies of the interview were slipped into the right channels by Oster and Dohnanyi. It read as if, somewhere and at some time, it had been published in the United States; as far as content was concerned it was perfectly genuine, the only non-genuine aspect being the fact that it had never appeared in print. Its contents, however, had the desired effect. Months later Beck asked me about the interview. It had been shown to him by an officer unknown to me who thought he had discovered in it the solution to our external political problems. Meanwhile, on the basis of information from an American acquaintance Ulrich von Hassell had assured both the military faction and the civilian dignitaries that Roosevelt had only one aim in foreign policy – to bring down Hitler. In this connection Popitz told me that the Americans had let it be known that replacement of the German régime by a constitutional monarchy under Louis Ferdinand would be favourably received in the United States, and not by Roosevelt alone.

On my suggestion Popitz discussed with Beck the question whether we should try to establish a direct link between Louis Ferdinand and Roosevelt via Louis Lochner. The latter did not know that there was already an organised conspiracy to overthrow Hitler, but he did know a whole series of influential politicians of the pre-Hitler period – he had been on close personal terms with Brüning, for instance. Owing to his long-standing friendship with Louis Ferdinand he could be guaranteed as completely trustworthy. It was therefore Louis Ferdinand's decision whether Lochner should be let into the secret – and he was in favour. Popitz, however, advised extreme caution.

In late September 1941 I invited Louis Lochner to meet Ernst von Harnack in my house. Harnack gave a most impressive exposé, choosing his words carefully. It gave Lochner the necessary insight into the conspiracy to enable him to inform Roosevelt personally. Harnack was outspoken in his criticism of the régime's crimes, and he made a most moving case against our military commanders who had been promoted to the highest rank and continued to fight for Hitler although they knew full well the criminal nature of the régime. As if pleading before a world tribunal, Harnack emphasised our moral disgust, but also our impotence, forcing us to look for allies among people in foreign countries who thought as we did. What was the object, Louis Lochner asked, and did we wish to re-establish the monarchy? Harnack's reply was: 'Germany must become a state based on law once more; everything else is secondary.'

Louis Lochner was a close friend of Major (as he then was) William Hohenthal, Assistant Military Attaché at the American Embassy in Berlin, whom I later knew well as Military Attaché in

Madrid. I also knew the American Naval Attaché, Commander Albert Schrader. Goerdeler wished to use these contacts in order to send his plans to Roosevelt with a covering letter from Louis Ferdinand, asking for American support in negotiations with Britain after a successful overthrow of the régime. Behind this was the thought that, if Roosevelt's reaction was favourable, our efforts to persuade one of the field marshals to lead the *coup d'état* would carry more weight. Commander Schrader lived in the Grunewald next-door to Louis Ferdinand's villa. Through a gap in the garden hedge Louis Ferdinand and I would often visit the Schraders after dark to exchange information and discuss the world political situation over a glass of whisky.

It seemed to me too risky to let the American service attachés into the secret, still more so to give them letters to Roosevelt – they were specially closely watched by Heydrich's secret service and also by the military Abwehr. I discussed the matter with Oster and Dohnanyi and they both consulted Canaris. Via Dohnanyi he sent an urgent warning to Dr Goerdeler not to let the American service attachés have anything on paper. I promised Dohnanyi to sever my connections with Hohenthal and Schrader.

In November 1941 the question of United States entry into the war still lay completely open. No sensible person dreamt that Hitler would go so far as to declare war on America. Nevertheless, in September Roosevelt had already ordered the American fleet to open fire on German ships found in certain American coastal waters and from then on it seemed to me only a question of time before we found ourselves at war with the United States. I consequently urged my friends to give Louis Lochner more detailed information about our plans and the members of our circle. In my view he should be in a position to give Roosevelt a first-hand picture of the men, the forces and the political tendencies gathering in Germany to overthrow the régime. Louis Lochner was well aware of the danger of making notes or writing memoranda and had developed his own technique to assist his memory. If we were discussing something he would note down a few key words which leapt to the eye as he wrote. Later he would destroy his note-sheet and carry in his head what he intended to pass to Roosevelt. He was due for leave in Switzerland in December and we wondered whether he should not contact Roosevelt from there.

Our requests were to be transmitted to Roosevelt by Louis

Lochner with a friendly covering note from Louis Ferdinand. They were as follows:

1. We were endeavouring to overthrow the régime with the help of disaffected generals, to end the war as rapidly as possible and to re-establish the rule of law in the State.

2. In the event of a rising we requested the enemy powers not to attempt to exploit internal unrest for strategic purposes.

3. The rights of the oppressed peoples and persecuted persons would be restored.

4. Our efforts could be assisted from outside by announcements or confidential communications to the effect that the Western Powers would be prepared to conclude peace with the German people once they were purged of Nazism.

5. We requested the President to support us in the interests of a rapid termination of hostilities.

Although according to the rules of resistance secret discussions should, if possible, take place between two people only, in this case we arranged a larger gathering for Louis Lochner in the house of Josef Wirmer. For security reasons he was not to come by car but was to meet me at a metro station in Charlottenburg. As I was about to leave, Louis Ferdinand telephoned unexpectedly. He had resigned from the Luftwaffe and was running the Hohenzollern model farm at Cadinen in East Prussia. His object in resigning was to anticipate a secret order issued by Hitler at Goebbels' instigation laying down that 'all members of the former ruling Houses with relatives in enemy countries were to be released from the Wehrmacht'. Goebbels had insisted on this since, after the death of Prince Wilhelm of Prussia, certain of the royal princes had distinguished themselves for bravery, and he feared that this might give rise to monarchist tendencies. I hurried over to Louis Ferdinand in the Prinzessin Palace on Unter den Linden, where he had a two-room attic apartment (he had given up his Grunewald villa). I told him that I was on the way to meet Louis Lochner in order to take him to a meeting of our friends *chez* Josef Wirmer and asked whether he would like to come along. 'Better not,' he replied, 'because you might want to talk about me there.' He accompanied me to the Charlottenburg metro station and then rode with me and Louis Lochner in the blacked-out train to Lichterfelde, whence he went home by himself.

At Josef Wirmer's, in addition to our host and myself, Louis Lochner met Jakob Kaiser, speaking for Wilhelm Leuschner, Klaus Bonhoeffer, Justus Delbrück representing Dohnanyi, Oster and also Beck, Max Habermann and Bernhard Letterhaus. He was able to discuss our plans and intentions in detail and, as a result of these personal contacts, be accredited as a sort of ambassador from the internal German resistance to Roosevelt. For Louis Lochner it was an impressive occasion which he has described in his book *What about Germany*. On the return journey he told me that he received regular information from a former trade-union official who had already apparently heard of 'the generals' who proposed to revolt once Hitler had suffered severe defeats. He had not taken much account of this since he knew that the hopes we had placed in Fritsch had come to nothing. Our best recommendation to Roosevelt, however, was the fact that, despite Hitler's victories, we had not ceased to work for his overthrow.

Roosevelt's mind was concentrated on Hitler's victories and his crimes against the oppressed peoples, for which he regarded the entire German people as responsible. After the Japanese attack on Pearl Harbor German journalists in the United States were interned; American journalists in Germany were arrested and interned in Bad Nauheim. I saw Louis Lochner once more on the night before his arrest. Shortly thereafter the Gestapo dragged him from his bed. He and his family did not reach the United States until June 1942. When I next saw him again, in London in the summer of 1945, he told me what had happened on his arrival home. He could no longer approach Roosevelt, who was already surrounded by a 'ring' which he could not penetrate. Roosevelt had lost interest in German resistance to Hitler and during his internment Louis Lochner had lost touch with political developments in the United States. Re-establishment of his contacts in Washington took time and he had been slandered by some of his 'dear colleagues' who had said that he had been 'on very friendly terms' with the Nazis. The fact is that he was the only American journalist whom we took into our confidence as a proven opponent of the régime. Not wishing to draw attention to himself, he had never been particularly forthcoming to the Nazis on the surface. In his 1942/3 diaries Goebbels said of him: 'I have never thought much of Lochner. We made too much fuss of him.'

Lochner eventually managed to speak to Mrs Eleanor Roosevelt, but she was distant and condescending, merely asking: 'Do these dear little children really think that there would ever be a chance for them to get back to the throne?' Our purposes could hardly have been more grossly misunderstood – Louis Ferdinand's support of the resistance sprang from pure moral indignation. The plan for a Hohenzollern restoration did not stem from him but from Beck, Popitz, Goerdeler and the other leaders; Leuschner, Jakob Kaiser and other prominent working-class representatives had subscribed to it with the proviso that a referendum should be held. In any case the Prince and his family had been risking their necks, as we all had for years. I wanted to explain all this to Mrs Roosevelt when she came to a United Nations meeting in London in 1946, but she wrote saying that she had 'unfortunately no time to speak to me'.

When Hitler, intoxicated with his apparent invincibility, had declared war on the United States, a vast coalition began to form against Germany. From far away, behind the Urals in the east and from America in the west, its forces gathered to drive the Wehrmacht from the *lebensraum* which it had conquered.

But our field marshals and senior commanders only realised this when it was too late. In Bridgend after the war Brauchitsch said to me: 'As long as I was in command in Russia operations there went according to plan.' He had ordered winter clothing for the troops, he said, well before the first Russian winter. 'The débâcle began,' he went on, 'in late August 1941 when Hitler began interfering with the operational command.' Was there ever any real chance of winning a war on two fronts, I asked him. He did not say 'No' but maintained that this was a question no one could answer. In his post-war monograph *Hitler als Feldherr* [*Hitler as warlord*] Halder explained how the war in Russia could have been won!

Brauchitsch felt himself in no way responsible for the disastrous German defeats, still less for the fate which overtook the German people as a result of the war. He said that in December 1941 during the heaviest fighting in front of Moscow he had 'fought to the limit of his strength to persuade Hitler to withdraw the front to a fortified winter position'. Hitler would no longer be advised. Keitel and Jodl, he said, 'with their sycophancy' had given Hitler megalomaniac ideas about his genius and infallibility as a commander. Owing to his continuous quarrels with Hitler he, Brauchitsch, had had increasingly frequent heart attacks and had resigned. That ended Germany's problems as far as he was concerned!

7
World War

On 18 November 1941 the world was told that Ernst Udet, Göring's Master-General of Air Ordnance, a First World War fighter pilot with the 'Pour le Mérite' [the German V.C.] and a reputation as an aerobatics pilot extending far outside Germany, had met with a fatal accident 'while testing a new weapon'. In fact he had shot himself with a service revolver. It was the sequel to a quarrel between him, Hitler and Göring over the Luftwaffe's failure in the Russian campaign. The Stukas had been ineffective in the vast expanses of Russia, and Hitler had told Udet to construct a strategic bomber fleet at once – '2000 at least'. Udet had replied disrespectfully that Hitler might just as well order him to construct 20,000 bombers – 'all you have to do is to give me the men and material'. No one had spoken to Hitler like that before and he stormed out of the room.

Göring, who had been taken aback, soon recovered his composure. Though Udet had been his fellow-officer in the First World War, Göring dressed him down, threatening him with proceedings for financial chicanery in a French aircraft factory under his control. Udet was furious that he should be accused of underhand dealings by Göring of all people, who had always made much of their war service together. He spent the evening with friends and a female companion, was very depressed and drank a great deal. On getting home late at night he called his lady friend and said: 'Come along with me.' She heard the shot over the telephone.

Udet was given a state funeral. Hitler made a funeral oration and Göring, wearing a suitably mournful expression, walked for several miles behind the coffin from the Ministry of Aviation to the Invaliden cemetery. I was not invited to the funeral. Later Leo Roth, one of the senior 'Old Eagle' pilots and a mutual friend of both Udet and myself, told me that he had torn up my invitation card since he was afraid that I might seize the opportunity to attempt to assassinate Hitler. The idea had never crossed my mind. No one knew beforehand that Hitler would attend the funeral. We had missed a unique opportunity of getting near to Hitler.

The nomination for Udet's successor as Master-General of Air Ordnance was Gablenz and so for the first time an uncompromising opponent of the régime had been appointed to the higher levels of the Luftwaffe. His remarkable capabilities, to which the German Lufthansa owed its world-wide reputation, were of more importance to Hitler, Göring and the equipment of the Luftwaffe than his political views. 'The right man in the right place at last,' Dr Goerdeler said – on his ministerial list Gablenz was already earmarked to succeed Göring. Goerdeler wished to talk to Gablenz, who was ready to receive him but sent word via me not to place too great hopes in him since he was certain to be turned out by Göring soon. He was impulsive and in the habit of speaking his mind; in the long run he was bound to have a row with Göring.

Until the departure of Brauchitsch we had been under the illusion that the Army Commander-in-Chief could be persuaded to lead a *coup d'état* against Hitler. Once Hitler had assumed command of the Army himself, however, there was no longer any question of a *coup* 'from the top'. Goerdeler now believed that the Army Group commanders in Russia could be persuaded to revolt and force Hitler to resign. Goerdeler's reasoning was that ever since the first severe setbacks before Moscow the Army Group Commanders had realised that 'Corporal Hitler's' strategy was disastrous and were cursing him heartily. Neither Beck nor Goerdeler were men of the temper of Hammerstein-Equord, the former Colonel-General, with whom I discussed the problem in January 1942. He thought nothing of such ideas and maintained quite simply that 'the march to catastrophe could only be stopped by a revolver bullet into "him"'.

The army commanders in Russia, he said, had no picture of the over-all situation as in the First World War. They did not know what was going on to left or right of their sector of the front and they were totally deceived by those above them. They believed what they were told in order to stifle their conscience. If they would get together they could be better informed but arrogance and jealousy kept them apart. Whenever they assembled in a headquarters – an Army Group headquarters or elsewhere – they arrived with a retinue of staff officers in whose presence they could discuss nothing confidential. There was no spirit of solidarity among the senior commanders, as there had been previously when they had understood each other without having to say very much. For these reasons Goerdeler would not be able to bring about any combined action by the army commanders.

There was one field marshal who would have been ready to do what Hammerstein had wanted to do in the autumn of 1939 when he had a command on the Western Front, in other words 'to eliminate Hitler once and for all without legal proceedings'. This was Field Marshal Erwin von Witzleben. He had been on Beck's side ever since the Sudeten crisis and was determined 'to act'. In the winter of 1941/2 he was Commander-in-Chief of the German troops in France, but he could not persuade Hitler to make a 'trip' to Paris. Witzleben had none of the moral scruples such as others used to excuse their reluctance to sanction the 'murder' of Hitler. I said to Hammerstein: 'I do not understand why fully fledged field marshals who, without a thought, send thousands of soldiers to their death in Russia every day, should have moral scruples about killing "him", if the entire people could be saved thereby.'

These gentlemen were not merely being hypocrites, Hammerstein said – 'if that were so, we could get somewhere very quickly'. It was something much worse, he continued; they had all been spellbound by Hitler and in their heart of hearts they could not now free themselves from him. They could no longer bring themselves to break with Hitler, with the possible exception of Fromm, the Commander-in-Chief of the Replacement Army. 'I know him very well,' Hammerstein said. 'He has gone off on the wrong tack. He will realise this one day when it is too late.' Fromm did not in fact come to his senses until the spring of 1944 when he asked Stauffenberg to be his Chief of Staff. It was indeed too late. Moreover, until the last moment Fromm blew hot and cold.

In support of his plan to incite the senior army commanders in Russia to mutiny Goerdeler used somewhat curious arguments. He maintained, for instance, that the oath sworn to Hitler early in August 1934 by soldiers, officers, generals and officials was valid 'only' in his capacity as Head of State, not as Commander-in-Chief of the Army. In the latter capacity they could refuse to obey him if he issued nonsensical orders. I commented that Hitler was nevertheless wearing the same uniform tunic without badges of rank and how should the field marshals distinguish between the 'corporal' and the Head of State? The object must be to free the field marshals from Hitler's spell. But that, Hammerstein maintained, could only be done in private talks out there at the front, man to man; it could unfortunately not be done by writing letters to this person and that about 'the situation', as Beck was in the habit of doing.

For centuries German officers and soldiers had pledged themselves to their King in person. They had similarly pledged themselves to Hitler under an oath which all, with certain exceptions, had sworn voluntarily. Did this mean, however, that the oath which the senior commanders had previously sworn to the King was now no longer valid? Could not Louis Ferdinand base his case upon it and, as Pretender, win the field marshals over to action against Hitler? Goerdeler and Ernst von Harnack argued the subject earnestly. Goerdeler continually returned to the idea that it should be possible to 'eliminate' Hitler, but he was not prepared to accept that this could only be done by murdering him. The idea that the commanders on the Russian front, now stabilised, could be induced to mutiny was unrealistic, Harnack said; the problem was simply one of killing Hitler. Harnack's retort to Goerdeler's scruples was a sarcastic witticism: 'The bashful man begets no children.'

After listening to this conversation between the two leaders I decided to arrange a meeting between Louis Ferdinand and Hammerstein. He had known the Prince as a schoolboy and I hoped that he would advise and inquire whether we could not still do something along Goerdeler's lines to exploit the traditional respect in which the senior commanders in Russia still held the House of Hohenzollern.

We visited Hammerstein in his house after dark on a cold winter's day in January 1942. The general still appeared alert and full of energy, although he was already suffering from the cancer of which he died a year later. With its hunting trophies and old family furniture his house might have been that of a senior forestry official – far more comfortable than the ostentatious villas which Hitler had had built by Speer for his field marshals. Was I reckless in taking the Prince to see the general who had once been Hitler's most powerful opponent? Hammerstein said that his house was 'still' not watched, though his telephone was certainly tapped. He would never telephone. Those who listened in on his telephone would hear nothing but his daughter talking to her friends about her homework.

Whereas Goerdeler was rather apt to turn a discussion into a lecture, Hammerstein was a good listener and he let the Prince talk. What he had to say about 'the situation' brought upon the German people by Hitler and his field marshals was very much to the point; it was a highly realistic description and appreciation of the over-all war situation. 'One is really ashamed to be a German,' Louis Ferdinand said; 'it can't go on like this. It must be brought to an end. I would like some indication from you as to whether I can do anything to halt what you call the march to catastrophe.' The discussion was a serious one and on a high level. Here were an ex-commander-in-chief of the Army and a prince of the Hohenzollerns united in their anxiety to avert what subsequently came upon us–proof that, in the mind of the true Prussian, morality and integrity were still powerful impulses.

It was not possible, Hammerstein said, to halt the 'march to catastrophe' except by immediate military action. Goerdeler's plan to persuade the 'gentlemen out there' to take action would fail simply because they lacked civil courage. 'I call it cowardice,' Hammerstein said to Louis Ferdinand. 'One can only proceed against "him" revolver in hand. But that is not your job.' After almost two hours of discussion we were forced to admit that, whether with or without the Prince, there was no prospect of persuading the senior commanders in Russia to take action against Hitler. Downcast over our impotence, we made our way home through the winter night.

Louis Ferdinand stayed in Berlin for a few more days. We had further talks with Jakob Kaiser, Josef Wirmer, Klaus Bonhoeffer and Justus Delbrück and for the first time included Captain Ludwig Gehre, whom Louis Ferdinand did not know. In the house of Rudolph Wahl, the author, we met Dr Rudolf Pechel, editor of the *Deutsche Rundschau*. He was on the way to Paris to meet Field Marßhal von Witzleben. Being a close friend of Hammerstein, he was sure that Witzleben 'would initiate some action'. His trip to Paris was fatal to him, however. On his return to Berlin the Gestapo arrested him. One of their French agents had discovered that, while in Paris, Pechel was proposing to contact Dr Rauschning, former President of the Danzig Senate, and Dr Brüning the ex-Reich Chancellor.

Meanwhile an entirely new function in the conspiracy had come my way. I had to fly to Madrid on duty for Lufthansa, since Iberia, our subsidiary there, was to be reorganised. Dr Goerdeler therefore sent word by Jakob Kaiser asking me to come to the Hospiz am Askanischen Platz opposite the Anhalter Station, where he stayed when in Berlin. Goerdeler wished to utilise the opportunity to establish links from Madrid to London and Washington, in particular, with Prince Louis Ferdinand's help, to Roosevelt. So far I had only met Goerdeler in the company of other people. This time, however, he insisted that we should talk alone. This I found surprising since I had been told that he did not set much store by the opinions of younger people. Meanwhile, however, I had become an important link in the chain of conspiracy; it could barely function as a whole without my assistance.

Dr Goerdeler received me in a small modest hotel room where he was still eating a frugal cold supper and drinking tea. He excused himself, saying that he had reached the hotel later than intended. He took the tea-cosy off the pot and clapped it on the telephone, adding one of the sofa cushions with the words 'better to be sure'. Everyone in those days was afraid of microphones hidden in the telephone. When he had finished his meal he gave me an exhaustive lecture, explaining all his plans for action against the régime and for the renewal of Germany. I was like the junior to whom the professor was explaining an elaborately designed programme of work. It was in fact a summary of his internal and external political programme, basically as set out in his memoranda published by his biographer, Gerhard Ritter.

Finally Goerdeler explained why he had asked me to come and see him privately. The importance to him of a link with Roosevelt, he said, could not be overestimated. He was already in touch with London and also the United States through Wallenberg, the Swedish banker, but direct contact with Roosevelt, vouched for by Prince Louis Ferdinand, was 'vital' and might 'mean our salvation'. The Americans were totally unfamiliar with circumstances in Europe and Germany. Misjudgements, with ultimately catastrophic results as in 1918, could only be prevented if Roosevelt was given a true picture of what respectable Germans were thinking. For the moment the American picture of the German people had not yet been distorted by war propaganda, but that would not last for ever. If the American propaganda machine were once turned on to whip up hatred against Germany, it would no longer be easy even for Louis Ferdinand to talk to Roosevelt.

Armed with Goerdeler's instructions I reached Madrid. As I entered the great dining-room of the Palace Hotel on the first evening it looked to me like a Hollywood film set – snow-white tablecloths and flower-decked tables, fluorescent lighting, beautiful well-dressed women, a plethora of tail-coated waiters, waitresses in black satin with white caps and aprons, soft music from a trio behind a screen of palms. It was all like a fairy-tale. Gerd Lindenberg, the Lufthansa representative in Spain, was no longer impressed; it was a daily occurrence for him. We soon discovered that politically we were of the same mind and became good friends.

A bell-boy called me to the telephone. On the line was Angel Ferrari-Nunez, my Spanish friend from my student days in Frankfurt University. We had not seen each other for nearly ten years and meanwhile the Spanish Civil War had taken place. He came round to the hotel at once and we immediately began to probe to see where the other stood politically. We had both remained the same. He said: 'I am the only liberal here.'

Angel's father-in-law was the Marques de Aledo, one of the most influential Spanish bankers; Sir Samuel Hoare, the British Ambassador, was often to be seen in his house. As far as the Germans and Gestapo in Madrid were concerned I was completely above-board as legal adviser to Lufthansa. To the British and American secret services in the Madrid 'international merry-go-round', however, I was obviously suspect from the moment of my appearance. Angel was harried by his family and others with: 'What's your friend Otto John doing here in Madrid?' My job was to protect Lufthansa interests in Iberia and work out new company articles, but it was generally assumed, Angel said, that I had come with some secret commission from the German Ministry of Aviation. I had better pretend to be a *bon viveur*. As such I should be more credible since Germans generally came either as agents or to enjoy 'a bit of peace in Madrid'.

Little discussion was needed to show that Angel and I were at one in thinking that sooner or later the war would end in fearful catastrophe for Germany. Why then, Angel asked, did I want to go back to Germany when I saw all this so clearly? I could not remain in Madrid, however, nor anywhere else in Spain. Only recently the Gestapo had kidnapped the son of a German industrialist who did not wish to serve in the Wehrmacht and carted him across the frontier into occupied France. If I wished, however, I could go to South America. He and his family would arrange money and contacts for me. I had to come out in my true colours or Angel, his family and his friends would have found it impossible to understand why I wanted to go back to Berlin despite my antipathy to the régime. I confided to him that I felt myself pledged to a conspiracy whose object was to overthrow Hitler.

After more than a week in Madrid I received the call for which I was waiting – from Colonel Don Luis Ruiz de Valdivia, formerly Spanish Military Attaché in Berlin and an avuncular friend of Prince Louis Ferdinand ever since 1921. At that time he had rescued the young Prince from his strict Prussian court upbringing in Potsdam and introduced him into Berlin musical circles, then becoming the Prince's mentor in a life based on music and cosmopolitanism. Don Luis came over at once to my Lufthansa office and invited me out to dinner, to which he brought Juan Terrasa, a Spanish diplomat who had been a friend of Louis Ferdinand's when they had been students together in Berlin late in the 1920s.

Juan was a Catalan from Barcelona, then in his late thirties. He was an accomplished musician, having studied both in Munich and Berlin among other places. Before the Spanish Civil War he had been in Belgrade where he was well acquainted with von Hassell who was his German colleague; he had also served in Moscow and Washington. As proof of his manifold academic interests, he painted and had composed a small volume of poems in English. Like Valdivia he had become an expert connoisseur of music. He read *Pravda* as regularly as he did the main newspapers from the Western capitals. In the upheaval of the Spanish Civil War he had been denounced as too liberal and socialistically minded and had been imprisoned, spending two years in degrading conditions. Eventually he had been rescued and rehabilitated by Ramon Franco, Franco's brother, the aviator, who had served with him in the Spanish Embassy in Washington.

I would really have preferred to talk to Valdivia alone beforehand. Over the aperitif I asked him in a whisper whether one could talk freely in this restaurant. Valdivia did not at first seem to understand what I meant and Juan Terrasa explained. Valdivia then said in German: 'We can say anything we like here.' I had much to tell Valdivia and he asked endless questions. He had not been in Germany for eight years and was particularly interested in my account of the war. Juan Terrasa listened, saying noticeably little. After dinner he drove me back to my hotel and said: 'You talk quite differently from all Germans here. We must take a walk and talk at greater length.'

About 9 a.m., when Madrid society and the Gestapo who had

adopted its habits were usually still asleep, Juan and I would walk through the Retiro, Madrid's central park, where we could talk undisturbed. Louis Ferdinand having vouched for his reliability, I did not have to trouble about telling him of our conspiracy and our purpose in seeking a link to Roosevelt. Juan knew of the personal friendship between Louis Ferdinand and Roosevelt from his time as attaché at the Spanish Embassy in Washington; he also had friends there who might be able to further our requests. He advised me, as a first step, to contact Willard Beaulac, the American Chargé d'Affaires in Madrid (the Ambassador had been recalled by Roosevelt), with whom he was on friendly terms.

Beaulac was a man in his early fifties who gave the impression of being a southerner and fitted well into Madrid society. When we met in Juan's apartment, he eyed me in a most undiplomatic manner. Realising that he had probably been briefed by the American secret service, if not wrongly, at least incompletely, I explained to him my position with Lufthansa and outlined to him the official business which had brought me to Madrid; I confided to him that I was a member with Prince Louis Ferdinand of a resistance group which was looking for a link to Roosevelt. He did not know Germany at all and had no conception of our politico-military situation; he said that for America the war in the Far East had priority. He also asked whether I believed that Germany could win the war. I gave him detailed reasons why this was an impossibility, mentioning the fuel problem, Hitler's planned offensive to capture the Caucasus oil-fields and my feeling that the first setbacks in front of Moscow were the beginning of the end. Nevertheless, I then said, as Gablenz had told me, that Germany could hold out for a good two years before her manpower and material were totally exhausted. Beaulac promised to place his Washington contacts at our disposal and to keep in touch with me through Juan Terrasa. As he left, he said: 'Good luck! You need it!'

On my return to Berlin early in April 1942 I rang up my parents to learn that my brother Hans had been severely wounded in Russia. He had a bullet in the head, another had gone through his shoulder and a third lodged in a lung; he was paralysed down the left side. My mother wept bitterly over the telephone. My father, though an anti-Nazi, had been an officer in the First World War and so was more militarily minded; he told me with some pride that Hans had been promoted N.C.O. for bravery in the field and had been awarded the Iron Cross 1st Class. I could not conceal my rage. There was no need for Hans to have become a soldier. Through Ludwig Gehre and his friends in Replacement Army headquarters I could have arranged for him to be placed in a reserved occupation. But he had not wanted that. In despair at the thought that Hitler might win the war he had enlisted shortly after the victory over France with the remark: 'Better to get hit by a bullet somewhere.'

Barely had I finished my evening telephone conversation with my parents an hour after landing in Tempelhof than a worried Klaus Bonhoeffer appeared to tell me that Dr Pechel had been arrested. He warned me not to ring Pechel, as had been agreed before my trip to Madrid. Pechel and his *Deutsche Rundschau* had long been a thorn in Goebbels' flesh. Between the lines he had continually criticised the régime; one had only to replace the word 'Stalin' by 'Hitler' in his articles, for instance, to see who was really being attacked as the wrecker of our culture. Many people thought that these intellectual *tours de force* were not justified in view of the appalling risks entailed in coming into open collision with the régime. Like Karl Ludwig von Guttenberg's *Weisse Blätter*, however, they were a moral support to many in their conflict with the régime.

Pechel's arrest proved to be a severe blow to the leaders of the conspiracy because for a long time we could not find out why he had been arrested and therefore who was endangered as a result. He knew, for instance, why I had gone to Madrid; he had known the leaders of the conspiracy for many years; he was a close friend of Hammerstein; he was among those who knew of Witzleben's intentions against Hitler. 'All who knew Pechel,' Klaus Bonhoeffer said, 'are in danger.' Dohnanyi was continually reminding us that no one could say whether, or for how long, Pechel could withstand the Gestapo's tortures. If Pechel had not proved so steadfast under arrest, the conspiracy might have been blown in the spring of 1942. The Gestapo could not compete with his intellectual ability, however.

At the end of April 1942 Hitler made a speech to the Reichstag in which he claimed to have saved the Russian front from military catastrophe. This was to some extent justified in that, by his brutal intervention, he had in fact brought the front to a halt once more. Beck, certain other generals and Goerdeler all forecast that the Wehrmacht would not survive another such winter in Russia. Goerdeler maintained that, as a result of their fearful experience of the Russian winter, the field marshals were coming to their senses. If only they would now bring themselves to take action against Hitler, the terrible casualties in Russia might subsequently prove to have been to some purpose. He had meanwhile met his confidant Wallenberg in Stockholm and, when I reported to him my conversation with Beaulac in Madrid, he thought that perhaps we might no longer have need of this link. However he now wished to meet and talk to Prince Louis Ferdinand.

I could not, of course, arrange a meeting either by telephone or letter and therefore drove down to Cadinen for a weekend. First, however, I wished to be clear whether the historic father–son problem of the House of Hohenzollern had been solved for our generation. Goerdeler said that he and Beck had finally opted for Louis Ferdinand, since the Crown Prince was 'no longer thinkable' owing to his role in the First World War. Angel Ferrari and Juan Terrasa had said the same to me in Madrid. I had no wish to become an intermediary for a restoration of the Crown Prince, although Popitz had pointed out to me that, as a monarchist, one should think on legitimist lines and the Crown Prince accordingly had precedence. This led me to make a sort of confession of political faith to Popitz and Goerdeler. I told them that I did not care what was the future form of German state; all I was interested in was finally ridding mankind of 'the scourge of Hitler'. My sole personal and political aim was to see this. I myself would like to stay in civil aviation. Josef Wirmer remarked that no doubt I would not be averse to being Chairman of a 'Royal' Lufthansa.

I drove down to Cadinen 'Castle'. It was in fact a simple country house which the Kaiser had bought together with the surrounding estate running down to the Haff, in order to make a model farm of it. It was situated in attractive rolling country and stretched down to the shore of the Haff. Elbing was the nearest town and railway station. Cadinen itself was situated away from any main road and was an ideal spot in which to live quietly and hold a meeting such as Goerdeler proposed. The Prince and Princess lived in isolation and could only keep themselves informed by listening to 'enemy stations' such as the London B.B.C. They were longing to hear the story of my experiences in Madrid and particularly my account of the overall war situation, on which I had been able to form a far better picture in Madrid than in Germany, having had access to the British and American press and radio.

'What will you do if the Russians come?' I asked the Prince. 'We shall get along even with them,' he said. 'We haven't done them any harm.' He would not hear of having to evacuate Cadinen one day. Why did Dr Goerdeler want to come and talk to him, he asked, if he had no real reason to believe in an imminent fall of the régime. Princess Kira was sceptical. She had no illusions any more.

In the light of the information on Germany's politico-military situation which I had gathered in Madrid there seemed no possibility that the Wehrmacht could win this war on two fronts, precisely as Beck had forecast to senior commanders before the war. In addition, for me and my political friends it was an appalling thought that Hitler might be able to perpetuate his régime of terror over Europe for an unpredictable period. If we did not succeed in overthrowing him, he would only fall with the unconditional surrender of the Wehrmacht to enemy forces. That was my view. As Goerdeler had commissioned me to tell Louis Ferdinand, however, there was now fresh hope of some action by the field marshals against Hitler because, after their severe setbacks during the Russian winter, they would be actuated by considerations of sheer self-preservation. Goerdeler had set down his views on this subject and on the increasingly menacing supply situation both of the Wehrmacht and the people in a series of memoranda which he had given me to pass to the Prince preparatory to their discussion. After we had agreed on a code-word so that we could arrange Goerdeler's visit by telephone, I set off back to Berlin.

On the return journey I went via Glogau since my brother had meanwhile been transferred to a hospital there and I was astounded to see the progress he had made. The paralysis of his left side was less marked and he was already allowed to get up. We were able to talk in the garden. The severity of his injuries had not reduced his interest in the politico-military situation. He assailed me with questions and criticisms and made sarcastic comments on the field marshals. He asked whether I was still 'playing about' with this conspiracy; if the conspirators intended to wait until the war was lost, they had better realise that Stalin would square accounts with them; no amends could ever be made, he said, for what we had done in Russia.

8

Illusory Plans

UNDER the impact of the severe German setbacks during the first Russian winter the question was raised within the military faction whether General Olbricht, as Colonel-General Fromm's deputy, should not simply seize the General's authority inside the Reich and initiate a rising against Hitler. But who would have followed this unknown armchair general? A military rising could only succeed if led by one of the field marshals who had become a popular figure through his lightning victories. Even before the war Field Marshal von Witzleben had declared himself ready to act – and these were no empty words on his part. In 1942, however, to ensure that he was physically fit for a *coup d'état*, he underwent an operation and was accordingly relieved as Commander-in-Chief in France. Henceforth he was a field marshal without troops. The other field marshals were cursing heartily about 'Corporal' Hitler's methods of command, but none of them gave any sign of being willing seriously to oppose Hitler, still less overthrow him. Colonel Henning von Tresckow, Chief of Staff to Army Group Centre, however, was making every effort to convince his commander, Field Marshal von Kluge, that it was both a necessity and a patriotic duty to do so.

Tresckow, now forty-one years of age, was a man of great intellectual and moral stature. He had fought as a young officer in the First World War and had then joined a bank; he therefore had experience of business life and considerable knowledge of the world. As described to me by Colonel Rudolf von Gersdorff, who had served with him on the staff of Army Group Centre, he was an outstanding personality from every point of view. He rejoined the Army in 1924 after a trip round the world and became a pupil of Beck's on the General Staff. The two were 'kindred spirits', Tresckow being a fanatical opponent of Hitler out of sheer moral indignation with the régime. He had systematically filled his staff in Army Group Centre with officers of similar views, appointing as his aide, for instance, Lieutenant (Reserve) Fabian von Schlabrendorff. The latter, a Berlin lawyer by profession, was a committed opponent of the régime; as one of Tresckow's closest associates he maintained contact with the military faction in Berlin and was therefore well known to my friend, Captain Ludwig Gehre.

When Schlabrendorff came to Berlin in the early summer of 1942, Gehre said that I must at all costs get to know 'this important person'. Justus Delbrück, our financier, invited me to lunch with Klaus Bonhoeffer, Gehre and Schlabrendorff and there I learnt why Schlabrendorff wished to make my acquaintance. He felt that he had been badly treated by Dohnanyi whom he had got to know through Colonel Oster; he said that Dohnanyi treated him 'as a lawyer would a junior clerk'. Dohnanyi was well aware of his own outstanding intelligence. He could be very cool and distant, particularly to generals and their staff officers who might be trying to play politics. Schlabrendorff had had a taste of this attitude when he had asked Dohnanyi to introduce him to Goerdeler – which he now asked me to do.

Dr Goerdeler was only too willing. The idea of a personal link to Field Marshal von Kluge via Schlabrendorff and Tresckow filled him with enthusiasm. He was convinced that he could win the Field Marshal over to his side and his plans for a *coup*. One evening I took Goerdeler along to Schlabrendorff's apartment where they got to know each other and could talk to their hearts' content. On the way home Goerdeler said to me that he would now like to talk to Prince Louis Ferdinand as soon as possible. After that he wished to visit Field Marshals von Kluge and Küchler, commanding Army Groups Centre and North on the Eastern Front.

To conceal his meeting with Louis Ferdinand, Goerdeler first visited his brother Fritz, who was municipal treasurer of Königsberg. Thence he went to Braunsberg where Louis Ferdinand and I awaited him and we all rode to Cadinen together in the Haff narrow-gauge coastal railway. Goerdeler was soon on good terms with the Prince and Princess. After lunch he gave them a succinct sweeping exposé of the catastrophic dangers threatening Germany. He assailed the leaders of the state as responsible for this situation, through their economic mismanagement and corruption; he explained the motives and purposes by which he felt morally compelled to overthrow the régime 'in order to re-establish law and decency in Germany'. There was no hint of sycophancy in his voice as he paid tribute to the virtues of the 'law-abiding, straightforward and clean leadership through which Prussia had become great under her kings'. Government on these lines must be re-established in Germany, he said. 'But how is this to happen?' Louis Ferdinand asked. Like me and the majority of my friends in the conspiracy he was quite clear that the murder of Hitler was an essential prerequisite to the *coup*. Even Beck had ultimately reached this conclusion, but Goerdeler still had most serious doubts. With a glance at me he said that he was not of the opinion that Hitler must necessarily be killed. A Christian should only kill in the most extreme emergency. A new German government should not incriminate itself beforehand by murder. One day murder might be necessary and even justified as an emergency measure in defence of the people, but it was a method to be employed only when all other methods had proved impracticable. 'If the army commanders will range themselves unanimously behind me,' Goerdeler said, 'I am entirely prepared to approach Hitler and demand his resignation to save our people and our country. If he refuses, we can always resort to the possibility of eliminating him by force.'

Beck had already tried in vain to instigate a similar mutiny against Hitler during the Sudeten crisis in the summer of 1938. Goerdeler knew this, of course, but he nevertheless believed that he could succeed where Beck had failed because meanwhile the Wehrmacht's potentially catastrophic situation had become fact. It was his mission, he said, justifying every personal effort and every personal risk, to convince the senior commanders that action must be taken at once. He was determined to visit these gentlemen in their headquarters and appeal to their consciences. They could hardly refuse to co-operate once it was made clear to them that total catastrophe could only be averted by the overthrow of the régime.

Louis Ferdinand reminded us of Hammerstein's remarks about the army commanders and said to Goerdeler that there was little hope of persuading the senior commanders at the front to rise against Hitler. 'But if we do not rid ourselves of Hitler of our own accord,' he said, 'the Allies will pursue the war ruthlessly until Germany is totally destroyed.' As an airman with knowledge of the American arms potential he could imagine very well what the American bombers would do to Germany once they were in mass production and ready for action. 'Then I propose,' Goerdeler replied at once, 'that the first thing to be done by every town and every village which acknowledges us after the *coup* is to lift its black-out.

The new government will ensure that such places are bombed no more. The people will heave a sigh of relief if the lights go up again.' Goerdeler's eyes lit up as he said this. That evening, after we had taken him by carriage to the station, Louis Ferdinand said: 'I believe Goerdeler will bring it off. He is the man to whom the German people's fate can be entrusted.'

Goerdeler's optimism proved illusory. In the first place the Wehrmacht won further spectacular victories in the summer of 1942. Rommel and his Afrika Korps captured Tobruk and pushed forward to El Alamein. According to Goebbels' grapevine propaganda his next offensive would carry him farther east through Egypt and Persia to join hands somewhere in Asia with the Japanese and drive the British out of Asia. People were only too ready to believe it all. In the Aero-Club I listened to young Luftwaffe officers carving up the world afresh – Egypt for the Italians, India for us! On the Eastern Front Army Group South captured Sevastopol, 'the strongest fortress in the world', drove into the Caucasus and came up against Stalingrad. But the more perceptive among the field marshals and General Staff officers knew that these were no decisive successes and that in the second winter of the war even worse defeats must be anticipated. When, therefore, disguised as a representative from the firm of Bosch with false papers provided by Oster, Goerdeler did actually visit Field Marshal von Kluge in his headquarters in Smolensk, Kluge was ready to listen. He, and still more Tresckow, were highly impressed by Goerdeler, who believed that he had won them both over. In fact, however, Goerdeler's only genuine ally was Tresckow; as was later proved, Kluge had only simulated determination to act against Hitler. Field Marshal Küchler, on the other hand, was quite honest with Goerdeler and refused to go along with him.

About this time Goerdeler began pressing for a talk with Gablenz. None of the leaders of the conspiracy had any contacts in the higher levels of the Luftwaffe. As Master-General of Air Ordnance Gablenz held a key position with ramifications throughout the armaments industry. He was quite ready to meet Goerdeler for a talk in my house one evening but had to call off the arrangement at the last moment because he had been kept late at a conference with Field Marshal Milch in the Ministry of Aviation. On the following Monday he invited me to dine at Horcher's with two of his nieces, the object being to agree on a fresh meeting with Goerdeler. The British raid on Dieppe had taken place that day and certain secret Luftwaffe navigational equipment had been lost. Hitler had been furious and Gablenz had therefore been kept very late in the Ministry. As he arrived he said: 'I hope the British won't spoil my weekend by invading.' The following Saturday, after a conference in Munich, he hoped to fly on to his farmhouse in Allgäu.

On the flight to Munich Gablenz, who was piloting the aircraft himself, crashed and was killed with all on board. The cause of the accident has never been explained. The word went round that the aircraft had been sabotaged in order to get rid of Gablenz. Göring ordered an inquiry and I saw its report since I had to deal with Gablenz's will; it said that 'the possibility of sabotage could not be excluded'.

Being a permanent and impetuous critic, Gablenz had long been expecting to be dismissed by Göring. Owing to the high regard in which he was held both in German and international aviation circles, however, Göring had not been able to bring himself to do this. Goerdeler said: 'This man is truly irreplaceable for us.'

Early in September 1942 Hitler dismissed Halder as Chief of the General Staff and replaced him by General Zeitzler. Among the leaders of the conspiracy and in the military faction this was regarded as a severe setback. Ludwig Gehre, on the other hand, thought that it served Halder right; he had missed his chance of departing honourably when he had failed to resign with Brauchitsch in the previous year. Even in 1918, Gehre said, Halder had been 'unwilling to leave the fleshpots' and ever since then had invariably complied with orders from on high; Halder had been obedient to the last and had always done his 'duty' for the Führer, at the same time talking treason and committing himself to the conspiracy. In fact, ever since Brauchitsch's departure Halder had been voicing increasingly frequent doubts and objections to Hitler's strategy in Russia. Hitler finally lost patience and screamed at Halder that his appreciation was 'idiotic blather'. This was told to Gehre and me by Major Schrader, one of our friends in the conspiracy who was a liaison officer and so had the entrée to the Führer's headquarters. Halder's departure was no great loss to the internal German resistance.

According to Hitler's ideas General Kurt Zeitzler, nicknamed the 'lightning bullet', was a general after his own heart. On one occasion when his sector of the front had begun to give way in face of a Russian counter-attack, Zeitzler had descended on the rear areas and personally driven up to the front all those who were skrimshanking around, even including the cooks. As a result this subservient, corpulent, mercurial man could do no wrong in Hitler's eyes. As he told me in Nuremberg in January 1948, he did not realise 'that all was in vain and that the war could no longer be won' until the spring of 1944. In April 1944, when the realisation had begun to dawn on him, he met Stauffenberg and, as Stauffenberg told me shortly thereafter, confided to him his doubts about winning; he began drinking and talking about shooting himself. Stauffenberg advised him to shoot Hitler first. But Zeitzler had not the courage, as he openly admitted. 'I wish I had,' he said to me in Nuremberg with a note of mild self-reproach in his voice.

In the autumn of 1942 Zeitzler would not hear of any defeatist ideas about the outcome of the war. He drove the Sixth Army on to Stalingrad because that was what Hitler wanted. But the army commanders in Russia and their staff officers viewed Hitler's strategy with increasing anxiety. They were quite clear that, if Hitler once again forbade the armies to withdraw in good time to winter quarters in the rear, severe defeats were inevitable during the Russian winter. In the light of this the military faction and the civilian dignitaries laid their plans: some well-known commander in Russia was to rise against Hitler and carry the entire Wehrmacht with him. The obvious choice was Field Marshal von Kluge, but he continued to make excuses to Tresckow. He was fully prepared to assume supreme command of the Wehrmacht in place of Hitler, but only if Hitler had been removed and the *coup d'état* had succeeded. Tresckow accordingly tried to win over Field Marshal von Manstein to his plans. Information from Gehre held out some hope, but this proved to be an illusion to which not only I and my friends in the conspiracy but also more influential people in the military faction succumbed.

After the war Manstein invariably, and usually with some indignation, denied that he had ever been approached by Tresckow, Gersdorff or other officers. I tried to clear this up when Manstein was a prisoner of war in Bridgend camp in Wales. I took him for walks through the sand dunes near the camp and sat with him for hours smoking and chatting. He insisted that no one had approached him to bring him into the anti-Hitler conspiracy, and in any case he would not have agreed to join. The overthrow of Hitler, he said, could only have led to chaos and the immediate collapse of the front; the catastrophic defeats at Stalingrad and elsewhere in Russia, however, could have been avoided if only Hitler had entrusted a single supreme commander with over-all leadership on the Eastern Front instead of forcing mistaken strategy and tactics upon the Army Group commanders. The clear inference from what he said was that he felt himself to be the best qualified to halt the advance of the Red Army into Germany, if only Hitler had handed over supreme command of the entire Eastern Front to him in good time.

The serious setbacks during the first winter in Russia had also provided food for thought for Himmler and the S.S. leaders. Our informant here was Dr Carl Langbehn, a well-known Berlin lawyer and a friend of Professor Popitz; his daughter went to school with Himmler's daughter. The two girls became school-friends, so even before the war Langbehn had spoken to Himmler and gained his confidence. From Oster and Dohnanyi we knew that, since the spring of 1942, the S.S. leaders' appreciation of the situation had been gloomier than that of many General Staff officers. Heydrich issued, for the benefit of Himmler's entourage, appreciations of the situation and political morale reports in which the position was set out with complete realism and with no attempt at whitewashing. For his personal information Canaris had received a series of these reports, though not all of them, and had passed them to Oster and Dohnanyi to read.

When Rommel's offensive in north Africa was brought to a halt and it became obvious that Hitler's dilettante and obstinate strategy was exposing the Wehrmacht to fresh and catastrophic dangers in Russia, Langbehn learnt from Himmler that the S.S. leaders 'were preparing themselves for any possible eventuality, even including the necessity to eliminate the Führer one day'. Langbehn had long been disgusted by the hesitations of the army commanders and this gave him the idea that the overthrow of the régime might be brought about through the S.S., which would later 'be purged of all unhealthy elements'. Popitz, Albrecht Haushofer and others found this plan by no means absurd. Goerdeler, however, refused flatly and categorically to co-operate with the 'blood-stained' Himmler. If Himmler thought the situation so threatening and was even considering the necessity of action against Hitler, he said, this was merely one additional reason for the commanders at the front to anticipate the S.S. and act at once. Goerdeler was still obsessed by his talk with

Field Marshal von Kluge, whom he regarded as his strongest ally in the fight against Hitler. We had only to await the psychological moment, Goerdeler said, since Kluge was determined to act. Popitz, however, said that we were nothing like so far forward as Goerdeler thought and that he was prepared to speak to Himmler. For the first time I sensed a latent rivalry between Goerdeler and Popitz.

9

Prospector for the Conspiracy

LUFTHANSA'S trustee in Madrid was a Spanish aristocrat, married to an Englishwoman, who held a block of shares worth millions in the Spanish aviation company Iberia. Not without reason, Gablenz's successor was afraid that these shares might be privately negotiated behind our back, and he therefore commissioned me to fly to Madrid to protect Lufthansa's interests. He gave me strict instructions to remain in Madrid until I had actually laid hands on the necessary securities; in view of the delaying tactics likely to be adopted by certain interested Spanish parties, the length of my stay in Madrid was indeterminate. This was an attractive proposition – and not solely because it enabled me to get out of Berlin for a few weeks, taste the peacetime life of Madrid and have a good sleep. I was still fascinated by my talks with Goerdeler and, like him, believed that with the help of Field Marshal von Kluge he would now really be able to initiate the *coup*. So that I might keep in touch with Klaus Bonhoeffer during my absence, we agreed on various ways of exchanging information through the official Lufthansa mail which was not subject to the normal censorship.

The members of the conspiracy had discussed how best to use the contact with Beaulac, the American Chargé d'Affaires in Madrid, which I had established in the spring. To my astonishment Goerdeler did not want to use it at all and said that this must be the prerogative of Prince Louis Ferdinand so that, as soon as the *coup* had succeeded, he could get into direct touch with Roosevelt via the American Embassy in Madrid. He was more interested in finding out Churchill's attitude. If I could establish a link to him, Goerdeler said, he (Goerdeler) would come to Madrid. Although he did not tell me so at the time, his contact to London via the Swedish banker Marcus Wallenberg had failed to provide any direct or clear information on Churchill's attitude to his plans. Popitz thought that there was no point in trying to find out, as Goerdeler was ceaselessly and vainly trying to do, whether the British were prepared to negotiate with us. Something must actually happen first – the installation of a new Reich government, for instance. Dohnanyi implored me to be extremely cautious and under no circumstances to mention names; the S.D. was continuously collecting secret information about 'the opposition among Hitler's generals', and the Gestapo might therefore be led straight to us.

In mid-October 1942 I flew to Madrid and immediately tested the ground with Juan Terrasa. Beaulac invited me to dinner in his house. I hesitated at first in view of Dohnanyi's warning. Madrid was swarming with agents. On the other hand I did not wish to give the impression that I was afraid of the Gestapo. So after dark I drove to Beaulac's house with Juan, naturally having first taken the usual precautions to evade observation. Conversation over dinner was general until Mrs Beaulac withdrew. Beaulac then referred back to our conversation in the spring and seemed highly impressed that Hitler had in fact advanced into the Caucasus to capture the Maikop oilfields, as I had forecast. He asked me for my ideas on future war developments. Referring to the views of our General Staff experts, I quoted Goerdeler (not by name) and said that the Wehrmacht could not survive another winter in Russia if Hitler once more forced it to hold the most advanced positions reached instead of allowing it to withdraw and await the spring. Beaulac showed me vivid pictures in American illustrated papers of the devastation we had left behind us in Russia but said no more on the subject.

We then discussed the war in north Africa. A few days earlier Montgomery had opened his offensive against Rommel. Although the desert war could in no way be decisive, Beaulac thought it of considerable significance for the future course of events that the Wehrmacht should be driven from Africa. 'If I were in Montgomery's shoes,' I said, 'I wouldn't do that. As long as the Afrika Korps is being hunted backwards and forwards in the Libyan desert, its troops and supplies are committed and are not available for employment in Russia.' This was a new idea to Beaulac. Naturally, however, he knew that the Allies were planning a large-scale landing in north Africa to take Rommel in rear and he merely remarked casually that he did not give Rommel much chance. Shortly thereafter the Allies landed in Morocco and Algiers.

Beaulac indicated that there was no prospect of an early end to the war by invasion from the Atlantic side and the formation of a second front on the Continent. This was considered a possibility both by the German 'Watch on the Atlantic' and by the conspiracy planners in Berlin. The latter were afraid that the Allies might exploit any military rising against Hitler to form a bridgehead on the Atlantic, Baltic or Scandinavian coasts. Wishing to warn them that 'All quiet on the Western Front' was likely to continue, I sent a report to Klaus Bonhoeffer for transmission to Oster via Dohnanyi. It was my first secret report to the conspirators from Madrid.

After this talk Juan Terrasa asked me somewhat testily why I had said nothing to Beaulac about the state of preparations for the *coup*. I replied that I was not authorised to do so. With Juan, however, I could and would speak frankly. I told him that Goerdeler had met Louis Ferdinand and, since at this time I still believed it true, that Goerdeler had won over Field Marshal von Kluge and would initiate the *coup* as soon as further severe defeats at the front had created the correct psychological conditions. What Goerdeler urgently needed was a completely safe undercover link to Churchill in order to concert matters with him. Juan was on very good personal terms with practically all British diplomats in Madrid. His immediate reply, however, was that he had a better link to London via Lisbon; I was to wait until he knew whether 'our man in Lisbon' was prepared to talk to me.

On Sunday, 8 November 1942, I left my hotel early for a long walk in the Sierra near Madrid. About midday I turned into a village and called Angel Ferrari with whom I had a rendezvous for the afternoon. I wanted to put him off and continue to enjoy this beautiful sunny autumn day. In great excitement Angel said: 'The Allies landed in north Africa this morning.' He knew no details but had already heard on the B.B.C. midday news that the Allies had gained bridgeheads on the African mainland. I hurried home and sat up till late at night listening on Angel's radio to the B.B.C. announcements of the progress of the landings on the Mediterranean coast of Africa. When I returned to my hotel I was clear that Rommel and his Afrika Korps were lost. But what had the Allies gained thereby? I could not understand what the basic object of their strategy was. A year later I talked this over with Colonel Hohenthal, the American Military Attaché in Madrid. His explanation was that, owing to the waywardness of de Gaulle and the eternal quarrels between the French generals in Africa, the Allied High Command had been forced to clear up the political situation. Only in this way was de Gaulle prevented from divorcing himself from the Allies and setting himself up independently with a French army in Africa.

Juan Terrasa called from Lisbon indicating that 'his man' in the British Embassy there was ready to meet me. I flew to Lisbon and Juan fetched me from my hotel. We first took a zigzag walk through the centre of Lisbon and then a taxi into the suburbs where my British interviewer was waiting for us in a car belonging to one of his Portuguese agents. Juan introduced us in the car, saying: 'This is Otto – this is Tony.' Tony was a middle-aged, tubby, decorous-looking gentleman, radiating *bonhomie*. His full name was Tony Graham-Meingott.

We drove out of the city into rolling country, left the car by the roadside and walked along country lanes between stubble-fields and vineyards with our eyes skinned for the approach of any unwanted observer. Tony did not speak German but clearly knew a lot about Germany and what he called the 'German opposition'. As we talked I gained the impression that he was not speaking freely and had been briefed for our meeting by London. He first asked whether I had been surprised by the Allied landing in Africa. I told him what I thought and he took note without comment, adding with great self-assurance: 'Montgomery's offensive will continue beyond Africa until we have won the war.' I told Tony frankly of myself and the reason for my stay in Madrid and then put forward my request. Without giving names I outlined to him the conspiracy to overthrow Hitler, its motives and aims together with its united political backing which I described as a concentration of the régime's opponents from all the former political parties under the leadership of a man known personally to both Churchill and Vansittart. This man was anxious for an answer from Churchill to the question whether the British government would be prepared to negotiate with a new Reich government led by him. Only in this way could the war be ended quickly and a catastrophe averted which would have unforeseeable consequences for the whole of Europe.

Tony stopped and gazed thoughtfully at the countryside. His silence irritated me. I was increasingly embarrassed at being unable to mention Goerdeler's name. I took from my pocket a letter from Klaus Bonhoeffer to his sister Sabine who was married to a professor of law named Gerhard Leibholz and had emigrated to Oxford before the war. Her brothers Klaus and Dietrich, I said, would vouch for me. George Bell, the Bishop of Chichester, could give the British government full details about them. I was not authorised to say more, I continued, but this should be enough to prove my identity. Finally I said that former German trade-union leaders, well known to Walter Citrine, their British opposite number, had joined the generals in the conspiracy.

'I see no reason,' Tony said, 'why I should not believe you. Juan has vouched for you. That is enough. But there are people here in Portugal claiming to belong to the German opposition who would like to mislead us. Before the war German opposition emissaries came to London and told us that they were in touch with German generals who wished to overthrow Hitler. But what happened? Nothing. The German generals are fighting for Hitler and they're not doing it badly either.'

At this moment a string of R.A.F. fighters flew very low over us in the direction of Africa. 'Do you see that?' Tony said. 'The Portuguese are now allowing us to fly freely over their country because they are convinced that we are winning the war. The landing in Africa is the turning-point. The German opposition must soon prove itself by doing something if it wishes to get a hearing in London.' This was unmistakably his answer to me; it was precisely what Klaus Bonhoeffer had meant when he had said during one of our discussions: 'We owe the Allies a payment on account.'

Back in Madrid I found a letter from Klaus Bonhoeffer. It included the remark that 'the pending tax case will be decided shortly' which, in our code, meant that the *coup* would take place very soon. The thought that I would not be in Berlin when it happened was nerve-racking. But I could not leave Madrid. The Spaniards' faith in a German victory had been shaken by the landing in Africa and this made my official mission in Madrid more difficult. No one wished to commit himself to Lufthansa any more. I offered the block of shares to a bank consortium, holding out hope of large profits as post-war civil aviation developed. But there were no takers.

By December the Stalingrad catastrophe could be clearly seen on the horizon and so the conditions existed for which, according to Goerdeler, we had to wait before initiating the *coup*. While I waited tensely I received a second letter from Klaus Bonhoeffer containing the sarcastic comment that he hoped I would enjoy Christmas in Madrid. So it had all been an illusion once more. For the first time, therefore, I did not spend Christmas Eve in my family's house in Wiesbaden, but in Madrid with the Lindenbergs with whom I was now on extremely intimate terms both politically and personally. Gerd Lindenberg had long held the view that Hitler must be eliminated and from our talks he had realised that I was involved in certain plans which were not confined to mere words. He offered to help, saying: 'You have no need to tell me what is going on, but if I am wanted, I am available.' I told him that the time would come very soon.

On 24 January 1943 Roosevelt and Churchill surprised the world. They met in Casablanca and then held a press conference. I read the text in the Spanish and English newspapers and learnt that the Allies proposed to insist on 'unconditional surrender' by the Wehrmacht. I did not at the time take this literally and thought it a piece of war propaganda to demonstrate Allied superiority over Fortress Europe. My recollection of it soon faded before the reports in the British and American newspapers of the Sixth Army's fate at Stalingrad.

About this time I obtained the Spanish signatures which I required to complete my Lufthansa job in Madrid. I arranged my return to Berlin, summarised my observations and discussions in Madrid and Lisbon and made up my mind that I would have to destroy some of the conspirators' illusions.

10

In the face of Hitler's 'Providence'

DURING the months in Madrid I had been on the touchline, observing the war from both sides; I had seen it from an angle which sharpened my wits and enabled me to look at the plans for the *coup* with greater realism. On my return to Berlin I found, to my consternation, that despite the catastrophe of Stalingrad those who should have been solidly together to carry out the plans for the *coup* were arguing with each other. Moreover, there was still no sign that one of the senior commanders had made up his mind to lead a military rising against Hitler. When I saw Dohnanyi again he was pale and dejected and said: 'They curse Hitler and his orders but they still have not realised that the war is lost.' Goerdeler was still confident of Field Marshal von Kluge and was scurrying round talking to his widespread circle of acquaintances arranging his government's programme.

Soon after my arrival I called on Popitz. He was not alone, and his daughter Cornelia therefore took me to another room. While I was waiting she brought in Adam von Trott zu Solz. He was surprised to find me in Popitz's house and began to talk about my experiences and impressions in Madrid. Popitz soon called me into his study where was Dr Günther Gerecke, the ex-Reich Minister and one of the Gestapo's first victims after the seizure of power. I had made his acquaintance early in the war through his cousin Irmgard Klewitz, whom my brother and I had taken into our confidence on political problems.

My purpose in coming was to arrange a meeting with Field Marshal von Witzleben for Popitz and Gerecke which both thought urgent owing to the excessive activity of Goerdeler. Since being deprived of his command Witzleben had been living near Lübben in the Spreewald, on the estate of his aide, Major Graf Lynar, and holding himself ready for the *coup d'état*. Through Ludwig Gehre I had made friends with Lynar and so had come to know Witzleben. To avoid attracting attention, Popitz did not wish to go himself but wanted Gerecke to go and act as spokesman for them both. Being a well-known horse-breeder, Gerecke could go to Lynar's estate to see some horses without being noticed by any spy. Popitz merely indicated briefly what he had in mind. Gerecke was to explain it all to me on the way to the station while Popitz kept his appointment with Adam von Trott.

Popitz had introduced Goerdeler to Beck and it had been agreed that he should have a voice in all planning, but he now felt himself increasingly driven into the background by Goerdeler. Goerdeler wished to arrange everything himself, Gerecke said. Beck had given Goerdeler a free hand in political matters for too long and now, although he realised that the formation of a new government could not be left to Goerdeler alone, Beck was unable to control him. Beck was too weak and in addition he was in bad health. He should be spared too much work but instead Goerdeler overloaded him with government programmes and ministerial lists. We should consider who could replace Beck if he fell by the wayside. For this reason a talk with Witzleben was essential; of all the field marshals he was closest to Beck.

In the meanwhile Goerdeler was behaving more and more as if he had plenary powers to form a new government. 'Who from?' Gerecke asked. 'Perhaps your friend Louis Ferdinand has a hand in this. Has the Prince said anything to Goerdeler to make him feel that he has some special authority?' I was astounded and explained that Goerdeler's visit to Prince Louis Ferdinand had taken place at the former's request and that the Prince had not said a single word which could indicate to Goerdeler that he had some sort of special commission from the throne. Up to this point I had always assumed that, on the fall of the régime, Goerdeler would become Reich Chancellor, but Gerecke said that this was by no means definite. Popitz had told him this after his last interview with Beck. Beck had recently been thinking of a provisional arrangement in the form of a Directorate in which political leadership would be assumed by Schacht and von Hassell in addition to Goerdeler, all three on an equal footing. Under them individual ministries would be run by State Secretaries pending the formation of a Reich government after fresh elections. During the state of emergency Beck would act as Reich Regent and under him Witzleben would exercise plenary powers as Supreme Commander of the Wehrmacht.

I knew that Popitz had no particular ambition to become Reich Chancellor. He had repeatedly told me and others that he would like to take over the Ministry of Culture. He did not, therefore, regard himself as a competitor of Goerdeler's but, after a talk with Beck, was determined not to leave the formation of the government to Goerdeler alone. Popitz was a highly educated and intelligent man and his dearest wish was to devote the rest of his life to the spiritual and moral restoration of the young, for whom he felt responsible because, as a minister under Hitler, he had set them a bad example. For his part in the resistance he, like Goerdeler, was hanged. His memory should not be overshadowed by that of Goerdeler. Despite their common political background (both came from the German National bourgeoisie) the two men were too different ever to have been able to work together as proposed.

Gerecke asked me whether I knew that Trott zu Solz, too, did not favour Goerdeler and the programme he had agreed with Louis Ferdinand. This was new to me but it explained why, when we met in Popitz's house, Trott had not been altogether natural. He regarded me as one of Goerdeler's adherents, whereas he had entirely swung over to Popitz's side during my absence. Earlier he had once said to me that on the fall of Hitler Niemöller should be Reich Chancellor; he was by far the most popular German both in Britain and America. I had replied that after years in a concentration camp Niemöller would be neither physically nor mentally capable of doing such a job and would also not be sufficiently *au fait* with the political problems which had arisen meanwhile. From the point of view of popularity in Britain and America Dr Brüning seemed the best choice for Chancellor of a new government. Trott had spoken to him in America in the autumn of 1939 when his advice to Louis Ferdinand had been that any question of the restoration of the monarchy should be submitted to a plebiscite. With this in mind I proposed to Gerecke that we should establish a link to Brüning via the American Embassy in Madrid – Gerecke had, after all, been a Minister in Brüning's government. If people could no longer agree on Goerdeler as Chancellor, I said, we should have to fall back on a man like Brüning. Gerecke showed no particular interest in this proposal. Only later did I realise that, like Goerdeler and Popitz, he had no wish to associate himself with émigré German politicians.

Jakob Kaiser and Josef Wirmer were both uneasy when I told them what I had heard of Beck's new plans. They and their friends were solidly behind Goerdeler as Chancellor-designate. They thought, as did Klaus Bonhoeffer and I, that the idea of a directorate was a ridiculous best-of-a-bad-job solution which would not gain the confidence of the German people. Leber and Leuschner, who represented the social-democrat wing of the secret anti-Hitler front, were nothing like so firmly in favour of Goerdeler. Leuschner particularly was disillusioned that the military action against Hitler promised by Goerdeler still did not occur in spite of Stalingrad. His confidence in generals had been shaken and he wished to see them do something. He had resigned himself to awaiting the collapse of the Third Reich as a result of an overwhelming victory by the Allies, keeping his hands free for the subsequent political reconstruction. He wanted to know from me something about the activity of his émigré political friends in London – for information rather than with the idea of concluding some agreement with them. In his circles there was some fear that the left-wing émigrés might try to form a German government-in-exile.

Graf Helmuth von Moltke and his circle, now well known as the 'Kreisau Circle', were also prepared to wait and plan for a fundamental political reconstruction after the collapse of the régime as a result of an Allied victory over the Wehrmacht. This circle was formed of men of the most varied backgrounds – Adam von Trott was one of them; they felt themselves pledged to certain ideals of society and ethics, the realisation of which they felt was imperilled by the personality of Goerdeler, whom they thought too reactionary. They considered that the moral rejuvenation of the people, which was their aim, was more likely to result from a total collapse of the régime following a catastrophic military defeat than from a military *coup d'état*. Since Stalingrad the military defeat seemed to be staring us in the face, but Goerdeler's reaction was to press all the harder for the *coup d'état* in private conversations, primarily with General Olbricht.

During my absence in Madrid the risk of betrayal of the entire project had grown. The Gestapo had uncovered the Soviet resistance and espionage organisation which has come to be known as 'Red Orchestra' and this had drawn their attention to Dr Curt Bley, his friend Adam von Trott and even more to Ernst von Harnack. Anxiety continued to grow after my return from Madrid; psychologically this was an additional burden for us all. In August 1942 a secret radio transmitter working for the Soviets had been 'blown' in Brussels and as a result the Gestapo arrested a resistance group of over one hundred men and women led by Arvid Harnack and Harald Schulze-Boysen. The judicial investigations and legal proceedings against them were kept secret under the code-name 'Red Orchestra'.

Harald Schulze-Boysen, a relative of Grand Admiral von Tirpitz, was a lieutenant on the General Staff of the Luftwaffe; Arvid Harnack, a nephew of Ernst von Harnack, was a senior civil servant in the Ministry of Economics. Arvid Harnack I had once met casually in a restaurant through Klaus Bonhoeffer, who had known him since childhood. Schulze-Boysen was a nodding acquaintance in the Aero-Club. 'Red Orchestra' Berlin, however, included doctors, officials, artists, writers, craftsmen and workers and there were many close connections with our group as a result of long-standing friendships from student days. By no means all of them were convicted of espionage, but the majority were condemned for high treason. Some of them were in touch with Dr Curt Bley whom Adam von Trott had recruited into the Foreign Ministry as an old political friend from his socialist student days. Bley, who was a friend of mine, was repeatedly interrogated by the Gestapo about his acquaintanceship with various of the prisoners. He felt it wise to disappear from Berlin and volunteered for active service with the Wehrmacht. Before leaving he gave me an urgent warning to be on my guard against the Gestapo. All personal acquaintances and connections of the prisoners were checked, primarily of course those of the Harnack family. Before his execution Arvid Harnack managed to send word to his relatives via one of his gaolers that the Gestapo were taking a special interest in Ernst von Harnack. With the finger pointed at him, Beck, Goerdeler, Dohnanyi, the Bonhoeffers, the Delbrücks, in fact everyone who was involved with him in the Resistance were all in danger.

Over fifty death sentences were pronounced as a result of the 'Red Orchestra' proceedings, including nineteen on women. Since the war erudite analyses have been made, based on a peculiar provision of German law distinguishing between treason against the government and treason against the country, to prove that resistance to Hitler should be judged by special moral standards. The German criminal code, however, can be disregarded in any judgement on the moral worth of these resisters; morally the only law is that enunciated by Henning von Tresckow shortly before he went to his death after the abortive *coup* against Hitler: 'A man acquires true moral worth when he is prepared to give his life for his convictions.'

On 18 February 1943 in a speech in the Sportspalast Goebbels announced total war. Through the loudspeakers he screamed to the world: 'Do you want total war?' An obedient chorus rolled out the answer: 'Führer, command! We follow!' On the same day Hans and Sophie Scholl distributed leaflets in Munich University headed 'Die weisse Rose' ['The White Rose'] protesting against the senseless continuation of the war and the tyranny of the German subhumans. They were denounced by a porter, arrested together with their tutor, Professor Huber, and executed. Sophie Scholl believed that her death on the gallows would lead to a popular rising against the régime and said to her mother: 'It will make the waves run high.' But there was no storm among the German people. They simply accepted the Scholls' sacrifice complacently. What more could be done to rouse the people and Wehrmacht to revolt against Hitler?

The senior commanders at the front seemed impervious to military, political and even moral argument. In spite of Tresckow's pressure Field Marshal von Kluge still refused to lead a rising against Hitler, saying that he was afraid that he would not have the confidence either of the soldiery or the people. Tresckow accordingly decided to act on his own. Together with Fabian von Schlabrendorff he rigged up a bomb for an attempt on Hitler's life in the headquarters of Army Group Centre. Meanwhile General Olbricht and his friends in the A.H.A. [Allgemeine Heeresamt – General Army Office] were preparing to proclaim a state of emergency throughout the territory of the Reich as the first step in our 'seizure of power'. It was to be initiated on Hitler's death which was to be the reason for it. My first indication that something was afoot came through hints from Ludwig Gehre. He invited me to his house one evening, swore me solemnly to secrecy and said that the time was now ripe to place a bomb in 'his' aircraft. He asked whether I knew the Führer's aircraft. I replied at once that no one could get near it; since Gablenz's crash all official aircraft were closely guarded. Gehre did not know this. At his request I obtained for him a detailed plan of the four-engined Focke-Wulf 200 of which there were two identically fitted out as 'Führer's aircraft'.

On another evening Gehre asked whether I possessed an accurate watch. He asked me to lend it him for a couple of days. I handed it over and he mumbled something. At first I thought that, in his comic way, he was about to play some practical joke on me. I only learnt why he wanted it on the evening of the day when Tresckow's and Schlabrendorff's bomb plot went awry – 13 March 1943. Gehre was to sit by his official telephone and pass to Oster code-words received from Schlabrendorff informing the Berlin conspirators of the progress of the *coup*. He needed a second accurate watch to keep a check on the time.

Hitler had swallowed the bait and, urged by Tresckow, had flown to Smolensk that day for a 'front-line visit' to headquarters Army Group Centre. Among his entourage from the Führer's headquarters was Colonel Brandt. Before the aircraft left on the return journey Schlabrendorff handed Brandt a package ostensibly containing two bottles of cointreau as a present from Tresckow to his friend General Stieff in the Führer's headquarters. In fact the package contained a live bomb. But its detonator failed. Hitler and his company returned unharmed to the Führer's headquarters.

When I visited Gehre that evening, he merely said: 'Blast it! It's gone wrong.' I thought he meant that the attempt to place a bomb in Hitler's aircraft had failed and remarked rather smugly that I had already told him that no one could get near the Führer's aircraft. Gehre gave me back my watch, paced the room cursing, opened a bottle and finally said that he did not yet know what had actually gone wrong. I only found out two days later when Schlabrendorff came to Berlin. He had flown to the Führer's headquarters in a courier aircraft and had exchanged the package for another which actually did contain two bottles of cointreau, saying that the wrong parcel had been handed over in error. Subsequently he established that, although the detonating mechanism of the bomb had functioned, the detonator itself had failed.

Schlabrendorff was able to obliterate all traces of the attempt and so nothing was ever discovered. This at least helped us to overcome our disappointment at the failure of the attempt – we were all very downcast in those days.

On 'Heroes Memorial Day' Hitler proposed to open an exhibition of captured war material and war pictures in the Berlin Arsenal. The exhibits had been collected by Army Group Centre's Intelligence Section and Colonel von Gersdorff, the head of the section, was to be there as 'the Führer's guest of honour'. Tresckow appealed to him to seize the opportunity for an attempt on Hitler's life. Gersdorff was prepared to blow himself up together with Hitler.

He obtained some explosive from Schlabrendorff, studied the details of the opening ceremony and, after the parade in front of the Arsenal, joined Hitler's entourage. In each overcoat pocket he carried a live bomb with the time-fuse set at ten minutes. Hitler's tour of the exhibition was due to last thirty minutes. For some unexplained reason, however, after eight minutes he suddenly brought it to an end. Gersdorff only just had time to extract the detonators from the bombs in a lavatory.

It was difficult to pacify those who had now twice been warned by code-words to hold themselves ready for the *coup d'état*. Fortunately they were confined to the comparatively small number of men who had under all circumstances to be ready to lend their political weight to the *coup* once Hitler had been successfully assassinated. They naturally expected some explanation of why nothing had happened. Owing to the overriding necessity for secrecy they could not be told that attempts had actually been made, and it fell to Dohnanyi to give them semi-plausible reasons. How he did it in each individual case I do not know. Leuschner later said indignantly to Harnack that he had had more than enough of being led up the garden path by generals.

Today it is not possible to tell what the effects of a successful assassination would have been. From the psychological point of view the right moment was undoubtedly chosen – after the catastrophic defeats of Stalingrad and Tunis. Germany's military position was such that a new government would still have been able to make offers of armistice and peace negotiations. These conditions had passed by 20 July of the following year. But since, in general terms, this was still the right time for a *coup*, we went on thinking of the form in which a state based on the rule of law could be re-established and the contribution which each of us would be called upon to make.

Talking over this problem among my friends, our main worry was Beck's dubious state of health. What would happen if he fell by the wayside? What were his own ideas for this eventuality? He had presumably discussed the matter with Oster and Dohnanyi who, as his immediate military and political advisers, were on the closest terms with him. We would have liked to ask Dohnanyi but the only person who could do this was Dietrich Bonhoeffer. When urged by his brother Klaus, however, Dietrich refused saying: 'Hans has other worries at the moment. Guttenberg has warned him that his telephone is being tapped.' This brought out into the open something which Klaus Bonhoeffer, with his excitable nature, was not intended to know. Gehre had a friend in the 'Reich Research Office', the telephone-tapping agency, who kept him continuously informed and he had asked Guttenberg to warn Dohnanyi.

Klaus Bonhoeffer became violently agitated and demanded a precise explanation as to who and what lay behind this warning. 'If Hans is under surveillance, this affects not only him and our families but all of us here and all those involved in this affair with us.' He asked Justus Delbrück and me to talk to Gehre since we both knew him well. We knew, however, that Gehre would give away no more than he had already said. He never confided to me the name of his friend in the 'Research Office', although as time went on he told me more than anyone else. Klaus Bonhoeffer's agitation was in fact fully justified and the threat to his brother-in-law Dohnanyi and his brother Dietrich far more imminent than we suspected.

This particular evening was the last occasion on which I saw Dietrich Bonhoeffer. Shortly thereafter he was arrested. Before we parted that night a particularly important subject was broached – the prospects, after a change of régime, of collaboration between the political Left and Right and between the two Christian churches. I hoped that, after the frightful experiences and sufferings inflicted on people by the war, some lasting solution would emerge and I pleaded in particular for reunification of the two churches. Dietrich Bonhoeffer, however, held such a development to be impossible; the Catholic Church, he objected, would never deviate materially from its dogma and its tradition, for it would then be renouncing itself. Reunification was only possible if we, the Evangelicals, were prepared without reservation to return to the fold of the Catholic Church.

11

Himmler Reaches Out

WHILE we were still ruminating over the fact that two carefully prepared attempts on the life of Hitler had failed, we learnt to our horror that Dohnanyi had been denounced to the Gestapo. The culprit was Dr Wilhelm Schmidhuber, a prosperous Munich businessman who liked to be addressed as 'Mr Consul'; on the outbreak of war he had done some work for the Abwehr and had been trying ever since to make his mark with Dohnanyi as a confidant of Canaris and Oster. I had met him once when talking to Delbrück and Guttenberg, and he gave me the impression of a self-important busybody.

Dr Schmidhuber abused his position with the Abwehr to do some illegal business, as a result of which the Prague customs got on his trail. He was dismissed from the Abwehr with an injunction not to travel abroad again. In spite of this he went to Italy and was arrested there by an Abwehr officer, Captain (Air Force) Brede, and brought back to Germany in handcuffs. He expected Dohnanyi to engineer his release through the Abwehr but, since his arrest had no political background and was due solely to unscrupulous business dealings, Dohnanyi did nothing. Mortified by this, Schmidhuber began to 'offload' about Dohnanyi.

'Mr Consul' had not been let into the secret of the conspiracy but he knew Oster's and Dohnanyi's views; he had kept his eyes and ears open and had done some quiet observation, particularly in Rome, where he had followed the trail of our friend Dr Josef Müller into the Vatican and wormed his way into the latter's confidence. So, 'like a mosaic' – as he put it to Pastor Eberhard Bethge in Windach after the war – he pieced together a picture of Dohnanyi's undercover activities in the Abwehr, and he gave Brede a very clear lead. The gist of his revelations was that Dohnanyi and Josef Müller 'had some murky business' in the Vatican, that Dohnanyi had helped Jews cross into Switzerland by giving them commissions for the

Abwehr, earning hundreds of thousands of dollars in the process, that he had placed his brother-in-law Dietrich Bonhoeffer in a 'reserved occupation' with the Abwehr and dispatched him to Rome and Stockholm to organise a link to the Bishop of Chichester. These were serious accusations against a man who was one of the closest confidants of Admiral Canaris, the head of the Abwehr. Brede passed them on to his friend Dr Manfred Roeder, the senior Luftwaffe judge advocate who had just obtained death sentences on the members of 'Red Orchestra', making a name for himself thereby. In Haltwhistle prisoner-of-war camp after the war Brede told me that he would not have done this, had he known of the resisters' intentions, since 'he had always been anti-Nazi'. Roeder seized the opportunity to make his mark in high places. He informed Göring who at once spied a chance of expunging the stain on 'his Luftwaffe' left by Schulze-Boysen and his 'Red Orchestra' – the Russian-run spy ring. Göring put Dr Lehmann, head of the O.K.W. legal department, on the mat, saying that now at last one knew where the traitors were – inside O.K.W.! This was aimed at Keitel whom Göring regarded as his rival ever since Hitler had appointed him Chief of O.K.W. Göring demanded that Dohnanyi be dismissed from the Wehrmacht forthwith and handed over to the Gestapo.

Keitel ordered court-martial investigation proceedings against Dohnanyi and declared the whole matter 'Top Secret'. Göring thereupon persuaded Hitler to allow 'his commissioner for political cases', in other words Roeder, to carry out the investigation on Dohnanyi. Dohnanyi heard what was brewing against him and the rest of us from Dr Sack, who had been an ally of Dohnanyi and Oster ever since the Fritsch crisis of spring 1938 and, as Head of the Army Legal Department, knew what was going on in O.K.W.

Roeder was a friend of the head of the Gestapo, the notorious S.S.-Gruppenführer [Major-General] Müller. He spread the word that Dohnanyi was a spy and was plotting treason through his sister-in-law, Sabine Leibholz, in Oxford. He swore to bring Dohnanyi to the gallows.

Even before 1933 Dohnanyi had become known in official government circles as an outstanding young lawyer. After the seizure of power the Gestapo's attention was soon drawn to him because he used his position as personal assistant to Dr Gürtner, the

Reich Minister of Justice, to help people who were being persecuted on religious, political or racial grounds. When he was appointed to the staff of the Abwehr on the outbreak of war, Heydrich had told Gestapo Müller to 'keep an eye on Dohnanyi'. Himmler did not think badly of Dohnanyi; he had once said to Dr Langbehn: 'I know that Dohnanyi is no National Socialist, but at least he says what he thinks and one always knows where one is with him.'

On 5 April 1943 Roeder, accompanied by a Gestapo official [Kommissar] named Sonderegger, appeared in the Abwehr offices to arrest Dohnanyi. Hitler's order exempting Wehrmacht officers and soldiers from Gestapo jurisdiction was still in force and, as a Section Head in the O.K.W. office 'Ausland/Abwehr' [Foreign Intelligence] with the rank of Major, Dohnanyi could only be arrested by the executive agencies of the Reich Court Martial. The presence of a Gestapo official was therefore illegal, but it revealed Roeder's intention to 'bring Dohnanyi to the gallows' with the assistance of the Gestapo. The latter had long since had information that Dohnanyi was 'getting large-scale bribes for smuggling Jews into Switzerland' but, having no proof, had been unable to take action against him. Dohnanyi was not expecting to be arrested. Only the previous day Dr Lehmann, who had a high opinion of Dohnanyi, had assured Canaris that his (Dohnanyi's) arrest was not even being considered for the moment. Dohnanyi had not therefore 'cleaned out' his safe.

In Oster's presence Roeder and Sonderegger searched Dohnanyi's office. Between the files and documents in the safe was a piece of paper setting out the Confessional Church's suggestions for a message from the Pope; they were to be discussed by Dietrich Bonhoeffer with the Rector of the Collegium Germanicum in the Vatican. They could well have been passed off as 'material' for an intelligence mission to the Vatican. This was Dohnanyi's intention and he laid the sheet of paper on the table so that Admiral Canaris might confirm that it was in fact 'intelligence material'. Oster, who knew its real significance, took it and put it in his pocket. Sonderegger, the Gestapo man, however, saw this. Roeder ordered Oster out of the office at once and placed him under house arrest. Dohnanyi was led away to the Wehrmacht prison reserved for persons under investigation.

Meanwhile Frau von Dohnanyi and Dietrich Bonhoeffer had also been arrested, simultaneously with Dr Josef Müller, his wife and secretary in Munich. This was the opening of the final dramatic phase of the battle between Canaris and Himmler. Ever since 1938 the military and political resistance groups had been held together and directed by Dohnanyi and Oster working under Beck. With their arrest the back of the resistance was broken. Beck, the leading brain, had just undergone a serious operation carried out by Professor Sauerbruch and was in no state to continue to head the conspiracy.

All of us in Dohnanyi's fairly widespread circle had made up our minds years ago that we might be arrested by the Gestapo one morning. With Dohnanyi's arrest, however, this possibility had become an imminent threat. Since the Gestapo was involved we had to assume that all friends and acquaintances of those under arrest would now be shadowed. The uncomfortable thought came to me that Roeder had accused Dohnanyi of traitorous connections with his sister-in-law in Oxford and that I had happened to take to Lisbon for forwarding to Oxford some purely personal letters from the Bonhoeffer family for the Leibholz family. Who was to know that Roeder might not find out about this through Gestapo agents in Lisbon?

Though we were extremely agitated over our friends' arrest, at least they were in Wehrmacht prisons and so safe from torture by the Gestapo. How often had I heard Dohnanyi say: 'No one can say how long he can hold out once the Gestapo has him in its power.' In fact he showed superhuman will-power in withstanding all the Gestapo's interrogations. Roeder had no proof against Dohnanyi but he hoped to extract it with the help of the Gestapo. We were kept continuously informed about his methods of interrogation by Dr Sack and Ludwig Gehre. Among their many friends and acquaintances were people in the Reich Court Martial; they kept their ears open and passed us on very reliable information.

By good fortune Major Maass, Commandant of the Wehrmacht Detention Prison, turned out to be an uncompromising opponent of the régime. He risked his neck daily for Dohnanyi, allowed him and Dr Müller every possible privilege and arranged for secret talks between them. Maass passed all his information to Dr Sack and he in turn passed it on to the Bonhoeffer family via Perels, the legal adviser to the Confessional Church.

At the end of April Roeder was obliged to release Christine von Dohnanyi, Maria Müller and her husband's secretary, since he had no proof at all against them apart from indications by Schmidhuber to the effect that Dohnanyi's and Müller's wives were 'in the secret'. When interrogated afresh, however, he could not substantiate this statement. The reports of these ladies on their release confirmed that Roeder had no really watertight proof. His interrogations brought him no proof against Dohnanyi either, so, not being allowed to torture him, he began to torment him.

First he was not allowed to smoke; then he was forbidden to read, write or draw; finally all the notes he had made about his interrogations to assist in his defence were confiscated. Major Maass did his best to alleviate these deprivations and meanwhile we had established direct communication with Dohnanyi. His wife was permitted to take food to him in the prison twice a week. Notes in hair-line writing passed between Dohnanyi and his wife under a jam-jar cover. Maass warned her that she must be prepared one day to be received at the entrance to the prison by two Gestapo officials who would take her and her parcel into custody.

Dietrich Bonhoeffer's family regularly received letters from him, smuggled out of the military prison at Tegel, frequently accompanied by poems and theological studies. He used his arrest to think and write as if in voluntary retreat. The warders were so impressed by his personality and his bearing that they granted him many privileges; three of them took the risk of smuggling out letters for him – perhaps encouraged by the fact that General von Hase, the Commandant of Berlin and therefore their ultimate superior, was Dietrich's uncle.

Major Maass and Dr Sack also kept us up to date on Josef Müller's condition. Being of robust health he, like Dietrich Bonhoeffer, took his imprisonment far more easily than did Dohnanyi, who was naturally delicate and sensitive and, as a result of Roeder's arbitrary restrictions, developed phlebitis in both legs. As Roeder told Maass over the telephone on one occasion, these irritations were designed to 'soften up' Dohnanyi. Roeder frequently gave way to such outbursts of rage because he was getting nowhere with his interrogations, Dohnanyi being both an expert on criminal law and the superior brain. As time went on it became clear to Roeder that the statements of the accused tallied remarkably. He tried to bring Maass to book for allowing Dohnanyi to communicate with the outside world, but Maass refused to be intimidated and continued to help as best he could.

My Lufthansa work brought me into daily personal contact with Klaus Bonhoeffer in a way which could not arouse Gestapo suspicions. It occurred to me that I might keep the civilian leaders, such as Jakob Kaiser, Ernst von Harnack, Josef Wirmer, Wilhelm Leuschner and their principal allies in the other civil resistance groups, informed of the progress of the investigations against Dohnanyi. They were all quite clear that Roeder and Gestapo Müller were on the trail of our conspiracy. Roeder was fanatically persistent with his inquiries into the 'Black Orchestra' – as the German resistance came to be called; he had the nose of a bloodhound and realised that he was on the right track. On his instructions the Gestapo's spy service went into action and we had to assume that one day someone would be caught and forced to talk under torture. In this situation Goerdeler wrote a letter to General Olbricht pressing for the *coup* and once more declaring himself ready to demand resignation from Hitler if the senior military commanders would line up behind him.

Meanwhile, on his own initiative, Dr Sack had taken steps to help Dohnanyi. As Head of the Army Legal Department he had friends in all divisions of the Reich Court Martial and they kept him fully informed of Roeder's investigations, helped by the fact that the latter was garrulous and came out with something fresh every day. During one of his interrogations Roeder had said to Dohnanyi himself: 'I shall not stop attacking you personally until I have destroyed you.' Roeder put a spoke in his own wheel, however, by boasting to his colleagues that he would 'bring Canaris to book as well as Dohnanyi'.

This remark moved Dr Sack to inform Keitel in person about Roeder's methods of investigation. He explained that, being Göring's minion, Roeder's purpose was to overthrow Canaris and thus discredit O.K.W. as a whole, together with Keitel as its Head, in the eyes of the Führer. Keitel lent a willing ear. He knew that Göring had always wished to become Chief of O.K.W. and so he ordered Dr Lehmann, head of his legal department, to examine the entire matter. For three days Lehmann closeted himself in the Reich Court Martial offices with the files on 'Black Orchestra'. Then he reported to Keitel that Roeder was actuated by blind ambition, had overreached himself and was clearly proposing to indict Dohnanyi for treason in order to expose Canaris and O.K.W.; there was in fact no case against Dohnanyi. Accordingly, on 23 July, Keitel ordered that Roeder's investigations be confined to possible abuse of his office by Dohnanyi.

We hailed this decision of Keitel's with relief. The only case now remaining to Roeder could easily be refuted. Dohnanyi, however, who was now in low water both physically and mentally, did not think that Keitel's decision improved his position. He sent us word not to harbour any illusions; Roeder would not capitulate to Keitel. Unfortunately, it proved that Dohnanyi's appreciation of the situation was more accurate than ours.

12

The Italians Do Better

DOHNANYI'S arrest dislocated the political structure of the conspiracy and the unity of the numerous resistance groups began to crumble. I was disillusioned and downcast. Now that Beck was ill, and Oster and Dohnanyi could no longer work for us, the conspiracy was leaderless.

Goerdeler felt himself called upon to assume the leadership in place of Beck and he began to act somewhat autocratically. No doubt he did so in all good faith, but it led to a breach between him and Popitz. Both found it necessary to see me to find out how Dohnanyi's case was faring. Of the two I saw Popitz more frequently since he lived in my immediate neighbourhood. He had never liked Goerdeler's hustle and bustle, he told me one evening, and had expected that, with Beck *hors de combat*, Goerdeler would discuss everything with him. When he introduced Goerdeler to Beck it had been agreed that they should work in double harness, but Goerdeler had not kept to this agreement. Internally he was tagging along behind the socialists and trade unionists; externally he now refused to accept the advice of men like Ambassador Hassell and Graf Moltke, who knew their Britain well. He (Popitz) had tolerated this for a while but had eventually had to have words with Goerdeler, after which Goerdeler had ceased to visit him.

Meanwhile, in May, Goerdeler had gone to Stockholm and, via the bankers Jakob and Marcus Wallenberg, had transmitted to Churchill a memorandum setting out his political plans. He returned convinced that he would soon receive a positive answer from Churchill. It never came. In the conviction that it would, however, he pressed Olbricht all the harder for the *coup d'état*.

Goerdeler apparently did not perceive our doubts on the subject. Only after Harnack had spoken to him did he agree to a discussion with Moltke and his Kreisau circle – but it produced practically nothing. He therefore redoubled his efforts to win the older politicians of the secret front over to his programme by means of personal talks. But he could no longer convince men like Leuschner and Leber. They had had more than enough of his promises that 'the generals would act because developments would force them to'.

In the summer of 1943 senior officers like Field Marshal von Kluge still believed that they could stem the Red Army's advance. Early in June Gehre, Schlabrendorff and I were together in Gehre's house and Schlabrendorff gave us a picture of the Russian front as seen from Army Group Centre. An offensive was planned for early July against the Russian salient around Kursk. Its objectives were limited, he said, and it therefore had every prospect of success. In the light of the Soviet victories this seemed to me pure military wishful thinking. The offensive opened a fortnight later, was held by the Russian defences and then thrown back. From this point the Wehrmacht was in full retreat everywhere in Russia.

One day during this summer I met Goerdeler with Jakob Kaiser. They were waiting for Josef Wirmer and were then to discuss constitutional questions, for which purpose Wirmer had borrowed my copy of Hermann Heller's *Staatslehre* [*State Doctrine*]. Although Goerdeler knew from our last meeting that Dohnanyi's health was critical, he did not even ask after him. Like many others he did not realise that Dohnanyi's fate was that of us all. I was angry that our leaders should treat the matter so lightly. One of them had even said to me that in a military prison people would be 'in safe protective custody'.

I handed to Kaiser the book Wirmer wanted and said that I was in a hurry as I was on the way to Klaus Bonhoeffer. Only then did Goerdeler ask after Dohnanyi. I purposely exaggerated and said that Dohnanyi was at the end of his tether and one could not say how long he could stand up to Roeder's interrogations; a single incautious word might bring us all to the gallows. Goerdeler stared at me in amazement.

Goerdeler was not the only one to be playing politics of a highly personal nature; the various civilian resistance groups were becoming increasingly independent. They acted as if the generals' *putsch* was a certainty. Gehre and his friends Colonel Freytag-Loringhoven, Colonel Fritz Jaeger and Major Graf Blumenthal told me that no real preparations of any sort were being made for a *putsch*. I, therefore, never fell victim to the illusion that the *coup* was only a question of time. It was not for me, however, to destroy the hopes of Klaus Bonhoeffer and his associates.

Klaus Bonhoeffer found it hard to stomach his enforced inactivity while his brother and brother-in-law were at the mercy of the Gestapo. In addition he had to restrict his contacts with his friends of the conspiracy. As a precaution against informers we ceased using the familiar *du* both in the office and at home. After Dohnanyi's arrest I had become his main link to the conspiracy. Being excitable by nature, he found our daily talks an increasing strain on his nerves.

I lived in a quiet side-street in Dahlem; the house had a garden in front and across the street was a small park 'Am Erlenbusch' [Elf-bush]. Ludwig Gehre accordingly gave me the code-name 'Elf-king'. The house proved ideal for the conspiracy. Anyone coming to me – and after Dohnanyi's arrest they were many from all the various resistance groups – could check whether the coast was clear by taking a walk along the edge of the park. If it was not, the fact could be indicated by broken pieces of flower-pot near the garden gate. In emergency two neighbouring underground stations could be reached through the back garden. At night I was often bicycling around until the small hours after nine or ten hours in my Lufthansa office. I had to keep in touch with a fairly wide circle of conspirators of various types, exchange information and arrange meetings, for which, of course, the telephone could not be used. Secret discussions frequently took place in my house, often with my brother Hans participating; after his release from the Wehrmacht he had once more become legal assistant to Professor Rüdiger Schleicher, another brother-in-law of Klaus Bonhoeffer, and was working in the Institute for Aeronautical Law.

On the day Mussolini fell my brother and I were alone in the house in the evening. We heard the news over the B.B.C. My brother jumped up, threw his arms round me and said that it would be ludicrous if we could not do what the Italians had apparently succeeded in doing quite easily. Soon afterwards Ludwig Gehre appeared with a bottle of champagne so that we could drink to Badoglio. We discussed the possible effects on our field marshals and came to the depressing conclusion that there was no Badoglio among them. In rank and reputation Field Marshal Rommel was his equal but he was now commanding the German forces in northern Italy and had not yet abandoned his belief in the Führer's ultimate victory.

During his soundings in Rome and the Vatican Josef Müller had come in contact with an Italian resistance group and, in agreement with Oster and Dohnanyi, had concluded a sort of mutual assistance pact – in the event of a rising in one Axis country a *coup* 'for better or worse' was immediately to be initiated in the other. The idea was to create a new political solidarity between Berlin and Rome and strengthen the position *vis-à-vis* the Western Powers in any negotiations for an armistice. After the fall of Mussolini, Dohnanyi and Müller accordingly pressed for a *coup*, Dohnanyi pointing out to the movement that we had 'a moral duty' to the new Italian government. Josef Müller wanted to go to Rome to co-ordinate armistice negotiations with the Western Powers as he had promised.

In order to free Dohnanyi, Müller and Dietrich Bonhoeffer from prison as soon as possible, Dr Sack, with the support of Canaris and Dr Lehmann, was to try to extract from Keitel a decision either to quash the proceedings or order a full-scale trial. Unfortunately, Sack was no longer in a position to influence Keitel. Keitel had told him that he would order the proceedings to be quashed if Himmler agreed, an agreement which Dr Langbehn hoped to obtain. One of Sack's staff drew up a memorandum for Himmler's information on the discussions between Sack and Keitel. Keitel heard of this and was furious; he forbade Sack to have anything further to do with the Dohnanyi case and the member of Sack's staff was relieved of his post.

Sack had no intention of knuckling under to Keitel, but for the moment he could do little. The fact was that all the prerequisites for fulfilment of our 'moral duty' to the new Italian government were lacking. Beck being ill, all military preparations for a *coup d'état* were at a total standstill. To set new preparations in motion through General Olbricht's staff, Tresckow took several months' sick leave and came to Berlin. Beck had meanwhile been released from his clinic and had been invited by Professor Sauerbruch to convalesce on his estate. I took Beck down a bottle of vintage burgundy. On this occasion Sauerbruch told me in confidence that he very much doubted whether Beck could ever be 'active' again. Sauerbruch did not, of course, know of the conspiracy, but he did know that Beck and his old friend Popitz 'had something under way'.

In view of Beck's dubious state of health Popitz felt it important to deal with the question of his successor. He wished Colonel-General von Falkenhausen, then Commander-in-Chief in Belgium, to head the conspiracy. In fact he thought Falkenhausen superior even to Beck because of his wide experience as adviser of many years' standing to Chiang Kai-shek and even more because of his outstanding intelligence. Falkenhausen had been a member of the military faction ever since his return from China in 1938. As a personality he was quite exceptional among the German generals.

I therefore understood very well why, in 1940, Popitz had suggested to Beck that Falkenhausen should take over command of the Wehrmacht in the event of a *coup* instead of Field Marshal von Witzleben who was sick. Beck had turned him down, however, because, although as Commander-in-Chief in Belgium he had given proof of good will and a sense of justice, in Allied eyes he was nevertheless identified with all that we had done in that country.

Popitz did not labour under Goerdeler's illusions about the resolution of our senior commanders. In the summer of 1943 he therefore took up Langbehn's idea of engineering a sort of palace revolution by the S.S. against Hitler. In this way the Wehrmacht might be persuaded to take action against the S.S. and proclaim a state of military emergency. He asked Langbehn to seek an interview for him with Himmler through S.S.-Obergruppenführer [Lieutenant-General] Wolff ('Little Karl'). The interview took place on 26 August with no one else present. Popitz told me what had happened and authorised me to pass it on to Goerdeler.

Popitz began by giving Himmler a detailed picture of Göring's ostentatious mode of life, proving with dates and figures that he was appropriating fantastic sums from the Prussian budget, of which Popitz was in charge. Himmler had listened in silence and had finally interposed: 'We must first put the lid on this stinkpot and then put it on one side.' Encouraged by this positive reaction Popitz had then explained in carefully chosen words his anxiety that the Führer was overloaded, the danger that he might become a casualty through sickness or collapse, finally the unsuitability of Göring as his successor in emergency and the incompetence of Ribbentrop. Himmler had listened to this also in silence. Having thus put Himmler in the right mood, Popitz came to the point. He besought Himmler to visualise the possibility of a 'Reich emergency' in which it might be necessary to end the war in the West in order to continue it against bolshevism. These were ideas which Himmler seemed to accept. He continued to listen in silence. Finally Popitz suggested that Langbehn be sent to Switzerland to sound out the attitude of the

Western Powers. For the most part Himmler had listened to all this without saying a word, leaving Popitz wondering whether his silence implied agreement.

Popitz later repented having tried to initiate a *coup* involving Himmler. Goerdeler was incensed and used this as an excuse to justify his break with Popitz. By going to Himmler, Popitz had put his head in the lion's den. Nevertheless, the idea of a 'Reich emergency' to which Popitz had referred accorded with Himmler's thinking; as we know from Walter Schellenberg's memoirs, in autumn 1943 he had perceived the danger threatening from the East and had authorised Schellenberg to contact Abraham Steven Hewitt, Roosevelt's plenipotentiary in Stockholm.

With these ideas in mind, after his talk with Popitz, Himmler allowed Langbehn to go to Switzerland to sound out the possibilities of negotiations with the Western Powers. This led to a fatal leak. A coded radio-message from Switzerland was intercepted and decoded by the R.S.H.A. [Reichssicherheitshauptamt – Central Security Department] intercept station. It read: 'Plenipotentiary of Reichs-führer-S.S. arrived here to investigate peace possibilities.' The radio message was passed to Gestapo Müller who, according to Schellenberg, was only too ready to denounce both him and Himmler as agents of foreign powers and so overthrow them both. Müller knew who the 'plenipotentiary' was and submitted the message to Himmler with the brief comment that Langbehn had obviously mis-used the Reichsführer's name and position in order to establish contact with the enemy. He must be arrested forthwith, he said. Himmler dropped Langbehn and agreed to his arrest. Popitz tried to intervene on his behalf; he telephoned and sent telegrams – but Himmler denied all knowledge.

In the summer of 1943 we were entirely convinced that the Western Powers would negotiate with us after the overthrow of the régime. But the chance was missed. This became clear to me when talking to Juan Terrasa, who came to Berlin at the end of July to find out how our project stood. He was dealing with the exchange of German and British prisoners of war in Lisbon and so his presence in Berlin was not suspect. I helped him gain a picture of the conspiracy by arranging meetings with all those within reach of Berlin and also telephoned Louis Ferdinand, who had not seen Juan for eight years. On the evening before his departure Juan gave me and Ludwig Gehre a summary of his impressions to be passed on to the members of the military faction. We still definitely had a chance, he said, of saving Germany from total destruction, but only on condition that the *coup* take place soon and we capitulate quickly to the Western Powers, thus saving them the sacrifices entailed by the conquest of Fortress Europe. Our generals must at last grasp the fact that unconditional surrender would be forced on them sooner or later.

The fact that Tresckow was working intensively with Olbricht's staff on military preparations for the *coup* inspired Goerdeler to high-pressure activity. He was vexed, however, that it was now August and he still had no reply from Churchill to the memorandum which he had transmitted through the Wallenberg brothers in May. He asked me whether I could inquire of Churchill through my contact with the British Embassy in Lisbon. I replied that, of course, I would try but attempted to explain to him that even Churchill could now no longer save us from unconditional surrender. Goerdeler stared at me flabbergasted. Internally he still had confidence in the good sense of the generals and externally in that of the Western statesmen. He still believed that they would ally themselves with us against bolshevism. On both counts his confidence proved illusory.

13

Mission for the Military Faction

THE Wehrmacht's continuing withdrawal in Russia, the Anglo-American landings in southern Italy and the air-raids on German cities during the lengthening autumn nights of 1943 shook the German people's confidence in ultimate victory. After the heavy air-raid on Hamburg Goebbels launched a propaganda campaign on the grapevine about the secret 'V' weapons, but this aroused more scepticism than hope since the weapons did not come into action. After the war Brauchitsch told me that Hitler personally was largely responsible for this. Before the war he had said the idea and development of 'V' weapons was utopian and refused to give the Army resources for their development. Had his own proposals been accepted, Brauchitsch said, the 'V' weapons would have been in mass production and in action in 1943.

But Germany could never have won the war. Development of the atomic bomb had started in America in 1942. Had 'V' weapons been employed against England in 1943, and particularly if the country was being devastated, Roosevelt would have been forced to use the atomic bomb on Germany. Germany could have manufactured the atomic bomb in theory but not in practice. We were told this in the summer of 1943 by Karl Friedrich Bonhoeffer, Director of the Max-Planck Institute for Physical Chemistry. An atomic bomb could not be tested in Germany nor indeed anywhere in thickly populated Europe since the effects of its chain reactions were unpredictable. 'But even if we could produce a controlled atomic bomb explosion,' Bonhoeffer said, 'we must take care that Hitler does not get his hands on such an instrument of destruction.' By 'we' he meant the German atomic scientists of the Uranium Association, particularly the Nobel Prizewinners Otto Hahn and Max von Laue.

By the autumn of 1943, it was clear to anyone who wished to see and hear that the war was lost. The sole remaining chance of avoiding

Germany's total destruction lay in the overthrow of the régime and rapid capitulation to the Western Powers in order to create a basis for armistice negotiations on the Italian model. I set out this point of view in a memorandum.

In it I stressed the change in the politico-military situation since Goerdeler's memorandum to Churchill. Popitz said that my memorandum would contribute just as little as Goerdeler's towards bringing about a *coup*. Ernst von Harnack thought that perhaps I was right. Jakob Kaiser was indignant that I had referred to our activities, in other words what is now called 'the resistance', as 'the opposition in Germany'; we were 'the German people', he said. Like Wirmer and Letterhaus who were also present at this discussion, he still believed in Goerdeler's negotiating abilities. Others, such as von Hassell and von Trott, the foreign-policy experts, did not react at all and probably regarded my memorandum as a purely academic exercise. Goerdeler never asked me to a meeting again.

People were simply unwilling to accept my arguments. But I was not to be shaken, not even when I heard from Gehre that Tresckow had managed to arrange a meeting between Beck, Kluge and Goerdeler in Olbricht's house. Beck had talked privately to Kluge and extracted from him a promise to head a military revolt as soon as Hitler was dead. In addition, Gehre said, someone had arrived on Olbricht's staff who would 'liven up the joint' – a certain Lieutenant-Colonel Graf Stauffenberg.

Early in October 1943 Walter Luz, then head of Lufthansa, told me that he would have to release me for the Wehrmacht. Many people thought it a scandal that, being barely thirty-five years old, fully fit and unmarried, I should still be in a 'reserved occupation' with Lufthansa, doing something which any retired lawyer could do. I had once been assaulted by a woman in the underground cursing loudly that 'well-dressed young idlers were still running around in Berlin while fathers of families had to go to the front'. I had sworn that under no circumstances would I fight for Hitler. Solely for this reason I had wished to go abroad before the war but had allowed myself to be persuaded to remain to assist in the *coup*. I reminded Ludwig Gehre of this and sent word via him to the gentlemen of the military faction that, if I received a call-up order, I should 'scram' to Lisbon on the next aircraft.

Hans Karl von Winterfeld, the pre-war head of the Lufthansa Traffic Policy division and a friend both of Prince Louis Ferdinand

and myself, was at this time a Luftwaffe major in charge of foreign air-attachés. He had acted on his own and had a desk job in Luftwaffe headquarters ready for me, should I be called up. Ludwig Gehre, however, discovered a means whereby, in my new guise, I could work for the military faction. In agreement with their friends on Olbricht's staff, Gehre and Major Graf Blumenthal, the desk officer for reserved occupations in the A.H.A., arranged a posting by Army Headquarters which cancelled my call-up. I was to be 'subject to defence regulations' and posted to the Abwehr Office in Stettin for special duty. My experience of foreign countries and knowledge of languages were given as justification for this army appointment.

The head of the Abwehr office in Stettin, a naval captain named Wiebe, and his assistant, Fürst Knyphausen, were firm opponents of the régime and were doing what they could to end the war by means of a *coup*. They accepted me like an old friend. I went to Stettin three times to get to know the Abwehr office. Otherwise I waited for my 'special duty'.

After swearing me to complete secrecy Gehre told me of the military preparations for the *coup* which was to be launched by the code-word 'Valkyrie' after the assassination of Hitler. Some younger officers had joined the conspiracy and were prepared to blow themselves up with Hitler on the occasion of the demonstration to the latter of a new winter greatcoat.

From the way Gehre spoke I had the clear impression that Olbricht's new Chief of Staff, Stauffenberg, had in fact livened things up. I too was to feel the effects. I did not know Stauffenberg; though an aristocrat, he was not one of the conspiracy's circle of Prussian counts which Gehre had nicknamed the 'Counts' Club'. He was a Swabian, Gehre told me, and 'could make a meal of the entire Counts' Club any time'. On his suggestion Colonel Hansen had already told Stauffenberg about me and my contacts in Madrid and Lisbon and as a result Stauffenberg was anxious to meet me.

For a time nothing happened since Stauffenberg had not a moment to spare. An assassination attempt was to be made on Hitler in November. It did not succeed because Hitler repeatedly called off the inspection of the new winter greatcoat. He had a remarkable instinct for security and had once said that his best protection was never to let anyone know when he would appear outside his own trusted circle. An aircraft, a special train and a motorcade were always standing ready for him and he only decided at the very last minute how he would travel. That November he clearly did not dare show his face outside his headquarters. About this period Gehre asked me on several occasions to be ready for a telephone call to meet Stauffenberg and his aide Werner von Haeften, who lived quite close to me, but each time he had to call it off.

About midday on 23 November Gehre came to see me; there had been a heavy air-raid on Berlin and the city was enveloped in smoke. This had spurred Stauffenberg and the military faction to fresh activity. The *coup* was still planned for 1943 and I was to fly to Madrid as soon as possible to find out whether rapid communications to Eisenhower's headquarters could be established through my American Embassy contact when the *coup* succeeded. I was to pass any positive reply to Klaus Bonhoeffer in an agreed code for transmission to Gehre.

This was a definite military task which pleased me. Hitherto my forays to Madrid and Lisbon had aimed at political links and information for the civilian dignitaries of the conspiracy. I had had enough of them since they refused to take seriously my estimate of the politico-military situation – which later proved correct. This task for the military faction, on the other hand, gave me the feeling that at last I was working with men able to set the military machine in motion to overthrow the régime.

I completed my mission in Madrid with the good fortune it deserved. Juan Terrasa immediately informed Beaulac of my arrival and he invited us to dinner in his house on his next free evening. There I met another tall American, in his mid-fifties, who greeted me in German like an old friend – 'How are you, Dr John?' He left me guessing, saying that we had mutual friends and acquaintances, such as Louis Lochner and Commander Schrader, the former American Naval Attaché in Berlin. He only made himself known after dinner: he was Colonel William Hohenthal, the recently appointed Military Attaché at the American Embassy in Madrid. He had previously been Assistant Military Attaché at the American Embassy in Berlin where he had once met me at a party.

Hohenthal had naturally been warned by Beaulac that he was going to see me. He did not, however, ask me any loaded questions, so I could talk quite naturally to him. But I had not been expecting to meet him, and meanwhile I had to think what I should say and how far I wished to get in the end. I had plenty of opportunity to do so during dinner. We discussed the war in general and I admitted quite openly what Beaulac already knew – that from the outset I had regarded it as lost. Hohenthal asked me whether the heavy air-raids on Hamburg and Berlin had not demoralised the people and led to war weariness.

I welcomed the question. I explained that with air attacks the Allies could neither destroy our industry nor cause our people to revolt. To do this they must land on the Channel coast, an operation for which the French, Belgians and Dutch had long been waiting in vain. He said that the time and space factors were of a different order of magnitude for the Allies than for us, primarily because of the war in the Far East. But they had learnt much from the Wehrmacht, he said, principally land/air co-operation. This would be made clear to our military men one day.

I quoted what Gablenz (whom Hohenthal also knew slightly) had said to me on the outbreak of war: that the Wehrmacht could fight for seven years before it was totally exhausted. I said sarcastically that we therefore probably still had three years to go before the Allies reached the Brandenburg Gate – unless we first contrived to end the war earlier 'through a change of régime'. Since he took this quite calmly, I said, without giving names, that 'we' intended to make an attempt 'to change the régime', before Christmas. For this purpose the outside support we needed was a declaration by the Allied High Command promising our field marshals the same treatment as had been guaranteed to Badoglio. This I thought was enough to raise the question in which I was interested – could we remain in touch? He willingly agreed, gave me his secret telephone number in the American Embassy and promised the strictest secrecy.

I passed the coded message to Klaus Bonhoeffer as agreed and then waited from day to day for something to happen to 'our Führer' or for some news from Klaus. This waiting got on my nerves, and on 16 December I flew back to Berlin. That same evening I learnt from Gehre that no assassination attempt had been made because Hitler had called off his greatcoat inspection. Hansen had not wished to bring Klaus Bonhoeffer into the matter because all Bonhoeffers were under surveillance because of Dohnanyi. I was to report to Hansen personally.

During the heavy air-raid on the night of 23 December Dohnanyi's cell had been set on fire and he himself had been found with partial paralysis of his speech and sight. This enabled Dr Sack to have him transferred to Sauerbruch's private clinic in the Charité. The files on the case had also been burnt during the air-raid. Keitel could now have ordered the proceedings quashed, but instead he ordered Roeder, at the latter's suggestion, to reconstitute the file on the basis of the Gestapo's material. Thus encouraged, Roeder appeared in the Charité to take Dohnanyi into custody once more, but Sauerbruch showed him the door. Two days later Hoffmann, an officer of the Reich Court Martial, appeared with an ambulance and some Gestapo officials, but Sauerbruch, who had general's rank as a medical officer, was not to be intimidated. He telephoned Keitel who said that he had issued no order for the transfer of Dohnanyi. So Sauerbruch simply sent the officer and his minions away.

About this time Graf [Count] Ledebur called me asking to speak to me. We met in the Adlon where he plied me with champagne and finally said that he had been commissioned to take me to Hansen. He then proposed that we should work together in Spain – which meant that he would like to appropriate my contacts there. I had neither need nor reason, however, to share them with him. I told Hansen this when I saw him in private. He was impressed that I had established contact with Hohenthal so easily and thought it important to maintain this contact through me without involving Ledebur. Finally he asked me to tell him in detail about my friendship with Prince Louis Ferdinand and the Prince's relationships with Roosevelt.

Finally Hansen proposed that I relinquish my Lufthansa post, leave the Abwehr office in Stettin and join his section as 'specially employed' with the rank of major. I had to argue him out of this since I knew that the professional officers in the Abwehr already looked askance at civilians like Dohnanyi, Delbrück and Guttenberg. Moreover, I could not be sure that Hansen would not be posted tomorrow or killed in an air-raid next day and in that case I might find myself under command of some colonel loyal to Hitler. More important still, I did not wish to let down Gehre, Wiebe and Knyphausen by cutting myself off from them. I accordingly told Hansen that as a member of Lufthansa I could move about with much greater freedom than as an Abwehr officer. As such it would be impossible for me to meet my opposite numbers in the American Embassy Madrid and the British Embassy Lisbon without embarrassment. This argument convinced Hansen and I was retained in Lufthansa service, at the same time remaining a member of the

Abwehr office in Stettin. Hansen felt it important that I should keep him informed personally and reserved to himself the decision on my future employment.

Four weeks later I realised how right I had been. Canaris was dismissed, the Abwehr disbanded and the rump of it incorporated into the R.S.H.A. as 'Amt Mil' [Military Office] under Schellenberg. As a member of the Abwehr I should have been swept into the S.D. under Schellenberg!

14
Gathering Clouds

WE thought that under Sauerbruch's protection Dohnanyi was safe from the Gestapo. He was in considerably better shape, and the impediment in his speech was now barely noticeable; Klaus Bonhoeffer had emphasised to me, however, that he must be treated with care. But Dohnanyi wanted from me an unequivocal answer to his burning questions. He was tortured by anxiety about what was happening and whether indeed anything was being done to overthrow the régime. I had several conversations with him and gave him all the details, trying to raise his hopes. He was sceptical, particularly since he realised the dangers now hanging over us. I had to promise him to destroy his notes which were kept in a safe in Zossen camp by Major Schrader, a friend of Gehre's; they included the 'X Report', intended to win Brauchitsch over to the conspiracy early in 1940. Schrader would not release the documents to me; Beck had said that they were historic and must therefore be preserved. This would cost him and all of us our lives, Dohnanyi said, and asked me to speak to Beck. Before I could do so, however, Keitel ordered Dohnanyi's transfer to the prison hospital at Buch, so we were once more reduced to communicating by smuggled notes. The documents were actually found by the Gestapo during their investigations into the 20 July *coup*, after Schrader had shot himself. They did, in fact, cost Dohnanyi his life later.

Gehre heard from his informant in the Reich Research Office that Halder's telephone was being tapped. Halder had, of course, been suspended from active service for more than a year but before that he had been so heavily involved in the conspiracy that, if the Gestapo were on his trail, they might easily be led to Olbricht and his staff. Alerted by this, Werner von Haeften, Stauffenberg's aide, came to me and asked me to tell him the background and circumstances of Dohnanyi's and Langbehn's arrest. Olbricht's staff had to think how to protect themselves, he said, if they were to continue; further setbacks resulting from arrests simply could not be allowed to happen. This first talk with Haeften brought us closer to each other. He was nephew to Field Marshal von Brauchitsch, about my age and, like me, a lawyer by profession. That evening we talked late into the night and parted as good political friends.

The year 1944 opened with fresh heavy blows to the conspiracy. Dr Otto Kiep, ex-Consul-General in the United States, was arrested; he was serving as an O.K.W. Reserve officer in Zossen camp and was a close friend of Oster, Dohnanyi and Langbehn. He was the first uniformed officer on active service to be arrested by the Gestapo. An officer of the camp had tried to send the Gestapo officials about their business but they refused to be deterred and telephoned the R.S.H.A.; at Himmler's insistence Keitel ordered the Commandant of Zossen by telephone not to oppose Kiep's arrest. This showed us all that there were no longer any barriers to the Gestapo, and that Wehrmacht uniform no longer offered any protection.

Kiep, together with all the friends and acquaintances of Frau Solf, widow of the last imperial Foreign Minister (later the ambassador), had been denounced by an informer, Dr Reckzeh. Frau Solf and her circle had been shadowed for nearly six months beforehand and, as a result, there was now no knowing who was on the Gestapo's black list and under observation. This also explained why Halder was under surveillance. Reckzeh had tried to involve him in compromising discussions with Frau Solf. In Frau Solf's circle Goerdeler was known as the driving force behind the resistance. Had we even a hope of keeping the conspiracy secret from the Gestapo?

In this situation Stauffenberg got away one evening to meet me in Werner von Haeften's house. The latter had told him that I had been one of Oster's and Dohnanyi's immediate circle and was also on good terms with the 'great men' and other leaders of the various civil resistance groups. Stauffenberg knew nothing of the political and personal complexities inside the civil resistance or of its development. He had not yet been in Berlin six months and wished to be briefed by me.

I got on well with Stauffenberg from the outset. I had imagined him to be older and was surprised to meet an officer whose personality overshadowed both his uniform and his rank. What he said showed clearly that he was now the focus of all organisation and initiative for the *coup* and that it was therefore important for him to be told all I knew about the conspiracy from its inception. As a result of his shrewd questions any gaps in my story were filled, and he eventually said that he was now fully in the picture.

We discussed my contacts in Madrid and Lisbon and the possibility of establishing a link between Louis Ferdinand and Roosevelt. Stauffenberg, who was a Württemberger, knew nothing of the Prince who was a Prussian. I briefly described him and his political attitude. We wanted no 'plans à la Goerdeler', Stauffenberg said; the vital necessity was to create a new situation. At this point he was not proposing to assassinate Hitler with his own hand but he was determined to initiate and carry through the overthrow of the régime. He therefore required some link to Eisenhower and Montgomery which, as Hansen had indicated, I was to provide in Madrid and Lisbon.

Before I could set forth to Madrid again, however, Himmler administered the *coup de grâce* to Canaris. As a result of the investigations into the Kiep case Dr Erich Vermehren, one of the Abwehr representatives in Istanbul, was summoned to Berlin with his wife by the Gestapo. They would certainly have been arrested. They defected to the British, but not in silence or in secret; they broadcast their reasons to the world over the British radio. Another husband-and-wife couple in Abwehr service in Istanbul together with a secretary, all less well known, followed the Vermehrens' example. Hitler was furious, and Himmler had only to remind him that he (Himmler) and Heydrich had already frequently pointed out the unreliability of the Abwehr, for which Canaris was solely responsible. On Hitler's orders Canaris was suspended from duty and sent on leave; the Abwehr was placed under Himmler, reorganised and incorporated into the R.S.H.A. as 'Amt Mil'. Colonel Hansen was appointed head of 'Amt Mil'; like his ex-master Canaris, he contrived to keep our conspiratorial activities secret right up to 20 July.

This was made considerably easier by the fact that, before his departure, Canaris had managed to put paid to Roeder in a somewhat peculiar manner. In one of Dohnanyi's memoranda Canaris had read that Roeder had referred to the 'Brandenburg' Regiment, the Abwehr's raiding and sabotage force, as a 'draft-dodgers' union'. When Canaris repeated this to General von Pfuhlstein, the regimental commander, the latter was furious and took it upon himself to avenge this insult to him and his men. He sought out Roeder in his office and asked whether he was Dr Roeder. When Roeder said he was, the general gave him a resounding box on the ear and went away. Completely at a loss Roeder ran down the passage after him and asked: 'Who are you anyway?' This public scandal made Roeder's life so impossible that he was relieved of his post. Dohnanyi's case was handed over to a judge of the old school whose investigations Dohnanyi found easy to deal with.

Early in February I flew to Madrid, feeling that I was now an associate of men who were really working towards the *coup* with some purpose. Hansen had impressed upon me that, in addition to contacting Colonel Hohenthal in Madrid and Tony in Lisbon, I should try to find out dates and plans concerning the military situation, in particular whether and when the invasion announced by Churchill would take place. I met Colonel Hohenthal straight away. He was just off on a lengthy tour of duty, but promised to let me know on his return in March whether he could establish a link to Eisenhower for us; he could not decide on this himself.

My mission to Lisbon was entirely unsuccessful. Tony was ostensibly away. Instead I met one of his staff, Miss Rita Winsor, with whom Juan Terrasa had arranged a meeting for me. We rendezvoused in a side-street after dark and I got into her car, recognising her by a grey streak in her hair which contrasted attractively with a pretty young face. As we drove through the town she told me that strict instructions had been received from London forbidding any further contact with emissaries of the German opposition. So there was no point in talking further. General Eisenhower had been appointed Supreme Commander for the invasion, she said, and the war would now be decided by force of arms. To sweeten this bitter pill she invited me to her home to say farewell over a glass of whisky. I went in order to put one last request to her. I asked her to arrange for the R.A.F. not to bomb Düppel camp between Berlin and the Wannsee so that at least we had one place where we could carry on our preparations undisturbed. She promised to pass on this request and got me to make a sketch-map.

Back in Madrid I woke in the night with badly smarting eyes; I had a severe attack of conjunctivitis. I had to stay in bed in a darkened room and sent a telegram to Klaus Bonhoeffer so that he could tell Hansen of this via Perels. The news made Hansen and Stauffenberg extremely uneasy. As I learnt on my return, Ludwig Gehre had been arrested but had escaped from the Gestapo. People on Olbricht's staff were afraid that I had somehow or other been warned by Gehre to defect to the Allies either with or without him and that this would give rise to a new scandal which would make it impossible for Hansen to retain his key position. Knowing nothing of all this, I flew back to Berlin as soon as my eyes were better, arriving on 10 March, a fortnight later than planned. My brother met me at the airport, watching from behind a pillar to see whether I would be arrested. This my friends thought quite possible since my close connections with Gehre might easily have become known to the Gestapo. Haeften was waiting outside the airport in an official car. Since nothing happened to me Haeften drove me home. What I heard during the drive and later in more detail from my brother at home sounded to me like a last warning. I was no longer safe in Berlin.

Months earlier Oster had put through a telephone call from Kiep's house. Gehre had heard from his informant in the 'Research Office' that the conversation had been intercepted. Graf Moltke, who was serving in O.K.W. as adviser on international law, was asked by Canaris to warn Oster not to use the telephone any more, not because he might compromise himself but because the clandestine listeners were intent on finding out to whom he was telephoning. From their investigations into Frau Solf's circle the Gestapo learnt that Oster had been warned by Moltke, who was immediately arrested. He was incapable of lying, and the Gestapo extracted from him the fact that his informant was Gehre, who was then arrested in his turn.

Gehre played the 'old Party fighter', referred to his previous acquaintanceship with Himmler and declared himself ready to transfer from the Abwehr to the S.D., saying that he had had enough of working 'with reactionary officers'. He asked for brandy and drank to 'the old comradeship' until the others were under the table. The next morning he was due to prove his readiness to collaborate by writing a political critique on all the Abwehr officers he knew, using the internal Abwehr telephone directory. This he promised to do but said that he would first like to go home to fetch a couple of things. Two Gestapo officials were ordered to escort him. In his in-laws' villa in Lichterfelde where he was living alone (his wife and family had been evacuated), he made the two officials drunk. When they asked for more liquor, he said that his stocks were exhausted but suggested that they go over to his brother-in-law, Paul Herpich, who had everything to eat and drink.

Paul Herpich quickly grasped what was happening and the carousing continued. Finally a film was shown and with the whir of the projector the two tipsy Gestapo men nodded off. Meanwhile Gehre disappeared. He went to my brother who first hid him in our house and after a few days in that of a reliable friend, Otto Lenz, later State Secretary to Dr Adenauer. There I saw him once more. He said that if the Gestapo found him he would shoot himself but before that he would go to Olbricht and give him hell unless something was done to bring the tyranny of the brown-shirts to an end.

This caused Stauffenberg and Hansen to ask me to find some hideout for Gehre in Spain; they feared that he might 'go round the bend'. In my view, which later proved correct, there was no danger of this. However, on the pretext of some Abwehr business, I went to Paris and there looked up a Spaniard whose address Juan Terrasa had given me in case one of us should have to go to ground. We could easily have given Gehre a forged military pass and movement order to Paris, and the Spaniard was willing to hide him. But Gehre utterly refused to leave Germany without his wife and child, although they were in perfect safety in his in-laws' country house on the island of Sylt.

I drafted two reports on my mission to Spain and Portugal. The first dealt with the Western Powers' attitude to Spain. In the other (see Appendix A) I predicted that the invasion would take place in June and said that there was no possibility of a split between the Anglo-Americans and the Russians. I tried to make clear that we could not evade a formal declaration of unconditional surrender. This was vehemently contradicted by Adam von Trott who quoted against me a speech by Churchill to the Commons in February when he had clearly distinguished between the Nazis and the German people.

Hansen contrived to play an intrepid double game between his new S.S. masters and the conspiracy. As late as 20 July Kaltenbrunner and Schellenberg were still regarding him as an efficient non-political intelligence officer; they left him a comparatively free hand in the expansion of 'Amt Mil' which continued until late spring. Meanwhile Canaris was appointed head of the Special Staff for Economic Warfare, a position in which he could do nothing for the conspiracy.

Meanwhile the Gestapo had stumbled on my trail. When talking to some S.S. people, one of Hansen's staff was told that the fugitive Gehre had been a close friend of a well-dressed blond young 'gentleman' whom Gehre always called 'Doctor'; he had often bicycled over to see Gehre in the evenings. The description fitted me; it originated from the caretaker's wife at the Herpich villa. To my great good fortune Gehre had never given the inquisitive woman the name of any of his visitors. Nevertheless, it was not a pleasant feeling that the Gestapo had my description and were looking for me.

This feeling was certainly not lessened when my brother and I were looking after Gehre. We had to change his hide-out frequently. Then late one evening Haeften collected me in an official car and we moved Gehre to a new hiding-place. This in itself was a risky operation since we might have been stopped by a military patrol or overtaken by an air-raid. As a precaution against such mishaps Graf Schwerin-Schwanenfeld, who was serving as a captain in the Quartermaster-General's department, arranged a paybook for Gehre with a false name and major's rank. To disguise himself he had grown a moustache and wore an eyeglass. He drove us to desperation by going out for walks at night and casually ringing people up from some call-box. He was continually threatening that, if the Gestapo caught him again, he would 'blow the whole Bendler-strasse shop skyhigh'. He thought that by such pressure he might accelerate the *coup*.

Once more Hansen proposed to me that I should join his staff as 'specially employed', this time giving as his reason that Schellenberg did not think much of the Abwehr office in Stettin. Now, however, I had every reason to avoid any position which might attract the attention of the S.D. I said that I was quite ready to leave the Stettin office but not to join 'Amt Mil'. Hansen found a solution. On his instructions I was appointed 'Special O.K.W. Representative', continued as a civilian and legal adviser to Lufthansa but was now in the innermost circle of the military faction.

Since Goerdeler no longer made use of me, I saw Popitz all the more frequently to hear from him what the civilian leaders were thinking and planning. Rumour had it that, since his interview with Himmler, he was under permanent surveillance, but there was nothing of the sort to be seen. His telephone was tapped, of course. He again asked me to arrange, via Lynar, an interview for him or Gerecke with Field Marshal von Witzleben. While discussing this

Lynar told me that the Field Marshal was annoyed that no one should have thought of having an aircraft ready for him in the event of his assumption of supreme command of the Wehrmacht when he would have to go to headquarters. I took my friend, Flight Captain Horst von Baumbach, into my confidence and he made arrangements to have a Junkers 52 on call.

During one of our talks Popitz proposed a meeting with Julius Leber. I had come to the conclusion that he was our most effective left-wing supporter as Popitz was that of the Right. Leber was quite ready to talk to Popitz, but the latter, with an obstinacy incomprehensible to me, insisted that Leber should come to him. This Leber refused to do since he was convinced that Popitz's house was watched. While discussing this, Leber told me that he had meanwhile met Stauffenberg. All of us should do all we could to support him, Leber said; if anyone could get the Wehrmacht to act, it was Stauffenberg; what happened thereafter would depend on the situation and that would certainly be quite different from what Goerdeler thought.

I was gratified that an experienced politician like Julius Leber, who had long since risen above his socialist party political background, should express my thoughts so exactly. During my first talk with Stauffenberg I had drawn his attention to Leber. In retrospect I believe that this was my most significant contribution to the political aspect of the plans for the *coup*. At my suggestion and through Adam von Trott Stauffenberg met Leber while I was in Madrid. In the last three months before 20 July the two came closer and closer together; after a *coup* they would probably have formed an important progressive force in German political life.

After the war all sorts of ideas were spread abroad about the possible or probable new directions which German policy might have taken both internally and externally; they were based on the available Gestapo records such as the Kaltenbrunner reports, memoranda, diaries, cases for the prosecution and sentences of the Peoples Court, and were all pure speculation. It is certain that Stauffenberg would not have implemented Goerdeler's plans. Since his nomination as Chief of Staff the entire initiative for the *coup* lay in Stauffenberg's hands. He had a high opinion of Beck and never questioned his position as leader of the conspiracy; moreover, he could not have acted alone. Beck, exhausted by illness, sceptical and wearied with the eternal haverings of the senior commanders, left Stauffenberg a free hand. The latter, after briefing himself thoroughly in Berlin until the spring of 1944, would accept no political tutelage and tried to resist Goerdeler's claim to authoritarian control. In the spring of 1943 the secret anti-Hitler front had disintegrated politically and was without central leadership. In their impotence the leaders of the civilian resistance concentrated their hopes on Stauffenberg.

Such was the situation when Stauffenberg and Leber met, two congenial personalities who appraised realistically both the over-all situation and their own ambitions. Both wished to overthrow the régime and, this done, negotiate with the Allies. The first step was to be a meeting between Beck and Eisenhower when an armistice would be negotiated. Everything else was left to the moment of decision. With this as the aim, in the spring of 1944 Stauffenberg's idea was to initiate the *coup* through one of the young officers such as von dem Bussche or von Kleist, who were prepared to sacrifice themselves in an attempt to assassinate Hitler. All these plans failed, however, since none of them could get near Hitler.

Hansen hoped that Stauffenberg would be able to initiate the *coup* very soon and urged me to fly back to Madrid immediately after Easter. I had every good reason to do so since I would have been safe from the Gestapo there, but initially this did not weigh with me, particularly seeing that I had a passport with authorisation for foreign travel and could climb on to a Lufthansa aircraft any day. I was held back by the question: what does Stauffenberg want – and what do I really want myself? Stauffenberg was proposing to come and see me one evening but had not the time. This was the first occasion on which I had the impression that he was taking too much upon himself because no one else could do things well enough for him.

Because of Stauffenberg's visit I kept postponing my departure for a day or two. He wished to talk to me and my brother about the use of my house 'Am Erlenbusch' for secret meetings, as I had suggested to him. But it never happened. While I was still waiting, Albrecht Haushofer arrived to take me for a walk through the Grunewald. He knew that I was planning to fly to Madrid and had been speaking to Hassell the day before. They were both agreed that Madrid and Lisbon were not suitable for our negotiations. They thought that Stockholm was the right place! There one could 'turn eastwards and talk to Stalin' if the Western Powers proved unwilling to negotiate after a successful *coup*.

Haushofer did not know what my specific mission was. He thought that I would still be reconnoitring for Goerdeler in Madrid and Lisbon. Moreover, he still believed that we had room for negotiation and explained to me in ingenious phraseology how we must bring home to the British that Hitler was merely a sort of super-Cromwell, whose elimination would create a basis for negotiation. On 17 April 1944 I flew once more to Madrid.

15
Eclipse

DESPITE the peace of Madrid, which was calming to the nerves, my feelings and thoughts were still in Berlin and I waited tensely for some sign of the *coup*. Gerd Lindenberg, the Lufthansa representative, thought and felt as I did. We often sat alone in some country inn in the evenings over a bottle of red wine.

At least, therefore, I had a kindred spirit in Madrid, with whom I could speak my mind. Nevertheless, this waiting around doing nothing became intolerable and on 15 May I returned to Berlin. Stauffenberg had made no further progress and had still found no one who could approach Hitler. I wrote an 'official' report for 'Amt Mil' and a true one for the military faction. In the latter I forecast once more that the invasion would take place on the French coast in June and again emphasised that unconditional surrender would be demanded. Many people were still under the illusion that it might be possible to split the Anglo-Americans and the Russians; Goerdeler used to say: 'The British simply cannot allow the Russians to enter Germany since this would make their world-wide political differences with the Russians insoluble for all time.' Even at this time it was already questionable whether the East–West alliance would continue after the war but there was not the smallest reason to hope that it would break up before Germany's capitulation. This I had already stated in my report for Stauffenberg of March 1944 (see Appendix A).

Doubt was cast on my forecast by a speech of Churchill's to the Commons on 24 May: 'We will all fight on together until Germany is forced to capitulate and until Nazism is extirpated . . . the principle of unconditional surrender will be adhered to as far as Nazi Germany and Japan are concerned.' The phraseology, according to von Trott zu Solz, showed that Churchill was still determined to differentiate between the German people and the régime.

One evening in the last week of May I wished to see Julius Leber.

He was not at home. I went round the house and suddenly came face to face with Stauffenberg. He also wished to see Leber and suggested that we take a walk together. We sauntered through the park near by and sat on a bench. This was the first time that I had had an opportunity of talking personally and at length to Stauffenberg instead of hurriedly discussing something to do with the situation and our plans.

On this particular evening Stauffenberg was wearing the normal Wehrmacht cape without badges of rank. He was lively without becoming excited and seemed to be assessing my reactions as we talked. We knew little of each other personally but, being both south Germans, understood each other quickly. I was particularly pleased to hear from him at first hand that he had a high opinion of Julius Leber and was fully prepared to receive suggestions and advice from him. This seemed to me the best guarantee for political reformation in Germany. After I had criticised the field marshals, Stauffenberg asked what I would do in their place. The question was academic, I replied, since I had never been an officer – and at once thought that, for a professional soldier, this answer was too categoric. How good it would be, Stauffenberg said, if our generation was not faced by such serious problems and duties. Why was I not married, he then asked. I replied that I did not wish to place my wife in the position of Hanna Gehre and had wanted to emigrate; I simply could not fight for Hitler.

Stauffenberg then asked me whether I knew Stefan George's 'Anti-Christ'. This led to an exchange of reminiscences of our younger days. As a schoolboy I, like Stauffenberg, had admired the poet and had met him once through a lecturer, Professor Richard Grützmacher. The thought of Stefan George, I said, made me wonder whether I would not have done better to emigrate as the poet had done to ensure that he and his poetry could not be misused for propaganda purposes by Goebbels.

On the contrary, Stauffenberg said immediately and with emphasis, I had taken the only correct course in remaining. This would soon be clear. He then asked what I planned to do in the 'new' Germany, a question which led me to think that he took some personal interest in me. I had no very definite ideas. I knew, however, from the British and American press that the Allies intended to break up Lufthansa and told Stauffenberg so, remarking that, as a lawyer, I should certainly not be unemployed during the chaotic post-war period. Could I not visualise myself as something else, he asked – fulfilling some function in the political reconstruction, for instance? I was under no illusions and said so quite frankly. With that Stauffenberg had to leave; his driver with his car was waiting in a dark side-street. As we parted he asked: 'Why are you so pessimistic? That is not like you. We must talk about this some other time.' I had the feeling that I had made a friend.

About this time Stauffenberg was faced with a far-reaching decision. Colonel-General Friedrich Fromm, Commander-in-Chief of the Replacement Army, asked him whether he would like to become his Chief of Staff. Initially, Stauffenberg told me and Leber a few days later, he had hesitated. He had had to weigh the fact that he and Fromm viewed the politico-military situation completely differently and he was not therefore particularly suited as Chief of Staff. Fromm had told him, however, that he, too, had had to revise his ideas about 'the situation'. Here Stauffenberg saw his chance: as Fromm's Chief of Staff he would be admitted to Hitler's briefing conferences. He agreed and Fromm accepted him. Stauffenberg was promoted Colonel and became Chief of Staff of the Replacement Army. 'One only becomes Colonel once and that must be celebrated,' Julius Leber said, opening a bottle of moselle. I was happy that Leber and Stauffenberg were on such good terms.

Stauffenberg was not convinced that an invasion of France was imminent. He said that it was possible but not probable. 'In any case,' he continued, 'we can be reasonably sure that we have at least a fifty-fifty chance of driving the British and Americans back into the sea. And then the British, who have suffered no significant casualties in this war, will negotiate.' I put forward once more all the arguments which Hansen and I had assembled pointing to an invasion. 'Let me be the devil's advocate for once,' Stauffenberg said. 'Trott has told me that he has seen a telegram from our embassy in Ankara. It records a conversation between the Russian Assistant Military Attaché and a Turkish general. The Russian complained that the British and Americans did not propose to invade at all this year and that Russia would have to continue to carry the main burden of the war against Germany alone.'

I remained unconvinced by this telegram – the Russian complaints were too superficial. Stauffenberg insisted that I talk to Trott about it and about the Churchill speech already referred to, which had raised new hopes of negotiations should a *coup* succeed. Such speculations meant nothing to Leber. An overthrow of the régime in Germany, he said, would fundamentally alter the whole world political situation. One could only form a judgement and act on the basis of the new situation which would then emerge. With this Stauffenberg agreed.

A few days later, on the morning of 6 June, the greatest armada in history attacked the European mainland. Surprise was complete. Stauffenberg and his staff were caught up in these great military events, had much to improvise and organise and were no longer accessible. Three days later Hansen sent word to me to meet him at the Rangsdorf metro station, whence he would take me by car to his weekend cottage. He did not arrive; instead Haeften appeared late in the evening and said that I was to meet Stauffenberg and Hansen in Olbricht's ante-room at midday next day for a final discussion, after which I was to fly to Madrid as soon as possible.

In Olbricht's ante-room there was high-pressure activity and the staff was obviously in turmoil as a result of the invasion. In addition the first V1 had been launched the day before. Stauffenberg was handing over his duties on Olbricht's staff to his successor Mertz von Quirnheim. He was rushing back and forth between Fromm and Olbricht, and said that he simply had no time; I was to discuss everything with Hansen. When the latter arrived he took me out of the hurly-burly into a small room near by.

Hansen complimented me on having forecast the invasion correctly. He had talked to Stauffenberg on the previous evening. Both now considered that the Anglo-Americans were firmly established ashore and could no longer be thrown back into the sea. The next three weeks would be decisive, Hansen said. By that time something must and would happen. I was to fly to Madrid and await him there. As soon as Witzleben had assumed supreme command he (Hansen) would come to Madrid to establish communications to Eisenhower's headquarters through Colonel Hohenthal. Quoting Stauffenberg, he emphasised to me that armistice negotiations were the business solely of the military command – 'soldier to soldier' – and that no politician was to take part. He was referring to Goerdeler.

Before leaving for Madrid I paid one more visit to Josef Wirmer. Politically he had veered towards Leber and now stood halfway between him and Goerdeler. Like the rest of us, he was disillusioned that no senior commander was prepared to bring the war to an end. Wirmer's explanation of this was that the Allies held us out no hope of reasonable peace-terms. He wished me to pass this on, and I was to transmit to London a memorandum from him and his friends of the former Catholic Centre Party. I promised to do this, although I thought it totally useless. On 26 June I passed the memorandum (see Appendix B) to the British Embassy in Lisbon through Juan Terrasa.

On my arrival in Madrid Juan assured me that once the *coup* had succeeded we could contact Eisenhower's headquarters at once through the American Embassy. He gave me a promise that any message or information transmitted to Eisenhower from our new high command would be placed on his desk immediately. Juan had once more been told, however, that Eisenhower's answer could only be a demand for unconditional surrender. Having informed Hansen of this, I could do nothing but wait.

To be able to talk freely I visited Mgr Boyen-Maas of the French Red Cross in Madrid; he was in close contact with the underground French resistance and with M. Truelle, General de Gaulle's representative in Madrid. I had made his acquaintance through Juan Terrasa and I told him of my commission from Josef Wirmer. He gave a warning against harbouring illusions and said: 'The British and Americans will definitely make no special effort to be in Berlin before the Russians. There are people who hold the view that Germany deserves punishment and they are quite happy to leave that to the Russians.'

I was dismayed and talked the matter over with Gerd Lindenberg. He had to fly to Berlin on business and so I asked him to look up my brother, get him to arrange an interview with Stauffenberg or Hansen and tell one or other of them of my talk with Mgr Boyen-Maas. He was to emphasise to them that there was no more time to lose.

On 13 July my brother took Lindenberg to the War Ministry to see Haeften. Stauffenberg was not there; Haeften telephoned Hansen to come across from Zossen camp. Before he arrived, Lindenberg had to go to Tempelhof for a Lufthansa board meeting. Haeften sent Hansen after him, and the latter summoned Lindenberg out of the meeting into my Lufthansa office where they could talk in private. Lindenberg flew back to Madrid next morning. From the aircraft he sent me an urgent radio-message that I was to go to Berlin at once. On landing Lindenberg passed Hansen's message on to me: Leber had been arrested.

A few days earlier Klaus Bonhoeffer had warned me in a letter not to come to Berlin. He was afraid that I would be arrested in connection with Gehre. I flew to Berlin, therefore, with very mixed feelings, convinced that this time I should not re-emerge in one piece. My brother had a message for me from Haeften that all was prepared 'for the great blow' on the following day. I was to hold myself in readiness either at home or in my Lufthansa office.

The next day, 20 July, there was an eclipse of the sun. In the morning the sky seemed grey and murky, the air oppressive. No weather for a revolution, I said. My brother, however, pointed out that the French had also stormed the Bastille in July. I was undecided and could not make up my mind whether to await Haeften's call at home or in the office.

Meanwhile my brother told me what had been happening during my absence. Shortly before, through Irmgard Klewitz and Lynar, he had succeeded in arranging the long-planned meeting between Field Marshal von Witzleben and Gerecke, acting as spokesman for Popitz. It had taken place on 18 July and was certainly of some significance for the political decisions to be taken on this day since Witzleben had shown himself open to suggestions and advice from Popitz. My brother did not know, however, how the conversation had gone.

The arrest of Leber I found quite incomprehensible. Months before he had once said to me and Harnack that, whatever happened, we must find out what the communist attitude to a *coup* would be. He had someone in his coal business, he said, whom he could probably use to make the necessary contacts. In any case over the last months and weeks Leber had busied himself with the question of what the communists would do if the Wehrmacht revolted. This was no ground for thinking that Leber had veered towards the communists, still less to the East. Even the most conservative leaders were inevitably interested in the possible communist attitude. While pursuing this question, my brother told me, Julius Leber had fallen into a Gestapo trap set by a communist spy.

I could not imagine what I could or should do in Berlin. I called Hansen in his office and was told that he was away. There was nothing to do but wait for Haeften's telephone call, and I drove to my Tempelhof office. Klaus Bonhoeffer was horrified that I had returned to Berlin instead of remaining in safety. I could not tell him a word about the *coup*, however, since his position was most perilous because of Dohnanyi. The latter was seriously ill in Potsdam Isolation Hospital with scarlet fever and diphtheria. Legally his case was not in bad shape; because of his serious illness proceedings had been postponed to the end of the war and he was to be interned in a sanatorium. On the next day, however, Himmler was master in Berlin. The Gestapo removed Dohnanyi and eventually murdered him on the grounds that he had master-minded the conspiracy against the Führer.

I did not go out to lunch as I usually did with Klaus Bonhoeffer but said that I had urgent letters to write. Eventually, between 5.0 and 5.30, came Haeften's telephone call. Quite casually and naturally, as if he was inviting me to lunch, he said: 'Come along here; we have executive authority.' For a lawyer this was an unusual, and therefore unforgettable, form of words; it meant that I should hurry. I quickly told Klaus Bonhoeffer, asking him to go to my brother and expect me or a phone-call from me that evening.

The iron grille at the main entrance to the War Ministry in the Bendlerstrasse was closed. I told the porter that I wished to see Colonel Graf Stauffenberg. He telephoned. A few minutes later a young captain arrived and said: 'I am to let you up, Doctor.' In the courtyard I saw an open black police BMW, obviously an official car from S.S. headquarters. I recoiled.

At the foot of the stairs stood a sentry with fixed bayonet. 'You can go on up,' the captain said, thus getting me past the sentry, and he then went back to the guard-room.

With my eyes on the stairs I went up to the second floor where Fromm, the Commander-in-Chief of the Replacement Army, and Olbricht had their offices. As I arrived I was brought up short once more. Facing me on the landing was Colonel Fritz Jäger, a friend of Ludwig Gehre, and on either side of him a sentry in steel helmet and with fixed bayonet; a few paces away was an S.S. officer with a revolver in his holster. It looked as if Jäger had been arrested. I thought I was running into a trap and said with deliberate ceremony: 'Heil Hitler, Colonel.' He took me by both hands and replied: 'It's good that you've come.' With a wink he gave me to understand that the S.S. officer was his prisoner.

I went into Fromm's spacious ante-room; the glass door leading to Stauffenberg's office was open. He was telephoning and waved to me. Generals and other officers were standing around in the ante-room talking. Haeften arrived, welcomed me, took me into a window-bay and said: 'Hitler is no more. Keitel maintains that he's not dead but only slightly wounded. It's not true.' I asked after Hansen. Haeften did not know why he was not there and replied: 'You just stay here now.' He left me standing and ran to one of the telephones manned by a secretary in the corner of the room. I felt uncomfortable, lit a cigarette and watched what was going on around me. I had always pictured the General Staff in action as purposeful, calm and relaxed, something very different from what I saw and heard – a flurry of telephone conversations, officers rushing to and fro, two small groups of generals standing talking as if in the mess. I recognised General Specht from his striking profile; he was talking to two others about some gun or other. Another general came in through the wide-open door from the passage, went up to the other group and asked: 'Do any of you gentlemen know why we have been ordered here?' Nobody did.

Graf Fritz von Schulenburg came slowly out of Stauffenberg's room smoking a cigar. He was surprised to see me, greeted me and said that he must go over to Olbricht's office on the other side of the corridor. The next to emerge was Stauffenberg's brother, Berthold, in blue naval uniform, looking out of place in the field-grey scene. We did not know each other personally. He bowed slightly towards me, said nothing and passed through the room deep in thought. I was wondering whether to speak to him when in came Graf Schwerin, the State Secretary-designate to Beck, the Head of State-designate.

Despite his apparent deliberation, Schwerin was highly effective in his quiet way; he seemed to have time to explain the situation to me. I offered him a 'Lucky Strike' from a packet which I still had in my pocket from Madrid. He drew up chairs and we sat down. He told me that Stauffenberg and Haeften had been to the Führer's headquarters and that Stauffenberg had blown Hitler up during the briefing conference. This was the news for which Beck, Olbricht and the staff officers in the conspiracy had been waiting ever since midday. They had received it only during the afternoon when Haeften had called from Rangsdorf airfield after he and Stauffenberg had landed.

Thereupon Olbricht had reported to Fromm that 'the Führer was dead' and had proposed that, since disturbances were to be anticipated, a state of military emergency be declared. To reassure himself Fromm had called Keitel who had said that there had in fact been an attempt on the Führer's life but that he had only been slightly wounded. Fromm had thereupon refused to proclaim the state of emergency. This, however, was the vital prerequisite for the initiation of the *coup d'état*. Olbricht withdrew to his office and waited for Stauffenberg.

Meanwhile Colonel Mertz von Quirnheim, thinking that rapid action was required, had issued the orders for the state of military emergency. Shortly after 5 p.m. Stauffenberg returned with Haeften. He insisted that Hitler was dead and that Keitel was lying. Olbricht, Stauffenberg and Mertz hurried to Fromm to force him to announce the state of emergency. Fromm refused and threatened to arrest them. He was then himself arrested by Olbricht, Stauffenberg and Mertz.

I asked who was now acting as Commander-in-Chief in place of Fromm. 'Stauffenberg, as you see,' Schwerin replied. In fact, as Fromm's Chief of Staff, Stauffenberg was exercising his master's command, still firmly convinced that Hitler was dead and determined to carry through the *coup d'état* by using Fromm's authority over the troops within the Reich. Beck, who had meanwhile taken Fromm's place, was equally determined – 'old Beck is totally determined to see the matter through to the end', Schwerin said.

Stauffenberg rushed into the room to the telephone table, seized the receiver out of the girl's hand and urged someone emphatically to carry out the Commander-in-Chief's orders, saying that these alone were authoritative. This convinced me that Stauffenberg had matters in hand and that Hitler must be dead. 'If only the occupation of the radio station had clicked,' Schwerin said. Continuous muted military music was to be heard from a loudspeaker in some other room. I took this to be psychological preparation for the state of military emergency.

Schwerin asked whether I had brought any fresh news from Madrid. I reminded him of my reports, of which he knew, saying that I had nothing to add but was ready to explain them in person to Beck. There could be no question of that at the moment, Schwerin said. The situation must first be clarified. But at this time – it was after 7 p.m. – none of those present was in a position to clarify the situation, nor did they know what had really happened in the Führer's headquarters. In fact Himmler was on his way to Berlin by air, Hitler having nominated him Commander-in-Chief of the Replacement Army in place of Fromm. Major Remer, commanding the Berlin Guard Battalion, was on his way to Goebbels to place himself and his troops at his disposal.

Schwerin was summoned to Beck and I followed him into the corridor. At this moment Beck came out of Fromm's room and stood in the open doorway looking past me down the passage. Before I realized what was happening Field Marshal von Witzleben came round the corner followed by his aide, Graf Lynar. Beck was clearly expecting them. Witzleben saluted Beck respectfully with his marshal's baton; Beck shook him by the hand and took him into Fromm's room. Lynar followed, whispering something ill-humouredly to me as he went by. I caught the words 'the whole thing has been bungled'.

I found it embarrassing having to sit around with nothing to do. I forgot that Hansen had still not arrived. One of the generals in the ante-room had seen through the open door into the passage that Witzleben had arrived and had been taken into Fromm's room. He told the others and they whispered together, taking umbrage that they should still be kept waiting. Finally one of them asked Stauffenberg whether he could go, saying that his time was too valuable to waste it here. Stauffenberg let him go and shortly afterwards the other generals took themselves off.

I still believed Hitler dead and could only have been convinced to the contrary by some word from Stauffenberg or Haeften. Both were far too busy to bother with my questions, but I could see and hear Stauffenberg issuing orders and instructions by telephone to set the Wehrmacht on the march against the Nazis. I never suspected that the Wehrmacht would do an about-turn as soon as it was clear that Hitler was not dead. Punctually at 8 p.m. I called my brother as agreed and told him to continue to wait for me at home with Klaus Bonhoeffer. He plied me with questions, wishing to know more, but a telephone girl asked me to hang up as the line was needed.

This really made me realise how useless I was being, and I wanted to go. One of the secretaries then arrived with a scratch evening meal for Stauffenberg and his staff – sandwiches and sausage salad. I must certainly be hungry too, she said, and put a plate down in front of me. I was thankful. Since breakfast I had waited tensely and eaten nothing, merely having drunk a cup of coffee in the office. After this I continued to sit there and wait; sometimes I was alone in the room, while the others had gone to eat either in their offices or in the mess below.

Once more Stauffenberg rushed into the room to the telephone table, saying to me, 'Counter-orders from Himmler.' He seized the receiver out of the girl's hand, dragged up a chair with the stump of his right arm, slumped into it and listened tensely. Then he spoke hurriedly and with great emphasis: 'Stauffenberg here – yes – yes – they are all C-in-C's orders – yes, that stands – all orders to be carried out at once – you must occupy all radio and signal stations forthwith – any resistance will be broken – you will probably get counter-orders from the Führer's headquarters – they are unauthorised – no – the Wehrmacht has assumed plenary powers – no one except the C-in-C Replacement Army is authorised to issue orders – do you understand? – Yes – the Reich is in danger – as always in time of supreme emergency the soldiers are now in full control – yes, Witzleben has been appointed Commander-in-Chief – it is only a formal nomination – occupy all signal stations – is that clear? – Heil.'

This conversation confirmed my impression that Stauffenberg would succeed in imposing the state of emergency and overthrowing the régime. If Himmler and the S.S. resisted, the Wehrmacht would break them – of that I was sure. Haeften was giving an elderly major instructions to organise a room in which to 'incarcerate the unreliable fellows for the night'. I was now quite certain that Stauffenberg would smash all resistance.

I now began to think of practical matters. Gerecke, as spokesman for Popitz, having had an interview with Witzleben two days before, I was vitally interested in knowing what the outcome had been. I therefore wished to go and see Popitz, and told Schwerin so. He agreed enthusiastically since none of the civil leaders had yet been told of the course of events. He promised to call me at home, should there be any important new development.

Stauffenberg was in Fromm's room with Beck and Witzleben. I accordingly told Haeften that I wanted to go and that, as a civilian, I was only in the way here. Should I get no call from Schwerin, I said, I would ring Stauffenberg's number sharp at eight o'clock next morning. 'By that time either we shall have done it or we shall all have been hanged,' Haeften said. I looked at him in perplexity. 'We're a long way from that yet,' he said with a reassuring chuckle. I felt better. He shook me warmly by the hand, saying: 'Auf Wiedersehen – till tomorrow.'

During my journey in the underground I thought over my experiences and impressions of the day. Among the differing and recurring figures I had seen, that of Stauffenberg stood out with increasing clarity. Through him and the deed which he had done I felt my confidence return and the hopes revive which had once decided me to stay in Germany and join the resistance.

I was brought sharply down to earth from my ruminations when the German Radio announced: 'The Führer speaks.' I listened to this speech by Adolf Hitler in the company of my brother, Klaus Bonhoeffer and our neighbour. I had assured them that Hitler was dead and we had celebrated our liberation in champagne. I felt a fool even in my own eyes. Our friends went home. I tested a revolver given me by Ludwig Gehre. I could not hope to escape yet again. We waited until the summer's day dawned. The Gestapo did not come.

That morning I went across to see Popitz and was told by his daughter Cornelia that her father had been arrested at 5 a.m. on orders from Himmler. It could not be long now before my turn came. While awaiting my fate I drove to my Lufthansa office and in the face of violent opposition from Klaus Bonhoeffer called Stauffenberg's number. A female voice said that he was 'away on duty'. Was he still alive and secretly being held prisoner by the Gestapo? Why would they shoot the leader of the military movement without trial? I must find out!

I called Adam von Trott. He came over to see me in the afternoon and told me what he had heard while on duty in the Foreign Ministry. The *coup* had been frustrated by officers loyal to Hitler; Stauffenberg, Haeften, Olbricht and Mertz von Quirnheim had been overpowered and handed over to Fromm who had had them shot by sentence of summary court-martial. Beck had shot himself. When Major Remer, commanding the Guard Battalion, arrived at the Bendlerstrasse with his men to suppress the revolt on Hitler's orders, he had only to complete what the officers had begun. The Wehrmacht throughout the Reich had voluntarily placed itself under the orders of its new Commander-in-Chief, the Reichsführer-S.S. Heinrich Himmler.

Still the Gestapo did not come. Perhaps they were using their well-tried method, I thought, and would go on shadowing me so that I could provide them with fresh clues. I hid myself in our neighbour's house. Klaus Bonhoeffer came and, together with my brother, pressed me to vanish to Madrid, saying that if the Gestapo caught and 'interrogated' me, I should endanger far too many people. Adam von Trott said the same. So on Monday, 24 July, I climbed on to the regular Lufthansa aeroplane for Madrid and escaped yet again.

16

On the Run

'A DAGGER'S the right way to murder a man like Hitler. If one of you had had the courage to do that, the *coup* would have succeeded. What you did was wrong and too late.' These were the words with which I was assailed five days after the failure of our rising against Hitler and my flight from Berlin to Madrid. They were spoken by a paternal friend of over eighty, Don Luis Ruiz de Valdivia whom I had come to know well during my previous visits to Spain. Now, with the dinner table cleared, I was sitting opposite Valdivia as a fugitive. We were drinking port.

I smoked and gazed into space. My friends in Berlin had urged me to escape so that I could tell the world 'what we had wished to do and why we had failed' – Adam von Trott's words during our last talk on the day before my flight from Berlin. But I could not do this to Valdivia. He had already grasped the background reasons why our rising against Hitler failed. This he made clear to me that evening in a few short strong words. I only understood much later. On this particular evening the imprint of my experiences in Berlin was still strong and I was convinced that Stauffenberg had tried to do the right thing and that this alone would justify him in the eyes of the German people and of history.

Old Valdivia sat at the table straight-backed. He kept stopping and pursing his lips as if to prevent himself saying what he thought. Old though he was, Valdivia was now angry, in a typically Spanish emotional fury. His eyes blazed at me through his thick spectacles and he repeated with angry emphasis: 'Wrong and too late. Have you understood that?'

I was completely confounded. Valdivia left me no time to think over his reproof. I saw the anger fade from his eyes and they filled with tears. Valdivia, bearer of one of the most famous names in Spain, was weeping, weeping over Germany's now inevitable fate. He loved Germany.

'Don Luis,' I said to Valdivia in an attempt to put forward my arguments, 'Stauffenberg had only his left hand and only three sound fingers on that. He could not have held a dagger nor even a revolver properly. In addition he had only one eye. He had to try with a bomb. It was the only possibility for him.' 'Stauffenberg was a cripple?' Valdivia asked. The question hurt me. I had only known Stauffenberg for six months, but it had never occurred to me or any of my political friends to refer to him as a cripple. It was obvious to anyone that he had been severely wounded; he had only one eye and half a left hand – but the man was unbroken. 'A cripple?' Valdivia had asked. I had to admit that it was so but I could not say it. I just nodded dumbly.

'And there was no other officer with sound eyes and hands? You allowed a cripple to try to attack with a bomb?! Shame on you!'

I wanted to explain to Valdivia how difficult it had been to approach Hitler at all, that we had not lacked men ready to sacrifice their lives to do away with Hitler. But Valdivia gave me no time to speak. 'I knew Colonel-General Beck very well,' he said, 'when I was Spanish Military Attaché during the First World War and you were still at school. The last time I spoke to him was in 1936 when our civil war broke out. I had a long talk with Beck. He was then your Chief of the General Staff, a man such as one would wish for Germany – intelligent, highly educated, a fine man. But I do not understand how he can have allowed Stauffenberg to make the attempt. That I shall never understand. I say to you once more: wrong and too late.'

I had nothing to say. Valdivia passed the cigarettes to me and said, 'Here – smoke!' I lit a cigarette and Valdivia recounted his experiences with the First World War generals, how in 1917 when America entered the war he had told Ludendorff that Germany could no longer win, how William II had dressed him down as a result and how finally, in September 1918, Hindenburg and Ludendorff had asked him to tell the Kaiser that the situation was hopeless since they lacked the moral courage to do it themselves. 'That was what the imperial army leaders were like,' Valdivia said. 'The Wehrmacht leaders are no better. The German Army is the best in the world, but your generals have no soul. They are good craftsmen, but not men – just as Hölderlin said.'

Valdivia knew that I was no longer safe in Madrid and that the

This photograph was taken by a friend of Otto John's in Berlin before he left Berlin for Madrid in March 1942. It was meant to be a memento for Dr. John's family in case he was caught by the Gestapo.

Otto John and his wife Lucie on his brother-in-law's trout farm in the Taunus near Wiesbaden after Otto's release from prison.

Spanish police would hand me over to the Gestapo. He reminded me of a counsellor at the German Embassy named Haeberlein who had been forcibly taken to Berlin the year before with his Spanish wife. I was able to reassure him that Juan Terrasa would get me to safety. He had gone to Lisbon on duty for the Spanish Foreign Ministry, but had called me at my hotel early that morning and had given me to understand that, with the help of his British friends, he would get me to Lisbon in the first instance, since it was safer there. I could rely on his word. Nevertheless, the wait for Juan's return played on my nerves. As a distraction I had spent the whole day before Valdivia's dinner wandering aimlessly through the city, sometimes by taxi, sometimes by underground and sometimes on foot. I was overwrought and felt that I was being watched. On one occasion my nerve nearly cracked. I was going up the staircase of an underground station when a shot rang out behind me; I felt sure it was aimed at me. My fears were soon set at rest, however, when a yelling swarm of children playing cowboys and indians rushed past me up the stairs with pistols crackling.

This shock was good for me. It showed me that I must lead a more cautious existence. For a few days, however, I could feel safe from the Gestapo in Madrid and so I had ventured to go to dinner with Valdivia. What I heard from him, however, shook my confidence in our ability to justify our rising in face of world publicity.

Such were my thoughts as I left Valdivia. I went down the brilliantly lit Granvia, threading my way through the light-hearted bustle of Spaniards who, as always, were turning the night into a long evening, in and outside the cafés and restaurants. Bullet scars on a church reminded one of the Spanish Civil War but, in their own way, the Spaniards had put their war behind them.

I wondered: my most important contact in Madrid over the last two years had been Willard Beaulac, the American Chargé d'Affaires, and his Military Attaché, Colonel William Hohenthal. To guard myself against any unpleasant surprises, should I simply go to the American Embassy and ask for asylum? I rejected the idea. What Juan Terrasa had said to me on the telephone implied no more and no less than an assurance that, with the help of his British friends, he would get me to safety in London. That was where I wished to go in order to tell the world over the B.B.C. 'what we had wished to do and why we had failed'.

My report on the failure of our rising against Hitler was already on its way to London and Washington. I had been urged to write it by Mgr Boyen-Maas, Juan Terrasa's friend to whom I have already referred. He was the first person I had called on my arrival in Madrid after failing to find Juan Terrasa at home, doing so from Juan's apartment to which I had a key. The jovial cleric hurried along to the apartment at once. Owing to the heat the shutters were tight shut and the room in semi-darkness. I described the events in Berlin. Boyen-Maas noticed that my voice frequently broke; he therefore interrupted our talk and took me into the kitchen to make coffee. Having calmed me down somewhat, he said that it was highly important that I should write a detailed report as soon as possible. He then left me to myself and returned in the evening to take my report to the British and American Embassies. Not until October 1966 did I learn that Boyen-Maas, loyal to de Gaulle, had done no such thing but had first taken the report to Truelle, de Gaulle's representative, who had forwarded it to Soustelle in Algiers. On his return from Lisbon next day Juan Terrasa independently sent copies of the report to London where it arrived after a three-day delay.

I thought that with this report I had taken the first, and promising, step towards explaining to the world at large 'what we had wished to do and why we had failed'. I did not realise that this was pure illusion until three months later when I had arrived in London and found myself clapped into prison there. When I drafted my report on the day after my flight from Berlin, I did not suspect that a secret agreement existed between the governments of the Western Powers to draw a veil over internal German resistance to Hitler and write off our rising as a sort of palace revolution. On 2 August 1944 in a speech to the Commons, for instance, Churchill merely said: 'The highest personalities in the German Reich are murdering one another or trying to.'

Since then a very different story has found its way into contemporary literature. In his book on 20 July Eberhard Zeller quotes a speech supposed to have been made by Churchill in 1946:

> An opposition movement existed in Germany, quantitatively growing ever weaker owing to casualties and a discouraging international policy, but it ranks among the noblest and the greatest of the movements ever produced in the political history of the nations. These men fought without assistance either from within

or without, driven solely by unease of conscience. . . . We look forward to the time when this heroic chapter of internal German history will receive due appreciation.

I found this so surprising that, in the autumn of 1949, I asked Churchill to specify when and where he had said this. On 19 November 1949 he replied: '. . . no record can be found of any such pronouncement by me. But I might quite well have used the words you quote, as they represent my feelings on this aspect of German affairs. . . .'

Naturally, five years after the failure of our revolt against Hitler, Churchill took a different view from that in his speech to the Commons of 2 August 1944. Among many German and foreign politicians, and not least among the German people themselves, opinion about the anti-Hitler resistance fluctuates. It will no doubt continue to do so, as does that of the German officer caste about the principle of questioning military discipline.

But after my flight to Madrid I was not thinking of this sort of problem as I waited for my friend Juan Terrasa to return from Lisbon.

17

Prison and Internment

JUAN TERRASA returned from Lisbon with a plan concerted with his British friends there. I was to be passed through to London by secret channels. The channels, in fact, led me to imprisonment in Lisbon – the first of many experiences to shake my confidence in the British Secret Service, in whose hands I had placed myself unconditionally by giving my agreement to this plan. I remained a further two days in the Palace Hotel, Madrid, where I had become a familiar visitor over the last two years. Germans and Spaniards I knew talked to me in the hotel bar about the attempt on Hitler's life and asked what had really happened in Berlin. I had little difficulty in throwing dust in the eyes of these inquisitive people. I merely said that I knew no more than was in the newspapers and that I had seen nothing whatsoever in Berlin of the '*putsch* against the Führer by an officer clique'. Some Spanish Air Force officers I knew were not so easily put off and refused to believe that, with my contacts in Berlin, I did not know more. Primarily, however, they were fascinated by the fact that the 'miraculous' secret weapon, the V1, was now being used against England, and they congratulated me on it. Many of them placed their hopes in it because they still wished Germany to win the war.

Such conversations in the hotel bar provided a good opportunity for putting the Spanish police and their Gestapo string-pullers off the scent of my proposed escape route. I said that I had to go to Paris next day, confirming this by showing my astonished questioners my O.K.W. 'Frontier Pass West' No. 89 274. This authorised me to travel where I wished in France, including restricted military zones. It was a vital document which Graf Schwerin-Schwanenfeld had provided for me when he was serving as a captain on the staff of the Quartermaster-General in Army Headquarters and was active in the anti-Hitler conspiracy. The next morning I took a hotel taxi to the Paris express. At the station a porter, who was in fact one of

Juan Terrasa's agents, took my bags, carried them straight through the express and out the other side. Juan was waiting in his car at a side entrance and took me to the private house of an Englishman working for the British Secret Service in Madrid. The Englishman said that that night I would be safely lodged with a reliable Spanish family, whence I would be taken by Embassy car to Gibraltar and thence flown to London.

The 'reliable Spanish family' turned out to be a lone widow, whose husband, an innocent republican, had been murdered by Spanish fascists. I was taken there by a charming young French girl who, for the next three weeks, formed the contact between me and the British Secret Service. She told the widow that I was a British pilot who had been shot down over Germany, had escaped from a prisoner-of-war camp and was now on his way back to England. The good woman told me that she had often hidden other R.A.F. pilots. She went to great trouble to spoil me with good food and drink, and the French girl brought me British and American newspapers. From these I learnt of the fake trials being held before the People's Court in Berlin and of the death sentences pronounced on my personal and political friends. This news made me impatient, but the good French girl could not say when I would be taken to Gibraltar. On every visit she had words of consolation.

In addition to the uncertainty I was tortured by the heat of the Spanish summer. Not a breath of air penetrated the little room in which barely four strides separated bed and table. For the most part I wore only pyjamas, the normal Spanish attire when at home in the heat. I was plagued by thoughts of my brother and our friends in the Gestapo prisons and in despair that I could not lift a finger to help them or mobilise any assistance from the Western Powers. For something to do, I began to draft a speech which I might make over the B.B.C. in London explaining to Germany and the world the motives and aims of the German resistance.

The young French girl looked after me with professional expertise. I was completely nonplussed, however, when she appeared one day and said that 'they' had decided that my strikingly blonde hair should be dyed black. She had brought the necessary tools, mixed her dye and went to work. I stripped to the waist and let her plunge my blonde hair into some black brew.

After these preparations for further flight I did not see her for a time but one day in the last week of August – the day of the liberation of Paris – she appeared late in the evening. A taxi was waiting before the door and in this she took me to a sumptuous Madrid apartment. We said goodbye and I never saw her again. My new host was a Frenchman who was astonishingly well informed about me. He personally provided me with food and drink and put me up in his spare room. I did not meet my unknown host again until eight years later in Paris when I was arranging contacts for the Federal Government with the French Secret Service, in which he was then occupying a senior position. On this occasion in Madrid, however, he handed me over early next morning to a member of the British Embassy, who drove me in his private car, not to Gibraltar, but into Asturia. He deposited me with a British agent in the port of Vigo and wished me a good journey to London, where I was eagerly awaited.

After dark a Basque took me to a little village on the Minho, the frontier between Spain and Portugal. That night I slept in the house of a smith who supplemented his income by the old-established trade of smuggling. He knew the location of the guard posts on the river and their patrol schedules and promised to bring me across the Minho without risk. Before dawn he had rowed me across the river. On the other side I found some friendly peasants waiting for me; they took me to their hut near the bank and gave me an enormous breakfast. Eventually a large limousine appeared with a Union Jack on the radiator and a C.D. plate behind. An elderly Portuguese gentleman got out and asked me for my 'proof of identity'. As agreed in Madrid, I showed him a matchbox in which was hidden a 100-peseta note. Without further ado I was driven to the British Embassy in Lisbon.

I was received by an assistant to the Naval Attaché. After I had proved my identity to him also by producing the matchbox with the 100-peseta note, he ordered tea and biscuits; we chatted for a while about his pre-war experiences in Germany, and he then told me that 'they' had decided to lodge me for the moment in a simple inn outside Lisbon. I asked when I should be flown to London, and he replied that the decision did not rest with him but with London and that I must wait for it. From a neighbouring room he summoned a Portuguese agent, Pedro Romero aged about thirty, whom he introduced as John Collinson. Pedro was a schoolteacher by profession and, as I found out later, a communist intellectual who had volunteered to work for the Western Powers in the fight against fascism. He drove me in a taxi out through the suburbs of Lisbon. To my astonishment he ordered the taxi to park on an open country road-side and asked me to get out. Seeing that he sent the taxi-driver away without paying, it was clear that the latter was in the game. I was experienced enough to ask no questions. Without a word I walked off down the dusty road beside Pedro, who had addressed me in Spanish. He was somewhat ragged and was carrying my small smart leather suitcase; I was wearing a light tropical suit. We were a highly conspicuous pair, I thought, a walking challenge to any gendarme. Fortunately none appeared.

After some half-hour's walk a small hamlet appeared behind a vine-covered hill and here in the inn, a Portuguese *pavoa*, we had reached the end of our journey. The fat slovenly innkeeper produced for us a meal rivalling the best Lisbon restaurants both in quality and quartity. Pedro departed assuring me that this was the safest lodging for me, if not the most comfortable – a bold prognostication which proved not entirely accurate. When I asked to be shown my room, the innkeeper led me to his barn where, in a corner between bales of straw and sacks of corn, he had rigged up a temporary sleeping-place for me with a tarpaulin. The thought of what my friends were undergoing in the Gestapo cells made it easy for me to accept this peculiar bedroom without demur.

About midday next day Pedro appeared, bringing English news-papers and some Spanish friends with him. They had all fought on the republican side in the Spanish Civil War and had fled to Mexico after Franco's victory. From there they had made their way back to Portugal with the help of a secret American organisation and were now awaiting an Allied victory over Hitler which they hoped would put an end to the Franco régime in Spain. Thereafter, with American assistance, they proposed to set up a 'democracy' in Spain. They were mostly ex-officers of the varied communist stamp thrown up by the Spanish Civil War. Pedro introduced me to them with the tale about my being a British pilot shot down over Germany and escaping to England. They admired me.

Being financed with American dollars, these Spaniards had a lot of money. They celebrated all Allied victories as if they were their own and a contribution to the expulsion of Franco. For them my appearance was a welcome excuse for a celebration. They ordered from the innkeeper a luxurious meal for that evening with excellent wines and had a large table set up in the barn. Naturally I could not evade this celebration in my honour. I had to tell stories of my operations over Germany and in particular of the heavy air-raids on Berlin. I knew quite enough to make the story plausible but I did not enjoy pretending to be a sort of Baron Münchhausen of the air war over Europe. I was glad when these eight or ten Spaniards went off to continue guzzling somewhere else. I did not imagine that they constituted any danger to me.

The next morning I was sitting in my barn between sacks of corn which I had arranged as a seat, reading an English book brought me by Pedro from the British Embassy. Suddenly, through an open trap-door in the barn, I heard voices in the garden. Tables and chairs were being moved about and people were speaking German. From the tone of voice I sensed that these were two Germans who still believed in the Führer's ultimate victory. As I listened tensely, one of them got up and his footsteps approached the doors leading into the barn. I was all ready to club him down as he entered, but he only opened the door a crack and then shut it behind him again this was not the place he was looking for.

After the two had gone the innkeeper, quite unconcerned, told me that they belonged to the German Gestapo and had taken a villa in the neighbourhood; they were less concerned with political matters than with an active smuggling trade in goods of all types to and from Germany. 'As an Englishman', however, the innkeeper said, I had no need to worry about the Gestapo! The following night Pedro took me in a taxi to his own house, a little place on the outskirts of Lisbon where he lived with his wife and children.

My movements were restricted to the inner courtyard of the little house. Day after day went by without Pedro bringing any firm reply from the Embassy to my invariable question – when should I at last be flown to London? I was told not to lose patience and that Pedro would look after me well, particularly as regards provision of reading material. It became horrifyingly clear to me that no one was really interested in getting me to England.

As some relief from the uncertainty of this waiting I began a systematic study of Portuguese literature and started to write the story of my experiences. Over the last three years I had assembled a pile of important notes and reports in Madrid and this seemed to me to be the time systematically to think over and analyse all that I had been through. As the prospect of speaking to the German people and the world over the British radio seemed to be becoming slimmer, it seemed to me all the more essential to get something published.

One evening, as I was sitting thinking over my notes, there suddenly came loud knocking on the house door. I heard Pedro open it and two men forced their way in. To me this was unmistakably the secret police in action. I hurriedly hid my notes among the books and crept under the bed-cover, thinking how ridiculous I must look. There was no possibility of escape. The two secret policemen soon came into my room and asked for an identity card. I said that I was an R.A.F. officer, had been shot down over Germany and was on my way to England. This must be checked, one of them said amicably in English. He asked me to follow him. A red car stood before the house and in this I was taken to a prison where I was housed, not in a regular cell but in a wooden construction between enormous thick walls. I was in the medieval fortress of Aljube. As I lay on the plank bed and ruminated upon my situation, I comforted myself with the thought that, at the worst, the Portuguese authorities might intern me but that they would not hand me over to the Germans. Having escaped Hitler's gallows, the idea of being interned in Portugal was not very terrifying.

Only after the war did I discover in complete detail what had led to my arrest and the fact that it had saved me from being taken to Berlin, dead or alive, by a special Gestapo detachment.

I was soon summoned for interrogation and stuck to the story that I was an R.A.F. officer who had been shot down over Germany and was escaping back to England. As agreed with the British Embassy for this eventuality, I demanded to see the British consul. My interrogator, a secret service officer named Captain Almeida who was in civilian clothes, gave his assistant a wink and drew a suitcase out from under the table. It was mine and it contained suits and underclothes which I had stored in Madrid in case I should be bombed out in Berlin. Without my asking for it, the suitcase had been forwarded to Lisbon and had been found when Pedro's house was searched. Captain Almeida was handed a dinner jacket from the suitcase, pointed to the label of my Wiesbaden tailor and asked with a sarcastic smile since when had it been normal Royal Air Force practice to carry such equipment for air-raids over Germany.

The game being up, I thought it best to put a good face on it and laughed. Captain Almeida had a sense of humour and he laughed too. He then asked me politely but very firmly to tell him the truth. I revealed my identity, but not the complete truth. I said that during the military *putsch* against Hitler I had happened to be in Madrid on duty for Lufthansa, as I had often been before. From a telephone call to Berlin I had learnt that my brother and several of our friends who had been involved in the *putsch* had been arrested. I had been friendly with Graf Stauffenberg and others who had been shot after the failure of the *putsch*. In Spain I had not been sure that I would not be handed over to the Gestapo and so had fled to Portugal. I asked that I be granted political asylum.

Captain Almeida was discretion itself. He did not even ask how I had reached Portugal or who had hidden me in Pedro's house. He asked me politely to write down what I had told him, if possible in French. Then he left me alone in his office, even placing cigarettes on the table. I drafted the letter he required and also wrote a letter to President Salazar since I knew that, as a Professor of Finance, he was a good friend of Professor Johannes Popitz and that each had a high opinion of the other. I therefore referred to my political friendship with Popitz, of whose arrest Salazar must meanwhile certainly have heard, and asked the President to sponsor my application for asylum.

Almeida read my report, paying particular attention to my letter to Salazar. Then he looked quizzically at me and asked: 'Then you're not a communist?' I had no difficulty in assuring him on that score. I said that it was pure chance that I had been lodged with a communist; I would very much like to know, however, how the Portuguese secret service had stumbled on my trail. 'Pure chance,' Almeida said with a grin and told me the story: the Spaniards who had given me that dinner in the barn had got above themselves, had drunk too much and had molested some girls in the village. As a result there had been a brawl with some Portuguese lads which had ended in a knifing match. Up to this point the Portuguese police had winked their eye and overlooked the fact that these Spanish Reds were in the country illegally, primarily because they were under American protection. The knifing match had led to an investigation, however, in the course of which they had come upon Pedro Romero's trail. The two policemen had in fact found me quite by chance when they came to arrest Pedro.

Almeida dismissed me, saying that he did not like having to send me back to prison but I would, of course, understand that this was how it must be; there were 'one or two formalities' to be completed before I could be granted asylum – and I was not to lose patience. Both what he said and the way he said it made me certain that I should soon be released from prison and should also be spared internment. I returned full of hope to my dark plank shack on the top storey of the old fortress on the edge of the city. As he locked me in, the warder expressed his personal regrets at the quality of accommodation provided, but this was the section for political prisoners, he said, actually intended for communists. Since I had been caught with communists, I would be treated as such pending proof to the contrary. When I asked for matches, he willingly gave me some, although it was against regulations, and left saying that he hoped I would soon be released.

My cell was not fit for human habitation – no water, no bucket, no light, a plank bed, a straw mattress full of fleas and bed bugs and a filthy blanket. For washing and shaving I was taken to a primitive washroom at uncertain times of the day. Twice a day I was given fish, soup and bread.

The semi-darkness of Aljube provided ideal conditions for reflection on my memories and experiences. Day after day went by without anything happening. The warder looked in at me occasionally and continued to be friendly but was in no position to say whether or when I would be released. Five days after my interrogation by Captain Almeida (to check the passage of time I made a mark on the wall each day with my spoon) another prison official appeared, obviously a senior executive. He began to address me as soon as he opened the door, asking where I had come from and where I was going. I was suspicious, told him only what I had already said to Captain Almeida and asked when I should be released. I should be under no illusion, the official said; most probably I would be taken to Berlin and that would cost me my head, as he signified with a dramatic gesture.

I have never discovered who this man was. Either he was a Gestapo agent or had been sent by the Gestapo to ensure that I was still there. As I learnt four days later in the British Embassy, the Gestapo were determined to kidnap me and take me to Berlin, having heard through their agents that I was in prison in Lisbon. The Portuguese government had refused a request from the Reich government for an extradition order and Kaltenbrunner had then ordered that I be brought to Berlin dead or alive. Himmler and Schellenberg, the head of his secret foreign intelligence service, were particularly interested in the contacts with the Western Powers which I had made for Stauffenberg. As Schellenberg told me after the war in the American prison hospital in Nuremberg, they already had certain secret ideas and were proposing to try to make contact with the Western Powers behind Hitler's back.

Dr Schröder, an S.D. commander, and Herr Cramer, an ex-Abwehr agent placed temporarily under his orders, were charged with my abduction to Berlin. For this purpose, as Cramer told me after the war, they had 100,000 escudos at their disposal. The plan was that a corrupt official in the Portuguese Ministry of the Interior should order my transfer from Aljube prison to another establishment and that, on the way there, I should be kidnapped and taken to Berlin.

Cramer told me the full story after the war – 'At first we cooked something up. Then we wondered how to get out of it. We didn't really wish to do it since we thought that the war would end before Christmas.' Accordingly they went to the Portuguese Ministry of the Interior, placed the 100,000 escudos on the table, revealed their secret mission and declared that they did not wish to carry it out. In addition they warned that another Gestapo group would assuredly try to take me to Berlin as soon as it was seen that they (Schröder and Cramer) had 'failed'.

Meanwhile the British Embassy had heard of the Gestapo's plans for me and had given the Portuguese Minister of the Interior to understand that this would not be viewed with indifference. The Minister of the Interior sent word to the Embassy that, in view of the intrigues against me, my long-term safety in Portugal could not be guaranteed and that, for security reasons, I should be taken to England. In the end I owed my life to Miss Rita Winsor. She was still working in the British Embassy in Lisbon and remembered me from my clandestine meetings with her and her master in the Secret Intelligence Service. She was the person who really took action to save me from the Gestapo.

The days and nights preceding my release from Aljube prison were, I think, the most agonising of my life. The manner in which the unknown official had prophesied my extradition to Berlin had been both definite and convincing. I knew that the Gestapo had already taken a corpse secretly by air from Lisbon to Berlin. In the years before the war I had always been prepared for arrest by the Gestapo and incarceration in a concentration camp because of my 'anti-State attitude'. Ever since I had joined the anti-Hitler conspiracy I had realised that I had been risking my neck. That I had not found terrifying. But now, having reached the westernmost point of Europe in my flight, I found it hard to accept the thought of being tried before the People's Court in Berlin.

One of Albert Schweitzer's sentences came into my head: 'Our existence is at the mercy of irrational happenings and can be destroyed by them at any moment.' I had always felt this to be incompatible with the Bible's promise that not one sparrow could fall to the ground without the will of God. Ever since my student days I had thought about this and had finally constructed an optimistic theory for myself, based on Albert Schweitzer: Prayer does not consist of asking and begging for what seems desirable at the moment. For me it implied trust in God summarised in the phrase: 'Thy will be done.'

This does not mean that I was upheld by a faith in deliverance by Christ. As a boy I had once seen in a large bible a picture of God portraying Him as an old man, and ever since then I had felt that my duty and responsibility lay towards the God of the Old Testament, not from a spirit of profound reverence but from fear of his punishments. Dietrich Bonhoeffer had once explained to me and his brother Klaus that this was an inadequate concept of the Christian faith; he said that it was not enough merely to accept the Christian code of morals and try to live accordingly; everyone must be prepared to die for his faith in salvation.

So on the morning of my last day in Aljube prison I prayed and suddenly something happened which I regarded as a miracle. The doors of my wooden shack were opened and beside the warder stood a man. He said that he had come to take me to the British Embassy. There I was given a British emergency passport and lodged for the night with a British couple. The next morning I boarded a regular British aircraft for Gibraltar accompanied by a friend of Rita Winsor named 'Alice', the American wife of the former British Ambassador, Henry Hopkinson. She was to vouch for me on arrival in Gibraltar. But, owing to gusty winds over the mountains, we could not land for safety reasons and back we flew to Lisbon. My reappearance in the British Embassy earned me the nickname of 'Boomerang'. The following night Rita Winsor took me to the flying-boat station at Tejo where there was a Clipper waiting. We took off during the night and so I reached England.

The flying-boat moored in Poole harbour and I was taken in charge by a secret service official. Everything I had in my pockets was placed in a large sealed envelope. I was given lunch and then had to wait. Finally I was handed over to another official who took me to London. We arrived at Waterloo late in the evening. My escort left me standing with my bags on the blacked-out platform. He was looking for a chauffeur who was to fetch us, but could not find him. Finally he organised an official car in which we drove through blacked-out London to the 'Patriotic School' on the outskirts of the city, where nationals of states allied to Britain and non-belligerent powers all over the world were trained for the fight against the Axis Powers.

The commandant, a colonel, asked in a friendly way who I was. I insisted that I could not tell him since the British Embassy in Lisbon had given me strict instructions to reveal my identity to no one who did not know of me already. The colonel sent me and my escort away. We drove back through London for a considerable distance, twisting and turning through the blacked-out streets. The car stopped before a blacked-out house and my escort led me hurriedly into a dimly lit entrance hall. Behind a shabby writing-desk against a wood-panelled wall sat a man in uniform, reading and smoking. My escort handed me, my bags and the sealed envelope over to the soldier with all speed and vanished.

When the soldier asked me who I was and I told him that I could not say, he was nonplussed. He pressed a button under the table and a sergeant-major came in, followed by an athletic-looking corporal. Again I refused to identify myself. The commandant's adjutant was then called, a slim elderly gentleman in major's uniform with a very well-groomed moustache. I gave him no information either. He opened the sealed envelope, examined the contents, started as he saw my German passport with its swastika, compared it with my British emergency passport and finally said to the sergeant-major: 'Take this gentleman to Captain ——'s room' – I did not catch the name.

I was led across a dark courtyard. Suddenly the night was lit by a dazzling white flash as if from a giant magnesium flare. There was an explosion larger than anything I had heard during an air-raid. 'That was a V2,' the sergeant-major said, 'not far off. We were lucky.' We crossed the courtyard still in darkness, went down a flight of stairs and through a cellar door into a guard-room full of soldiers. One of them opened a door. It led to a whitewashed, brilliantly lit corridor with a row of heavy brown wooden doors. A prison!

'Where am I?' I asked. 'Questions don't get answered here,' the sergeant-major answered drily and handed me over to a warder with the keys. The cell into which he locked me was tidy, scrupulously clean and the camp bed was comfortable. In one corner was an armchair.

Late the next morning an Intelligence Corps major appeared. He said that I had 'unfortunately' been put in prison owing to a misunderstanding. The telegram about me from Lisbon had gone astray. I should have been taken to an internment camp. He took me there; it merely entailed going up one flight of stairs. The internment camp consisted of the rooms of the house, the cellar of which was used as a prison. I was in Chelsea Oratory School, rechristened 'Camp 001', in which enemy nationals and doubtful foreigners, primarily Germans and Italians, were screened.

I was lodged in a communal room with about a dozen other Germans. Some of them still actually believed in the ultimate victory of the Führer. For the first fortnight no one took much notice of me. I was quite glad to be left in peace by the others but had little hope of emerging from this camp before the end of the war.

My first interrogation took place a fortnight after my arrival in the internment camp. I was faced by a young Intelligence Corps captain and proposed to tell him of the background to the 'generals' putsch' and the course of events; I suggested that I should write a detailed report including the dates he required concerning my political career, if I could be provided with paper and a typewriter. That would suit him very well, the captain said, but I must first answer one or two questions in person, in particular how long had I been a member of the Nazi Party.

'I thought you knew all about me,' I said ill-humouredly – he was clearly taking me for a Nazi renegade. The captain said that he knew who I was but that I must nevertheless answer his questions. My anger boiled and I let go, saying: 'I simply do not understand why I have been brought to England. I could have answered your questions just as well in Lisbon. I had hoped that, here in England, I should be able to do something against the Nazi régime, whereas I have simply been locked up.' He said acidly: 'You came to England to save your skin. What more do you want?' This was the end of the interview for me, I replied; I got up and went out. I was convinced that I now had no chance of being released from internment before the end of the war.

I was well provided for in this camp, particularly with newspapers and radio bulletins on the progress of the war which seemed to be nearing its end. The prospect made my stay in the camp more tolerable. Far less tolerable, however, was the fact that I had no possibility of correcting the erroneous picture of a so-called 'generals' *putsch*' created by the Allied war propaganda.

18

A False Name

I HAD already resigned myself to remaining in the London internment camp until the end of the war, when the turning-point came.
On a gloomy November day a corporal summoned me from the
dormitory and led me through the guard-room into an interrogation
room. A corpulent gentleman in mufti was awaiting me; he greeted
me in perfect German and seemed very friendly; his speech belied
his somewhat bohemian appearance. He congratulated me on my
escape from the Gestapo and asked me how I had done it. I told my
story and he threw in questions which made it clear that he knew all
about me – did I know Flight Captain Baur, for instance? As reporter
for the *Daily Express*, he said, he had flown all over Germany with
Baur and Hitler during an election campaign. He gave me his name
– Sefton Delmer.

The name was familiar from the B.B.C.'s German-language
broadcasts given by him, Lindley Frazer and Hugh Carleton Greene.
I had to tell him about the effects of the broadcasts in Germany. He
took note with apparent indifference when I said that they were a
source of information and encouragement to opponents of the régime both in Germany and territories occupied by the Wehrmacht. I
did not suspect that he was the head of the 'black' station known as
'Soldatensender Calais' [Forces Network Calais].

We discussed the progress of the war. Delmer did not share my
view that Germany had already lost the war when she invaded
Poland. He did think, however, that an Allied victory was now certain but said that it would still require much effort and sacrifice. This
was where I could help. He asked me whether I was ready to do this,
alternatively what ideas I had for employment in England.

I said that, ever since my escape from Berlin, I had had no peace
of mind. I needed a few days' complete rest somewhere in the country and then I would be ready to do all in my power to bring the
madness of the German war leadership to an end. I could certainly

do that, Delmer said; he was in charge of certain special radio operations and I could provide useful assistance; he did not wish to say more until I had really made up my mind to work on radio propaganda with no reservations. I thought that he was referring to the B.B.C.

I did not fully realise what Delmer's proposition meant until I had joined the staff of 'Soldatensender Calais'. Initially I merely saw my long-awaited chance to tell Germany and the world over the B.B.C. 'what we had wished to do and why we had failed'. I therefore placed myself unreservedly at Delmer's disposal. He promised that I would be released from the camp in a day or so and would then meet him again.

Weeks passed and nothing happened. I was eventually released in December 1944 when one or two incorrigibles in the camp were celebrating the Ardennes offensive. A corporal took me to the camp adjutant where I met a handsome captain. He had an identity card made out for me in the name of Oskar Jürgens and asked me to pack. I was then taken to a military car which was waiting at the door with a woman driver at the wheel.

It was cold and wet and I had no overcoat. The captain bought me a hat and coat which he paid for, saying that this was a matter of course. He treated me quite differently from the other British military with whom I had come in contact. He told me that he was taking me to a house in the country where I would be put in the picture by people I knew. I asked no more questions and hoped that I might find Rita Winsor in the house; she had told me two months before in Lisbon that she would shortly be going back to England and would like to meet me again.

We drove out of London on the Great North Road, stopping for tea in a small town, and in the evening arrived at the great gates of a park full of ancient tall trees. A blonde girl in uniform was at the gate and she directed our driver through the blackness of the park. Finally the car stopped before an iron grille behind which was a door leading into a guard-room. Through the half-open door I could see men in uniform and sub-machine-guns with their barrels glistening against the wall.

A policeman came up to the car, took a careful look at our guide to identify her, opened the grille and let us through. A short distance farther on the car stopped once more in front of a hermetically blacked-out building. The girl in uniform asked me to get out, the captain and driver to wait in the car. I felt rather uneasy. The girl led me through a dark entrance and then along a brilliantly lit corridor to a door above which was a red light.

She knocked on the door and someone said: 'Come in.' She opened the door and let me go into the room alone. Behind a large desk covered with telephones, dictaphones and papers sat Sefton Delmer. He apologised that I had had to wait so long in the internment camp for my release. He had been at Allied Headquarters in France, he said, and had been held up there. He had not wished to leave my welcome as a member of the staff to anyone else. I was now in the offices of the 'Soldatensender Calais' of which he was in charge.

I was dumbfounded. In Germany I had listened to this station almost every day. I knew from the Abwehr that it was located in England and that very many German soldiers listened to it.

Delmer said that he was very busy with the evening broadcast. I would now be taken to the house where he lived and he would discuss everything with me over breakfast next morning. He hoped that I would be happy with them and said that I would be getting to know people whom I would certainly like; I must, however, undertake to preserve the strictest secrecy about my identity and everything I might hear or see on the station. I signed a pledge of secrecy.

The blonde girl took charge of me once more at the door and guided the car through a village to a country house situated on rising ground on the outskirts. There I was handed over to Mrs Maddy, Delmer's housekeeper. She showed me to a room in a wooden hut in the garden and then took me into the living-room. A thin middle-aged man wearing an eyeglass was sitting in front of the fire. He introduced himself as Mr Halkett. Later he told me that he had previously been called von Fritsch and was a cousin of the von Fritsch who had been Commander-in-Chief of the Army and who, we had hoped, would take action against Hitler.

Being an anti-Nazi, Halkett had emigrated to England where he had assumed the name of his Scottish grandmother; he had become well known for his book on Hitler, *The Dear Monster*. We talked generalities, and I had the clear impression that he was summing me up. Meanwhile a bearded Catholic priest wearing metal-rimmed spectacles and in a short black habit came into the room. He shook me by the hand, saying: 'I am the Father.' I looked at him in puzzlement at this introduction, but he merely said: 'Yes, just like that.'

He was in charge of a secret transmitter, 'Christ the King', over which he broadcast to Germany and the world the crimes of Hitler and his followers.

Delmer's house was named 'The Rookery', in German 'Krähenhorst' which in underworld jargon means 'den of thieves'. It had been requisitioned by the British government as had many houses in the village of Aspley Guise together with the mansion and park of the pacifist Duke of Bedford. The actual studios of 'Soldatensender Calais', which was under police guard, was located near the village of Milton Bryant, a few miles away.

Sefton Delmer has told the story of its origins and the work of 'black' propaganda in his book *Black Boomerang*. It was, in fact, a sophisticated technique, thought up by Delmer himself, to subvert the Wehrmacht; it was known by his 'white' propaganda rivals as the 'Delmer circus'. On this I worked, though actually only on the fringe, from Christmas 1944 until April 1945 when it was in its final and most highly developed phase.

The members of Delmer's staff who lived in the 'Den of Thieves' gradually assembled during the evening. From their accents they were obviously German. Halkett, who was now also speaking German, introduced me and everyone eyed me curiously. One of them, in sloppy civilian clothes, was introduced as 'The Sergeant' and another, in uniform slacks and mufti coat, as 'The Corporal'. The names of the others were, I thought, genuine, but in fact they were only partially so. During dinner I acted very British, saying little and asking no questions.

On my first day there I had to sign certain official forms and was then issued by Delmer's secretary with a 'Certificate of Registration' and a pass entitling the 'enemy alien' Oskar Jürgens to work and travel in Britain without obligation to report to the police. 'You are now a temporary civil servant on His Majesty's Service, as we all are here,' Delmer said, and asked what I would like as a salary. This I left to him, particularly seeing that I had free board and lodging in his house. Initially I received just under £12 a week.

I had no qualms of national conscience in continuing the fight against Hitler in the service of the King of England. I had merely changed my habitat and in no way renounced the moral principles to which I had felt myself pledged in Germany. Moreover I had to assume that, having fled Germany, I would meanwhile have been deprived of German citizenship by the régime in accordance with current practice. This was of no consequence to me.

To introduce me into the work of the 'Soldatensender Calais' Delmer handed me over to his assistant Clifton Child, a philologist and historian whose duty it was to assemble, sift and evaluate the intelligence coming to 'black' propaganda from Allied agents and intelligence services in Germany and elsewhere. Child took me to the daily conferences, usually run by Delmer himself, at which the broadcast programme was discussed. Questions were put to me, but I found it difficult to answer naturally since this was the first time that I had been expected to express my opinion in public before a circle of men whom I did not know. Ever since 1933 I had only been able to talk politics in secret with trusted friends.

I was an object of suspicion. In the first place I refused to tell anyone who I was or whence I had come. Secondly, someone had suggested that I was an S.S. officer deserter, rather like S.S.-Obersturmführer Zech-Nenntwich, who later became notorious in the Federal Republic and was at this time working a secret short-wave transmitter under Delmer's supervision in a special section of 'Soldatensender Calais', trying to rouse the S.S. to revolt against Hitler. I was later told by Joe Lederer, the authoress, who was working in the 'Soldatensender' on a programme for German women, that this theory seemed credible because of my Teutonic appearance.

The station contained a number of German ex-officers and soldiers who, for moral reasons, were working to subvert the Wehrmacht, but I found it impossible to form close personal ties with them because I was not allowed to give my name. Most people, of course, have an urge to pass on information, find it difficult to keep secrets and like to talk. Accordingly over the years the staff of the station and their female helpers had formed themselves into little groups. As a late arrival I remained an outsider. Only once did I attempt to hint at my background when I told Freiherr von Guttenberg, one of the announcers (later State Secretary in the Federal Chancellery in Bonn), that I had been a friend of his uncle Karl Ludwig Guttenberg, the editor of the *Weisse Blätter* who had been executed. But this got me nowhere.

I was less upset by this than by the growing conviction that, although my advice was asked on specific questions and problems, I was not to be allowed an opportunity of acting on my own initiative and speaking over the 'Soldatensender'. I was disillusioned since

I had placed myself at Delmer's disposal purely with this in mind. My first step was to give Child the draft of an address which I might make in my own name explaining to the German people and the Wehrmacht the background and the reasons for the failure of our rising against Hitler. I was given to understand that the B.B.C. alone was responsible for such overt propaganda and that I could not speak over the B.B.C. since I was working for secret 'black' propaganda and this might be 'blown' if I were heard speaking, which was the first time that I had been told this. Early in the new year Delmer told me that an official British directive existed forbidding him to allow me to speak over the radio.

I made one more attempt, drafting a factual report, with comments, on the events of 20 July. This I showed in the first instance to one of the staff who, I knew, had once been a member of the German diplomatic service. I wished to have his opinion. I later found out that he was Wolfgang von Puttlitz. He merely said contemptuously that he would have nothing to do with it. I then passed the draft to Child. What happened to it I have never discovered nor did I inquire since I had meanwhile sensed, though not really grasped, the fact that no one wished to discuss the subject of 20 July.

I had little else to do other than answer the various specific questions put to me. I simply explored the station's files and waited for the end. The fate facing Germany was clear to me. Captain Molly Fitzpatrick, an Irish girl in charge of a group of German officers working in the station, said that Montgomery had been all set to reach Berlin before the Russians. The fanatical German resistance had, however, made it hard for him, and he would now risk no more casualties on the capture of Berlin; the Germans could expect no mercy from him.

As his forces advanced into Germany, Eisenhower issued an announcement ordering the civilian population to remain in their houses both for their own protection and to avoid hindering Allied movements. On Churchill's instructions Delmer had to issue through his station, now transmitting through Cologne and Frankfurt frequencies, orders purporting to come from the Gauleiters calling upon the civil population to take to the roads with all their goods and chattels, carts, bicycles and perambulators. The idea was to reduce the Wehrmacht's capacity for resistance. When I protested, Delmer reminded me, not without justification, that in 1940 during the invasion of France the Wehrmacht had made similar use of the radio to drive the civil population on to the roads and so impede the French defence. The Wehrmacht had shown the Allies what to do! After it had been made clear to me that I would not be allowed to use the 'Soldatensender Calais' to call for a rising in the name of the victims in the Resistance, I hoped until the bitter end that such of the internal German resistance as still existed would make some move. I hoped in vain. On the night of 14 April 1945, when Berlin was already surrounded by Soviet armies, the activities of 'Soldatensender Calais' ceased. Nothing remained for me but to watch Germany's death agony from a distance.

Meanwhile Delmer and a section of his staff had gone to London to prepare for their new duties, the reconstruction of the press and radio in the British occupation zone. He left me behind by myself in the 'Den of Thieves' under the care of his housekeeper, Mrs Maddy. My case must be decided by more senior authorities in London, he said, but he hoped that I would be able to join him in Hamburg.

Early in May Delmer returned once more to pack his things. On 5 May the signal for cessation of hostilities on the British front was given and broadcast over the radio. I was sitting by the set. Delmer, who had been inoculated, had gone to bed. As the cease-fire came over the air the door opened and Delmer looked in wearing British uniform and with a sporting rifle under his arm. Blinking sleepily he said: 'Herr *Geheimrat*,' – (Mr Privy Councillor), that was what he usually called me – 'I am now going out into the garden to shoot rabbits.' I countered that the cease-fire order had just been given. He yawned and went out into the garden.

To celebrate their victory over Hitler the heavens gave the British an exceptionally fine spring. In the Duke of Bedford's park were rare and exotic trees and shrubs, all in full bloom. Mrs Maddy pampered me, even lending me her bicycle so that I could get farther afield. Nevertheless, I felt constricted. The station security officer, whom I had never even met, sent word that I must remain where I was pending further instructions from London. In any case, with neither money nor passport, I could not start for home on my own. People in London seemed to have forgotten me.

Meanwhile from the British press reports and the B.B.C. I got a very vivid impression of what was going on in Germany, better probably than most Germans on the spot, for whom a general view was impossible with the breakdown of all communications and news media. I knew nothing about my friends or relatives and could not even write home like any ordinary prisoner of war. My feelings ranged from exultation at the final end of the brutal slaughter to depression at the thought of the innocent having to suffer with the guilty.

Early in July Commander Donald McLachlan called at the 'Den of Thieves' and said that I was to go to London for an interview. I had known him as Delmer's friend and deputy in the 'Soldatensender Calais' but had then lost touch with him since he had mostly been in France as liaison officer to Eisenhower. He confirmed that I had 'nearly' been forgotten and told me that a 'German–Austrian division' of the Foreign Office was to be set up under his direction in Bush House, which also housed the German Section of the B.B.C.; the task of this Division was to establish the theory upon which 're-education' of the population in the British-occupied zones of Germany and Austria would be based and direct the necessary measures on the Continent. I was to work in this Division until higher authority had decided whether I could join Delmer in Hamburg.

I agreed at once. Frank Lynder, whom I had known in Delmer's house as 'The Sergeant', arranged a lodging for me in London. McLachlan installed me in a back room on the sixth floor of Bush House with a desk, chair and well-stocked bookshelf. He left it to me and my imagination to propose to him what should be published in the British zone of Germany.

This was the time of the election campaign in Britain and it provided me with the material for a brochure entitled 'The Possibilities and Limitations of Democracy'. Churchill had been toppled from the pinnacle of fame because, demagogically, he had over-reached himself during the campaign when warning the British not to elect Labour. He argued that the socialists could not rule without a political police and that they would set up a Gestapo régime. His electoral defeat was the perfect example of democracy in action. Despite his overwhelming power and his reputation he had to bow to the will of the British people.

But my brochure on the subject was never printed. Donald McLachlan, who had said to me at 10 a.m. on polling day: 'Our country's going red,' left the office, and his place was taken by a much-bemedalled officer who knew neither me nor anything about me. On instructions from above he allowed me to continue in office. I planned a 'German Weekly for Culture and Politics'. Rudolf Pechel heard of this and suggested that we work together to revive his *Deutsche Rundschau*. I was enthusiastic since I had a high opinion of Pechel. Military government, however, drew a red pencil through our plan. Someone did not like the fact that Pechel was so loud in his support of the 20 July martyrs. At this period the Allied Military Governments seemed determined to draw a veil over internal German resistance to Hitler. I accordingly occupied myself with the translation of English books on politics and history.

One day I was asked by the Ministry of Information to attend a private press showing of the film of the liberation of Belsen concentration camp. They wished to have my opinion on it afterwards. I could not utter a word. I did not even know the name Belsen but I knew enough about Buchenwald and other camps. Nevertheless, the film was a severe shock to me. For the first time it showed me with stark clarity what had gone on in the concentration camps. I now found it painful, as a German, to live among the British. I wanted to go home.

My German passport had been removed when I was interned and so I now had to prove my identity. Weeks went by before I could obtain a birth certificate from my home town of Marburg in the American zone and almost a further six months before I was provided with a Nansen passport as a political refugee. Then at last I was myself once more. I wished to go to Wiesbaden where my parents lived but could not obtain an entry permit from the American Military Government since at this time the Americans were not, on principle, allowing entry to German civilians from abroad. A British official suggested to me that I should allow myself to be repatriated as a prisoner of war – but I refused. Why should I acknowledge the Wehrmacht even in retrospect?

19

Between Victors and Vanquished

ONE of the oddities of the military bureaucracy was the fact that it lay within the province of a sergeant in the American Military Permit Office in London to refuse me entry to the American occupation zone of Germany. Apparently I had failed to give an adequate explanation for my frequent journeys abroad on behalf of Lufthansa before and during the war. Fortunately, the man responsible for liquidating the remnants of the 'black' propaganda organisation in London was Leonard Ingrams, a banker doing his war service with the Foreign Office, and he came resolutely to my assistance. He granted me the status of a British war reporter, fitted me out with a uniform without badges of rank, as was obligatory at the time for all Allied journalists in Germany, and dispatched me by air to Bad Homburg accompanied by a certain Major John Gwynne, with an introduction to the American General Robert MacClure who was in charge of psychological warfare in the American Army.

General MacClure, his aide said, could not remember receiving any information or recommendation about me from the British. My escort Gwynne, however, had distinguished himself as a parachutist with the Partisans in the Balkans and he acted with energy. He forced his way in to MacClure and insisted on a search for the letter announcing our arrival from London. When it was eventually found the general gave us a jeep, K-rations and 'Travel Orders' for a three-week journey through the American zone.

So at last, early in 1946 and disguised in British uniform, I reached my parents' house in Wiesbaden. I saw some of the few survivors among my personal and political friends; I also saw several others who later raised a hue and cry against me on the grounds that I had become a British officer. What I saw and heard during this first post-war stay in Germany considerably reduced my confidence in the ability of military government to reconstruct Germany as a state based on Christianity, social order and the rule of law such as those with my faith in the ideals of Western democracy had hoped for. I came to realise that any government run by generals must, by its very nature, be constituted on military lines. Eisenhower was no exception.

When the trial of the major war criminals was held at Nuremberg Major Gwynne obtained tickets for us in the gallery reserved for distinguished Allied visitors. The scene below made far less impression on me than I had expected. There were the men for whose downfall I had so often longed. But what good could this trial do to the peoples and individuals who had been tormented, murdered and otherwise ruined by these war criminals? John Gwynne thought that it would at least do something towards establishing the rule of law and so contribute to peace in the world.

In fact these efforts were vain. This does not mean, however, that the major and minor war criminals should not have been tried, nor does it imply agreement with the view, born of neo-German patriotism and often heard today, that the criminals should have been tried by German judges and under German law. The German people had made no contribution to its own liberation – its unconditional surrender is irrelevant – and it had therefore forfeited any right to sit in judgement on the leaders it had once acclaimed so enthusiastically. Remilitarisation, however, has now reduced the sentences of the Allied military courts to an absurdity and therefore their legality has not impressed itself on the minds of the German people. In many German minds they still rankle as an injustice.

At about that time, Professor Geiler, the Minister-President of Hesse, suggested that I take office in the Hessian government. Everyone else with whom I discussed the matter, including von Schlabrendorff and von Preuschen, a lawyer friend from our junior barrister days in Wiesbaden, urged me to remain in London and work for a sensible reconstruction policy on the lines advocated by those who, by their resistance to the Nazi régime, had at least earned the right to be heard by the Allied Military Governments. This seemed to me a worthwhile task.

I returned to London in the realisation that, as in Goethe's time, Germany was now no more than a geographical expression and would remain so for a long time. Leonard Ingrams invited me to tell him in detail, over a glass of whisky, of my experiences and impressions in Germany. He proposed that I write a report for the

British government but said that it would be unlikely to improve matters since the government had trouble enough in dealing with their own problems in the British zone which was costing the British taxpayer a lot of money. Nevertheless, I wrote a full report. Leonard Ingrams thought it 'highly significant' and passed it 'on up'. What happened to it I have never discovered. Undoubtedly I did not make myself popular with this report. It included severe criticism of the dismantling policy in the British-occupied Ruhr and a statement to the effect that by this policy a workers' government in Britain would be depriving German workers of their livelihood.

The Labour government had set up a 'Control Office for Germany and Austria', known as COGA. In addition to political direction of the British military régimes in Germany and Austria it was responsible for the care of German prisoners of war in Britain. It provided for the prisoners books, periodicals and newspapers, and lectures to demonstrate to them the type of régime for which they had fought; even more important, it gave them ideological instruction on the nature and functioning of British democracy with the object of providing ideas for democratic reconstruction in Germany. Under the direction of Colonel Henry Faulk, a highly qualified philologist, German émigrés, mostly of the academic variety, and German-speaking Englishmen familiar with the German way of life were sent down to the camps to give lectures.

A gigantic staff was responsible for checking the camps at regular intervals to ensure that the prisoners of war were well cared for, to find out their attitude and their complaints in open discussion and to report on their findings to COGA. In addition to these camp inspectors, from the spring of 1946 special teams were employed to screen the camp inmates politically; each individual prisoner was examined and classified according to his attitude into categories A, B and C – anti-Nazi, politically indifferent or Nazi. An active anti-Nazi was included in Category A and an incorrigible Nazi in Category C.

In Wilton Park near Beaconsfield, an hour's drive north-west of London, the British set up a sort of political college for prisoners. This 'Training Centre', as General Strong said at the opening ceremony, was 'a novel attempt to build a bridge between victors and vanquished'. It was directed by Dr Heinz Koeppler, an Oxford lecturer of German origin, and the professorial body consisted of fifteen British academics. Well-known politicians and authors came down from London to lecture. Instruction was on the lines of the British 'residential colleges', and numbers were limited. Only about one per cent of the 400,000 prisoners in Britain could be selected. The criterion was their potential aptitude for democratic reconstruction in Germany.

All in all the treatment of German prisoners in Britain amounted to a generous attempt by the British government, at considerable cost in personnel and money, to help set German democracy on its feet. When I was asked, therefore, I had no hesitation in working for this end. Initially I evaluated the inspectors' reports forwarded to Bush House from the relevant division of COGA. I frequently drove to this or that camp to inspect or categorise the inmates; my primary duty, however, was lecturing. Almost two years after the failure of our rising against Hitler I spoke on the subject for the first time to German ex-soldiers in Wilton Park.

After this I was invited by Hugh Carleton Greene to participate in broadcasts on the 20 July *coup* by the German section of the B.B.C., also in a programme in memory of Dietrich Bonhoeffer and in various other broadcasts. In the legal department of COGA I met Ernst Cohn who had been my common law tutor at Frankfurt University. At the time he had been the youngest and best-qualified freelance lecturer in Germany and had therefore been a special target for the Nazi students; he had finally emigrated to London when he found that his final lectures in Breslau could only take place under police protection.

As a political refugee I had now been given a Nansen passport and could therefore once more use my own name. As a result my activities in the resistance became public knowledge and I realised how inhibited I had previously been in my dealings with the British and even more with German émigrés. I had always been afraid of being taken for a Nazi turncoat. Now once more I found it easy to make friends among the numerous people, both British and German, with whom I came in contact in COGA, in the B.B.C. or socially. I began to feel happy in London.

I had no hesitation, therefore, in refusing proposals to work with British Military Government in Germany, particularly since I felt that I had neither the will nor the ability to identify myself with military bureaucracy. Early in 1946 I was visited by a Major Lancashire who brought me greetings from Jakob Kaiser in Berlin and a request that I return to Berlin to assist in reconstruction. It was clear to me that under the increasingly severe pressure of the Soviet occupation one would be unable to pursue any independent policy in Berlin in the long run and I therefore refused. Shortly after I was invited to lunch in a Soho restaurant by a Colonel Smith from the British Military Government in Hamburg. He had been commissioned to offer me a key position in Hamburg reorganising the press and radio. I was not even tempted.

I gradually began to feel at home in London, particularly after meeting Lucie Manén, the singer, who was later to become my wife. She had come over to the Glyndebourne Opera with Fritz Busch in 1934 and, after singing engagements in Switzerland, Austria and Czechoslovakia, had settled in London as she was Jewish. At our very first meeting we found that she had known many of my friends in Berlin in her young days. She had long been living with her daughter Gisela in a flat in Hampstead which she had turned into a typical example of the old Berlin West End culture. She would often invite me to come in and talk about the past now buried in the ruins of Berlin.

In September 1946 I was commissioned to organise the first repatriation convoy in an assembly camp between Bristol and Weston-super-Mare. I met there a young prisoner who had heard my lectures in Wilton Park. Ever since he had been mulling over the question: 'How *could* our parents have voted for a man like Hitler?' The Germans who had elected Hitler, he said, should be politically disfranchised and never be allowed to vote again – not even his father. I am convinced that many young prisoners had had their eyes opened by the 'novel attempt to build a bridge between victors and vanquished'. I was happy to think that I had made some small contribution.

My readiness to help in dealing with German prisoners of war in England, instead of thinking of my own career, later became the basis of much slander against me and earned me the enmity of many who, together with the first Federal Chancellor Dr Adenauer, aimed to re-create the old 'establishment'. The start of this was a faulty decision by me – to assume responsibility for welfare in Camp No 11 at Bridgend in South Wales; here were held several hundred former German field marshals, generals, admirals and senior S.S. officers. When this was proposed to me, I postponed a plan which I had already discussed with Professor Cohn whereby I might resume my legal activities in his chambers and improve my knowledge of English law by attending lectures at the London School of Economics. For me the deciding factor was the thought that, working in

Bridgend Camp, I would have a unique opportunity to clarify the burning question why our senior military commanders had served Hitler to the bitter end, although by the time of the great murders of 30 June 1934 at the latest they must have realised that he was a criminal. Numerous applications by the inmates had been necessary before welfare in Bridgend Camp had been handed over to COGA by the War Office. Previously it had been kept strictly isolated from the outside world. In the camp itself high-ranking military personalities enjoyed all the privileges accorded them by international usage – they had batmen, for instance, who were housed in a separate section of the camp. Field Marshal Montgomery had allowed Field Marshal von Rundstedt's son, who was a reserve lieutenant, to accompany his father into imprisonment; the only one in camp still permitted to wear his badges of rank was S.S.-Obergruppenführer Karl Wolff ('little Karl'), Himmler's ex-Chief of Staff; this concession had been promised him by Field Marshal Alexander as a reward for his early surrender with the German forces in Italy. The badges of rank and decorations of the others were deposited in cardboard boxes in camp headquarters.

The German camp leader was Georg von Seidel, ex-Quartermaster-General of the Luftwaffe, whom I knew; I shared mutual friends with many others. I also knew from my friends in the Resistance that many of them had been opponents of the régime but had not been recognised as such after the 20 July *coup*. Soon after my first visit to the camp, therefore, quite a number of the ex-generals were willing to talk openly with me; they helped me to gain the confidence of the more suspicious. Rundstedt opened up completely after I had arranged that his son should be repatriated. He was a librarian by profession and, when in Freiburg, had belonged to a students' association which, to demonstrate its opposition to the beat-up gangs, had adopted an umbrella as its symbol. Since he had nothing to do with Nazi ideology, and in addition was suffering from a throat cancer, I was able to arrange for his release to Germany.

Starting in October 1946 I spent a total of forty-six days in Bridgend Camp, interspersed with absences of varying duration. At the outset I made it clear that my personal reason for coming was to assemble material for a book on militarism and National Socialism in the interests of historical clarification. On my suggestion, but also on their own initiative, quite a number of our former army commanders gave me full and detailed answers to my questions. I held seminar sessions with a group of seven generals to examine in free discussion the causes of, and responsibility for, Germany's defeat. If I thought fit, I could take one or other of the camp inmates for a walk outside the wire. This happened very frequently, when I wished to discuss more personal questions, which was best done outside the camp atmosphere. With many of them, therefore – on one occasion with Field Marshal von Manstein – I would sit smoking and chatting in the dunes bordering the Bristol Channel. Manstein complained that in his book *Revolt against Hitler* Fabian von Schlabrendorff had spread false tales about him. He had never been approached, he said, to take action against Hitler. I gave him the opportunity to send an amendment via me to Schlabrendorff. Neither would budge from their point of view.

During these discussions in the sand dunes, much became clear to me that many of those to whom I was then talking will now no longer accept. At the time the field marshals and generals were grateful to me for trying to obtain for them the 'equal treatment with the rank and file' for which they had argued with the British War Office for so long. The majority quickly forgot this once released. Only a few remained grateful to me for bothering with their personal and family affairs.

As soon as I was familiar with internal conditions in the camp I began the 'screening', in other words political examination and classification with a view to repatriation. All admirals were excluded, decision in their case being reserved to the British Admiralty alone; also excluded were the 'automatic arrest cases', the S.S. leaders, for instance, and others, such as the field marshals, who were on the Allied war criminals list.

My duty during 'screening' was to discover the genuine opponents of Nazism with a view to their early repatriation. I employed the same technique as I had in the other camps. It was always easy to spot two or three anti-Nazis with certainty. These I took into my confidence and asked them to give me the names of those who, while in prison, had shown themselves to be confirmed opponents of the régime. Having lived at close quarters with each other in the camp, the generals' judgement on this issue was quite as reliable as that of the rank and file. Having thus, and by additional questioning, established the Category A priority repatriation list, I categorised the remainder by questioning them, in all cases of doubt writing them down as politically indifferent.

Hohenburg, near Igls in the Tyrol, where Otto John and his wife now live.

Otto John in his study in the Hohenburg—a portrait taken in 1965.

Based on their own answers I then placed in Category C those who still seemed to be in the grip of the Nazi spirit. This list I checked with an appreciation given me confidentially by the proven anti-Nazis and in not one single instance did it turn out that I had been mistaken. Finally a man presented himself for political interview who had previously refused to do so. He had been talked round by General von Seidel. He was one of the youngest, a parachute general, and he still seemed to me to be under the influence of the Nazi ideology, as all the seven generals whom I had asked about him confirmed. His name was Heinz Trettner. He later became Inspector-General of the Bundeswehr [Federal Armed Forces].

In addition to those in Bridgend Camp I had special cases in various other camps, primarily in hospitals, where I was entitled to approve premature repatriation on health grounds. I also had to clear up the more obscure cases in an officers' camp at Featherstone Park, Northumberland. There the Commandant, Colonel Vickers, and his Intelligence Officer, Captain Herbert Sulzbach, who had been a German officer in the First World War and is the author of the book *Zwei lebende Mauern*,* had instituted a remarkable version of the 'attempt to build a bridge between victors and vanquished'; they had removed the barbed wire and allowed the prisoners freedom of movement on parole within a considerable area.

In Featherstone Park I met Gunter d'Alquen, the ex-S.S.-Sturmbannführer, editor and chief leader-writer of the S.S. newspaper *Schwarze Korps*. I had no need to categorise him since he was an 'automatic arrest' case and was due to be removed to a camp in Scotland reserved for men of his category. He asked for an interview and I took him out for a walk. He tried to explain to me that our revolt against Hitler would have succeeded if we had first made common cause with the opposition in the S.S. It was a friendly talk. Afterwards he spread the story that he had been badly treated by me and that I had sent him into internment.

Until autumn 1947 I was travelling almost continuously between London and various prisoner-of-war camps. I learnt to know both the country and the people, but my bridge-building operation earned me only the most meagre livelihood. It seemed to me time, therefore, to think of my own future and return to my legal profession.

* To be published in English by Leo Cooper under the title 'Two Living Walls'.

20

Back Home

IT had never been my intention to spend the rest of my life in England. I had not emigrated but had merely landed up in London as a political refugee. Meanwhile, however, I had come to like the British way of life and I had it in mind to spend some time in London and there build myself up a practice as an international lawyer. To join me I wished to recruit my colleagues in the Western capitals with whom I had worked as legal adviser to Lufthansa, but this could not be done from Germany owing to censorship and other Military Government restrictions.

Ernst Cohn, my Frankfurt University lecturer, was enthusiastic at the prospect of our work together. He paved the way for me, introducing me to Gerrard Holland, a solicitor originating from Berlin, who taught me the rudiments of his profession. I was taken on as 'Adviser on German and International Law'. In this way I could have made a more or less profitable living – but I was still tormented by the question: Why had it all happened thus and why had no one been able to stop it?

I had obtained no real answer to this problem from our senior military commanders although, in their deep humiliation, they had talked to me in Bridgend like a father confessor. The fact remained that none of the field marshals would acknowledge any responsibility. Brauchitsch, Rundstedt and Manstein, once the most eminent among them, had all tried to prove to me – as Halder had tried in his monograph *Hitler as Warlord* – that the war would have been won, had Hitler left the military leadership to them.

I had noted down their self-justifying arguments and in some cases I had used them in articles and lectures. This came to the notice of General Telford Taylor, a lawyer in uniform who headed the American Military Courts in Nuremberg, and early in January 1948 he invited me to Nuremberg for an exchange of ideas on German militarism. I was fascinated by the records of the American

Military Courts and I remained there almost six months with breaks at Easter and Whitsun. This gave me the opportunity to question a further series of generals. It was borne in on me that, to justify themselves, our former senior commanders were building up new false tales.

As an example: the demand for unconditional surrender was not the decisive reason for the continuation of the fighting until the bitter end. That this was so was confirmed to me in Nuremberg by General von Sodenstern who had been Chief of Staff to Field Marshal von Witzleben. I asked Sodenstern to write a note on the subject for my files and he willingly agreed. When I met him a few days later he was embarrassed and eventually admitted that he could not give me the note. He had discussed the problem once more with other generals and in fact the Wehrmacht had been forced to continue the fight in the West because of the demand for unconditional surrender and in the East to stem the advance of bolshevism!

The German generals, however, were not the only ones to tamper with history. In the October 1947 number of that highly respectable British periodical *International Affairs* appeared an article to the effect that, as legal adviser to Lufthansa, I had been one of those leading industrialists – like Dr Schacht and Ewald Loeser the director of Krupps – who had allied themselves with the Nazis in 1933 and only turned against them when the German collapse was obviously imminent. I owed this ridiculous accusation to a summons to appear as a witness in the Krupp trial. Dr Loeser had cited his Resistance activities as part of his case for the defence, but with the best will in the world I could not vouch for him as a Resistance fighter. I knew, of course, that Goerdeler had considered him as a possible Finance Minister but he himself had done nothing whatsoever towards the overthrow of the régime.

Senior Wehrmacht commanders found it quite compatible with their consciences, some even thought it their patriotic duty, to make false statements to the Allied Military Courts, even under oath. While in prison in Nuremberg they had concerted their defence tactics and agreed that they would categorically deny all knowledge of the genocide of Jews, Poles and Russians. Rudolf Freiherr von Gersdorff, however, one of the youngest of the senior officers, admitted the truth – that they had all known of these atrocities. He had himself sent reports on the subject to Army Headquarters, but in Nuremberg there was a concerted loss of memory on the subject.

The others simply ignored the fact that one man had had the courage to confess to the truth. Von Gersdorff told me all this in confidence. He was outlawed, and later when he applied for employment in the Federal Republic's rearmament programme was refused on various pretexts.

While I was pursuing my inquiries in Nuremberg the trial of Ernst von Weizsäcker, former State Secretary in the Foreign Ministry, and other senior officials was taking place. Weizsäcker's defence counsel and another diplomat who was assisting in the defence asked me to obtain a sworn statement from Lord Vansittart. It was to prove that Weizsäcker had done all in his power to save the peace in that in 1939, through Erich Kordt, then a foreign service officer [Legationsrat] in Ribbentrop's office, he had authorised Erich's brother Theo, the German Chargé d'Affaires in London, to conduct secret negotiations with Vansittart.

The story was new to me. However, when next in London, I went to see Vansittart. The Kordt brothers, he said, had tried to persuade him to dissuade the British government from concluding a mutual assistance pact with Poland 'in order not to provoke Hitler to war against Poland'. He had already heard, Vansittart commented sarcastically, that according to the latest story in Nuremberg responsibility for the war was being laid at the door of the British government because of their pact with Poland. Vansittart thus demolished the idea that Weizsäcker's defence might benefit from a sworn statement about the activities of the Kordt brothers. This earned me the enmity of Weizsäcker and his friends and they later protested against my employment under Dr Adenauer. I had, however, merely intervened with Vansittart at their request, though admittedly without success.

In my spare time in London I began to work on my material about the resistance and wrote a number of articles. I kept up a regular correspondence with the Oxford historian John (now Sir John) Wheeler-Bennett whom I knew through his book on Hindenburg, *The Wooden Titan*. He had lived for some time in Germany and knew Kurt von Schleicher well. Through this valuable book he had made his name as one of the best-qualified experts on German contemporary history, to a large extent due to the fact that Dr Brüning, the former Chancellor, had kept him fully informed on German policy.

I placed all my material at Wheeler-Bennett's disposal and over the course of two years discussed with him all the problems and questions arising therefrom. The outcome of this detailed work was his book, published in 1953, *The Nemesis of Power*, in my view the most authoritative book available on the nature and working of the German military hierarchy.

In the autumn of 1948 Brigadier Shapcott, head of the British Army's Judge Advocate Department, proposed to me that I become adviser on German law and interpreter for the trial of Field Marshals von Rundstedt, von Brauchitsch and von Manstein. I agreed since this did not entail abandonment of my private legal activities.

I had neither patriotic nor moral scruples in taking on this task. I felt no obligation towards the German generals, but I did feel myself bound by a Christian ethic transcending nationality and it was entirely in accord with this that men who had wished to conquer the world by genocide, and had brought about frightful calamity, should be brought to trial and sentenced. I was well qualified for the post through my legal training, knowledge of languages and researches into German militarism.

Preparations for the trial dragged on. Brauchitsch died, Rundstedt became very ill and it seemed likely that only Manstein would be in the dock. To familiarise myself with the case I studied Manstein's wartime operations in all the books, memoranda and documents I could find in libraries and the War Office Historical Section. I wrote a memorandum on the subject entitled 'Field Marshal von Manstein's Campaigns in the East'.

In 1948, at Winston Churchill's instigation, the United Europe movement had started. I discussed the subject with Duncan Sandys, Churchill's son-in-law, who at this time was acting as a sort of promoter for the efforts to bring Europe together. He thought, however, that as a German I could only work within the framework of some German organisation. I realised how strong the national prejudices against a united Europe still were.

New Year's Day 1949 I spent in Hamburg occupied in translating the cases for the prosecution against ex-Field Marshals von Rundstedt and von Manstein and ex-Colonel-General Strauss. I drove to the British Military Hospital, where the accused were lodged, with Colonel Luff, head of the War Crimes Unit in Hamburg. Responsible British government quarters had been unenthusiastic about fulfilling their international obligations and proceeding with the trial. Rundstedt and Manstein – I did not know Strauss – were astounded to see me again as the mouthpiece of the prosecution. They did not know whether to take it as a good or bad sign.

In the presence of their defence counsels I read the indictments to the accused, first in English, then in German. With that I had done my duty. Defence counsel, however, now wished to discuss with me various questions concerning the defence; they asked me to try to arrange British defence counsel for the accused. As we were talking Rundstedt lost his temper. He banged his cane on the arm of a chair and said: 'This trial and everything else here is only possible because of the occupying authority which lays down the law here. Such a thing would not happen in England.' Colonel Luff had not understood. I had no wish to make a scene but nevertheless felt compelled to ask Rundstedt what would have happened if a Frenchman had insulted the Wehrmacht like this when he, Rundstedt, was in command in France. Rundstedt mumbled something unintelligible. I thereupon declared the interview at an end and I never saw Rundstedt again. He was in fact spared trial owing to illness and died shortly afterwards, as did Strauss.

Manstein's trial did not open until August 1949; it took place in the Curio-Haus in Hamburg. The West German politicians were forming the Federal Republic at the time, and elections for the Bundestag took place on 14 August. The 'economic miracle' was burgeoning. The vast majority of people in West Germany were totally indifferent to the Manstein trial; during the Nuremberg trials, too, they had mostly shown complete callousness about the atrocities in the East.

The officers of the British Military Court were quite clearly on Manstein's side; the trial aroused little interest in England, and Churchill had come out in favour of Manstein. The case against him was so overwhelming, however, that the court eventually sentenced him to eighteen years' imprisonment. The severity of the sentence was largely Manstein's fault since he had insisted on flying in the face of the truth, even when presented with irrefutable evidence to the contrary.

I reached Hamburg three weeks before the opening of the trial, bringing with me the files of Eleventh Army, which Manstein had commanded in Russia. These files and most of the other documents brought in evidence were on loan from the American Army archives. My duty was to safeguard these files, acting as a sort of trustee, and make them available on demand both to the prosecution and the defence. Apart from this I had no legal function in the trial except to provide occasional clarification on matters of fact – for instance the question of the ethnic origin and significance of the 'Krimtshaken' or Crimean Tartars, a racial group in Manstein's area of command which had been 'liquidated' like the Jews.

Manstein paid me an unexpected compliment when he admitted that my memorandum on his campaigns in the East, apart from two geographical amendments, was factually correct and agreed that it might be used as a source of information for the evidence. Never in my wildest dreams had I imagined that my effort at General Staff work would be approved by a field marshal, said to be the ablest in the Wehrmacht. After the trial my memorandum was reproduced in the British Army periodical, the *Army Quarterly*.

Eventually, however, through my work at the trial, I became an object of Manstein's wrath. One of the main subjects raised in evidence was the question whether and to what extent Manstein had been responsible for the murders of Jews, gipsies and Tartars committed in his area of command. The prosecution produced an order signed by him to the effect that watches taken from Jews before 'liquidation' should be made available for junior leaders in Eleventh Army since they were inadequately provided with watches. Though he had signed this order, he denied knowledge of its significance.

Manstein insisted, as had been agreed in Nuremberg, that he had only learnt of the genocide of Jews and other peoples while in prison after the war. Elwyn Jones, the prosecuting counsel (later, as Sir Elwyn, Attorney General) summoned me into the courtroom with a volume of Eleventh Army War Diary, asked me to open it at a specific page and read to Manstein a passage which he indicated. It ran: 'A new Commander-in-Chief arrives. . . . He is an autocrat and somewhat difficult. However one can speak frankly to him.' Subsequent lines were pasted over. Elwyn Jones asked me to hold the page up against the light and challenged Manstein to read the words that had been pasted over. They were: 'The new Commander-in-Chief does not wish officers to be present at shootings of Jews. This is unworthy of a German officer.' Manstein was unable to explain how this passage came to be pasted over, but had to admit that he had regularly signed the War Diary.

As a result of this incident in court Manstein had clearly contradicted himself and therefore lost all credibility in the eyes of his

judges. In his book *Lost Victories* he did not admit to this but maintained that the pasted slip concealed merely the previous sentence –
'he is an autocrat and somewhat difficult. However one can speak
frankly to him.' His book makes no mention of what was really
beneath the slip.

On several occasions I had heard Dr Goerdeler say of our military
leaders: 'After this war the field marshals and generals will not be
able to draw their pensions and write their memoirs if they do not
act against Hitler.' I had thought that, under Allied control, the
people of the Federal Republic would not be deceived by generals'
memoirs as after the First World War and that history would not be
distorted; I had believed that the military and official hierarchy of
the Third Reich would not be allowed to revive and that in the
Federal Republic a liberal social democracy would grow up based on
the Christian ethos. For these reasons I decided to return to Germany earlier than I had intended.

The start of the process was the receipt of a postcard from Theodor
Heuss, the first President of the Federal Republic. It arrived before
the end of the Manstein trial and invited me to visit him on the
Venusberg, his temporary official residence near Godesberg. He
wished to discuss with me my employment in the formation of the
Republic. I had made Heuss's acquaintance shortly before the war
in the house of Klaus Bonhoeffer, whose wife was a cousin of Heuss.
In addition I had other connections with his family.

Lucie Manén had known the Heuss family from her youth, her
father, Dr Ferdinand Mainzer, having been a friend of Heuss's
brother when the two were medical officers together in France
during the First World War. The two families had been on friendly
terms ever since. When Theodor Heuss and Elli Heuss-Knapp,
being anti-Nazis, could no longer pursue their profession, Lucie
Manén, as a singer, had helped to produce advertising gramophone
records for Elli Heuss-Knapp and their sale had helped the Heuss
family eke out their meagre income.

This being so, my first talk with the Federal President was an intimate one. He thought that I must hear much more in London than
he did in Bonn and asked me a whole series of questions. He was
primarily interested in the problem whether the Federal Republic
would have an army again. I thought it possible that there might be
a sort of auxiliary force to assist the occupying powers and said so.
Heuss asked at once: 'What should I be then? Commander-in-

Chief?' The thought amused him. This would produce a remarkable piece of alliteration, I said – Hindenburg – Hitler – Heuss. He laughed. When I reminded him of this later, however, he pulled a long face.

To a direct question by Heuss I replied that my first choice would be work in the field of international relations. I proposed that we follow the British example and form an Institute for International Relations on the lines of Chatham House, which would be the basis for a new Foreign Ministry. Heuss was very taken with this idea. As a former lecturer at the Berlin Political High School, he knew Chatham House. He asked me to send him my personal details as soon as possible.

This I did but for a time received no answer. This gave me time to settle a highly personal problem – I wished to marry Lucie Manén. It was difficult for her to return to Germany with me, however. On the outbreak of war her work permit as a singer in London had been withdrawn because she was a German. During the war she had worked in a hospital, had studied medicine and had taken an examination as a physio-therapist. With this background she had become a singing instructress in Oxford after the war and had also worked on research into the human voice at the Nuffield Institute for Medical Research and the Institute of Phonetics in London University. Was she to give up all this?

She had to work out the answer to this problem herself. She decided in favour of me and Germany. The deciding factor was that, shortly before his death, when the Allies landed in north Africa her father had written: 'This is the turning-point. The Nazis will be defeated and then we can go back to our country.' Since a close friend of her father had now become Federal President, she found it easier to place confidence in the new Germany. We were married at Christmas 1949.

In February 1950 I had legal business in Germany. I called the Federal President's office, and von Herwarth, the Chief Protocol, told me that my personal details had been forwarded by the President with his recommendation to Counsellor [Staatsrat] Haas. Haas was a former Ribbentrop diplomat who had been entrusted by Dr Adenauer with the preliminary work for the formation of a new Foreign Ministry. When I tried to see him he was 'not available'. Melchers, his deputy and another ex-Ribbentrop diplomat, was evasive. He said that the organisation plan for the new Ministry was not yet ready and that I would be sent further information in London.

In fact Haas did write to me saying 'Your details are under consideration', but this was mere subterfuge. Through a friend well versed in affairs in Bonn I heard that Dr Becker, Weizsäcker's defence counsel, together with other diplomats of the Hitler period were trying to stop my employment in the new Foreign Ministry because I had not assisted Weizsäcker's defence in Nuremberg. Eventually, in September 1951, through an article in the *Frankfurter Rundschau* the closed-circle activities of ex-Ribbentrop diplomats became public knowledge. The Bundestag instituted a Commission of Enquiry which criticised the fact that my employment had not been considered – but that was all.

I found it distasteful to force my way into Bonn through some intervention by the Federal President. Gerard Friters, now Professor of Political Science in Quebec, had just published a monograph on the newly formed Ruhr Authority and he suggested to me that I should apply for a post with this novel international institution. I discussed this with Sir Ivone Kirkpatrick, later British High Commissioner in Bonn; his comment was that, if I wished to twiddle my thumbs, I should go to the Ruhr Authority. When I showed surprise, he confided to me that the life of the Authority would be a short one; a European Mining Union would shortly be formed, with which I should find far better opportunities of employment and I should wait.

This I decided to do and gave no further thought to obtaining employment in Bonn. In October I had further business in Germany and in Bonn I met John Wheeler-Bennett; I was to introduce him to President Heuss who had heard of him through his book on Hindenburg. The previous day I had talked to Jakob Kaiser, now Minister for 'All-German Questions'. He proposed that I should take over direction of the Federal Office for Internal Security [Bundesamt für Verfassungsschutz – lit. 'Federal Office for Protection of the Constitution']. I went to Kaiser's Ministry and examined the official documents setting out the duties and scope of this office. It had only been set up a fortnight previously and its purpose was to provide the Federal government with secret intelligence on radical anti-State tendencies.

Chancellor Adenauer had intended to appoint to this office his personal assistant, Dr Ernst Wirmer, a brother of my friend Dr

Josef Wirmer who had been hanged after 20 July 1944. The Socialist Party, however, had objected, not because they had anything against Ernst Wirmer personally but because they suspected that, by appointing one of his own entourage, the Chancellor was trying to reinforce his personal power – Dr Heinemann, the Minister of the Interior and now President had already resigned because of Adenauer's high-handed rearmament policy. At this time Dr Adenauer still had to take account of the opposition and so he left it to the Minister responsible, the Minister of the Interior, to find a head for the political secret service.

Over a dozen candidates had already applied for the post. None of them, however, were under consideration since, the Federal Republic not yet being a sovereign state, the appointment had to receive the agreement of the three Allied High Commissioners, which none of the applicants had been able to obtain. Since, as far as I was concerned, no objection to my past could be raised, I agreed that Jakob Kaiser should propose me to the new Minister of the Interior, Dr Robert Lehr. On the morning of my visit to Heuss with Wheeler-Bennett, Lehr gave me an appointment to present myself at the Ministry of the Interior.

Heuss naturally asked me what was the position with regard to my employment in Bonn. I did not wish to burden him with complaints about the intrigues of Ribbentrop diplomats and told him briefly that the Minister of the Interior had asked to see me about the post of Head of the Federal Internal Security Office. That would be a very important job, Heuss said, 'to ensure that we don't have another 1933'. Then he plunged into a discussion with Wheeler-Bennett. As we left he said that he hoped shortly to see me and my wife in his house.

My reception by Dr Lehr and his State Secretary Ritter von Lex in the Ministry of the Interior was friendly. Both had obviously briefed themselves about me in detail beforehand and they also knew that I had been visiting the President. The interview did not last long and ended with a request that I send them details of my career as soon as possible. The agreement of the High Commissioners would then be sought at once. I already had the details in my briefcase.

For three weeks I heard nothing from Bonn. Then a friend called me in a great state of indignation and said that I must come to Bonn at once since 'people were sniping at me furiously', not merely the 'Wilhelmstrasse gentlemen' but also the generals. I had recently (October 1950) published an article entitled 'The Military and Militarism' in Rudolf Pechel's *Deutscher Rundschau*. I saw no reason, however, to justify myself to these military gentlemen and so did not go to Bonn.

Meanwhile the Allied security chiefs had set their various secret services to work examining my personal and political past and a more precise check could hardly have been made. Everything was examined but nothing was found. At the end of November 1950 the three High Commissioners declared themselves in agreement with my appointment as Head of the Federal Internal Security Office. Ritter von Lex summoned me to Bonn by telegram. When could I take up office? It was a Saturday. I sensed that they needed me and wanted me, so I replied: 'The day after tomorrow – Monday.'

21
Secret Service

THE office which I was to organise was provisionally established in a block of flats amid the ruins of Cologne. There, on 4 December 1950, I found waiting for me the acting Deputy Director, Albert Radke, an ex-colonel, together with the heads of sections. The establishment comprised only some fifty to sixty personnel including drivers and cleaners. Journalists and press photographers appeared. I did not want publicity, but the interest of the press in my appointment as head of the Federal Republic's new political secret service was no mere sensation-mongering; after their bitter experiences with the Gestapo the citizens had a right to be informed about me and my office by the more sober press. I did not, therefore, avoid press interviews; with the advent of the Cold War the fascination exerted by spy novels and films amounted almost to a psychosis. My office did not exist to carry on espionage; that remained the duty of the Federal Intelligence Service, which at this time was still an American Army organisation.

Espionage aims to discover the military, political and economic capacity of a potential enemy. It is carried on by secret agents or spies who work underground and disregard morality and legality as they feel inclined; their motto is 'the end justifies the means'. Whether they are working for money or for idealistic reasons, their lives are always at stake. Success is their reward. They are paid either in money or by decorations. Such spies are mostly born adventurers.

The task of my office, laid down by law, was confined to Federal territory: to investigate left-wing and right-wing extremist intrigues directed against the State or designed to overthrow the constitutional order and to inform the Federal government thereof. For this purpose secret agents had to be employed. They were to work, however, not illegally in some foreign country, but legally within the frontiers of the Federal Republic. They had to observe the law and could not play about like the secret agent of the film. Personally and morally they had to be above suspicion or they would become use-less – as a result of blackmail, for instance. They had to school themselves in the art of seeing and hearing more than anyone else as they observed the world around them.

For some people the formation of my office awakened horrible memories of the Gestapo and its horde of informers – a considerable disadvantage to me and my staff. I therefore kept a very sharp eye open to ensure that the limits imposed on us by the law were ob-served. We were not allowed to use any political pressure or make arbitrary arrests, as the Gestapo had done. While I was in office these rules were never infringed. All executive measures were the prero-gative and responsibility solely of the Federal agencies of justice; as will be seen later, however, they contrived in every case to brand us as the scapegoats in the eyes of the public.

It is generally regarded as perfectly legitimate to spy in a potential enemy's country. When someone is caught spying for our enemies in our own country, the cry – rightly – is 'treason'; people protest in tones of the deepest moral indignation if they feel that agencies of their own government are breathing down their necks. But, with the international ideological complexities of today, no state can exist which does not make permanent use of secret agents in the political underground to search out those who are aiming to overthrow the constitutional order or discover state secrets.

My staff had to follow up clues indicating underground political activity whether in legal political parties, public institutions, private associations, firms, societies or any other form of organised human activity; any of these might be a target for subversive political infiltration and espionage. My office had its men, appointed by their superiors, in ministries, agencies and offices and also in political parties and organisations. In a far wider range of activities, however, not under state organisation or supervision, the employment of agents – paid informers – is the only method of keeping track of subversive political activity. In the process innocent citizens may come under suspicion and that is understood by all who have no-thing to hide. Protests come only from the fanatics who moralise about political rectitude as a matter of principle; the loudest come from those who are sailing close to the legal wind. It is both mischie-vous and pharisaical to label any legally accredited agent as 'a spy'.

Counter-espionage, in other words secret investigation of foreign spies, was not initially one of the responsibilities of my office. The

Allied Control Council had suspended the relevant provisions of the criminal code. Liability to punishment for treason against the government or the country was only reintroduced in August 1951 when the code was first amended.

In addition to this defensive activity I planned, when I assumed office, to promote a democratic outlook among young people to prevent them becoming influenced by totalitarian ideas. I planned the formation of an Albert Schweitzer Youth League to which Schweitzer was prepared to lend his name, but this never materialised. Financial support came from the Swedish industrialist Axel Wenner-Gren and President Heuss was prepared to be patron. With the repercussions of the Cold War, however, the work of the office became increasingly concentrated upon investigation of extremist elements in the political underground and upon counter-espionage.

When I returned to Germany I found a full-scale process of political rethinking under way influenced by the Korean crisis. The Western Powers had decided to rearm the Federal Republic. Under Article 131 of the Basic Law all persons in public service prior to unconditional surrender, including former professional soldiers, were entitled to apply for re-employment. By Article 65 of the Basic Law the Federal Chancellor had been given the prerogative of 'laying down policy directives'. This created the basis for the transformation of the Federal Republic into an authoritarian state on nineteenth-century lines – the old state administrative structure resting on the same officialdom, a Federal Chancellor with whom ministers were not equal but whom they must obey, and the State 'under the aegis' of a Wehrmacht, rechristened, but still commanded by the old-style generals.

Reinstatement of the old officialdom could easily be made to seem plausible in the eyes of a 'nation of craftsmen' by pleading the need for experienced men. Rearmament, however, brought confusion to the minds of many Germans who had not only taken off their Wehrmacht uniform but had also disarmed themselves mentally. A newly constituted newspaper, the *Deutsche Soldatenzeitung*, attempted with growing success to steer the people of the young republic in the desired direction. It was financed from American sources and was liberal in the distribution of its available money among former Wehrmacht propagandists.

The first public attacks on me were made in the *Deutsche Soldatenzeitung* – when 'an émigré' in England I had interrogated German prisoners of war. I could well afford to overlook such crude accusations. After all, every politician and official working to build up the Federal Republic was doing so only with the agreement and authorisation of the ex-enemy powers. The duties of my office had been checked beforehand by the High Commissioners' security chiefs and the fact that I had been entrusted with them showed that they had every confidence in me. I had certainly not gained this confidence by categorising German prisoners of war in England – to the American and French directors of security this was of no interest whatsoever. For them the decisive factor, in addition to my professional qualifications as an international lawyer with wide experience and knowledge of languages, was that I had been a resolute opponent of National Socialism and had proved myself in the resistance.

I had been installed in office by the Federal Minister of the Interior with the agreement of the Federal Chancellor and the three Allied High Commissioners. I was therefore pledged to loyal cooperation with the Allies. I had no need to suppress nationalistic rancour against our ex-enemies, since I had never regarded them as the enemies of my people. Even in the Berlin air-raid·shelters under a hail of bombs I had felt myself more closely allied to the Americans, British and French than to the Nazis. The German collapse was not necessary to teach me how to think and feel as a European.

When I took over my office Dr Adenauer had already laid down the broad lines of his policy. Internally – exploitation of the Marshall Plan dollars and German efficiency to consolidate the burgeoning economic miracle; here Professor Erhard, the Minister responsible, assisted him adroitly by giving the entrepreneurs a free hand. Dr Adenauer left the reconstruction of Ministries and other agencies to the Ministers responsible, using the Third Reich's experienced officials who were ready to hand. In internal policy, rearmament was the primary consideration. General Graf Schwerin, however, his first military adviser who resigned shortly afterwards, had never been a disciple of Hitler; he did not seem forceful enough to Dr Adenauer.

As far as foreign policy was concerned Adenauer turned his back on the East. He aimed at reconciliation with France and incorporation of the Federal Republic, as an equal, into a Europe which would gradually unite itself and into which German forces would be integrated. This was in line with the policy being pursued in Washington, London and Paris aimed at averting the threat from the East, now obvious with the outbreak of the Korean War. 'We need German soldiers like those we knew at Anzio and Nettuno,' General Truscott, the American who had commanded the landings in Italy, said to me. Dr Adenauer, who had originally pleaded for the total demilitarisation of Germany, wholeheartedly adopted the rearmament policy. He called back into State service men who had been 'prejudiced' by denazification and demilitarisation. This needed no particular statesmanlike qualities. Reconciliation was merely an offshoot of the people's acceptance of the economic miracle.

At the beginning of 1951 it was still not possible to see where this policy would lead. It was not Adenauer's brainchild, but a political product of the tense world situation. The Chancellor neither could nor would implement it except under the aegis of the Western Allies. This was some consolation to me. Moreover, at this time Allied efforts were directed towards the creation of a firm base for democratic principles and institutions in the Federal Republic and the revival of a democratic outlook among the people. In a private talk in mid-March 1951 McCloy, the American High Commissioner, assured me that democracy had made good progress in the Federal Republic.

To guarantee the development of democracy in the Republic, the formation of a strong opposition seemed to me more important than the German–American honeymoon. The obvious leaders were Dr Kurt Schumacher, Chairman of the Social Democrat Party, and Hans Böckler, the trade-union leader. Although I knew neither of them personally, I felt that there were links between us since I had worked in the resistance with their predecessors in the Party and the trades unions. Shortly after I had assumed office Schumacher and Böckler invited me to a discussion in their home. As a result the Chancellor suspected that I was a 'secret member' of the Socialist Party. This was confided to me by Dr Otto Lenz, whom I had known in the resistance and who was then State Secretary in the Federal Chancellor's office.

Dr Adenauer showed no particular interest in the work of my office. At first this seemed to me quite understandable; the office was in its infancy and could only grow into an independent instrument of internal policy within the framework of co-operation with the Allied security services. In addition Dr Adenauer and my master, the Minister of the Interior, were both clear, as was I myself, that the internal security of the Republic could be guaranteed only by the occupation forces. I felt that I was on firm ground and I had the confidence of President Heuss, of my Minister, Dr Robert Lehr, of his State Secretary, Ritter von Lex and, last but not least, of the Allied directors of security. Moreover, I found it easy to manage the people with whom I had to deal officially. So I went about my work with no particular worries.

A secret service must remain unobtrusive. Its achievements cannot be trumpeted abroad like those of some municipal water- or gas-works. When notice is taken of a secret service because something has gone wrong, public opinion and those who guide it react with all the greater hostility. The duty of my office was to inform the government of left- or right-wing extremist tendencies in the political underground. This was usually done by means of secret monthly reports to the Minister of the Interior, with separate reports in special cases. The Minister of the Interior then decided whether he should take action and, if so, what – for instance whether to use the police against some illegal demonstration by the communist Youth Organisation or whether to ban some neo-Nazi meeting. If agents from my office discovered spies, they were reported to the Federal Attorney, whose responsibility it was to procure arrest warrants from the High Court.

Walter Lippmann, the well-known American journalist, once asked me 'off the record' whether neo-Nazi or communist intrigue represented the greater danger to the Federal Republic. The reply which I gave him early in 1951 is, in my view, still valid today. I said that a seizure of power on the Hitler model could not be repeated, in other words an extremist Nazi movement could not revive in the Federal Republic; the danger of communism consisted only in the threat from outside; people in the Federal Republic were not as susceptible to communism as they had been in the 1920s; many Germans had had bitter experience of the 'blessings' of communism as prisoners in Russia or under Russian occupation; the Federal Republic, however, could not of course resist an invasion by the communist super-power from the East.

In the early 1950s various neo-Nazi groups and circles formed in the Federal Republic, particularly in the north. A Deutsche Reichspartei appeared in the Bundestag. One of its deputies was discovered to be a former Nazi, elected under an assumed name. He had even remarried his 'widow' who had applied for his death certificate. This scandal broke the party. Thereafter a Sozialistische Reichspartei was formed; its 'Führers' were a certain Graf Westarp and ex-Major-General Remer who had been commander of the Berlin Guard Battalion at the time of our rising against Hitler.

One day Graf Westarp asked me for an interview and I saw no reason to refuse. He tried to convince me that his party was democratic and that on 20 July 1944 Remer had merely been doing his duty as a soldier. I told him that it was no business of mine to discuss the past with Herr Remer or any other Nazi and that, although basically liberal in outlook, I would continue to keep his party under close observation. A year later, in the summer of 1952 my staff had assembled sufficient evidence to enable the Minister of the Interior to make successful application to the Federal Court for the banning of the Sozialistische Reichspartei.

During this case the activities of my office came to the notice of the public for the first time. Everyone could judge for himself whether we were correctly fulfilling our function of spotting anti-constitutional tendencies so early that they could be nipped in the bud. Graf Westarp made the mistake of calling me before the court as a witness for the democratic integrity of his party. This was my first public appearance in the Federal Republic, and I had no difficulty in refuting Graf Westarp's arguments. Everything seemed to be going as planned. Only the Chancellor seemed to be taking an increasing dislike to me. Otto Lenz told me one day that the 'Old Man' – as Adenauer was referred to by the Bonn politicians – was furious with me, but it had all been 'a misunderstanding' which he had cleared up. What had happened was this: Hans Schlange-Schöningen, the former Reich Minister, who was Adenauer's main rival in the Federal Republic and had organised food supply in the Western zone, had become the Republic's first diplomatic representative in London; Oskar von John, his amanuensis, had provided confidential information for Dr Robert Platow in Hamburg, editor of the *Confidential Information Letters [Vertrauliche Informationsbriefe]*, the files of which had been seized in late August 1951; the cabinet had discussed the case, and at the time Dr Adenauer had confused me with the other John.

Dr Adenauer was continually opposing my appointment as Head of the Office. For nearly a year I was only 'acting'. In the hope of bringing this transitional arrangement to an end my Minister, as Otto Lenz told me, had frequently sung my praises to Dr Adenauer.

Thereupon the Chancellor asked whether there was nothing whatever to say against me – after all, every man had his debit side. After some thought Dr Lehr had said that I was perhaps somewhat phlegmatic. Then I was not suitable for the job, Dr Adenauer had replied; a live wire was required in this post.

Other quarters also made my position difficult. The decision of the Western Powers to rearm the Federal Republic had put new heart into my militarist enemies. General Busse, Field Marshal von Manstein's former Chief of Staff, asked Dr Lehr for an interview and brought a protest from 'the generals' against my appointment as Head of the Office, saying that in Nuremberg I had 'interrogated German officers on behalf of the Americans'.

My office, and therefore I myself personally, became a bogey for all those now awaiting re-employment in Bonn. They were afraid that I might discover their Nazi past, which has of course long since been forgotten today except for cases of participation in genocide. People feared my office's 'secret card index'. This was, however, not a register of enemies of the state but, like any other card index, a cross-reference library. No telephones were tapped and no mail was opened; we also kept no files on bedroom secrets or other dirty linen, as many politicians suspected.

My greatest difficulty in the expansion of the office lay in lack of personnel. The Allied security authorities checked every new appointment in detail, even in the case of subordinate posts; most men with experience of the business were not approved because of their political past. This check on applicants by the Allied authorities, however, was a safeguard for the Office against the entry of unreliable people, but it did not prevent me from taking stern action when this seemed necessary. Accordingly in 1951 I dismissed one of my section heads. Dr Müllenmeister, the head of my Personnel Department warned me against doing so since the person concerned had close ties with the Adenauer family; Dr Sauer, a civil servant [Ministerialrat] in the security section of the Ministry of the Interior, he said, was the Chancellor's watchdog. This man became my enemy when I dismissed an inefficient public relations desk officer shortly after taking over.

Dr Sauer hinted to the criminal police that they should inquire whether I was carrying on illegal East–West transactions through the well-known firm of Otto Wolff in Cologne and whether I had a secret bank account in Switzerland. He thought up this idea because he had heard from a student that I had intervened with the Finance Ministry on behalf of a German secret agent who had been working for the British. This might have been the moment to resign. I did not do so however, because I felt some obligation to my Minister, who had always defended me. Moreover, it did not accord with my sense of duty to abandon a job which I had taken on.

I had every opportunity to return to civil aviation. Many of my Lufthansa friends urged me to do so, and Hans Christoph Seebohm, Federal Minister of Transport, was anxious to have me for the reconstruction of the new Lufthansa. He was enthusiastic over a plan which I had worked out during the war to organise all European airlines into one international concern capable of holding its own against American competition; B.E.A. and B.O.A.C., with whom I also discussed it, were particularly in favour. I would have been very happy to return to Lufthansa, had I not felt it wrong to desert my office.

As the Federal Republic took shape it was easy to see that political morality and democratic principles were being sacrificed to avert the nightmare of a Soviet invasion of the West. As an instance – a 'People's League for Peace and Freedom' appeared, run by Dr Taubert, an ex-member of Goebbels' staff; it was tolerated by the government and financed by the Americans. Taubert produced anti-communist brochures and posters, bringing the 'stirring soul of the people' on to the streets whenever he wished to demonstrate popular indignation against communism – just as in Goebbels' day. He would hire students and others prepared to go on to the streets for a couple of marks; they would form well-drilled choruses and throw rotten eggs or tomatoes – when a delegation from the East Berlin parliament came to Bonn, for instance. I could do nothing against such political hooliganism. Dr Taubert and his merry men were under police protection.

After the ban on the Sozialistische Reichspartei the right-wing extremist groups sang small and there was no need to use the resources of the State to keep them in check. Pro-Nazi sentiment evaporated in face of the economic miracle. Dr Adenauer did what he could to incorporate the nationalistically inclined, including in particular the refugees. In this he had no difficulty after the elections to the second Bundestag in September 1953, when he included the B.H.E. [Bund der Heimatvertriebenen und Entrechteten – League of Refugees and Dispossessed] in his government.

During the electoral campaign he had said to one of his colleagues in the Christian Democrat Party, Christine Teusch, Cultural Minister in Düsseldorf and a politician of genuine Christian Democrat opinions: 'Why are you always inveighing against the Nazis? We need them. They are, after all, the voting populace'.

From among my friends and acquaintances I had selected as my personal advisers people from various walks of life. They included generals, historians, politicians, lawyers and also the late Dominican Father, Laurentius Siemer. I had met him during the war in Klaus Bonhoeffer's house, when Jakob Kaiser had brought him to make contact with me, and had later come to know him as a member of the resistance. He was my adviser on all questions to do with the Catholic Church. My wife and I would often sit talking to him in the evening over a glass of wine.

Father Laurentius was a close friend of Dr Brüning, the former Chancellor; he knew his politics and had known Dr Adenauer as Burgomaster of Cologne, where he had lived for many years in the Andreas Monastery. Adenauer could not stand him because, on one occasion in the 1920s, through a misunderstanding he had kept Adenauer waiting at the gate of the monastery. Adenauer had left a note saying: 'An Adenauer does not wait.' In view of the dissension between my Minister and the Chancellor (they had been rivals when Burgomasters of Düsseldorf and Cologne respectively) I asked Father Laurentius' opinion. He said, weighing his words carefully: 'Unfortunately it is a fact that in politics nothing happens without prevarication.'

I asked someone else for his advice as to whether I should remain in office – Ernst Reuter, the unforgettable Burgomaster of Berlin. His reply was: 'You must. We all need someone like you in Bonn.' That decided me not to capitulate to Dr Adenauer.

22

Conflicting Trends

IN March 1952, when Dr Adenauer was campaigning for the European Defence Community, Stalin took the Germans and the world by surprise with a proposal for the reunification of Germany. He offered free all-German elections under four-power control, a peace treaty, national armed forces and withdrawal of all occupation forces – all on the sole condition that Germany did not adhere to any military alliance. How serious Stalin was with this remarkable proposal we shall never know. Dr Adenauer simply waved it away. The Western Powers had opted for a 'policy of strength' and were arming 'their' Germany. Eisenhower, then N.A.T.O. Supreme Commander, came to Bad Homburg to shake the German ex-generals by the hand. The former Waffen-S.S. reformed itself as HIAG, the 'Hilfsgemeinschaft auf Gegenseitigkeit' [Mutual Aid Association]. It organised demonstrations and marches and presented itself as Europe's front-liners against bolshevism. Fuel was added to the fire of the Cold War.

This being the climate, ex-Major-General Remer felt able to label me and my friends who had been hanged after 20 July as 'traitors'. I did nothing to counter this since I thought it no part of my official duties to institute proceedings for libel in order to clear up the past. Meanwhile, however, General Tresckow, a cousin of Henning von Tresckow, had publicly challenged Remer, accusing him of being a deserter who had left his troops in the final stages of the war, disguised himself in civilian clothes, and sought asylum with Russians.

Remer had brought a case for libel and slander before the court of Bückeburg, formerly a Nazi shrine, and I drove down to listen to the proceedings. The evidence given produced no clear case. Finally one of Remer's former staff officers was called as a supplementary witness; from his Nazi jargon his background was clear but he swore that Remer had never left his troops in the lurch. The presiding magistrate was in obvious embarrassment and adjourned the verdict until the afternoon. During the lunch break he had a long telephone conversation, discussing the case with a former fellow-officer living in Hamburg – this I was told by an acquaintance whose girlfriend was a telephone operator and heard the conversation. Tresckow was sentenced to a nominal fine, but Remer was thereby publicly rehabilitated, as the magistrate's friend had advised. Nothing could be done to reverse this verdict, even though it had been reached as a result of outside pressure.

During this period the communists were able to pursue their activities just as 'legally' as Herr Remer. Their members of parliament, functionaries and members sailed as close to the legal wind as they dared without providing grounds for a ban on the party by the Constitutional Court. Underground, however, and directed from the East, innumerable communist agents were active, spying and agitating against remilitarisation. They organised pseudo-democratic disruptive manoeuvres such as the collection of signatures in favour of a 'plebiscite for the peace treaty', protest marches and chain letters; in all this they were assisted by the 'useful idiots', honest citizens who had fallen victim to the propaganda from the East.

Even today the overlap between right-wing and left-wing extremists remains one of the peculiarities of the German underground jungle. It arose from the fact that, immediately after the war, the Military Governments in all three zones made use of many communists in the denazification process. As a result communists had knowledge of numerous personal records and were able to blackmail former Nazis into serving them as agents. Classic examples of this were ex-S.S.-Obersturmbannführer Heinz Felfe, ex-S.S.-Hauptsturmführer Hans Clemens and their assistant Erwin Tiebel. With a promise of an amnesty from all their Nazi crimes these three were blackmailed by the K.G.B., the Russian secret service, and infiltrated into the Gehlen organisation, which formed the basis of the present-day Federal Intelligence Service. Over a period of ten years they were able to tell the Soviets everything for which this Service was spending millions of the taxpayer's money, first American and then German, to discover.

I knew that ex-S.S. officers were working in the Gehlen organisation and that they were in contact with former comrades in the Eastern Zone. At this time, however, the Gehlen organisation was financed from American Army funds and directed by the American

Secret Service. For me, therefore, it was taboo. Had the Western Allies exerted the same degree of control over the Gehlen organisation as they did over me and my office, Felfe could never have infiltrated it and the resulting, well-nigh immeasurable damage would have been averted.

Against this, the argument was used that 'professionals' were needed, the very men who had become expert in the service of the Gestapo and Himmler's secret intelligence service. American generals were blinded by the halo with which General Gehlen had managed to surround himself as '*the* Russian expert'. They overlooked the fact that he could neither read, write nor speak Russian. But he had appropriated the Wehrmacht files on the Soviet Union and Red Army and handed them over to the Americans. They, therefore, gave him a free hand to recruit his staff among the 'professionals' without regard to their political past.

Immediately after capitulation all 'professionals' who had worked in the Nazi régime's secret services were forbidden by Military Government to take any post connected with intelligence. Meanwhile, however, they were quietly recruited by the Allied secret services. They maintained close and friendly contact between themselves, no matter whether they were in the service of the Americans, the British or the French. They swapped their information as if on a secret stock-exchange, working on the principle 'You give me something, I'll give you something' and were thus able to throw dust in the eyes of their Allied masters as they wished. None of the Allied secret services could be sure that its intelligence was its own private property.

During the hungry years the temptation to enter an Allied secret service for the sake of cigarettes, whisky and other luxuries was great; later other privileges became an attraction. An agent who had a really important piece of information could always sell it to at least one of the four Allied secret services, in addition to the internal security offices of the *Länder* and my own office. To stop this swindle I proposed to the Allied security chiefs that a secret central register be maintained, open only to heads of agencies and one named member of their staff, from which everyone could see who was working for whom as a secret agent. The suggestion was not accepted; even the security offices of the German *Länder* were against it and I had no authority to issue instructions. Nevertheless, I am convinced that, even today, there are agents in Germany working for more than one secret service and earning a good wage thereby.

At this point the citizens of the Federal Republic were subjected to a second process of re-education – from anti-militarism to defence preparedness and readiness to fight against bolshevism. One of the main agencies active in this sense was an American-sponsored youth organisation known as German Youth Activities. In the early post-war years it had selected for training as youth leaders primarily pacifists, conscientious objectors and even ex-soldiers who had been punished for subversive activities against the war effort. Now, however, the pacifist ideals of the starvation years had once more to be eradicated in the young.

For this purpose a German Youth League [Bund Deutscher Jugend – B.D.J.] was formed in Frankfurt, backed by American money. The psychological indoctrination given to it by Paul Lüth, its leader, was directed not solely against communism but also against all neo-Nazi tendencies. Nevertheless, the B.D.J. was a militant organisation, intended as a counterweight to the Free German Youth [Freie Deutsche Jugend – F.D.J.] which was communist-run though ostensibly independent of the communist party. This organisation was directed from East Berlin and was intended to infiltrate West German youth.

Ever since the outbreak of the Korean War the B.D.J. and F.D.J. had been carrying on a sort of cold war with each other. They canvassed for their 'ideals', the B.D.J. passing letters and brochures through the Iron Curtain, the F.D.J. abusing democratic freedom by protest demonstrations in Federal territory. The F.D.J. would go round at night daubing their 'peace slogans' on houses, fences and street walls. The next day the B.D.J. youngsters would paste or paint on their counter-slogans.

This infantile psychological warfare, using brochures, paint-pots and stickers, was expensive. My office possessed more than enough evidence to enable the Minister of the Interior to ban the F.D.J. by law because of its pseudo-legal and pseudo-democratic backing and methods, but even more because it was financed and directed by communist agents from East Berlin. The F.D.J. was the cause of my own first setback. One Sunday groups of F.D.J., coming by bus from all over the country, assembled on the Siebengebirge and converged from all directions on the Hotel Petersberg, the office of the three High Commissioners, where they proposed to demonstrate 'against rearmament and for a peace treaty'. They were dispersed by rapidly alerted motorised police units.

Chancellor Adenauer was furious with me once more. I had failed, he said, to give the government timely warning of this forthcoming action by the F.D.J., and the High Commissioners' lives had been in danger. I was summoned to my Minister. He was easily reassured since none of the Allied intelligence services had heard of the F.D.J. action in time for police precautions to be taken. Moreover, there could have been no danger to the lives of the High Commissioners since they never foregathered in their communal office on a Sunday and in fact only used it at intervals for conferences.

I suggested yet again to the Minister of the Interior that he apply for an official ban on the F.D.J., also that the B.D.J. be offered some better prospect than competing with communist propaganda by democratic slogans in brochures or on posters and stickers. I asked him to assist in realising my ideal of a humanitarian Albert Schweitzer Youth League. He replied that we must not cut across the American concept for the defence of Europe. In fact he had bowed to the Chancellor, who wanted the Cold War and therefore wished to use the militant B.D.J.!

Not all German politicians, however, were prepared to follow the American strategists quite so implicitly. In late September 1952 I received an urgent call from Dr Georg August Zinn, Minister-President of Hesse, asking me to come to his house in Wiesbaden at nine o'clock that very evening. He had a most serious matter to discuss with me which he could not talk about over the telephone. In Zinn's house I found his State Secretary and his public relations officer, Zinnkann the Minister of the Interior, his State Secretary, the Police President of Frankfurt and three or four others.

Zinn said that he must wait for a telephone call before beginning to talk. It soon came, and Zinn merely said 'Thank you' to the caller. Then he turned to me and said that, on his personal instructions, a wave of arrests was in progress in Hesse at that moment. The Hessian government had uncovered a neo-Nazi organisation. It consisted of members of the B.D.J., was run by Peters, a member of the B.D.J. committee, and was organising secret firing exercises and training for partisan warfare at night in the Odenwald. It had drawn up a blacklist of left-wing socialists who were to be arrested or even murdered in the event of attack from the East, to prevent them collaborating with the communists.

I was dumbfounded. There had been an undertone of agitation in Zinn's voice. The others watched my reaction in silence. The illegal activities of these partisans, Zinn continued, were organised and financed by the Americans; the Federal government and even my own deputy, 'our friend Colonel Radke', knew all about them. The Hessian government was not prepared to tolerate these partisan war games on their territory, he said. What had I to say about it?

I made it clear that all this was news to me, that I did not approve of such illegal civil war preparations and would order an inquiry. 'But,' I then asked, 'why was I not told of this illegal activity by the Hessian internal security office long ago?' 'We did not wish to let the matter out of our own hands,' Zinn replied. 'If it had become known in your office Bonn would have been told about it next day and Herr Adenauer would certainly have found ways and means of stopping the arrests and house searches which are now under way.'

What was happening in Hesse that night was, in fact, a revolt by the *Land* government against the Federal government and the American occupation authorities. I was less worried by this, however, than by the realisation that illegal military training for partisan warfare had been going on behind my back with the knowledge of the Federal government. This was the way my own generation had been misused by the Reichswehr after the First World War in pursuit of their secret rearmament; then it had been kept secret from the occupying powers, but this time it was actually organised by one of them.

I had taken office determined to co-operate loyally with my Allied colleagues in the unification of Europe. I had no wish to allow an open quarrel to develop between the indignant Hessians and the American authorities. I therefore proposed to Zinn that a mixed German–American commission of inquiry be formed and that he await the results of its investigations. He agreed. Dr Lehr, to whom I reported the matter, told me that Dr Adenauer had also agreed. Two days later I brought Zinn and the responsible American general together round a table. They agreed to my proposed commission of inquiry and both promised to keep the matter secret until the commission's report was available. General Truscott, the senior American secret service representative in Germany, was very pleased and sent me a bottle of whisky.

But then, a week later, Zinn blew the affair wide open in the Bundestag. I was ordered on to the government bench in support of my Minister. Outwardly Zinn observed the secrecy agreement with the Americans since he did not refer to their background role. As a result, however, his criticism of the Federal government and its security agencies was all the sharper, since, he said, they had tolerated these illegal 'anti-constitutional' partisan war games. Inevitably, all who heard this assumed that he was referring to me, and my Minister showed no inclination to defend me in front of the Bundestag. Not being a member of parliament, I could not speak in the Bundestag in my own defence.

Zinn's outburst in the Bundestag against the B.D.J. as an illegal underground organisation preparing for partisan warfare had most unhappy results. The commission of inquiry had become a farce and never reached a conclusion since its sittings were suspended. The B.D.J. was banned in Hesse and other *Länder* with Social Democrat governments. The Federal Attorney initiated investigation proceedings against the central committee of the B.D.J., but these were eventually stopped. Meanwhile, as a result of the publicity given to the affair, East German agents had acquired material and information about the activities of the B.D.J. in the Soviet zone and the East Berlin security service tracked down a number of B.D.J. members. They were sentenced to savage terms of imprisonment even though they had had nothing to do with events in Hesse. A whole year afterwards a twenty-one-year-old in East Berlin was sentenced to nine years' hard labour for belonging to the 'fascist' B.D.J.

At the same time the communist F.D.J. was allowed to continue to abuse democratic liberties and pursue its illegal pseudo-democratic activities in the Federal Republic. The double standards applied were absurd. The fact was that the Federal government was not master in its own house. In the post-war starvation years the Americans had voluntarily and generously come to our aid. The German economic miracle had been financed by the American taxpayer.

I was pleased to note that I was still on particularly good and friendly terms with my American colleagues. I therefore took special pains to co-operate with Gehlen, head of the American Army espionage organisation which carried his name. Gehlen visited me and invited me to inspect his headquarters at Pullach near Munich. In the evening I was his guest at dinner with the members of his immediate staff. He raised his glass for a toast: 'We wish to forget the past. To good co-operation.' I had nothing to 'forget', but I knew very well what he meant – the fact that I had participated in the trial of ex-Field Marshal von Manstein, now in a British prison, whom Gehlen regarded as a great commander. Since Gehlen seemed so willing to forget his grudge against me, however, I said 'Prosit' and shook him by the hand.

Throughout my period in office the main aim of Adenauer's policy was equal status for Germany and the incorporation of a German contingent into the European Defence Community (E.D.C.). The 'Blank Office' was the germ of the present-day Ministry of Defence. Under Blank as Minister the former generals Heusinger and Speidel were working on plans for the Bundeswehr. Gehlen hoped that one day he and his organisation would be taken over by a German Ministry of Defence. Meanwhile, however, Blank had already formed a cell intended as the basis for a secret military intelligence service. According to the letter of the law it was illegal but both the Federal government and the occupying powers turned a blind eye.

Blank's position as a Minister was very strong. More than anyone else he had Adenauer's backing. He had been a trade-union official and had risen no further than 2nd Lieutenant during the war, but Adenauer made him a Minister and his 'Representative for Questions concerning the Occupation Forces' – alias rearmament – because he thought him best suited to convert the demilitarised citizenry to a policy of remilitarisation.

Just at this time Fritz Aurel Goergen, one of the great captains of industry in the Ruhr, managing director of Phoenix (now Thyssen-Röhrenwerke AG), offered me a very highly paid post in the Mining Union. Seebohm, the Minister of Transport, once more urged me to return to civil aviation. Friedmann, his 'right-hand man' in the German Party, which basically I did not like, pressed my British friends in London, including Terence Bird the former Permanent Secretary of the Ministry of Civil Aviation, to persuade me to pursue my plan for a European Airlines Company.

I would dearly have liked to return to civil aviation, but not as someone who had been dismissed from office nor as someone who had abdicated, and only after I had fulfilled the task I had undertaken – to build up my office. I was regarded as 'a British protégé'.

When I was attacked in the Press, however, my moral support came from my American rather than from my British colleagues. My French colleague remained somewhat aloof in Baden-Baden. Ivone

Kirkpatrick, the British High Commissioner whom I had known for years, told my friend John Wheeler-Bennett that he was avoiding all personal and private contact with me, so that I should not be regarded as 'a British stooge'.

He pursued this policy so rigidly, however, that he did not even tell me when he had Dr Naumann, Goebbels' ex-State Secretary, arrested for alleged subversive activity. The affair became a scandal and I was later accused of having engineered the whole thing, acting as a 'British agent'.

23

Divided Loyalties

A SECRET service must not be visible to the public eye; it must work silently and remain unobtrusive. I had no difficulty in following this rule in the daily round of collection and evaluation of intelligence for the current information of the Federal government. In general I had the full support of a favourable West German and international press. I was the target for one or two ludicrous slanders in the communist press – for instance that I had 'been commissioned by Göring, the 'fire-raiser, to investigate the Reichstag Fire', but these disturbed me as little as did the attacks of the hard-core Nazis.

After an interview with the Zurich *Weltwoche*, the paper described me as 'a calm character who seems to have no trace of nervousness'. Fortunately, I did possess the strong nerves required for the job. I remained completely unmoved by criticism and attacks against me and about me.

As a result of the Basic Law, the Occupation Statute and the Petersberg Agreement, sovereignty in West Germany was shared between the Germans and the Allies. I never ceased to emphasise that we owed our loyalty not solely to Dr Adenauer, his government and our country but also, according to an unwritten law, to a united Europe. This was the spirit in which I ran my office.

There was much that I found difficult to grasp or explain. My personal adviser on rearmament questions was Colonel-General Freiherr Geyr von Schweppenburg, a confirmed anti-Nazi with considerable experience of foreign countries, having been Military Attaché in London. One day he told me that Colonel-General Guderian, Hitler's last Chief of Staff, had been spreading the story among his friends that he was the 'secret' personal adviser on rearmament questions to McCloy, the American High Commissioner. I wished to know what lay behind this and asked McCloy. He said that he had no German ex-general as a military adviser. I asked him to publish the fact in the German press, and this he did. Later Guderian told Geyr 'in strict confidence' that of course McCloy could not admit in public that he, Guderian, was his adviser. But he was! Very secretly of course!

There was much spiteful talk about me among those who had lost their jobs through demilitarisation and denazification. Rudolf Diels, Göring's first head of the Gestapo, told me about this with complete frankness. Former members of Diels' staff in the Gestapo had been re-employed in the Criminal Police Forces of the various *Länder* and some were even in the Gehlen organisation. I was standing in the way of all these people, Diels said. They expected that Dr Adenauer would replace me by Gehlen.

This might have been an occasion for me to accede to the proposals of Seebohm, the Minister of Transport, resign my office and return to civil aviation. But I felt it my duty to remain with my Office and complete the task assigned to it. I felt strong enough to stand up to anything that might happen, since I had the confidence both of my minister and the Allied security chiefs. Diels prophesied that Adenauer would bring me down. He knew Adenauer very well. After his dismissal as first Head of the Gestapo in 1934 Diels had been Government Representative [Regierungspräsident] in Cologne and had married a sister-in-law of Göring. At that time he had taken Adenauer under his protection and accordingly, when the Federal Republic was formed, expected that Adenauer would give him the office which I now occupied. When this did not occur, Diels became an embittered man.

Someone had put it into Adenauer's mind that I and Prince Louis Ferdinand, who was, after all, one of my few surviving friends from the Resistance, were out to sabotage his policy. We were said to be trying to smear him by a whispering campaign to the effect that he was a slave of the Americans. This was one of the more malicious rumours spread about me, but Adenauer seemed to believe it, so Otto Lenz told me. We discussed what to do. It was obvious nonsense that Louis Ferdinand, one of the Roosevelt family's closest German friends and a man who had largely adapted himself to the American way of life, should be accused of adopting an anti-American attitude. Otto Lenz arranged a private discussion between the Prince and Adenauer. Louis Ferdinand had little difficulty in convincing the Chancellor that not only did he approve of the latter's pro-American policy but also that whenever he had opportunity he supported it. Adenauer's dry comment was that 'he would not have expected anything else from a Hohenzollern'.

My office was invariably subject to the glare of publicity whenever some espionage affair came to light and this was particularly so in the case of the 'Vulkan' incident in April 1953. In a single round-up the Federal Attorney had had fifty-five persons arrested on suspicion of espionage. The general public naturally assumed that my office had been responsible for smashing what the Press called 'the greatest espionage ring so far'. On the morning after the arrests I had to report to the cabinet since both my Minister and his State Secretary were on leave. Dr Adenauer, who was on a trip to America, was in San Francisco.

Vice-Chancellor Blücher presided over the cabinet meeting. In the interests of secrecy I felt that I should not reveal to the ministers the background to the arrests, since the action had been initiated through a secret service agent employed by the Americans and on the run from East Berlin. I therefore submitted to the ministers a draft of a government statement couched in general terms and comprising only five lines. This was all that remained of a draft which I had made for the Press during the night and which covered two sheets of paper. In my briefcase I had a list of those arrested.

Dr Lehr had ordered his senior official, Egidi, a director in the Ministry, to accompany me to the cabinet meeting. I had unfortunately been unable to contact and brief him on the previous evening. He was, however, an experienced administrative lawyer and I had only to whisper a word or two to him for him to grasp the point. Meanwhile Vice-Chancellor Blücher had read my draft of the government statement. He registered indignation and declared that 'this matter should not be handled by bureaucrat methods'. He continued: 'We must explain to the people. The people wish to know what is behind all this.' He asked if I knew who the arrested persons were. Fearing that the information would be misused, I replied, untruthfully, 'No.'

Blücher clearly saw an opportunity to emerge from the shadow of Adenauer and act the Vice-Chancellor. He ordered Otto Lenz to inform the Chancellor in San Francisco by telegram. Then he stated that it would be necessary to hold a press conference after the cabinet meeting, at which Egidi and I should be present. I had a lunch appointment in Cologne with a senior American police official.

Blücher accepted this, allowed me to leave the meeting and commissioned Egidi to prepare the press conference.

While I was driving down the autobahn to Cologne Egidi used the authority of our Minister, whom he was representing that day, to demand from my office all secret data about the 'Vulkan' affair. He accordingly obtained the list of those arrested and the two-page draft of the press statement which I had reduced to five lines. Armed with this information, which personally I would never have released, Blücher held his press conference. Contrary to custom he even gave the names of those arrested. There were headlines in the German and foreign press with tributes to my office. Two days later, however, severe criticism began to pour in.

The Federal Attorney and investigating judge had gone too far with their arrests. They had accepted the statements of the American agent who had defected from East Berlin and, in addition to genuine spies, had arrested highly respectable industrialists and businessmen who would never have been touched had any sort of conscientious check been made. My only participation or responsibility in this notorious 'Vulkan affair' was that I had informed Dr Wichmann, the Federal Attorney, of the defection of the American agent from East Berlin, adding the specific comment that my office had no information about the man or his reliability.

One of those arrested committed suicide and a storm of press criticism burst over me and my office. I could have organised a press conference or informed certain reputable journalists of the truth of the affair. I did not do so, however, since it seemed to me mean to expose either my American colleagues or the irresponsible manner in which the Federal Attorney had failed to make a reasonable psychological or material assessment of a secret agent.

Dr Lehr, my Minister, was particularly vexed over an article in the newspaper *Zeit* since it included a sharp attack on the minister responsible to parliament for my office. Dr Lehr sent word to me through his State Secretary, Ritter von Lex, that I was to answer the *Zeit* by open letter. I resisted this because a newspaper editor is always one jump ahead, but the Minister insisted. My draft was so heavily amended in the Ministry that the letter was no longer mine. Nevertheless, I signed it as a matter of duty. It was easy for the editor to refute the letter in an article since it had left the background to the 'Vulkan affair' still totally obscure.

In September 1953 elections for the second Bundestag took place.

They were a great victory for Dr Adenauer and the Christian Democrat/Christian Social alliance. The voters opted for Dr Adenauer's party because he had become the symbol of the economic miracle. He had no opponent of any stature, Dr Kurt Schumacher, leader of the Social Democrat opposition, having died a year earlier. Policy was now dictated by the old Prussian administrative machine with no new spirit behind it. The appointment of Dr Globke, interpreter of the anti-Jewish legislation in the Third Reich, to the post of State Secretary in the Federal Chancellor's office was symbolic.

After the second Bundestag elections my minister, Dr Robert Lehr, retired from politics. His successor, Dr Gerhard Schröder, was unknown to me. He asked me to brief him, gave me a friendly reception and afterwards spoke favourably of me to his State Secretary. I had therefore started well with him, and all the statements that I was averse to him because he had been a Nazi Party member are untrue. With the second Bundestag elections, however, I lost my informant in a key governmental position – Dr Otto Lenz.

The political climate also changed with these second Bundestag elections. Apart from a few small insignificant groups the government's potential opponents of the extremist Right had been absorbed by the government parties. Dr Adenauer's success reaped its reward – in the new Bundestag his party had 243 seats as opposed to 139 after the first elections. The communists now had not a single seat in the Bundestag. Since the outbreak of the Korean War they had completely forfeited their credibility in the eyes of the German people. They worked all the harder, however, in the political underground and through their camouflage organisations.

Ever since the ban on the Sozialistische Reichspartei the government had been considering banning the communist party – the K.P.D. I was against this, in the first place because it was so weak as to represent no threat to government or state, secondly because it was far easier to keep a check on it as a legal party. Those communists who had occupied important positions in the early post-war years, primarily in the *Länder* police forces, had long since been dismissed. The Party, however, anticipated that its organisations would be banned and, after its total failure in the September 1953 elections, concentrated on expanding its secret underground activity, financed and directed from East Berlin. Accordingly my office was concerned primarily with left-wing radicalism and espionage, the 'national opposition' having been integrated into the government parties, at least for the moment.

With the strengthening of the Adenauer government's position as a result of the elections the Federal ministries and their administrative machine were expanded. Nazi fellow-travellers hurried along and occupied new positions in Bonn. Much democratic phraseology was used to cover up the re-establishment of the conservative authoritarian tradition. Yet, had the Republic been submitted to a test of its democracy, it would have withstood it, since people were happy with its obviously increasing economic success. Only from the refugees from the East were nationalist overtones to be heard, and these could not be disregarded.

These circles were the source of sharp attacks on me because, in one sentence in a certain article, I had described 'the refugees' as a potential camouflage organisation for illegal political activity. *Der Friedensbote*, the newspaper of the Nationale Partei Deutschlands (N.P.D.) published a virulent article against me. The League of Refugees and Dispossessed (B.H.E.), a new party with twenty-seven seats in the Bundestag, sent a letter of complaint to Dr Adenauer, and he ordered Dr Globke to reprimand me. The latter read the article and realised at once that I had had no intention of insulting the refugees. This he explained in a letter to the originators of the complaint.

I was also given some highly peculiar assignments. Before capitulation, a certain well-known firm had buried drawings of the latest Luftwaffe equipment in a coffin in a village cemetery. These I had to dig up on the pretext of a secret 'exhumation' of the supposed dead man. Another assignment made my office an object of public ridicule. A demented hospital nurse 'confided' to a senior ministerial official that she knew the hide-out of the former Reichsleiter Martin Bormann; he was concealed in the Bavarian mountains behind an electrically operated slab of rock. The American secret services had apparently searched for it on many occasions. On the instructions of my State Secretary I dispatched a search party which hunted for the hide-out in the snow-covered mountains. Only then did it become known that the nurse had invented the entire story.

In March 1954 Sefton Delmer arrived in Bonn to write an article for the *Daily Express* entitled 'How Dead Is Hitler?' I had not seen him for years and met him quite by chance in the Schwarzer Adler restaurant in Bad Godesberg. He visited me in Cologne. I was reticent because I did not wish to be quoted in his newspaper, which was anti-Adenauer, and I would only have irritated the Chancellor further. Delmer said that he had spoken to a whole series of important and well-informed people in Bonn and continued (I quote): 'It will not get any easier for you here in the Federal Republic. You have many more enemies than you think. But I will also tell you that the *Daily Express* and Lord Beaverbrook will always be at your disposal if you need help.'

About this time Wolfgang Ganz Edler von Puttlitz, the former foreign service officer [Legationsrat] whom I had known in the Soldatensender Calais, was also in Bonn. Immediately after the war he had returned to Germany and had been employed with the Schleswig-Holstein government. There he was denounced by his former colleagues as a British agent and, enraged by this, had returned to England. He took out British nationality but failed to make his way in Britain and took a post in East Berlin. He called saying that he wished to speak to me.

I agreed to meet this odd political crank in a restaurant. He produced all the slogans which could be read daily in the East German press – the division of Germany, reunification, against rearmament, in favour of a peace treaty. I asked him what all this had to do with him, since he was now an Englishman. He replied: 'I am as much a German as you. I have torn up my British passport.' I pointed out that he had not thereby lost British nationality and told him that, if he wished to talk politics, he should get in touch with Sefton Delmer, his ex-master in the Soldatensender Calais, who was in the Federal Republic; he could find him at the Breidenbacher Hof Hotel in Düsseldorf. I said that I had no more to discuss with him.

I reported my conversation with Puttlitz to Randall, the British director of security. He saw no reason to take any action against Puttlitz. Delmer then attacked Puttlitz in the *Daily Express* because he had boasted that he, Puttlitz, was a friend of Burgess and Maclean, the two British diplomats who had spied for the Russians for years inside the Foreign Office and had defected to the Soviet Union. In the same article Delmer also severely criticised the British secret service for failing to keep a check on Puttlitz. As he was a British citizen I could not touch Puttlitz. Randall was very cross, however, because he suspected that I was behind Delmer's article against him and his service.

Once, and only once, I was summoned to Dr Adenauer's private house with Dr Globke. We drove there together in my official car. Dr Globke could not say what Adenauer wanted from me. The Chancellor received us in a small study. On his desk lay a religious picture at which he gazed, apparently deep in thought. Globke and I sat there waiting. Then Adenauer said: 'You start, Herr Globke', to which Globke replied: 'Chancellor, I don't know what about.' Adenauer then looked up and told me that he had information that Ulbricht had obtained copies of the drafts of the European Defence Community treaty. They had been passed to him by Jakob Kaiser, then Minister for All-German Questions, perhaps even by Frau Kaiser or at any rate from Kaiser's Ministry. This was a monstrous accusation. The Federal Chancellor was accusing one of his own ministers of treachery. I had known Kaiser for years in the resistance. He was the only minister who opposed Adenauer's unilateral West-orientated policy. I regarded it, however, as totally impossible that Kaiser should go behind the Chancellor's back to Ulbricht, who had chased him out of East Berlin, and conspire in any way against Adenauer.

To evaluate a piece of information, one must know its source. But Adenauer would say nothing about his informant. Dr Globke said not a word throughout the interview. It was clear that someone had denounced Kaiser, and Adenauer believed it. It occurred to me that we might here have come across the trail of certain Belgian Nazis who were peddling intelligence both in the right-wing and left-wing extremist underground in Germany; they were also in touch with interested circles in East Berlin to whom they passed French-language information. We had heard that they had sold to East Berlin a French text of the E.D.C. treaties – it was, in fact, a forgery. This might explain, I said to Adenauer, how Ulbricht had laid hands on the alleged drafts of the E.D.C. treaty; I thought it impossible that Jakob Kaiser should be involved in such a matter with Ulbricht. It did not seem at all 'impossible' to Adenauer. He would believe anything, he said, of Thediek, Kaiser's State Secretary. He had already spied on him on behalf of the Prussian government when he was Burgomaster of Cologne. He ordered me to clear the matter up and dismissed me.

I was in a difficult situation. Was I to tell Jakob Kaiser of these serious accusations against him? That would have been a dereliction of duty *vis-à-vis* the Chancellor. But what was my duty to my friend from the Resistance? On the way back I agreed with Dr Globke that, since we were the only people who knew of the matter apart from Adenauer, we would keep it completely secret, at least until it was cleared up. We wished to avoid an open breach between Kaiser and Adenauer.

It soon proved that my suspicions were correct. Ulbricht had paid a considerable sum for French-language drafts of the E.D.C. treaties forged by Degrelle Nazis. The Belgians were arrested and sentenced. Dr Adenauer accepted the report on the subject from Dr Globke without a word. He was apparently not in the least disturbed at having slandered Kaiser. I was shattered and I discussed the affair with Father Laurentius Siemer. He advised me to say nothing to Kaiser; if it came to a public scandal I would not be able to stand up to Adenauer; he would deny everything in front of the Bundestag and brand me as a liar. This was exactly what in fact he did when I later cited him as a witness.

From mid-May to mid-June 1954 I visited the United States at the invitation of the American government. After a three-week tour I spent a week in Washington where I was most cordially received. The main preoccupation of the American government at this time was the formation of the European Defence Community which was to include the Bundeswehr. While walking in his garden after a lunch to which he invited me, Allen Dulles asked me what could be done to bring the E.D.C. into being as soon as possible. The French, he said, were doing nothing towards it and were adopting a policy of delaying tactics. I told him that a very senior French official in Paris had said to me quite openly that there were enough strong-minded politicians in France to put a stop to the E.D.C.

Dulles wished to know whether and how German forces could be constituted without French consent. I spoke in favour of the formation of a Federal armed force since in the present-day world no state could exist without forces for its defence; I assured him that the 'leave-me-out' propaganda and other forms of resistance to re-armament in the Federal Republic would not succeed. The great problem, I said, was that rearmament should be controlled effectively and carefully. It should be organised by proven democrats and not 'from the top downwards' by some Federal Ministry of Defence; it should spring from the grassroots with the formation of small local units which could gradually be allowed to grow into major formations in the various *Länder*. The E.D.C. failed, as had been prophesied to me in Paris. The rearmament of the Federal Republic

was then carried through far too hurriedly and on the old Wehrmacht pattern. After the Bundeswehr had already passed its
formative phase a general said to me: 'Everything is being done
exactly as we tried to do it in the 1930s.'

After my return from America a debate took place in the Bundestag
on the notorious 'Vulkan affair'. Once again I was ordered on to the
government bench by my Minister. He made a statement on behalf
of the government. It had been drafted in the Ministry during my
absence and did not make clear that my office was in no way responsible for the arrests, whereas responsibility lay entirely with the
officials of the Federal Court. Parliament and the general public
were therefore confirmed in the view that my office, and therefore I
myself personally, had been responsible for the dubious evidence
which had led to the unfortunate blunders over the arrests.

Instead of the Minister of the Interior, the government statement
on the 'Vulkan affair' should really have been made by the Minister
of Justice. The arrests had been made on the sole responsibility of
the judiciary. Since the Minister of Justice did not know the background, however, during my absence my Minister had declared his
readiness to make the statement. I could easily have argued him out
of it, but now it was too late. I had to sit behind him on the government bench as a scapegoat, a target for public censure, while those
really responsible, Dr Wichmann the Federal Attorney, and Dr
Weber the investigating judge, sat quietly hidden under the visitors'
gallery.

Encouraged by the criticism of my office, a member of the B.H.E.
rose and again complained that I had insulted the refugees in the
article already mentioned; he demanded that I be publicly reprimanded. My Minister knew nothing of the incident since it was
before his time and I could not tell him about it in the House. He
listened to the B.H.E. member's statements and then rose to say that
he was sure that I had had no intention of insulting anyone. If this
were proved to be so, the Federal government would express its
disapproval. The 'national opposition' press thereupon maintained
that I had been reprimanded in the Bundestag.

None of this, however, disturbed or shook me. The previous day
I had visited President Heuss and he had said a few words of
encouragement, knowing of the attacks against me. Because of our
long-standing acquaintanceship and mutual friends, my wife and I
repeatedly received private invitations from him and his wife. In

private I addressed the President as 'Herr Professor' and could speak perfectly frankly to him.

During this particular visit the President was primarily interested in my impressions of America. He made me tell him everything in detail and was particularly struck by my comment that in Washington it was odd to find the Pentagon, the greatest War Ministry in the world, standing next to Arlington, the greatest military cemetery in the world. Rearmament still being the main plank of government policy, he was amused when I told him that I had said to an American general that I should never be able to rearm in the Pentagon, looking out all the time on this vast military cemetery. Finally we discussed some of his ideas for the speech he was to make in Berlin on 20 July, the tenth anniversary of our abortive rising against Hitler. As we left he said: 'Well then, auf Wiedersehen in Berlin.'

Early in July I was visited in my office by two flight captains, Hans Werner von Engel and Hannes Rathje. They came on behalf of our mutual friends and acquaintances in civil aviation with a further urgent request to resign 'this office which gives you nothing but trouble' and return to Lufthansa. Wolfgang von Gronau, famous as one of the first to fly the Atlantic, arrived with a similar request. A week later Kreipe, the ex-Luftwaffe general and a close associate of Seebohm, the Minister, asked for an interview.

They all wished to 'prise me loose from my office' and persuade me to devote myself to the reconstruction of a new Lufthansa. My answer was still the same as that which I had given Dr Seebohm months before: I would, of course, very much like to return to Lufthansa, but only on completion of the expansion of my office, when my departure could be vindicated in public and not celebrated as a capitulation by my enemies. I had already called a conference for August of all internal security officials and state attorneys from the *Länder*; I proposed to address them on my plans and ideas for the ultimate structure of the office in the light of experience so far and then open the subject for discussion.

The re-election of Professor Heuss as President was scheduled for 17 July in Berlin. Thereafter there was to be a memorial celebration for 20 July 1944. For this reason, and also on grounds of duty, I had arranged to fly to Berlin on the fifteenth. Two days before this Father Laurentius Siemer telephoned and asked me to see him in the monastery; he did not sound very friendly – and I knew I was at fault. Urged by Frau Eckert, widow of the well-known Cologne notary, who did typing for Father Laurentius, I had deceived him.

Father Laurentius wished to go to the 20 July celebrations in Berlin and had asked me to reserve a place for him on the aircraft which the United States Air Force was making available for the less well-to-do. Father Laurentius' doctor had told Frau Eckert that, owing to his state of health, he should under no circumstances fly. He had a weak heart and would not be able to stand the exertions of the Berlin festivities. Frau Eckert had said to me: 'If you wish Father Laurentius to remain with us, find some excuse why he cannot get a place on the aircraft.'

So I had told a lie – as seemed necessary. On the way to the monastery I thought that Father Laurentius must somehow have found out, for I knew that he was very anxious to attend the ceremonies in Berlin. I was not expecting a very friendly reception. What I heard, however, was the most disgraceful thing that had happened to me since I had been working in internal security. Father Laurentius came out with it at once: he must register the most serious protest with me on behalf of Dr Brüning (whose acquaintance I had made with Jakob Kaiser); for some time Dr Brüning had realised that he was being watched – his telephone, his mail, every step he took; he no longer dared move from his university desk or telephone even from a public call-box. 'It is intolerable, Dr John,' Father Laurentius said, 'that you should be doing this – and for Adenauer too!'

I was deeply offended that I should be suspected of such a thing, particularly since I had always respected Brüning. I said: 'Father Laurentius, I give you my word of honour that none of this is true. No one in my office would do such a thing, not even behind my back. But, of course, I do not know whether Dr Brüning is being watched by other people. This I will investigate. If it is so, it is a real scandal.'

'I believe you,' Father Laurentius assured me. 'Dr Brüning also regards you as an upright man. But he has seen something – and he has experience of being hunted by the Gestapo.' I knew of Dr Adenauer's animosity towards Dr Brüning. He was the only man with sufficient reputation to set himself up as candidate against Adenauer, had he wished to do so. Adenauer having once tried to smear Kaiser, as already related, I thought it not impossible that, without my knowledge, some students had been recruited by one of

Gehlen's agents to keep Dr Brüning under observation on behalf of Dr Adenauer. The Federal Chancellor's office maintained its own secret intelligence service, in some cases using the People's League for Peace and Freedom.

I would have liked to go to Dr Brüning forthwith but I had to go to the Ministry. On the next day I had a summons for a minor traffic incident which I could not evade. The remaining two days before my flight to Berlin were full till late at night with appointments and preparations for Berlin. I accordingly asked Father Laurentius to explain to Dr Brüning why it had not been possible for me to see him before my trip to Berlin; I hoped that he would accept my assurance that I was not having him watched on behalf of Dr Adenauer; I would clear the matter up and come and see him immediately on my return from Berlin.

24
The Kidnapping

EARLY on the morning of 21 July all Western secret services were alerted. On the night after the ceremonies commemorating the tenth anniversary of our abortive rising against Hitler I had not returned to my hotel. I was in fact lying heavily drugged in a house in Berlin-Karlshorst belonging to the Soviet secret service, the K.G.B. I still do not know how long I was unconscious, but it must have been between twenty-four and forty-eight hours. Only very much later did I discover the background to my kidnapping by the Soviets.

Only over the course of several years and by laborious investigation was I able to reconstruct events prior to the time I was drugged. The key figure was Dr Wolfgang Wohlgemuth. I had known him in August 1942 when he was assistant to the famous surgeon, Professor Ferdinand Sauerbruch. He had previously been assistant to Dr Theodor Morell, Hitler's personal physician, but had left him, thinking his future lay in the succession to Sauerbruch as head of the surgical clinic, the Berlin Charité.

When I first knew Wohlgemuth he was regarded as Sauerbruch's model pupil. However, after almost two years had gone by, in August 1944, Sauerbruch forbade him to continue to work in his clinic. Wohlgemuth anticipated his dismissal. He reported sick and took himself off to Professor Zahn's private clinic in Prague, where he was under treatment for six months. On his return Sauerbruch forbade him to work further in his clinic. He would not even give Wohlgemuth a reference because of his 'lack of moral aptitude for the doctor's profession'.

I only learnt of all this fifteen years later. After my first meeting with Wohlgemuth in Sauerbruch's house I saw him by chance some four or five times during the war, before he left for Prague. In July 1942 my brother Hans was released from the Wehrmacht, having been severely wounded in Russia; he lived with me and worked at the Institute of Aeronautical Law and for Lewinski, a barrister who was a friend of Sauerbruch's. From time to time, particularly with a change in the weather, my brother had trouble with the bullet lodged in his lung. Lewinski asked Sauerbruch to examine him and, if necessary, operate on him himself.

Dr Wohlgemuth was among those assisting at my brother's examination in the Charité. As Sauerbruch told me, he did not think an operation advisable since the bullet had satisfactorily encysted and, being lodged near the heart, an operation would entail some risk; the scars from the operation would probably cause more trouble than a well-encysted bullet. He commissioned Wohlgemuth to follow the progress of the encysting process by X-ray photographs. Accordingly at varying intervals in 1943 my brother met Wohlgemuth two or three times in the Charité. They discussed politics, and Wohlgemuth was most outspoken about Hitler, saying: 'The brute must go.'

Wohlgemuth was what, in our student days of the early 1930s, we called a 'drawing-room bolshevist' – one of those intellectuals whose pro-communist attitude contrasted sharply with a middle-class existence aiming at a successful career and a good salary; they preached marxism but were not prepared to make personal sacrifices for it. Over the years I had come to know their type, first in the circle of Ernst Gläser, the author who wrote *Jahrgang 1902* [*The Class of 1902*], and then with Hermann Kesser, the Swiss poet living in Wiesbaden, who became known for his play *Der Strassenmann* [*Man in the Street*]. This type of do-gooder, as Kesser once said to me, aimed 'not to descend to the level of the proletariat, but to raise the proletariat to their own level'. Wohlgemuth was one of these and I knew no more about him except that he was a violent opponent of the Nazi régime.

One evening Wohlgemuth appeared uninvited in our house. He had to let himself go, he said, and that he 'could best do so with us'. Although we had not invited him to do so, he used the familiar *du* as if we had been close friends for years. In this he was aping his master Sauerbruch who always used the *du* to his patients, my brother among them. In Wohlgemuth's case this was pure playing to the gallery. I did not object because he was an entertaining comic storyteller, because he was refreshingly outspoken about the Nazi régime and last but not least because, as Sauerbruch's assistant, I regarded him as a future authority in the medical world.

I was somewhat flabbergasted when Wohlgemuth let fall the fact that Dr Walter Nehlsen, a mutual acquaintance and one of his patients, had hinted that I was in touch with anti-Hitler generals. Dr Nehlsen, who was a lawyer by profession and was serving as a captain on the reserve with the Berlin garrison, was a cousin by marriage of Flight Captain von Baumbach, an old friend of mine. Even before the war Nehlsen had been known to me as a genuine anti-Nazi and had introduced me to certain officers of a similar turn of mind who were prepared 'to go along if things got under way against the Nazis'. This was during the Fritsch crisis of February 1938 when we had hoped that the Commander-in-Chief of the Army would liberate us from the Nazi régime by a *coup d'état*.

I did not, however, follow up Wohlgemuth's hint, but said that hopes placed in 'the generals' had proved illusory. I had good reason to wish to tell him nothing about the anti-Hitler conspiracy in spite of the fact that he was a genuine anti-Nazi. Carla Boucneau, a friend of Dr Margot Sauerbruch, had warned my brother to be cautious in Wohlgemuth's presence; because of his reckless outbursts against the Nazi state, she said, he could be a danger to us. Moreover, I knew nothing about Wohlgemuth personally except that he had twice been divorced. I thought him a clever and gifted doctor but not suitable for initiation into the conspiracy.

After this first visit Wohlgemuth took to arriving uninvited. On one occasion he brought with him a film starlet, on another he wished to borrow petrol coupons, and on a third he asked me to help his Jewish friend Oskar Tramm. I was able to assist Tramm to escape to the Balkans, but he fell into a Gestapo trap and thereafter I avoided all contact with Wohlgemuth. Nevertheless, he continued to arrive, and one evening gatecrashed a secret discussion I was holding with Prince Louis Ferdinand, who had come expressly from East Prussia for the purpose. We had to interrupt our talk until Wohlgemuth departed after a glass or two of wine.

The last time I saw Wohlgemuth during the war was in early 1944 before he moved to Prague. He told my brother and me that he had fallen out with Professor Sauerbruch's deputy and (untruthfully) that he was going to Bad Nauheim for a cure of his heart trouble. He showed us a letter to Sauerbruch asking for leave owing to his heart condition, and asked whether the letter was sound from the legal point of view. We told him that the cause of his leave was not a legal question but a medical one, which he was best able to judge.

After this my brother never saw Wohlgemuth again and I did not do so for seven years, until I went to Berlin on duty in February 1951. This being my first post-war visit to the old Reich capital, I took the opportunity to call on all my surviving friends and acquaintances. So I had a short talk with Wohlgemuth in his house at 175 Uhlandstrasse, near the corner of the Kurfürstendamm, where he had set up his practice. By this time he had already been a secret agent of the Soviet K.G.B. for a year. This was confirmed in 1959 by ex-K.G.B. Major Peter Deriabin, now living in the United States, who at my request was sworn in as a witness in New York on 6 August 1964. Before his defection to the West, Deriabin had been K.G.B. desk officer for subversive activity against me and my office. He confirmed that Wohlgemuth provided secret intelligence on West Germans and West Berliners.

As far as I was concerned Wohlgemuth played his agent's role to perfection. I was in no way suspicious since I regarded him merely as a clever pupil of Sauerbruch and was therefore prepared to excuse his somewhat peculiar behaviour. Sauerbruch himself, after all, though in daily contact with him, had taken two years to see through him. I knew Wohlgemuth merely from seven or eight entirely superficial conversations. When I returned to Berlin on this occasion Sauerbruch was no longer alive or he would probably have enlightened me about Wohlgemuth. Early in 1950 Sauerbruch had written to me in London congratulating me on my marriage and saying that it was time that we saw each other again and had a talk.

Wohlgemuth was obsessed with the idea that he might one day become Sauerbruch's successor in the East Berlin Charité. All his efforts were unsuccessful, however, since Professor Felix, another pupil of Sauerbruch, who had succeeded him, did not like Wohlgemuth; in addition, Wohlgemuth's behaviour had not made him popular with the functionaries of the Socialist Unity Party (S.E.D.) of East Berlin. Even the communists did not consider him politically reliable since he was not a member of the S.E.D. and did not attend their indoctrination courses. His last hope, therefore, of achieving his life's aim of becoming Head Surgeon in the Berlin Charité lay in proving his worth to the Soviet secret service.

Wohlgemuth knew from the Press of my appointment as head of the Federal Internal Security Office and at this very first meeting after the war he began to cover up. After we had exchanged a few reminiscences he said with great emphasis that he was no longer interested in politics but solely in his practice and in cancer research. He bemoaned the miserable state of the West Berlin hospitals and the lack of equipment and funds for research. He wondered whether I could help through my contacts and obtain some Marshall Aid funds. I proposed that he send me a detailed memorandum on the subject to Cologne and said that I was only too ready to help.

When I asked whether he was still working in the Charité, he said with some scorn: 'That lot over there only make a hash of things. What do you think? – they wanted to educate me politically. I sent them packing.' He then told me that he was no longer allowed to operate in East Berlin hospitals because he had told the matron of one of them that she was 'an old bag' and knew nothing of her profession. He tried to convince me that he had totally given up politics, particularly those of the East. 'I don't want to have anything more to do with it,' he said. 'I am getting older. I must now be able to work on my cancer research in peace.' In fact, he had done nothing whatsoever in the field of cancer research, but I believed Sauerbruch's 'model pupil'. As a layman I did not realise that for years cancer research had only been carried on by teams of specialists from the medical, pharmaceutical, chemical and other professions.

In 1953 I received a letter from Frau Else Nehlsen, the widow of Dr Walter Nehlsen who had died in 1949; to claim her pension she needed a certificate from Wohlgemuth, who had treated her husband. She had spent over two years trying to extract it from Wohlgemuth but had invariably been fobbed off with empty promises. She begged me to ask Wohlgemuth for the certificate as a matter between friends.

Since she was completely penniless, I wanted to help her and wrote to Wohlgemuth. He did not react.

One day in late January 1954, to my complete surprise, I received a telephone call from Wohlgemuth in my office. He was in Bonn, he said, to examine the father of one of his former nurses and would like to say 'How do you do' to me. In order to lay hands on Frau Nehlsen's certificate at last, I invited him to Cologne to dinner in our house. I warned my wife over the telephone, reminding her that I had already told her about Wohlgemuth, that he had been assistant to Sauerbruch and was now engaged on cancer research. Wohlgemuth kept us waiting a long time that evening. Eventually he arrived, accompanied by a girl whom he introduced as his former nurse. This was something of a poser for my wife but she coped with the situation very well and laid another place.

Over dinner a lively discussion took place between Wohlgemuth and my wife about her medical research work into the human voice. Over coffee I reminded Wohlgemuth that he still owed Frau Nehlsen her certificate. He had not prepared it, he said, because, in view of certain aspects of Nehlsen's medical history, it was difficult to find a legally watertight form of words; perhaps I could help. Was I coming to Berlin for the four-power conference in February? If so, we could draft the certificate together. Still quite unsuspecting, I said that this conference was nothing to do with me and that my wife and I were going to the Engadine the following week.

Wohlgemuth apparently accepted this quite happily and shortly thereafter left with his girl-friend, my wife and I having declined to go on somewhere else with them. 'What a character!' my wife said, Wohlgemuth having borrowed fifty marks from me as he left. She had taken an instinctive dislike to him. My later investigations showed that on this occasion Wohlgemuth had come on behalf of the Soviet secret service specifically to pump me; he had no genuine reason to pay me this sudden visit. Had I gone to the four-power conference in Berlin in February 1954, the Soviets would undoubtedly have used this occasion to lay hands on me with Wohlgemuth's assistance – as they succeeded in doing six months later.

For a long time the Soviet secret service had had a master spy in the Gehlen organisation, ex-S.S.-Obersturmbannführer Heinz Felfe. He was not exposed until Anatole Golytsin, a K.G.B. colonel, defected to the West in November 1961. Until then he had been giving the Soviets precise information about the Gehlen organisation's agents working in the Soviet-occupied zone. The Russians could have arrested all Gehlen's agents at any time but they did not do so because, had there been a wave of arrests, Felfe, their master spy, would have been blown, being Gehlen's desk officer for all agents in their zone. In order not to jeopardise Felfe and enable him to continue working for them inside the Gehlen organisation, the Soviets allowed all Gehlen's agents in their zone to continue, though of course under permanent observation. In any case they knew through Felfe everything the agents reported and in addition they could easily mislead the Gehlen organisation by feeding in false information. For ten years General Gehlen was duped by the Soviet secret service in this way.

In this cat-and-mouse game Wohlgemuth had been commissioned by the Soviet secret service to recruit prominent ex-functionaries of the Nazi régime to work as agents in the Gehlen organisation. Wohlgemuth knew a number of them very well, having operated on their wives. As a pupil of Sauerbruch he was on close terms with (for instance) ex-S.S.-Brigadeführer and Major-General Heinz Jost and Schmidt-Eckert, founder and head of the Reich Foreign Propaganda Office under Goebbels. During 1954 he tried to infiltrate both of these into the Gehlen organisation as Soviet agents; he also tried to recruit a school-friend, offering him a guarantee of 20,000 marks when he was in financial difficulties after his release from Russian captivity in December 1953. All this, however, I only learnt after I had succeeded in escaping from the Soviets in December 1955.

After our second post-war meeting in 1952 Wohlgemuth had offered to abduct me. After he had succeeded in doing so, a record of his political career was found in his house, in which he had noted that he had become friendly with me 'through the Resistance' and had added the comment that I was 'not yet polarised', whatever that may mean. Deriabin reported that in the Soviet secret service files on me and my office Wohlgemuth was described as 'the star agent'.

Having found out in January 1954 that I was not going to Berlin for the four-power conference, Wohlgemuth reappeared in Cologne in May. I was in America at the time but he sought out my wife in our weekend cottage in Hohkeppel and told her stories about his cancer research. Thinking him competent since he was an ex-pupil of Sauerbruch, my wife sent him to Düsseldorf in our car to visit a friend of ours who was suffering from cancer. It later emerged that, although Wohlgemuth's theories about cancer and its cures seemed plausible to my wife in the light of her medical knowledge, they were in fact mere plagiarisms of the research achievements of Professor Domagk, the Nobel Prizewinner.

On 9 July Wohlgemuth called me in my office about midday and said that he was about to leave Berlin by car and had to call at the firm of Bayer in Leverkusen for some preparation for his cancer research; he would like to drop in on the way that evening. As was usual on a Friday, my wife had gone to our cottage in Hohkeppel. We had a British friend staying with us but he was out that evening. Wohlgemuth did not appear, so I went to bed to read. Shortly thereafter he called from Cologne-Mülheim, asking whether he might still come. I said 'Yes', adding that I had no bed available for him. I could, in fact, easily have put him up but did not want to. I felt that

I did not know him well enough. I got up and took a bottle of beer out of the ice-box.

Wohlgemuth arrived and said that it was now too late to visit Bayer in Leverkusen; he had been held up in his consulting-room in Berlin. I asked if he wanted something to eat and what he would drink. He refused beer, wine and even cigarettes but asked for a cup of coffee, which our maid produced. He said that he would not go on to Leverkusen till next day and then had to go to Heidelberg for something to do with his cancer research. I was amazed that Wohlgemuth no longer smoked and would drink nothing. He began to lecture me about the iniquities of nicotine and alcohol. Meanwhile our British guest returned and I introduced him to Wohlgemuth. They exchanged a few generalities and then the Englishman went to bed. 'You really ought to give up smoking,' Wohlgemuth said, adding that since he had given up smoking and drink he felt quite different and could work much harder; that was very important for his research work. He asked whether I were going to the 20 July ceremonies in Berlin; if so, I could come to him and he would examine me; he would make a cardiograph. He asked whether my wife was going to Berlin with me this time, saying that he knew that she had not been with me for the ceremonies in previous years. During his first visit to us she had, in fact, told him that she had no wish to see the ruins of the city in which she had grown up.

I replied that my wife would probably not go to Berlin. Then we could go out together, he said. As I lit another cigarette, he began once more to condemn smoking – these American cigarettes were poison! He could give me some tablets which would make it quite easy to give up smoking. I felt perfectly well and saw no reason to give up anything. He took a little box out of his pocket and passed me a couple of tablets, asking me to try one and take the other next morning. I took a tablet for fun.

Wohlgemuth asked whether I did not find my duties very trying to the nerves; I should go on a cruise with him; that was the real way to relax. Once more he offered to examine me when I was in Berlin. I had no need of that, I said somewhat crossly – it was already late and he had annoyed me with the remark that I had reached the age when people should have a medical check-up. What I wanted from him, I said, was not a cardiograph but a certificate for Frau Nehlsen. When in Berlin I would call on him and not leave his house without it. He promised to produce it if I would help him with the legal wording.

It was fairly late before Wohlgemuth went off to the Dom Hotel, having drunk nothing but coffee and soda water. I was amazed at the energy of this *bon viveur*. As he left he said that he would go to Leverkusen early next morning and call again on his way to Heidelberg. I said that I would be lunching early and driving down to Hohkeppel to my wife immediately afterwards; if he was in time he could lunch with me. He arrived punctually for lunch next day.

During lunch, so our maid said later, I had been 'most peculiar'; my head had hung down and I had also been odd during the drive to Hohkeppel. I know nothing of all this. I merely remember taking Wohlgemuth to the front door and showing him the way on to the Berlin autobahn. He had telephoned Heidelberg but had been unable to obtain the call he wanted and had said that he would drive straight back to Berlin. Four years later, during the proceedings against him, it emerged that he had never been to Leverkusen and did not go back to Berlin but had set off in the opposite direction to Bonn to see his 'former nurse'. As I later discovered S.S.-Brigadeführer Heinz Jost was living in Heidelberg at the time.

What was all this about? With the pills which he had given me to stop me smoking Wohlgemuth was testing my resistance to some form of drug. This he involuntarily admitted in September 1964 when being questioned by a reporter for an illustrated paper who accused him of having drugged me and abducted me into East Berlin; he replied that one had 'first to test out' the possibilities of abducting a man.

My wife flew to Berlin with me. She had unwillingly decided to do so because, on our return from our weekend in Hohkeppel, she had found a message from the firm of Siemens to say that their special X-ray apparatus was available to her to take photographs of the larynx – an important opportunity for her research work, since the apparatus was unique in Europe. She accordingly overcame her aversion to visiting her ruined native city. We arrived in Berlin on the morning of 15 July and stayed in a private hotel in the Grunewald, the Haus Schätzle. We knew Frau Schätzle well; she and her late husband had previously run the world-famous Eden Hotel in the Budapester Strasse. Prince Louis Ferdinand was in one of the adjacent rooms and my secretary, Vera Schwarte, in the other.

My engagement diary for Berlin was full and Frau Schwarte had also prepared for me a memo sheet on which were the telephone numbers of Frau Nehlsen and Wohlgemuth. I first called Frau

Nehlsen; her lodger told me that she was away and would not be back until next week. I then called Wohlgemuth to remind him about the certificate. I asked him if he would like to dine with us that evening and he accepted at once. As it later emerged, Wohlgemuth had secretly tape-recorded this conversation. In his subsequent defence he said that he had done this 'for fun'. The truth is that he wished to have some proof for the Soviets that he had 'got me on the hook', in case I did not fall into his trap. The Soviets had thought that Wohlgemuth was merely 'blowing his own trumpet' with his stories of his friendship with me – this much the Soviet Colonel Gutshin admitted to me quite openly after my abduction to Moscow. When in Moscow, I also remembered that during this conversation Wohlgemuth had asked whether my wife was with me in Berlin.

The fact that my wife was also in Berlin had ruined Wohlgemuth's plan. From the outset he was determined to lure me into a trap in order – as in fact he did – to drug me in his consulting-rooms; this was why he had suggested a check-up to me. But now my wife was an obstacle. Undoubtedly his reason for coming to dinner with us in the Schlichter restaurant was to test the ground. He drank coffee and suddenly asked my wife whether she would not like to have a check-up from him one day. She could come to his consulting-rooms with me!

I thought that this meddlesome attitude was due to mere medical vainglory. My wife said that she felt very well and had no need of a doctor. Had she no confidence in him, Wohlgemuth then asked. 'Why should I have confidence in you?' my wife replied. 'I don't know you at all.' Wohlgemuth, the 'ladies' man', was not used to such an answer. He proposed that we go out somewhere nice with him, but we refused with thanks. Wohlgemuth then drank his coffee and left, saying that he still had a patient to visit. This was a lie. After my kidnapping it was established that he had gone to his girl-friend; she later told the court that he had behaved oddly that evening. Had we 'gone out' with him, he would simply have driven us to some spot in the Eastern sector previously agreed with the Soviets. There was still no Berlin Wall.

All this happened on Saturday, 17 July 1954. On the following Monday I was sitting over after-lunch coffee in the Haus Schätzle with my secretary and a member of my staff, when the head waiter announced that Dr Wohlgemuth was in the hall and wished to speak to me (my wife was visiting Siemens and lunching in the canteen there). I sent word to him to come in for coffee. The head waiter brought back the answer that he was in his hospital outfit and so could not come into the dining-room; he only wished to speak to me for a moment. I therefore went out; Wohlgemuth was standing at the hall door with a mackintosh over his hospital clothes. He said that he had been visiting a patient in the neighbourhood and only wished to say that he would be free the next evening to draw up the certificate. I proposed that he postpone the matter for a week since Frau Nehlsen would then be back in Berlin and I should be there also since I had another conference on the twenty-seventh.

He would not be in Berlin at that time, Wohlgemuth said, since he was going to Leipzig to see his mother. I had an appointment for the next afternoon with a couple from Potsdam, for whom I had messages from their daughter in Washington. I did not know them but had said to my wife that, if I liked them, I would invite them to dinner. I therefore told Wohlgemuth that I did not know whether I was free next evening. He left saying that he would be in his house and at my disposal from seven o'clock next evening, if I wanted to come. He had come to the hotel simply to be sure of me next day; there was no truth in his story of a visit to a patient in the neighbourhood, as one of his nurses stated in evidence.

On 20 July after the official ceremonies, at which Heuss made a speech and I sat behind Adenauer, there was a lunch at the Schöneberger Ratskeller. After that I drove with my wife and Colonel-General von Falkenhausen to the B.E.A. office on the Kurfürstendamm to postpone our air ticket reservations by a day. Helbig, Head of Berlin Finance, and his wife, whom my brother and I had known as opponents of the régime during the war, wanted to see me again and make the acquaintance of my wife. They had invited us to lunch next day. To make use of my time in Berlin I also made a rendezvous for the following day with a French colleague. A British colleague had invited us to dinner the following evening.

Having dropped Falkenhausen, we drove back from the B.E.A. office to our hotel, where I was expecting the Potsdam couple and my wife a Siemens engineer. The latter was the first to arrive. My wife introduced me to him and then went to talk to him in another room. The Potsdam couple appeared and had tea with me but refused my invitation to dinner since they were otherwise engaged. I went up to our room, took off my suit which was far too hot, and lay down.

I awoke thinking that I might as well use the time to go and see Wohlgemuth. I ordered the hotel car and asked Frau Schätzle to tell my wife, who was still talking, that I was going into town but would be back for dinner. In Wohlgemuth's consulting-room I had to wait. A young lady was in the big waiting-room as well as me. Suddenly Wohlgemuth came rushing in and greeted me effusively: 'My good chap, you're here! I didn't think you'd come. I'll be ready in a moment.' He took the young lady out and whispered something to her.

Wohlgemuth soon returned. 'I must just have a quick bite to eat,' he said. 'I haven't had any lunch. Then we'll go over to my house in the Litzenburger Strasse and do the certificate.' He took me into his private room and ordered a tray, offering me coffee. Since it was a rainy day I had on a mackintosh which I had not taken off in my hurry. I asked Wohlgemuth how he came to have another house in the Litzenburger Strasse, only 500 yards away. He had taken it on from his ex-wife, he said. I knew nothing of her but believed what he said. He called a nurse and asked her to bring in the Nehlsen files.

While Wohlgemuth ate I smoked and drank my coffee, standing in order to hurry him along. At one moment I went to the lavatory next door, still without taking off my mackintosh. 'Come along,' Wohlgemuth said, putting on his mackintosh and placing the Nehlsen files under his arm. His Ford was standing outside the door and he asked me to get in. As he turned the ignition key he said: 'I have forgotten something. I must just go over to my accountant and fetch something,' mentioning a street in the neighbourhood which I knew but can now no longer remember. I really had not the time, I said; would he please drive me back to the hotel since my wife was waiting for me for dinner. 'It won't take a moment,' Wohlgemuth said, and drove off; he crossed the Kurfürstendamm and turned into Grolmann-strasse with screaming tyres; I saw large drops of rain on the windscreen and the bonnet. Then I remember no more. When I came to myself I was lying on a sofa in a house in Berlin-Karlshorst belonging to the Soviet secret service.

25

Escape or Suicide?

I WAS lying in a darkened room. What I saw as I woke up seemed to me like a bad dream. The double doors to the adjacent room were wide open and in it I could see three strapping men in blue uniform; somewhat apart from them was a buxom woman in a white smock with a white kerchief over her head; beside her was a small dark-brown leather suitcase. Her head hung down; she was asleep. The men were smoking; one was reading a newspaper, another a book and the third was watching me. The door to a farther room was ajar and I could hear men speaking Russian. I was suddenly wide awake but I did not move.

I was lying under an army blanket without coat or shoes; my shirt-collar was open and my tie had gone; so had my wristwatch. I turned on my side as if sleeping uneasily. Through the crook of my right arm I could observe my surroundings precisely. The men thought that I was still asleep. I understood a few words of Russian from the other room – when Hitler and Stalin had formed their alliance against the Western Powers I had begun to learn Russian since a Berlin–Moscow airline was to be set up. Whenever I had flown to Berlin after the war I had wondered what I should do in the event of an emergency landing in the Soviet zone. I had always provided my staff with false papers for these journeys, but I could never have concealed my own identity from the Russians.

I considered my situation. Never before in my life had I been unconscious. I could remember Wohlgemuth putting his raincoat on over his doctor's white coat and saying, 'Come along.' He had delivered me into the hands of the Russians. Why? With what object? I could find no answer. Seventeen months later, after escaping back to the West, I heard that that night Wohlgemuth had left a letter in his West Berlin apartment saying that he 'might come under suspicion' because I had wished to remain in East Berlin. In the middle of the night he told his lawyer over the telephone that he was going into East Berlin since he had an appointment in the Charité.

He hoped that my abduction would bring him the position refused to him by Sauerbruch in the surgical clinic of the Charité. But he never got it. Professor Felix, Sauerbruch's pupil and successor, knew Wohlgemuth too well to employ him in the clinic. Wohlgemuth maintained that Felix had refused him simply because of his communist views. The Soviet secret service, however, demanded that Wohlgemuth's medical qualifications be checked by Russian doctors in Moscow and Wohlgemuth must have made a bad impression. One of the Russian doctors had apparently said to his face that he was 'a filthy fellow'. Instead of his post in the Charité he was given as reward for my abduction a well-paid job in a People's Police hospital in Bad Saarow in the Soviet zone.

What did the Russians want with me? I mulled over the problem but, as I lay on that sofa, could not make head or tail of it. Better lie quite still, I thought – I did not know how best to behave. Should I jump up and make a scene? Madness! The three men would seize me and hold me while the fat woman in the white smock pushed into me a needle from her bag. The whole thing is unreal, I said to myself. I knew what ways and means the Russians could use to put an end to me, but I also knew that I was powerless against drugs, some chemical in my food or injections.

Should I commit suicide? I could not have done so. My every movement was closely watched – even my sleep. The most disturbing thought was that I had no idea where I was or what these Russians wanted with me. Finally I made up my mind to wait for the morning to find out what they did want. So I went to sleep again. But, as I later found out, it was daytime, not night.

When I next woke a man was pacing up and down the room. He was dressed in Western fashion and had a pleasant face with a striking white streak in his hair. Here is someone I can talk to, I thought, so I stood up and asked: 'Where am I?' 'With good friends,' he said; 'How do you feel?' I lost my temper. 'Where am I?' I asked again; 'Where is Dr Wohlgemuth?' He did not answer. I shouted at him: 'With good friends, you say! What's been done to me is pure gangsterism. I want to get out of here!' The presence of the three men in the adjacent room reminded me how totally helpless I was. I could achieve nothing by shouting and raging. I lay down on the sofa again.

The man with the white streak in his hair continued to pace up and down, went into the adjacent room, came back again and turned on a radio which stood in a corner. Apparently he could not find the station he wanted and turned it off reluctantly. Then he came across to me, stood in front of me on my sofa and said gruffly: 'Doctor, we can't go on like this for ten days. Otherwise we shall have to do something else!' He had lost patience. I stood up and asked for a glass of water.

He went into the next room and spoke to the others. Then he returned with a bottle of soda water, followed by three young fellows carrying glasses and a bottle of brandy. I was given a glass of soda water. Then 'White Streak' offered me a brandy which did me good. Meanwhile I saw my coat hanging over a chair. There were conspicuous marks on the right breast and sleeve and I later found similar caked patches on my trousers. At some stage while unconscious I must have been sick.

'White Streak' drank to me saying 'To good friendship'. I answered him and the atmosphere changed. He called himself Michev and introduced me to the other 'friends' by name, but I took little notice since the names were all certainly false. Michev asked if I was hungry and would like something to eat. He took me into the next room where was a sumptuously laid table with caviare and other *hors d'œuvres*.

On the walls of the dining-room were incredibly tawdry copies of some pictures of the Rhinemaidens. They leapt to the eye and drew my attention to a thick, but threadbare, red curtain covering the window. At the top I noticed a small slit through which I could see that it was twilight outside. I thought it was dawn but it got darker and darker. I had therefore been unconscious for a whole night and a whole day. The Russians invited me to eat, saying that I must 'build myself up' since I had eaten nothing for over forty-eight hours.

Initially the Russians were clearly out to treat me well and I had no difficulty in putting on an honest poker-face. Michev was the only one who spoke German; the others conversed in Russian but they too toasted me with 'good friendship'. After the meal we went back into the room where I had woken up. My attitude had undoubtedly contributed to a relaxation of the atmosphere.

In my office, and also in the Ministry, we had often considered how one should behave in the situation in which I now found myself.

I had always insisted that, once a prisoner of the East, resistance was futile and that anyone caught should seek ways and means of escaping by collaborating without giving away any important secrets. I based this view on the memory of my friend Captain Ludwig Gehre who, early in 1944, had successfully outwitted the Gestapo by this method. All I knew at the moment was that the Russians clearly wanted me alive.

I asked Michev what they really wanted from me. 'Well now,' he said, 'we will work together. You will be all right, Doctor.' 'What am I to work on?' I asked. 'The General' would discuss that with me, he said; if I worked well with him, we should become good friends. I wanted to speak to 'the General' at once, but he said that that would only be possible next day. So I still did not know what the Russians wanted. While we were talking another man came into the room. He called himself Scholz and presented himself as a Volga German. He asked me how I felt. I pointed to the bottles and said that nothing could be better. He replied, equally sarcastically, that he quite understood that I must first become accustomed to my new surroundings.

I could 'work' for them far better, I said to Scholz, if they would release me; I would give a written undertaking to that effect; after all, I could be far more useful to them in my office. 'You can't go back,' Scholz said. 'You've already been here two days.' This confirmed that I had been unconscious for the previous day and night at the least. On behalf of 'the General' Scholz obtained my confirmation that I was ready to 'collaborate'. Having thus ostensibly committed myself unconditionally, a bed was rigged up for me on the sofa. Two men remained in the adjacent room to watch me through the open door as I slept.

On the next morning the thick curtains covering the windows had disappeared and the room was airy. I wanted to wash and shave. Some telephoning took place and after a time a young man brought me a brand-new electric shaver – they were clearly not prepared to trust me with a razor blade! For breakfast I was given a cup of coffee with lemon. Then I had nothing to do but wait, still under guard, for 'the General'. Meanwhile I tried to find out where I was by walking up and down in front of the open window. The garden round the house was a complete wilderness. A few hundred yards away I could see lower middle-class houses with gardens, but no recognisable landmarks. Somewhere in the distance, behind the houses and gardens, I could hear the familiar sound of the metro. I could not, therefore, be very far from Berlin.

A waiter in a white coat and apron came in from the kitchen and laid the table in the dining-room with all sorts of cold food and drink. Then 'the General' appeared accompanied by an interpreter. He was tall and slim, in a dark blue suit and with gold-rimmed spectacles and greeted me in friendly fashion; he offered me cigarettes and vodka and said that he was glad that I had decided to collaborate with him; that was a 'good decision'. His name was Eugen Pitovranov.

He invited me politely to the table, urged me to eat and then said through the interpreter that from now on I should 'no longer think backwards – never think back – only think ahead'. This meant that he did not wish to enter into any discussion with me about my kidnapping. I asked him where I actually was. 'In Karlshorst' (East Berlin), he replied and this answer I had to accept from him.

I tried to convince the General that I had resigned myself to my situation. Tactically I thought it best to ask him as few questions as possible and let everything come from him. Since he talked to me through the interpreter, I had time to think up my answers. Fortunately I still had both the energy and strength of nerve to remain calm.

Over after-lunch coffee Pitovranov broached the subject of 'the work'. 1 was a clever and experienced man, he said, and a good German patriot; he knew how I had fought against Hitler and I could be proud of that. I should now think of my brother and my friends who had been murdered by the Nazis for their part in the Hitler plot and I must pursue my struggle against the Hitler fascists. That was my duty – 'For a new Germany!' the interpreter concluded. Pitovranov added in German: '*Deutschland über alles* – but another Germany!'

I asked what he proposed. If I worked well, he said, I need have no worries; I would be quite all right with them. In addition, under Soviet protection, I was now secure against my deadly enemies in the Republic, the militarists and the fascists. General Gehlen and his people had always been set on getting rid of me; he had precise information on the subject. Even during my absence in America, he said, Gehlen agents had tried to approach my wife; I must think of her safety and take steps for her to join me as soon as possible.

Pitovranov's story seemed to me to lack all credibility. Nevertheless, on that very day General Gehlen was asked by the Bonn

Ministry of the Interior what explanation he would give for my disappearance. 'Once a traitor, always a traitor,' was his answer. Dumbfounded by this, Ritter von Lex, the State Secretary, asked him to explain. He was clearly referring to my wartime contacts with the Western Powers on behalf of my friends in the Resistance. For four years, von Lex objected, he had always stressed how well he had been able to work with me; if Gehlen had always thought me a traitor, why had not he and the Minister been informed? Gehlen had no answer.

So long as I was in the power of the Russians I would not admit, even to myself, that 'my colleague' Gehlen and his staff had been working against me. Through its agents in the Gehlen organisation, however, the Soviet secret service knew better. I only realised all this after my release from prison in July 1958. Until then I had not really understood either the motives or the purposes of the Russians in abducting me. The full explanation only appeared with Kim Philby's and Trevor-Roper's books – but this will be dealt with later.

The fact that after my disappearance from West Berlin Herr Gehlen had described me to my superiors as a 'traitor' was no slur on my honour. I had never been pledged to Hitler either ideologically or by personal oath – as he had. Herr Gehlen fought for Hitler's Germany until total catastrophe had become inevitable. Then he went over to the Americans, taking with him the Wehrmacht's files on the East.

At the time, therefore, General Pitovranov's remarks about Gehlen seemed absurd. I was none the less astonished that in this very interview he should launch out into a disquisition about the reunification of Germany. It reminded me of Stalin's proposals of March 1952 and sounded quite sensible and serious. But I still had no idea what I was really to 'work' on. Pitovranov summoned a batman and gave him instructions which obviously concerned me. To me he said that he must get back to work; everything I needed could be provided.

In the late afternoon I was taken by a circuitous route to another house. It was a stately villa in the Tresckow-Allee, Karlshorst, in the Soviet restricted zone. Here I found a new house staff and new guards. They were all very young, reticent but invariably polite; the house manager and General's interpreter was an ash-blonde young Russian named Iroff. A *soigné* Russian in his late thirties appeared.

He was called Chernov and belonged, so he told me, to the diplomatic service.

Chernov brought West Berlin newspapers with him, and so I could read for the first time about the sensation caused by my disappearance from West Berlin – and also the abuse and slanders hurled at me. I was completely defenceless and found these accusations in the Press more agonising than all the pictures of what the Russians might do to me which, with my knowledge of their resources and methods, I had conjured up for myself.

The campaign against me in the Federal Republic after my disapperance from West Berlin provided the Russians with a welcome occasion to put pressure on me and argue that existence had now become completely impossible for me back there; I should now place my confidence in them and start an entirely fresh life 'under their protection'. Pitovranov said: 'All your enemies are in the Federal Republic and all your friends in the People's Republic. If you "work" with us, the Soviet Union will be behind you – many millions of people, the entire "peace camp". You must continue to fight with us against the Hitler fascists.' He held out to me the prospect of a career as a 'patriot' in a reunited Germany. I did not understand what his proposal really was.

I visualised, of course, that sooner or later the Russians would try to find out as much as they could about my office and my previous existence. I was prepared for them to try all sorts of methods, including brain-washing, but was determined to do away with myself if I ever felt that I was losing control. The only possibility I could see of 'working' usefully with the Soviet secret service was to evaluate for them agents' reports from the West. That would mean, I thought, that I should not return to the West empty-handed, if I contrived to escape.

My 'work' began with a 'proposal' by Pitovranov. I was to state over the radio that I had fled to the People's Republic because of continuous persecution by the Gehlen organisation. I said at once that no sensible person in the Federal Republic could or would believe this. Pitovranov thought for a moment and said: 'We must think about that.' I must, however, make some statement over the radio, he said. It occurred to me that this would entail a move from Karlshorst to the transmitting station and that this might provide an opportunity to escape. I accordingly agreed to make some statement over the East Berlin radio.

I said to Pitovranov that I must first be given an opportunity to inform my wife and prepare my broadcast, that my wife was not safe in the Federal Republic and should join me. In the office we had agreed that, if any one of us were caught in the East, he should try to indicate the fact to some person in the West, but we had unfortunately not established a code-word for this purpose. Pitovranov was pleased that I was willing to speak over the radio and departed, commissioning Chernov to ensure that the letter to my wife was delivered in West Berlin at once.

I asked for a sheet of paper and on the spur of the moment wrote: 'Circumstances which I cannot yet explain have compelled me to take a step which I will explain later. . . .' The words 'yet' and 'compelled' were underlined. Then followed a couple of perfectly innocent sentences about power of attorney for my wife and a request to inform my father. Chernov cast his eye over the letter and made me write the address on the back, saying that he would have the envelope typed. Then he hurried away. My wife received the letter by airmail from West Berlin on the next day; she grasped its meaning correctly, as did my staff in the office and my Allied colleagues. This was clear from my wife's letter in reply, sent to a post-box number given by Chernov. My wife had realised that, in my situation, I might commit suicide. In her letter she said: 'The gift of life is the greatest of all possessions. Think of this and look after your health.' These words subsequently prevented me committing suicide during my moments of deepest depression while in the Soviet Union; for the moment they encouraged me to pursue the tactics on which I had embarked *vis-à-vis* the Russians.

Pitovranov arrived fairly early next morning with two other Russians and asked what my ideas were for my broadcast statement. A call to reunification, I replied. This he found excellent and I was pleased that he had dropped his idea about a 'flight from the Gehlen organisation'. He now had another 'proposal', however – his tactics towards me were always concealed behind 'proposals'. He showed me a cutting from a West German newspaper reporting that Dr Schröder, the Federal Minister, intended to relieve me of my office as soon as the Republic was a sovereign state. One of the Russians accompanying Pitovranov, clearly a propaganda expert, said that this provided the best reason for 'my flight' to the People's Republic. I resisted this since I had no wish to attack Schröder. Eventually, however, I gave way since the Russian propaganda expert, who

spoke German, began to draft: 'To my German fellow-citizens. . . .'
Anyone over there who heard this form of address, I thought, could
only laugh. It was typical Russian jargon translated into German. So
I gave the 'expert' best.

This was the background to my radio statement that I had 'taken
a deliberate step and established contact with the Germans in the
East in order to safeguard the German people from a new war and
to reunite them'. The primary reason given was that 'with his
statement to journalists to the effect that, on the achievement of
sovereignty, only persons above all suspicion could be entrusted with
internal security duties, the Federal Minister of the Interior had
rendered it impossible for me to work in my office'.

My radio broadcast was one of those really big lies of which Hitler
said in *Mein Kampf* that 'in politics they will always win because the
big lie is invariably believed by the masses'. The only part which
could have made my statement plausible to the unthinking masses
both in the West and the East was the passage attributing my
flight to this pronouncement by Dr Schröder, the Federal Minister
of the Interior.

The drafting of my twenty-six-line radio broadcast took the entire
morning. Following my tactics of asking no questions, I waited to be
taken to the radio station. Instead of this Michev appeared with two
other Russians and a tape-recorder. I had not thought of this; I had
merely imagined that there would be some security arrangement such
as I had known in the Soldatensender Calais whereby transmission
could be interrupted instantaneously, had I deviated from the agreed
text by a single word or shouted into the microphone that I had been
kidnapped. Since, however, I had stated my readiness to broadcast,
I now had to speak on this tape if I was to abide by my tactics *vis-à-
vis* the Russians. Those in the West who heard it and knew me said
that I had spoken quite differently from normal and had sounded
completely unnatural with audibly heavy breathing.

It may be that, after my radio broadcast, the Soviets believed that
there could be no going back to the Federal Republic for me. In any
case Pitovranov now made a new 'proposal' – that I apply to the
East German government for political asylum. Purely a matter of
form, he said! This I did at once in a three-line letter to Grotewohl,
the Minister-President, for which a typewriter was made available.
In doing so I tried a trick, in the hope that one day the letter might
serve as documentary evidence that I had been under Soviet

constraint. In addition to my name in the letter heading I typed the address of the house in the Soviet restricted zone in which I was – '67 Tresckow-Allee, Berlin-Karlshorst'. Pitovranov took the letter and drove off in his SIM. Half an hour later Michev appeared with a request to rewrite the letter to Grotewohl with the heading showing only 'Berlin, 24 July 1954'.

My few words over the radio were followed by a flood of correspondence from the Federal Republic, from communist and non-communist countries and from the Soviet zone. The mass of appreciative, indeed effusive, letters filled me with dismay, primarily at the ease with which men can be manipulated. My wife later told me that one of our neighbours, an ex-colonel, appeared and kissed her hand, saying that I had done heroic service to the reunification of our country. It must have been the chorus of applause from the West which induced the Russians to make a new 'proposal' – that I should give a press conference in East Berlin. This could not have been their original intention and was certainly not the motive for my kidnapping – they could not, after all, know how I would behave as their prisoner. The care with which my every movement was watched until my arrival in Moscow showed me that they had considered the possibility of suicide and were determined to prevent it. I agreed to this press conference since I would have to be taken out of the Soviet restricted zone to give it.

The press conference was rehearsed for almost three weeks. Its theme was: Against remilitarisation and renazification in West Germany and for reunification. I knew the East's propaganda slogans on the subject like my ABC and I put them all down on paper for my address. A group of eight, sometimes ten, Russian journalists were in the house from morning to night in order, in Pitovranov's words, 'to advise me'. In the office I had read the Eastern press and reports of East Berlin press conferences almost every day and I was confident that I could trot out the current phrases and platitudes and so present the Eastern journalists with a masterpiece of communist propaganda. My appearance in East Berlin became a world sensation, but only because the Western press of the time, as indeed that of today, was no match for Soviet psychological warfare methods.

I started on the assumption that I should be speaking only to Eastern journalists or those from the West who would be invited to East Berlin because of their left-wing tendencies but who would be of no significance in the formation of opinion in West Germany. I had no inhibitions about speaking to such an audience. I never imagined that the more serious Western press would send their best-known representatives to my conference. I was, however, perplexed about Pitovranov's 'proposal' for a press conference when I found that I was being 'advised' by Russian press experts.

My draft of my statement was translated into Russian and two copies of it taken from the house. An amended draft returned and was translated back into German. Obviously my Russian 'advisers' were being steered from the background. I played the imbecile, proposed certain other general propaganda slogans against re-militarisation and in favour of reunification and then became an onlooker while these were translated and taken away once more. However, the Soviet background functionary soon perceived that my 'advisers' were getting nowhere with me. He suddenly appeared with General Pitovranov, who introduced him as 'Comrade Michailov' from Moscow.

Michailov was a senior functionary, treated with respect by all the other Russians; he was a tough type, of that intermediate generation now ruling Soviet Russia. Instinctively I sensed in him a tough opponent, which he later proved to be in the Soviet Union. When he arrived with Pitovranov he sat down at the dining-room table without further ado, took the various drafts of the press statement and compared the German and Russian texts. He spoke quite good German but insisted on every phrase being explained in detail by a perfect interpreter.

Michailov wanted 'names and facts' from me, but I was not able to help him very much. He was not interested in obvious cases of renazification such as Adenauer's appointment of Dr Theo Oberländer, a man with a conspicuous Nazi past, as Minister for Refugees. He involved me in a discussion on the E.D.C. treaties. I had not read them; the drafts had not interested me since I knew that the French were opposed to the E.D.C., as the voting in the French parliament had shown. He was afraid that the E.D.C. might become a reality – the Soviets were genuinely anxious about this at the time. I was sure that Mendès-France would 'torpedo' the E.D.C. and said so, but Michailov was sceptical.

He then gave me a disquisition on the E.D.C., NATO policy and the aims of the West German 'revanchists'. He knew his subject very well. I found this astonishing and was at a loss to explain it. The mystery was eventually solved by Anatole Golytsin, the Soviet secret service colonel already mentioned: through ex-S.S. agents in the Gehlen organisation who owed their lives to the Russians the latter knew everything which was or might be of importance to them in West German politics. 'Where is Bormann?' Michailov asked in passing. To this day no one knows whether he is dead or alive. I told him so, adding that I would also like to know where Müller, the head of the Gestapo, was. Was he perhaps in Russia? I received no answer.

Michailov prepared the conference according to his own ideas. Unknown to me, Dr Adenauer had handed him a propaganda *coup*. While in his holiday home Bühler-Höhe, near Baden-Baden, Adenauer had given an interview on the radio of which I knew nothing; referring to my radio statement he had said that the worst feature was that I had said that 'I knew of a secret clause to the European Defence Community treaty'. I still do not know who or what induced Adenauer to say this. Subsequently he could not remember having done so! In my radio statement I had said not a word about a secret clause to the E.D.C. Michailov, however, knew how to exploit Adenauer's *faux pas* and bring it into my press statement using his own words.

I tried to stop this and told him that, although of course the E.D.C. treaties were secret, there were no special 'secret supplementary agreements'. Nevertheless, what Adenauer had said was more important to Michailov. He dictated the following for my press statement: 'Contrary to what Dr Adenauer has said, I declare, on the basis of my knowledge as President of the Federal Internal Security Office, that secret E.D.C. agreements do exist, which Dr Adenauer is trying to safeguard.'

Michailov was especially insistent that in my press conference I should mention the Gehlen organisation's illegal activity in France; I had only read of this in Swiss press reports, although I had been approached on the subject by a French officer. At the time I placed no more credence in activity by the Gehlen organisation in France than I did in Gehlen's activities against me. Today I am convinced that Michailov knew exactly what he was talking about. When I was hesitant to accept his drafts for the press statements, he would say with heavy sarcasm: 'Hit out or you'll be hit.' This was not the reason, however, why I accepted his drafts; to do so accorded with the tactics I was following and I could see no harm in proclaiming from the communist propaganda stage something which had already been published in the Western press.

Michailov frequently addressed me in somewhat unctuous tones as 'Mr President'. On one occasion, for instance, apparently without relevance to the press conference texts on which he was working, he said: 'You have, of course, received reports from the People's Republic, Mr President?' It would have been stupid to deny this. 'Of course,' I said. 'I'm glad you said that', he replied, stopping his writing and looking up. His expression showed clearly that he had been trying me out. He knew far more about me and my office than, for instance, the Federal Chancellor.

To enable me to carry on a dialogue with the journalists my 'advisers' had drawn up a list of questions and answers for the press conference. The questions included some to be put by Eastern journalists selected for the purpose and others which might possibly be asked by Western journalists. For a final rehearsal Dr Wilhelm Girnus appeared; I knew him by name and also as the secretary of the communist-run East Berlin Committee for German Unity. He had been placed in charge of the press conference by the Russians in order to give it the appearance of a German occasion. Girnus, now teaching in East Berlin University, is an intelligent and highly educated philologist. In September 1964, at an interview during a conference of the International Hegel Society in Salzburg, he told of his introduction to me by the Russians. In this he admitted quite frankly that he had never thought that I had really defected to East Berlin but had believed that I had come on behalf of the British secret service!

For an experienced propagandist like Girnus it was child's play to turn the press conference into a specious world sensation. It proceeded according to plan – until a blonde young female journalist stood up and asked me: 'Have you not written to your wife to say that "circumstances which I cannot yet explain have compelled me to take a step which I will explain later"?' 'Yes, I wrote something like that,' I stammered. 'Even including the word "compelled"?' she then asked. She had discovered the exact wording of my letter to my wife when in Dr Schröder's ante-room. Girnus instinctively sensed danger and shut the girl up, cutting short any further questioning.

The conference took place in the East Berlin Press Club near the Friedrichstrasse Station; my journey there was a grotesque camouflage operation. A convoy of three cars drove ahead of us out of

Karlshorst, a Russian SIM with German number-plates and two Wartburgs. I was driven in an armoured SKODA, as I was told ten years later by an East German official driver who had defected to the West. Ahead of us drove an official East German Government SIM with flashing blue light and a passenger who resembled me half-hidden behind the curtains. Three Russian guards were with me in the SKODA, which looked like an escort vehicle. Clearly the press conference would provide no opportunity for escape. Should I shout out that I had been kidnapped and was a prisoner of the Soviets? It would have been sheer madness. Though Stalin was no longer alive, Stalinism still ruled and I wished to return to the West alive in order to prove that in everything I did in the East I had been under psychological pressure.

Soviet secret service officials were sitting behind curtains on either side of the stage from which I spoke. The first row of seats was occupied by members of the East Berlin security service which also had men scattered among the journalists. None of the leading Western journalists who, to my astonishment, had come to the conference, noticed that the girl who asked her question had spoken the vital word which could have blown the whole conference sky high. Most of them knew me personally and they knew all about me. Yet, obsessed with the sensational aspect, they simply listened to the speech written out for me by Michailov and then asked questions which did not include a single one for which I had not been re-hearsed by the Russians. Years later, after my release from prison, Sefton Delmer, the *Daily Express* star reporter, said: 'It was complete nonsense for us to put questions as if we were in Bonn. I ought to have said: "Doctor John, what you tell us here does not interest us. Come across through the Brandenburger Tor. Then we can talk".'

Commenting on my statements to the Press, Chancellor Adenauer said: 'They carry the stamp of falsehood.' Allen Dulles declared: 'What Dr John has said behind the Iron Curtain is not of interest.' General Clay, the former head of United States Military Government in Germany stated: 'What Dr John said in East Berlin contradicts everything which he has so far said and done in his life. There's something wrong here.' It was, therefore, possible to perceive the truth about my appearance in East Berlin, particularly since I then disappeared from the scene and a whole series of people tried in vain to contact me in East Berlin. In fact, shortly after the conference, I was taken to Moscow. The world press had helped the Russians score a considerable victory in the Cold War. My Russian press 'advisers' were pleased. One of them remarked how stupid the people in Bonn were not to have sent a delegation to East Berlin immediately after my radio broadcast with a demand to the East German government for an interview with me – as the K.G.B. does in the case of Russian defectors. I had never set eyes on any of the 'responsible East German politicians' to whom I was supposed to have talked when asking for political asylum – not even on Herr Ulbricht!

26

'Rest-cure' on the Soviet Riviera

AFTER the press conference I was taken back at once to the Soviet restricted zone under the same security arrangements. I was deeply depressed at being totally cut off from the outside world. Pitovranov said that I must now rest and recover. This suited me; I said that I would like to go to the Harz or the Thüringer Wald, hoping to escape from there. Pitovranov, however, said that a rest-cure in the Crimea would do me more good and held out the prospect of an 'invitation' there.

In fact, after the press conference, I did feel totally exhausted. Heinz Stöckert, an ex-Wehrmacht captain who was working for the Soviet secret service in Karlshorst at the time and three years later defected to West Germany, told me that I had been 'prepared' for the press conference with artificial ingredients in my food. When he said this I remembered that, one day before the press conference, I had felt very unwell; I had had to lie down and the Russians were very solicitous about me. At the time I had thought that this was mere nervous exhaustion resulting from the extreme and continuous tension. I still felt myself strong enough, however, to hold on and try to obtain sufficient freedom of movement to escape. For this reason I had slipped into my press statement the words: 'I am *intellectually* as free as I have ever been.' Anyone hearing this could have realised that I was not otherwise free but was still in control of my senses. This 'invitation' to the Crimea, however, considerably reduced my hopes of escape.

It could not have been the original Soviet intention simply to use me for propaganda purposes, since they could not know how I would behave as their prisoner. However, I found it disquieting that even after the press conference they did not begin to question me. Probably, I thought, they are reserving this until they can do what they like with me in the Soviet Union.

I was kept under strict guard as if in prison and had lost all contact with the outside world. Pitovranov, Chernov and a colonel named Vadim Vitoldovich Gutshin rang the changes in talking and eating with me. We mostly talked generalities but I realised that Gutshin was the secret service man specially detailed to deal with me. He was rather thick-set, in his mid-thirties, spoke perfect German and knew his Berlin intimately since his father had been stationed in Berlin as a diplomat and he had grown up there. If I had met him on the Kurfürstendamm it would never have occurred to me that he might be a Russian.

Gutshin said that he would accompany me to the Soviet Union and spend his holidays with me in the Crimea. Pitovranov arrived one evening and said that they had arrested an agent on the Potsdamer Platz who was carrying two revolvers and some poison and had been sent from West Germany to liquidate me; for security reasons I must therefore be secretly removed from Berlin as soon as possible and taken to the Soviet Union. Perhaps he wanted to frighten me; he can hardly have genuinely thought me so gullible.

Before being taken to Moscow in an aircraft of the Soviet secret service I was the centrepiece for a number of occasions designed to make the general public believe that I had crossed into East Berlin of my own free will. One morning I was driven, under the usual convoy arrangements, to the Stalin-Allee where Henselmann, the municipal architect, showed me his plans for the reconstruction of Berlin; we then proceeded on to Professor Correns, the noted chemist, who in his capacity as Chairman of the National Front, served the East German régime as an 'extra'. I walked with both of them a few paces down the Stalin-Allee to the Warsaw Café where the security service had cordoned off a balcony and I was photographed with Henselmann and Correns. Shortly thereafter these pictures were broadcast to the world to show that I was a free man in East Berlin, whereas in reality I had already been taken secretly to Moscow. The security precautions for my public appearance in the Stalin-Allee and the Warsaw Café resembled those for a prominent politician. Apparently innocent passers-by walked in front of and behind us, but they were in reality secret policemen with their female counterparts.

A few days later I was taken by the familiar convoy, this time reinforced by two security cars, along the empty autobahn to Dresden. There I was to talk on television with Friedrich Paulus, the ex-Field Marshal and Commander-in-Chief of the Sixth Army annihilated at Stalingrad. The evening before Gutshin told me how Paulus had been converted into a 'freedom fighter'. When taken prisoner he had initially been unapproachable and had refused to discuss politics; he had insisted on being recognised and treated as a field marshal and had demanded that the necessary badges of rank be obtained for him through the Red Cross. Hitler forbade the Red Cross to do this, whereupon prisoner craftsmen had manufactured field marshal's badges for Paulus. Exasperated by Hitler's petty vindictiveness, Paulus had become increasingly accessible for political discussion. 'After wrestling with himself and as a result of vehement discussions,' Gutshin said, 'Paulus has turned himself into what he now is, a soldier and fighter of the peace camp.'

The meeting with Paulus took place in the office of Herr Weidauer, the Burgomaster of Dresden. Michev and another Russian who had guided the convoy remained in the cars outside. Microphones and cameras had already been installed in the Burgomaster's room. Paulus was led in by an attendant and 'Comrade Burgomaster' spoke a few formal words of greeting for the occasion of 'this historic meeting between two German fighters for peace'. Cameras whirred and clicked. Paulus made a gesture of dissent, saying, 'I have agreed with the Ministry of the Interior that I should give no interviews without their consent.' Comrade Burgomaster was taken aback.

Scholz, to whom I have already referred, came forward as my manager and said to Paulus: 'You need have no worry on that score; I will settle it all in Berlin. We will in any case take a picture or two and I will take the sound-track with me.' Nobody questioned Scholz's authority. Paulus and I discovered that we both came from Hesse and, when I asked him about the reasons for the failure to relieve the Sixth Army at Stalingrad, a lively and objective discussion developed. He laid the blame on Hitler and Manstein. The photographers and cameramen were then dismissed and Comrade Burgomaster took us in to lunch. Afterwards, with our entourage, we took 'a walk' to the Zwinger restaurant. Paulus and I were never allowed to say a word out of earshot of the others.

I was able, however, to observe Paulus closely and I thought back to the descriptions of his appearance eight years before, in field marshal's uniform and full decorations, in front of the International

Military Tribunal in Nuremberg as a witness for the Soviet prosecution. Now he was a broken man; he no longer even had the strength to play with any conviction the puppet role allotted him by the Russians. Hitler had demanded that he commit suicide as a patriotic example to the German people. Stalin had regarded him as an advertisement for the officers and men of the Free Germany National Committee and the League of German officers in the Soviet Union. During the drive back I ruminated over the fate of this man. Finally I said to myself that he was not to be condemned unless one really knew what means and methods had been employed to turn him into the man I had met.

Did the Russians intend to turn me into a political puppet, a political tool like Paulus? This idea was always in my mind and I could find no reasonable explanation for the fact that I had not been allowed to meet any of the 'influential Germans' with whom I had ostensibly collaborated in order to reunite our Fatherland and save it from war. Two further events seemed to support these ideas.

A few days after my radio broadcast Schmitt-Wittmack, a C.D.U. Bundestag deputy from Hamburg whom I did not even know by name, fled to East Berlin. According to Pitovranov he had done so in order to follow my 'patriotic' example; in fact, as I found out from the West German newspapers a year later after my return from Moscow, my office had stumbled on the trail of his illegal contacts with the East. He was 'cared for' not by the Russians but by the East German security service and was not subjected to a three-week preparation for his press conference as I had been. He appeared at a press conference only two days after his flight into East Berlin and thereafter was a completely free man.

It seemed to me suspicious that Schmitt-Wittmack, my alleged young disciple, was not brought to see me nor did he try to make contact with me. I asked Chernov, and after some beating about the bush he confided to me that another Bundestag deputy would come 'over to us' in the next few days; he was politically far more important than Schmitt-Wittmack and would speak with me. This was the reason why I had not yet been taken to the Soviet Union for my 'cure'. Some days passed but no further Bundestag deputy arrived. Then one evening Pitovranov appeared for dinner. The table was laid with particular care and the *hors d'œuvres* were especially choice. Behind him came a thick-set man with a bloated face and very light hair; he was dressed in the dark-blue suit which was apparently regulation for Soviet secret service functionaries. In his hand he held a bunch of red carnations.

Pitovranov greeted me and made as though to introduce his visitor. The latter, however, anticipated him, bowed awkwardly and said: 'Wollweber.' From press and other reports I knew that he was head of the secret service in the Soviet zone. He handed me the carnations and said that he brought me the congratulations of his government on my 'patriotic step'. Pitovranov poured out vodka and we drank to 'Good Friendship'. Wollweber, once a man full of energy who had set up an underground organisation before the war to sabotage shipping in the major Western ports, was now a sick man; because of his illness he could neither eat nor drink much. Being a reliable Soviet agent and a Soviet citizen, he had presumably been selected to meet me so that at least someone could tell the other East Berlin functionaries that he had spoken to me personally. Perhaps, however, there was another, quite different, motive behind Wollweber's 'visit'.

Dr Harry Soedermann, the world-famous Swedish detective known as 'Revolver Harry', had become a friend of mine in 1951 when Dr Lehr, the Minister of the Interior, had summoned him to Bonn to advise on the formation of a new Federal Criminal Police headquarters. When the news of my disappearance broke, he had at once hurried over from New York, where I had breakfasted with him in the Mayflower Hotel only a month before, and had gone to Cologne to see my wife; he had promised her that he would get me out of East Berlin. He thought that he had a lever since he had saved Wollweber's life during the war.

When the war broke out Wollweber was in Sweden, in prison for illegal subversive activity. At the end of his sentence he was due to be extradited to Germany. His term would have run out at a time when people in Sweden were by no means convinced that Germany would be defeated and, had Wollweber been handed over to the Nazis, he would have faced certain death. Soedermann visited him in his cell and advised him to engineer a quarrel with the warders shortly before the end of his term and to strike one of them. Wollweber did so and was accordingly sentenced to a further term of imprisonment; he therefore continued in prison in Sweden. He repeated these brawls with the warders and so remained in prison until Germany's eventual defeat was obvious. Then he was handed over by the Swedes to the Russians who, after the war, installed him as head of the East German secret service. Soedermann did not succeed in contacting Wollweber, however. He personally delivered a letter to the East Berlin Ministry of State Security asking for an interview with me, but received no answer.

On 24 August I was flown to Moscow accompanied by Gutshin, his nice blonde wife and Pitovranov's mother, a friendly old lady who had been on a visit to Berlin. The evening before Chernov had called on me to say that he would be following shortly to take a holiday in Yalta with his wife and daughter. He also urged me to 'work' in Moscow, once I had recovered, but did not vouchsafe what this 'work' was to be. This was apparently not his province. Since he had always been very approachable, I asked him the whereabouts of the other Bundestag deputy who was due to come 'over to us', what he was called and whether I should know him.

Chernov did not tell me the name but said quite frankly that the deputy had not arrived because the 'rumour' had been spread by the Bonn Ministry of the Interior that I had not gone voluntarily to East Berlin. He chuckled that neither my office nor the Gehlen Organisation knew where I actually was. I then asked when the television interview between Paulus and myself was scheduled for transmission. All he could say was that the 'take' had not been good. As far as I know the interview was never shown.

On the way to Moscow we stopped off in Minsk. Just before we landed Gutshin said: 'You may possibly be asked for your name. You are called Werner Bertram.' I had no travel documents. The aircraft was minutely searched by uniformed frontier police. They found two flower vases which Pitovranov's mother had bought and confiscated them. Foreign pottery is not allowed into the Soviet Union without special authorisation. I was vouched for by Gutshin and asked no questions by any of the police.

Before we landed at a military airfield near Moscow Gutshin told me that we would not be going to a hotel but to a 'villa' outside the city. I had often heard descriptions of these 'villas' in which the Soviets accommodated their 'guests' – a guest-house above ground but with prison cells in the basement fitted out for all sorts of interrogation. On landing Mother Pitovranov said goodbye and drove off in a waiting car; Mme Gutshin departed in another car with her bags. Gutshin and I were received by three civilians who looked as if they were dressed in their Sunday best.

We drove off in a large black limousine with curtained side-windows, into Moscow and through the city; some of the cupola towers seemed familiar to me from pictures. We drove out into wooded country, by which time it was dark. We stopped at a wooden gate, opened by an old peasant on a horn signal from the car. We entered a garden which was suddenly brilliantly illuminated. Among tall pine trees lay a small wooden house, a *dacha*. I was taken into a reception room and then to the first floor to my bedroom.

I was soon summoned down to dinner – a sumptuous table with Russian *hors d'œuvres* of all sorts, hot dishes and beer or wine to taste. This exaggerated hospitality was a fresh mystery to me. What for? In addition to Gutshin two of those who had received us at the airport were present. The third, the driver, had disappeared into the kitchen. The meal was served by a stately matron in a black satin dress with white cap and apron. She was introduced to me as Anna Sergeyevna.

The three Russians were thoroughly enjoying this 'official' banquet; they conversed with much loud laughter and were continually drinking toasts to me. I looked at the crests on the silver and napkins, and Gutshin said with a laugh: 'We liberated those from a castle in Mecklenburg.' Then, pointing to one of the others, he said: 'This young man will look after you here. He is called Vadim Konstantinovich.' Shortly thereafter Gutshin drove back to town to his wife. They lived in Moscow. As he left he said: 'You are a sensible person. I trust you'll do nothing stupid or make diffi-culties for me.' For a long time I sat at the open window of my bed-room, gazing out at the dark pinewood before me and the beautiful starlit sky above. It was the first night that I slept unguarded.

The next morning Vadim Konstantinovich took me down to an over-generous breakfast. He spoke very good German and I asked: 'What is going to be done with me here?' He replied that he could not say and that I must wait for Gutshin. He took me for a walk down to the Moskva river which flowed by only a few hundred yards away. We strolled along the bank and then back and forth through the pines and birch trees which gave the area its name, 'Silverwood'. When we got back to the *dacha* I asked Vadim Konstantinovich to teach me some Russian. I wanted to have something definite to do in order to take my mind off things.

Vadim Konstantinovich was very approachable; he was in his mid-twenties, a good-looking southerner, intelligent, educated and proved a thoroughly decent fellow. He was very pleased to teach me Russian and said that he would have liked to become a teacher but, since he had passed his examinations with high marks, he had been 'called up into our service'. He was a lieutenant in the secret service and showed me quite openly his official pass with a photograph of himself in full-dress uniform and also a photograph of his wife. We thus established personal contact and were able to talk quite freely on all sorts of political and literary subjects. During my crisis period he proved a real friend and prevented me committing suicide.

Gutshin returned from Moscow with the news that I must be patient for a few more days and remain in the *dacha* until accommodation for our rest-cure on the Black Sea had been arranged. He announced that I would be thoroughly examined next day. Next morning he appeared with three women, one fairly old with a gnarled face, the other two young and pretty, dressed in good, but remarkably old-fashioned, style. They were two female doctors with their nurse. They examined me most conscientiously, one physically, the other neurologically. The nurse took a couple of blood samples from a finger and an ear. Gutshin, acting as interpreter, said that I was in perfect health. Nevertheless, the doctors prescribed drops and powders for me and warned me not to smoke too much. The neurologist said that I needed a good rest but should not lie in the sun.

The days dragged on. To keep me occupied Gutshin brought me a complete edition of Heinrich Heine. Vadim Konstantinovich gave me lessons morning and afternoon and in the intervals took me for walks. He was a sensitive person and sensed my depression which he tried to alleviate by discussing German literature and philosophy with me.

Gutshin also tried to provide some recreation for me, combining his official duty to 'look after' me with his personal interests. He took me by car to the opera where his wife was waiting at a back entrance. We climbed up some back stairs to a box and saw Ulanova dance *Swan Lake*. Looking through a curtain during the interval, I could see in the stalls the 'Red Dean of Canterbury' who was a guest of the Soviet government at the time.

One of Gutshin's duties clearly was to maintain the fiction *vis-à-vis* my wife, my office and the general public both in the West and the Soviet zone that I was still in East Berlin. He informed me that 'it was not desired' that anyone, even including my wife, should find out where I was. I was to answer such letters as still arrived from the 'useful idiots' as if I was in East Berlin. They were addressed, as were those from my wife, to the East Berlin post-box number arranged for me and thence forwarded to Moscow by the secret service courier aircraft. Every morning one of Gutshin's people went to the airport to collect my mail and deliver my letters for Berlin. This pretence was entirely incomprehensible to me and it proved a complete failure. As she later told me, my wife had realised from my letters that I was in Russia, though she did not know where. The Russians have only recently been prepared to admit that I was in the Soviet Union; in the spring of 1969 someone who alleged he was Soviet Lieutenant-Colonel Carpov attempted to prevent the reopening of my case by contacting a representative of the German illustrated weekly *Stern*; he maintained that he had been my Soviet watchdog and tried to prove by photographs that I had walked around Moscow as a free man – but the pictures showed that I had never been alone and had invariably been accompanied by someone.

After ten or twelve days in the *dacha* – I had meanwhile lost all sense of time and date – Gutshin called from Moscow one afternoon and told Vadim Konstantinovich to get me and himself ready for departure for our 'rest-cure'; he would fetch us shortly after midnight. Vadim Konstantinovich could not say where we were going. Gutshin appeared in good time but equally did not say where he was taking me. My apprehension verged on the intolerable when, on entering the black SIM limousine, I saw that Gutshin had with him a German 'Erika' typewriter. I thought this a sure sign that I was being taken for interrogation and that he would draw up the record in German. Why else would he be carrying a German typewriter about in the Soviet Union?

As we emerged on the other side of Moscow and drove on through the night, I asked Gutshin why he needed a German typewriter on our 'rest-cure'. 'We will work together a little,' he said. It sounded so innocent, just as if he had said: 'We'll play a few games of cards together.' I was startled when the car turned down a drive and we alighted in front of a brilliantly lit building, obviously an airport. We went into a large waiting-hall where there was a varied assortment of people, some in oriental garb, the majority dozing while waiting for their flight.

Gutshin made for a door before which stood a militiaman. He opened it on a word from Gutshin and we entered a special waiting-room where we found Mme Gutshin sitting. As her husband remarked, 'she was coming with us because she, too, hadn't had a holiday'. I was now completely nonplussed. What did it all mean? I had had some experience of the use of women in secret service work. Could I be sure that she was really Gutshin's wife? These were my thoughts as I followed her into a twin-engined civil aircraft.

We flew off through the night under a beautiful starlit sky, making an intermediate stop in Kharkov. The machine flew on and, in the silvery glow of dawn, the Black Sea appeared behind a range of mountains. The aircraft flew lower, turned eastwards and passed along the Russian Riviera, a remarkably beautiful sight. Now at last Gutshin told me that we were not taking our 'rest-cure' in the Crimea but farther east along the Black Sea coast. 'Sochi,' he said, pointing to a seaside resort. Shortly thereafter we landed on an emergency airfield. A car with chauffeur was waiting and took us across the Georgian frontier to Gagra. As we drove along the sea front Vadim Konstantinovich waxed lyrical about the local wines, women and dances.

Numerous government holiday homes had turned Gagra into a real spa. We dropped Mme Gutshin at a dazzling-white establishment ornamented with classical pillars and oriental stuccoes. We drove on up into the Caucasus along a mountain road, through an iron gate to a country house surrounded by tall trees, colourful flower-beds and heavily laden orange trees. It had once been the country seat of some Georgian prince. The house manager was waiting for us – a spare old man, still recognisable as an ex-Czarist officer despite his ragged shirt and shabby straw hat.

I was allotted a sitting-room and bedroom on the first floor. A basket of appetising southern fruit stood on the dresser and a bust of Stalin on the writing-desk. Many of the guest-rooms in the house were empty. I asked why Mme Gutshin did not stay with us. This was only permitted for the wives of senior and most senior functionaries, Colonel Gutshin said. Although she was in no way ill, his wife had to take her cure in a government holiday home where regulations were strict and she must take meals as prescribed by the doctors. She might only visit her husband in 'our' country house in the day-time.

For the first few days I was treated as an honoured guest – all one could wish to eat and drink, sea bathing and drives in the Caucasus. In the evenings Gutshin and Vadim Konstantinovich played billiards with astonishing concentration and much excitement on both sides. I watched them but had no wish to play. I drank a great deal of the wine provided but was never drunk. One evening, while playing billiards, Gutshin said: 'Doctor, we won't go out tomorrow. Tomorrow we'll start to work.' So here we were!

After breakfast next day I was taken into a sort of sitting-room with a round table and green leather chairs. There was writing-paper on the table. Gutshin opened a briefcase and took out a thick wadge of photostat copies, threw them across to me and said: 'Look at that.' Before me lay a complete copy of my office's last monthly report to the Federal government, signed by my successor and not yet three weeks old. I was dumbfounded. 'You're a bit surprised?' Gutshin asked triumphantly. The monthly report was a top secret account of my office's latest discoveries. Originally we had made only two copies in addition to the original for the Minister, one for the Federal Chancellor's office and one for my own safe. Later, however, on request from Federal and *Land* Ministers, my Minister had ordered a wider distribution and for almost three years we had been distributing over seventy copies in the Federal Republic as a whole. I had told my Minister and his State Secretary that, with such a wide distribution, I could not guarantee the secrecy of the report. I was therefore not surprised that the Soviet secret service should be able to show me a copy, but I was completely speechless at the speed with which the Soviets had been able to obtain a copy of the last report, now little more than a fortnight old. I could not solve the mystery at the time. The explanation was eventually provided by the Soviet secret service Major, Peter Deriabin, who defected to the Americans in 1954; in his book *The Secret War*, published in the United States in 1959, he said that a Soviet agent had been working in the Federal Internal Security Office ever since 1952.

Gutshin then extracted from the briefcase a copy of my office's internal telephone directory and showed it to me saying: 'There are changes here which you don't yet know about. I tell you quite frankly: we know everything about your office. You can't hoodwink us.' He thumbed through the monthly report, opened a page and indicated some intelligence which showed clearly that it must have originated from one of my office's agents in East Berlin who must have had access to the innermost secrets of the Socialist Unity Party. He wished to know who the agent was. I did not know because it was not my business to deal with agents. I told him so, adding that it obviously could not be my business. Gutshin seemed to accept this. He put the photostat copies back into the briefcase, murmuring: 'We'll find the man without you. We know more than you do.'

I was not prepared for such a confrontation. I felt that I was being made a fool of and said no more. Gutshin broke the silence by offering me a cigarette and saying: 'We would like to talk of something else. What are your personal relations with Gehlen?' I replied that I had always regarded Gehlen as a colleague. Vadim Konstantinovich began to make notes. I had at the time no reason to doubt Gehlen's attitude towards me. 'We will open your eyes,' was Gutshin's comment. 'We have proofs.' I could not make head or tail of this. Gutshin then asked me to tell him everything about my background and my life.

My paternal grandmother came of a Russian family and my father had been born in Warsaw. His father, who came of a Huguenot family, had managed the first steamship company on the Vistula. My mother's ancestors had been pastors in Hesse ever since the Reformation. I began my story with these facts, said that I was a European cocktail and then proposed to give only the salient points. But Gutshin wanted to know everything in detail; he interposed questions showing that he was very well informed about me. The interrogation proceeded on these lines for a couple of days. In betweenwhiles Gutshin drove down to Gagra every morning in order – as he admitted to me – to telephone Moscow. Every morning he also sent a driver to the airfield to fetch the mail, including mine from Berlin.

Communications continued to arrive, both from the West and the Soviet zone, from people who supported me enthusiastically. I had to answer these, as also the letters from my wife, as if I was still in East Berlin. My letters were still taken by fast courier aircraft to Berlin and posted there. Meanwhile my interrogation on every detail of my previous personal and political existence continued, with Vadim Konstantinovich making notes all the time. But this was of minor importance. From the questions which Gutshin would put to me next day it was clear that every word I uttered was recorded on tape through a hidden microphone; undoubtedly Gutshin spent the evenings when I was alone upstairs, listening and analysing in order to be ready with criticisms and questions for our next day's 'conversation'.

I had nothing to hide in my previous political existence. I could therefore answer Gutshin's questions truthfully – I merely found them tiresome when they went into too much detail. Finally he concentrated on questions about my wartime contacts with the Western Powers. Primarily he wished to know what agreements I had reached with the Western Powers on behalf of Stauffenberg so that, in the event of a successful *coup*, Germany could continue the war against the Red Army alongside the Anglo-Americans. From the way in which he questioned me it was clear that this was an important point for him. I was able to prove the opposite – that Britain and the United States had remained loyal to their agreements with the Soviets and, even in the event of a successful *coup*, would have demanded 'unconditional surrender' on all fronts from any government formed from the internal German resistance.

Gutshin cross-examined me on this subject. This seemed to me ludicrous since, as I tried to explain to him, I had been the one who, in March 1944, had attempted to point out to the resistance day-dreamers that we could expect nothing from the West other than a demand for unconditional surrender; I had also maintained that, despite all potential military opportunities and all German offers of an armistice, the Western Powers would continue to fight alongside the Soviets until unconditional surrender. I became quite heated in trying to convince Gutshin of this. He gave no sign of what he thought of my arguments but for the first time ceased to play the know-all.

Gutshin now adopted a new approach. After some discussion he said that it was vital for the Soviet Union to uncover the 'West's military conspiracy' against the U.S.S.R.; I must assuredly be able to give him proof of that. I could say absolutely nothing about NATO or the E.D.C., their backgrounds or politico-military intentions, since I did not know. Gutshin was unwilling to accept this and pressed me so hard on the subject that I eventually said that he could have me injected with a 'truth' drug if he liked but would still learn nothing from me. He looked at me as if he thought that I was treating him with contempt. I realised, however, that, at this period at least, Soviet anxiety about a fresh attack from the West, using German soldiers and American equipment, was genuine.

It seemed to me that Gutshin was trying to test my veracity. He therefore asked when, where and how I had been trained by the British secret service, with what duties I had been charged by the secret service when assuming my appointment and to whom I had to report. I thought that I could write these questions off as ridiculous, but Gutshin became angry. He pointed out that I had been described in the West German press as 'the man of the British' and 'their agent' and that the Bonn government had never once denied this.

Gutshin, and therefore the Soviet secret service, could not and still cannot believe that I had not returned from London to the Federal Republic as a trained British agent and had assumed my appointment as such. Gutshin thought that he could trap me and asked: why then did I always listen to the B.B.C. news? I was undoubtedly expecting secret instructions that way. In fact both in Karlshorst, in the Moscow *dacha* and during our 'rest-cure' in Gagra I had listened to the B.B.C. news every morning and evening. This was a long-standing habit, and I followed it even in the Soviet Union because, of all the Western stations, the B.B.C. came through best. There was no more to it than that. It was immaterial to me, I said to Gutshin, whether he believed me or not.

I had no difficulty in coping with these interrogations by Gutshin. They were comparatively easy since I was not questioned about my office but even more because I merely had to tell the truth and could not be involved in contradictions. These interrogations, however, led to increasingly vehement discussions, particularly when Gutshin persistently tried to expose me as an 'agent' of the British secret service. I was probably to blame for his suspicion since, in answer to one of his questions, I had said that the British Navy possessed the best intelligence service in the West. This was not merely my own opinion but originated from an Englishman who had lifelong and world-wide experience of intelligence.

With the discussion of my alleged activity on behalf of the British secret service my interrogation was at an end. Gutshin said that we would stay another two or three days and then fly back to Moscow and that this would be the end of our 'rest-cure'. But it turned out quite differently.

27

The Threat of Lyublyanka

I SAT in the garden among the orange trees and gazed out over Gagra on to the Black Sea below. On the other side was Turkey. Should I try to take a boat and escape from the port of Gagra? I saw no real chance. I could not even have left the premises for they were enclosed by tall iron railings. The gate was guarded by old women who sat with the keys in their pocket and would not have opened for me. Frau Gutshin and Vadim Konstantinovich were sitting a little way off and arguing, as they sometimes did, over Vadim Konstantinovich's provocative theory that women were not clever enough to play good chess. Gutshin had once more gone off to telephone.

I thought about Gutshin's interrogations, and their object was still not clear to me. If I had been a British ex-agent the K.G.B. could well have confronted me with Guy Burgess and Donald Maclean, the two British diplomats who had defected. Both had been working for the Soviets inside the British Foreign Office until their flight in 1951. Even though they did not know me personally, they knew that I had worked in England. In addition the K.G.B. could have put pressure on them – they had placed themselves in its power for better or for worse; Burgess in particular would undoubtedly have been ready to say that I was working for the British secret service. But Gutshin never mentioned their names.

While I was thus ruminating Gutshin returned and said, as though he were giving me a pleasant surprise, that Michailov and his wife were on holiday in Sochi and were coming over to visit me. Michailov, it will be remembered, was the functionary who had come from Moscow to Berlin to prepare me for my press conference. His name was certainly not Michailov. Equally certainly he was not in Sochi by chance. It was obvious to me at once that he was the man to whom Gutshin had telephoned daily to tell him of the progress of my interrogation.

The next day Michailov appeared with his wife, an elegant symbol of the Soviet upper class, dressed in Western style. She was allowed to stay in the house. She spoke good German and liked to laugh. On their arrival a lunch took place at which Mme Gutshin was also present.

After lunch Michailov sent me down to Bizunda with Vadim Konstantinovich to bathe. He and Gutshin went into the conference room to discuss the results of my interrogation – as became clear next day. In the evening we sat for some time over the dinner table talking generalities like any set of hotel guests who had got to know each other on holiday. The next morning Vadim Konstantinovich took me down early to the conference room where Michailov and Gutshin were already sitting at the round table. Michailov said that I had now quite recovered but had 'worked' too little with Gutshin. He advised me to think of the great tasks which awaited me in Germany; I would not be equal to them if I did not myself make great efforts to conclude our mutual work successfully.

Michailov first asked me if I had known Arvid Harnack and Harro Schulze-Boysen and what my relations with them both had been (they were the two leading members of the communist 'Red Orchestra' already referred to). I told him that I had made Harnack's acquaintance since he was a cousin of Klaus Bonhoeffer's but did not know Schulze-Boysen; in any case, I added, I had only learnt of their illegal activity through the 'Red Orchestra' trial. Michailov took note without comment. Then he put a series of questions to which I was forced to reply with the same old explanations which I had already given in complete detail to Gutshin: the nature of my war-time contacts with the Western Powers; that there were no secret agreements with the Western Powers to fight on against the Red Army in the event of a successful *coup* against Hitler; that I had not been trained by the secret service or drafted into my office by them; that I knew nothing of the politico-military aims of N.A.T.O. or the E.D.C.

I had to talk for hours, continuously interrupted by questions from Michailov. My throat was dry; I was given some soda water but had to go on talking, rejecting Michailov's accusations over and over again. He smoked all the time and listened very attentively. His cigarette stubs piled up in the ashtray in front of him. Only once did he express an opinion – when he said that I could do the Soviet Union a great service if I would now tell him what I knew about the

Bonn government's 'revanchist plans'. Gutshin and Vadim Konstantinovich said not a word. When it was well past lunchtime Michailov
looked piercingly at me and said: 'One could believe all you tell us
if you had come over to us voluntarily.' Such cynicism made me
furious. I stood up in a rage, swore at him and marched up to my
room.

After some time Vadim Konstantinovich came in and said that we
were all going down together to bathe. I refused and said that I had
nothing further to say; they had much better send me straight to
Siberia! Vadim Konstantinovich tried to calm me down, saying that
Michailov was a bit rough sometimes but was nevertheless a good
friend of mine. I said, 'You can keep that sort of friendship,' and
insisted that I was not going to bathe. Vadim Konstantinovich gave
up and departed.

Late that evening I was summoned down to dinner by Vadim
Konstantinovich. The ladies clearly sensed the atmosphere but I had
meanwhile decided to adhere to the tactic I had adopted. I talked
through and past Michailov. He was obviously trying to propitiate
me and drank to me repeatedly. Finally he said that I had not yet
really recovered and should pay a visit next day with Vadim
Konstantinovich to a *kolkhoz* in the Caucasus lowlands. I did so to
keep out of Michailov's way.

On our return late in the evening Gutshin showed me the text of
the Bundestag debate on the 'John case'; it had taken place on 16
and 17 September and had been broadcast over the radio. I took the
report up to my room at once, read the record through a couple of
times and then asked myself what game the people in Bonn were
really playing. For two days speakers from all parties had discussed
the 'John case' but none of them had anything concrete to report
about me or my disappearance from West Berlin. The debate had
been initiated by Dr Walter Menzel, a member of the Socialist Party
committee; he had long been an opponent of Dr Schröder, the
Minister of the Interior, and saw here a chance to bring him down.
Schröder had in no way been responsible for my appointment since
he had not been a minister at the time, but the Socialist Party was
trying to hold him responsible.

The attacks on the Minister of the Interior, however, developed
into a more general discussion, and Reinhold Maier, the impetuous
Liberal leader, seized the occasion to launch a savage attack on the
Chancellor. He regarded the 'John case' as symptomatic of the

ineptitude of the government and therefore attacked the Chancellor himself as personifying the state – 'We are baying at the moon in concerning ourselves with John. . . . What has to happen in the Federal Republic before something is done?' The Chancellor was not prepared to discuss these basic questions and evaded the assault – he had to go to the airport to receive John Foster Dulles.

Dr Schröder had quite rightly described my appearance in East Berlin as 'a setback in the Cold War'. The embarrassment which all government agencies showed over my 'case' was almost ludicrous; by aggressive and belligerent statements the opposition, both on the Left and the Right, were able to bring the government to the verge of a serious crisis. When, therefore, I was told through Michailov that my answer to the Bundestag debate must be broadcast over the East Berlin radio, the Soviets were clearly aiming to inflame the situation.

As before the press conference, Michailov spent a couple of days with me drafting the answer to the Bundestag. Ought I to have resisted? It seemed to me no longer worth the trouble. I had no inhibitions about adding to the general ignorance in the Federal Republic concerning me and my 'case' by a few communist propaganda phrases – which would be clearly recognisable as such. In any case, isolated as I was, I could not tell in what vein the West German press would comment on my appearance in East Berlin nor what conclusions public opinion would draw from it. Today I think I can view the matter in the correct historical perspective and I am sure that I was not the cause of all these disputes. I and my 'case' merely provided the occasion which exposed the obvious weaknesses of this democracy – weaknesses which, in my view, had their roots in the political personalities concerned and the administrative machine so closely associated with them.

Having drafted my 'Answer to the Bundestag' two Georgians appeared and tape-recorded my speech. The tape was then flown by courier aircraft via Moscow to Berlin. There a hitch developed. The tape was of Georgian manufacture and, as Gutshin told me a couple of days later, could not be played back through the machines of the East Berlin radio. Instead my 'Answer to the Bundestag' was printed in one of the East Berlin newspapers. I have never read it.

After Michailov had listened to the tape-recording and approved it, he drove off with his wife. On leaving he advised me to 'work' seriously with Gutshin from now on; the words carried an unmistakable threat. I was all the more astonished, therefore, when next day, instead of the old housekeeper, our meal was served by a curvaceous local beauty – red lips and fingernails, thin richly coloured dress, no attempt to hide the sex-appeal. I asked Vadim Konstantinovich why we were being waited on by 'so fine a lady'. The old woman was sick, he replied, and this was a substitute, a nurse from a Gagra sanatorium; one could not let any old body into the house.

Very soon I found another explanation for her appearance. The day after Michailov's departure Gutshin began my interrogation all over again from the beginning. Undoubtedly Michailov had left him instructions to this effect. Eventually my whole being revolted against listening to, and discussing, the same questions and accusations over and over again. Gutshin's obvious purpose was to involve me in contradictions, but this he simply could not do because I merely had to stick to the truth and I have a very good memory; as a result I did not deviate from the facts by a hair's breadth, even inadvertently.

Since he was making no progress, Gutshin was under increasing pressure; the prospect of being compelled to admit failure to his master Michailov grew daily nearer. He became nervous and irritable. The harder he tried, the more I felt myself in control. Whenever he cast doubt on my statements, I countered coolly that he had better give me a 'truth' injection at last; this was presumably why the nurse was in the house, I said. What nurse did I mean, he asked. 'Our waitress,' I said. He was vexed that Vadim Konstantinovich, who was listening to this conversation in some embarrassment, had given me this information.

I did not take the presence of the 'nurse' quite so light-heartedly when Michailov returned, this time without his wife. I concluded that Gutshin had told him that nothing new had emerged from his interrogations. Michailov himself accordingly took me once more into the conference room. I had the definite feeling that he was determined to use other methods of interrogation. He concentrated on my connections with the British secret service ever since my first contact with the British Embassy in Lisbon in March 1942. Almost reluctantly he asked yet once more about the secret agreements between the Western Powers and the German resistance and about my training by the secret service; he particularly wished to know who was my 'boss' in London. I had already been over all this in detail with Gutshin. Finally I said: 'There are surely other colleagues of Burgess and Maclean in London from whom you could obtain information about me.' Michailov's face froze and it seemed to me that he was suppressing an outburst of rage. Gutshin, on the other hand, was clearly relieved that Michailov's methods of interrogation were no more effective than his own. Michailov then sent me out of the room and held a long discussion with Gutshin and Vadim Konstantinovich. The reason for Michailov's fury only became clear to me fifteen years later (see pp. 313 et seq. below).

During our late dinner Michailov suddenly asked me: 'Mr President, you are really a spoiled person, aren't you?' I replied that that depended on what standards one judged by. I did not understand the point of his question until he was about to go into the billiard room after dinner with Gutshin and Vadim Konstantinovich. He turned to me once more and asked what I had actually earned in my office. I told him that my monthly salary after all deductions was 1800 marks. Michailov took a step towards me and spat out contemptuously: 'Bah, that's ridiculous! Money?! The Soviet Union is rich. Money plays no part with us. You can have what you want – money, gold, currency, a bank account in Switzerland. But you must work!' With that he left me standing and went into the billiard room.

On the next morning we all went down fairly early to the sea to bathe. Michailov was probably expecting that I would refer to his offer but I acted as though he had never said a word. On return to the house I was dispatched to my room while Michailov, Gutshin and Vadim Konstantinovich went into the conference room. Vadim Konstantinovich summoned me to lunch earlier than usual, saying that Michailov would drive off afterwards. I felt as if a weight had been lifted from me.

Hardly a word was spoken at lunch. When it was over Michailov said that he was very displeased with me and also with Gutshin and Vadim Konstantinovich; we had 'worked' far too little; moreover, he did not believe me. Then he stood up and said: 'I have telephoned to the head of our service in Moscow. I have suggested that you should not be allowed back into Germany until you have told us what duties you were given by the British and who your "boss" in London is. The Chief agrees. So think it over.' As he went out he turned to me once more and said: 'We can be good friends but we can also be very nasty.'

The threat left me totally discouraged. Gutshin had been hauled over the coals and was cross, so he left me to myself. How was I to convince Michailov that I was not a British agent? I saw no escape and made a noose for myself in the bathroom. Then Vadim Konstantinovich opened the door; he was looking for me to take me down to bathe. 'What are you doing there?' he asked. I could not answer him but threw the cord behind the bath-heater. 'Come on,' Vadim Konstantinovich said, 'we'll go for a walk.'

For some time we walked side by side along a track in silence. On the left were the trees of the Caucasus in their beautiful autumn colours and on the right open slopes leading down to the sea. I thought of my wife's words: 'The gift of life is the greatest of all possessions. Think of this and look after your health.' Vadim Konstantinovich broke the silence saying, undoubtedly after much thought: 'Well, if I were you I know what I'd do. Think of it – the great Soviet Union stands behind you.' He seriously meant that I had great things to do in Germany, if only I would 'work', in other words place myself at the disposal of the K.G.B.

'I am your prisoner,' I said. 'You can do what you like with me; you can send me to a labour camp in Siberia or condemn me to death as a British spy. I can do nothing about it.' Vadim Konstantinovich said nothing for a time and then replied with great deliberation: 'Of course we can do that. We have the power. But we do not do that sort of thing. After all you have committed no crime.' After a time he said: 'Let's go back and play chess.' I tried but could not concentrate and gave up.

I cannot say how long we were in Gagra. It could have been five, possibly seven, weeks. I had no calendar and lived from day to day. One morning Gutshin came back from his telephoning and said that we would be flying to Moscow next day. What then, I asked. That I would learn from Michailov, he replied. I was clear on what I could expect from him – his words rang in my ears: 'We can also be very nasty.' I prepared myself for the notorious interrogation methods of the Stalinist years.

We flew next day to Moscow to find beautiful autumn weather. I was taken to the *dacha* where I had been before and where the cook and Anna Sergeyevna greeted me like a dear old friend. Vadim Konstantinovich tried to occupy me with Russian lessons, billiards and chess. He sensed very well what I was feeling and he himself did not know what was going to happen to me, as he told me quite frankly. I waited for Michailov from day to day like a man in the condemned cell waiting for the executioner. Gutshin appeared once more and tried to open up new subjects on which we could 'work'.

'You know a lot of people in Bonn,' he said, 'and you certainly know all their weak points. We must talk about that one day.' I asked what he meant. 'You know perfectly well,' he replied. 'Don't play the idiot.' I did, of course, know what he was driving at. 'I don't concern myself with other people's private lives,' I countered. Did I know that the Americans concerned themselves with my private life, he asked, and showed me a photostat copy of a report on me allegedly originating from an American secret service.

This was intended as a sweetener to persuade me to name to Gutshin people who were approachable or could be put under pressure because of some personal weakness. I must certainly have heard this or that, he said, which did not come to other people's ears. I told him quite plainly that I did not deal in scandal or rumour. Did that mean, he asked, that I would tell him nothing. He could make what he liked of it, I said, and got up. Gutshin hurled his fountain pen furiously on to the table and said: 'You've got a nerve!' He took a few steps and then turned to me again: 'I have failed in my profession with you. I give up. I shall say so to Michailov. Then other people can deal with you.' Once more I visualised Stalinist methods and collected a store of sleeping tablets.

Meanwhile, however, although I did not know it, a political thaw was in progress in the Soviet Union. Backstage preparations were being made for the end of Stalinism. I was never to see Michailov again. His place was taken by Chernov, whom I had long since forgotten. He told me that he had been on holiday in Yalta with his family and there had seen Dr Wohlgemuth with his girl-friend. In astonishment I asked after Wohlgemuth and Chernov replied: 'Now, go on with you. I don't know. I don't know people like that' – with a marked note of contempt in his voice.

This made it easier for me to talk to him. He asked: 'Why don't you work?' I had been invited to the Soviet Union by General Pitovranov for a rest-cure, I replied, not to be interrogated. Surely, he said, the invitation was a mere pretext. No, I replied; I was told I had been brought here primarily for my own security. And could I not do some 'work' after I had recovered, he asked. Then I would soon get back to Berlin. I pricked up my ears. I had promised Pitovranov to 'work', I said, against remilitarisation, against war and for reunification. I stood by that. But I could only do it in Germany.

Chernov thought for a moment and replied: 'All right then. I will suggest that you are shown Leningrad. That may make you change your mind.' To show him what I was really thinking I said that I did not want to go to Leningrad but to Berlin and that I was fed up with sitting around. I continued: 'I know that Michailov can do what he likes with me. He can also stop me returning to Germany. But he cannot stop me making an end of it all here in some way one day.'

Chernov understood and said that I must not talk like that; great tasks awaited me in Berlin; he would be there, too, if I returned, and we could once more 'work' together. As he left he said: 'Well then, auf Wiedersehen till Berlin, Otto.' It seemed to me that he meant what he said and it revived my hope that somehow I would get out of the Soviet Union. Then, however, days passed without anything happening. I sensed that the people in Moscow were undecided what to do with me, whether to follow Michailov's proposals or Chernov's.

One day Gutshin asked jovially whether I would like to see the great Red Army parade in Red Square on Revolution Day. Normally military parades do not interest me, but in this case I said yes. If I was seen in public in Moscow now, they could hardly just do away with me later. I was reinforced in this opinion by a question from Gutshin as to what I would say if I were recognised and spoken to by a foreign journalist. That I was doing very well in Moscow, I replied at once, and would shortly be returning to Berlin.

So as not to be caught totally unprepared by Western journalists as at the press conference in East Berlin, I drafted two notes – a handwritten letter to the Federal Minister of the Interior in an addressed envelope and a copy of it on a small slip which, when screwed up, was no larger than a walnut. I said that I had been kidnapped and was held prisoner in Moscow.

On the day of the parade I was shepherded across Red Square with Vadim Konstantinovich and Gutshin through several militia controls into a fenced-off enclosure in which Russian civilians were standing. To our left I could see a square of Russian generals in full-dress uniform with heavy curved sabres, some with shaggy moustaches. In front, but separated from us by a wooden fence, were the foreign military attachés including those of the Western Powers represented in Moscow. I could not approach any of them, however, without attracting attention nor even throw my little screw of paper.

During the parade I tried to draw attention to myself by loud and enthusiastic applause in German, but no one took any notice apart from the Russians immediately around us. At the end of the parade we had to push our way across Red Square through the crowds. Dinner in the evening was a festive occasion with a special tart and Crimean champagne. I felt that I was over the worst. Having put me on show in front of the Western military attachés, 'they' could hardly now simply do away with me. Later it appeared that none of the Western military attachés had noticed me. At the time I had thought that one of them, in French uniform, had looked at me very hard and had recognised me.

As time went on the Russians treated me better again; I travelled in the underground with Vadim Konstantinovich; we inspected their brand-new stations and once even visited the opera and a couple of restaurants.

I regained hope. Winter had already set in, and I liked going for walks with Vadim Konstantinovich across the frozen Moskva. I no longer thought of suicide. I felt sure that I would eventually return to Germany and my home one day.

Early in December there was great excitement. Gutshin said that I must return to him the passport made out for me in the name of Werner Bertram. I had never had it in my possession but Gutshin maintained that he had given it to me. The *dacha* was turned inside out. 'The passport must be found for your return to Berlin,' Gutshin fumed. I told him that he had never even shown me the passport but that I had seen him put it into his briefcase when we were checked out in Minsk during our flight to the Soviet Union. He emptied his bulging briefcase and there found the passport. Gutshin heaved an audible sigh of relief. He admitted to me that it would have been very unpleasant for him, had he been unable to produce the passport straight away. 'Our Chief has decided,' he said, 'that you should be taken back to Berlin, but before that he wishes to meet you personally.'

The Chief appeared for lunch next day, a tall slim man in an expensive fur coat with Anthony Eden hat and elegant, but very old-fashioned, buttoned shoes. He might have come from any English club. He was General Panyushkin, formerly Soviet Ambassador in Washington. With him came a young aide in flannel trousers and sports jacket who was introduced to me as Volgi.

Through Volgi as interpreter Panyushkin said that he was glad to meet 'so famous a colleague'. I replied that the general was paying me too great a tribute; I had never been a soldier, still less a general. 'I am a lawyer,' I said. 'Good, better still,' Panyushkin replied. 'You are a lawyer general.' Even now, twelve years later, I still do not know if it was in fact Panyushkin to whom I was speaking. During our conversation I asked whether, like Michailov, he took me for a British agent. He waved my question wearily away and said that we should talk about the future; what would I do when I was back in Berlin? I replied that I would probably set up as a lawyer there and, as agreed with General Pitovranov, work against re-militarisation and for the reunification of our country. 'Your plan is good,' Panyushkin said. 'Reunification is a great task for you.' I was thinking more of being nearer my wife. As he left Panyushkin clapped me on the shoulder with 'Auf Wiedersehen till Berlin, Mr President of Germany'.

When Panyushkin had gone Gutshin was clearly relieved that he had passed the test with his most exalted master. He gave me coffee and brandy and, as if he was giving me some personal present, said: 'And now pack this evening. Tomorrow we fly to Berlin.' I did not sleep a wink all night.

Vadim Konstantinovich accompanied Gutshin and me to the airport where Mme Gutshin was waiting. This time we did not fly in a secret service courier aircraft but on an ordinary Aeroflot flight. As I said goodbye to Vadim Konstantinovich I kissed him on both cheeks and gave him my gold cuff-links as a token of my gratitude.

28
Escape to 'Freedom'

MICHEV and Scholz were waiting for us at East Berlin airport. This was an unwelcome reunion which somewhat spoilt my private pleasure at being closer to the West once more. They took me, with two guards from the East Berlin security service, to a small house on Zeuthen Lake, south-east of Berlin. There I was introduced to Comrade Paul Voigt, his wife and his mother-in-law who were to take care of me. The entire family were long-standing communists, now employed by the East German security service. Voigt would see to everything I wanted, I was told, and a 'protective escort' was available outside the house. I at once attempted to rid myself of this supervision, remarking that I really did not need protection any more. 'We could not let you go out alone on the streets,' Scholz said. 'We are responsible for your life.'

My illusions about escaping from East Berlin quickly evaporated when I tried to open the shutters that evening before going to bed and found them firmly bolted on the outside. My rattling the shutters brought Voigt running along; he entered my bedroom without knocking and said that the shutters must not be opened at night. He was still under thirty, spare and sickly looking, but a tough security service functionary who took his job and the responsibility of 'looking after' me most conscientiously. The whole place was surrounded by electrified wire concealed in the hedge which set off an alarm if touched. The house was also guarded by a highly trained Alsatian dog.

I only discovered all these security measures gradually, by circumspect observation and questioning. At first I hoped that I might escape across the frozen lake during the Christmas period but this idea was checkmated by the vigilance of Voigt and his dog. Not once could I leave the house unnoticed, not even 'to get a breath of fresh air', as I tried to do on several occasions. Voigt and his dog were always at my side. Because of the dog I could not strike him down and escape; in any case, like all my guards, he had a pistol in his pocket. In addition, only fifty yards from the house the East German police had a watch-tower from which the lake and its shores were kept under observation day and night, since the boundary between the Soviet sector and the Soviet zone of Berlin ran through the middle of the lake. I had to resign myself to the fact that escape from this house was impossible.

Other opportunities offered, however, since I was driven into Berlin daily. In January 1955 I occupied an office organised for me in the building of the National Council of the National Front, Goebbels' former Propaganda Ministry; it was in a remote wing and well guarded. I had an office for myself, an outer room for a short-hand typist and another room for my guards. I could not leave my office without being seen by them. The office was only 500 yards from the Brandenburg Gate, then still the gateway to freedom. One day, I thought, I must succeed in shaking off my guards and escaping through that gate.

I could not even guess what the Russians had in store for me. I saw little of them. Occasionally General Pitovranov, Gutshin or Chernov, who had meanwhile arrived in Berlin from Moscow, would appear, usually in the evenings after dark, and inquire about me and my 'work'. My duty was to appear as a patriotic showpiece at National Front meetings, in so-called intelligentsia clubs, cultural associations or factories in the Soviet zone and sell the illusory story of reunification. Nevertheless, these meetings gave me the opportunity of moving around in the zone, observing my guards very closely and so gradually probing for means of escape.

My activity was directed from the background by Professor Albert Norden, then head of the East Berlin Unity Committee, and his executive director, Dr Girnus. They commissioned me to draft a memorandum on the possibilities of reunification. This constituted my office work, but in addition I had to answer numerous enthusiastic letters both from East and West Germany. In my office I read everything published in East Berlin and also various newspapers and periodicals from the West. At home I was allowed to switch on Western radio or television stations as I liked. I was therefore fully informed and intellectually a free man, but I felt like a prisoner in solitary confinement.

I received a salary for my work in the Unity Committee and fees for articles or radio broadcasts, but I myself never saw a penny.

Everything was paid into a secret account run by Voigt, who doled me out pocket money for cigarettes and meals as I needed it. Thirty thousand Eastern marks had been paid into the account for a pamphlet in my name published by the firm of Kongress without my knowledge while I was away in Moscow; it was entitled *I Chose Germany* and was a partially doctored account of my press conference. John Peet, the Reuter correspondent who had defected to the East, was introduced to me in the Press Club one day with the statement that he had translated my pamphlet into English and that it had been published in Britain.

I was continually thinking: How can I get into West Berlin? Since my journeys into the Soviet zone for lectures offered no possibilities of escape, I considered drinking my guards under the table. But Voigt, with his responsibilities always in mind, remained vigilant and sober. Only when a group of younger guards came on duty later did I once more hope to be able to shake them off one day. Meanwhile I thought up a new plan for escape through the Brandenburg Gate.

The manager of the State Opera on Unter den Linden had invited me to see the work of reconstruction going on there, and while doing so I discovered that the Opera and the management building a little distance away were linked by an underground passage. The manager had also invited me to the reopening, scheduled for the autumn. It seemed to me that here was a chance of escape through the underground passage. My plan was that a diplomatic car with British markings should be ready in the car-park near the Opera and in that I would escape through the Brandenburg Gate. I knew a British secret service officer who, I thought, would be prepared to leave me a car alongside other Western cars in the Opera car-park during a performance. I 'only' needed some agent through whom I could make contact with the Englishman. It was a long-term plan but it seemed to me practicable. To keep up my contact with the manager of the Opera, at his invitation I gave an address in the Admiral Palace to the 'creators of art'.

I mulled over this plan for months but was not assisted by news printed in the Federal Republic prophesying my return to the West. A leading article in a West German newspaper, complete with cartoon, stated that I had been exploring through a 'senior cleric' in Bonn the possibilities of my return. Obviously uneasy over this, General Pitovranov came twice to see me in the evening 'to find out how I was getting on'; his real object was to tell me that I must not lose patience since 'the great task for which I was destined, awaited me'. In passing he threw out the warning that my enemies in the Federal Republic were more powerful than ever.

I made somewhat closer personal contact with an elderly couple, Gabriel Brügel and his wife. He was highly educated, very musical and had previously been director of a glass firm. Early in the war he had been a reserve officer in Norway and, being a confirmed opponent of the régime, had come into conflict with a Nazi and had been denounced by him. On his way to Berlin to appear before the People's Court he had escaped and had been hidden in East Berlin by communists until the end of the war. He decided to remain there and worked as lecturer and specialist on Scandinavian questions in the East Berlin Institute of Contemporary History. He was an honest decent man and had remained faithful to the Evangelical Church.

Brügel told me that he had been asked to concern himself with me 'because the ordinary comrades could not do so properly', being inexperienced in society! I discussed many things with Brügel, since he often knew from the Scandinavian press what rumours Moscow was spreading. We talked over almost every known literary, musical and even political subject, avoiding only one over which Brügel was cudgelling his brains: Why and how had I come to East Berlin?

Brügel generally accompanied me to my lectures. After hearing me speak he was frequently inclined to believe that I really had come voluntarily to preach peace and reunification. He was the only man who could tell me, after my lectures, what effect they had had on the very varied audiences in the provincial towns. I invariably spoke completely extempore, sometimes for forty-five minutes or more, and always had a number of critical questions to answer.

Weeks and months passed while I continued this political play-acting in favour of peace and reunification. Meanwhile the only distant opportunity of escape which I could see was via the underground passage after the reopening of the Opera. This waiting was a severe nervous strain. I smoked a great deal and became jumpy. I could only sleep if I had drunk several brandies or vodkas, bottles of which General Pitovranov sent me from time to time together with a tin of caviare. The security service officials simply 'looked after' me according to Soviet regulations. Not once, however, did any of them try to embarrass me by entering into conversation or asking awkward questions. And the Russians kept themselves in the back-ground.

During a walk along the lakeside one day Chernov said to me that I would not be invited to the Soviet Embassy since the time for that had *not yet* arrived. A couple of days later, however, he drove me to a cinema in the Karlshorst restricted zone to see the film *Canaris*. When the film ended and the lights went up I had tears in my eyes; I was incapable of saying a word. Chernov said that I must now at last realise that in the long run I would not be safe from Canaris' murderers in the Federal Republic. Clearly he was wishing to make my existence in the Soviet zone more acceptable to me. Perhaps the Soviets had it in mind to allot me some political role in a neutralised reunited Germany. From various conversations with Chernov it was clear to me that they still clung to Stalin's proposals of March 1952 and were determined to prevent the incorporation of the Federal Republic into the Western economic and military system, even at the price of the neutralisation of all Germany.

Still seeing no possibility of escape to the West, I had another idea. In May 1955 I read in the Western press that a four-power conference was to be summoned in Geneva to discuss the reunification of Germany, European security, disarmament and the relaxation of tension. For months now I had been appearing as the propaganda showpiece on these subjects for the communist Unity Committee and the pseudo-patriotic National Council of the National Front. This seemed to me good enough reason to put my masters to the test. I asked Professor Norden and Dr Girnus to send me to Geneva via Prague and Vienna as an observer and *rapporteur*. Norden said that he would think it over but he would, of course, have to have the agreement of the Russians; he tried to dissuade me in a friendly way. I, of course, was set on reaching the Federal Republic from Geneva and I therefore emphasised that I must go to this conference if my appearances on behalf of peace and reunification were to remain credible.

A few days later a 'Comrade Beater', Voigt's master, appeared to talk me out of my proposed trip to Geneva on security grounds. I countered that in Geneva I would really be able to convince the Western world of the sincerity and political significance of my flight to East Germany. In helpless desperation he pleaded: 'Oh, Doctor, don't make things so difficult for me.' 'How so?' I asked. He was not a bad type, just one of those typical East German functionaries who was 'doing his duty', as innumerable former officials had done for the Nazi régime. 'You know what I mean,' he said. 'We can't let you out into the West.'

Professor Norden, of course, knew this too. He tried to sidetrack me, saying that it was time that I concerned myself with something other than the West for a while. He proposed that I be sent on a trip to China. I pricked up my ears since I could see here an admittedly roundabout but perfectly practicable route back to the West. I would not have been at all averse to a trip to China as a method of getting out of East Berlin. Humphrey Trevelyan, a British friend of mine, was Chargé d'Affaires in Peking at the time. His intelligence officers could easily have found some way back to the West for me via Hong Kong. However, nothing came of the visit to China.

One of the reasons may have been that Norden was now concerning himself less and less with me, particularly since he had found my memorandum on the possibilities of reunification to be of no use and had pigeon-holed it; thereafter he left it to Dr Girnus to deal with me. He had more exalted political ambitions and was working his way at the time into the Central Committee of the East Berlin régime. As Norden's successor Dr Girnus was more active. He wished to publish an ostensibly independent periodical entitled *Berliner Politische Korrespondenz* which would appear under my name but be edited by him. I let this drag on for a time since Girnus was busy with preparations for the Geneva conference. After his return from Geneva at the end of July, however, I was forced to take some part in it and wrote articles for trial numbers of the *Korrespondenz* which were widely distributed in the Federal Republic by the Unity Committee. The first issues announced that the *Korrespondenz* would appear regularly from then on.

I was completely astonished by the reaction from the Federal Republic to 'my' periodical. I was overwhelmed with letters and requests for contributions; Dr Girnus was overjoyed. I succeeded, however, in postponing the regular appearance of the *Korrespondenz* until after my escape. At a meeting of the Hegel International Society in Salzburg ten years later Dr Girnus told a Western journalist that he had always known that I was anti-communist and had not come across voluntarily but had arrived in East Berlin as a British agent with some specific task; moreover, he had always wondered why I had not 'fled' back to the West earlier.

One day Gutshin appeared and, with unconcealed excitement, showed me a most comprehensive and detailed report on Allied and German troops in the Federal Republic; he wished to know what I thought of it. In some astonishment I told him at once that, as he knew, I understood nothing of military matters, but he insisted that he wanted my opinion; General Pitovranov had sent him to me for that purpose, he said. I thumbed through the report and as I did so noticed that every page carried a red stamp 'Geheime Bundessache' ['Federal secret']. 'This report is a forgery', I said, since as far as I knew no such security grading as 'Geheime Bundessache' existed. Gutshin was relieved and thanked me; his top-level masters had disagreed over the genuineness of the report.

Even today I dislike thinking back to this period when my entire thoughts were centred on the possibility of escape. The continuous nervous tension increasingly became a physical as well as mental torture.

The first genuine assistance I received came from the Danish journalist Henrik Bonde-Henriksen, editor of the Copenhagen *Berlinske Tidende*. He helped me throughout the six months leading up to my eventual escape which was continuously postponed owing to bad luck, misunderstandings and the timorousness of some who could have helped. I had made Henrik Bonde-Henriksen's acquaintance on the day before I was kidnapped. He was a member of the Foreign Journalists' Club in West Berlin and had invited Prince Louis Ferdinand to address the club. I had not attended the occasion since I thought it incompatible with my position to appear before the Press as a partisan of my friend Louis Ferdinand.

On the evening before my abduction Henrik Bonde-Henriksen had come into the Haus Schätzle Hotel where I, my wife, Louis Ferdinand and my secretary Vera Schwarte were living. We talked for a time about my impressions of my trip to the United States, which I had not yet given Louis Ferdinand. Since I referred so favourably to the United States and the people I had met there, Henrik Bonde-Henriksen wished to interview me in the hotel on the next evening after the Prince's address to the press club, but when he arrived in the hotel with the Prince I was already lying unconscious in Karlshorst. The two hunted for me until late into the night, assuring my wife, who was distraught, that I must be somewhere and would soon turn up.

In the spring of 1955 I made my first reappearance in public at a press conference given by Professor Norden who was in the habit of organising such occasions on behalf of the Unity Committee from time to time in order to expound some anti-West German inflammatory theme. I was merely to appear in the audience, primarily to be shown to Western journalists, but to say nothing myself. While Norden developed his theme in his usual belligerent manner, I was frequently photographed and so attracted the attention of all those present. At question time Henrik Bonde-Henriksen, whom I had not noticed myself, stood up and in somewhat challenging tones demanded information on the fate of a German-born woman, a Dane by marriage, who had been arrested in Magdeburg. His self-assured manner made an indelible impression on me.

After the end of the press conference Henrik Bonde-Henriksen pushed his way quickly through to me and greeted me. We were surrounded by journalists and I asked him to come out into the hall with me. Most of the journalists followed. Bonde-Henriksen asked me to come down with him to his car since there we could talk alone. I indicated to him that this was not possible and that I could not even come down the staircase but must use a back flight of stairs. As he told me later, he realised at once that I was not a free man. Since other Western journalists were now besieging me with questions, I excused myself from Bonde-Henriksen saying that he might come to the Press Club near the Friedrichstrasse Station one day, since I lunched there almost every day.

A few days later I met him there. I wanted to explain my situation to him, but only after I had made sure of him. At first I talked to him like any other journalist who wanted an interview from me. I told him of my voluntary decision to work for reunification in East Germany. Under the watchful eye of my guards he made notes. He promised not to publish a word without my approval. He was continually trying to find out, however, what had happened during that night when he and Prince Louis Ferdinand had searched for me in vain. I gave the excuse that I must withhold these details from publication.

In July, on the anniversary of my disappearance from West Berlin, the *Berlinske Tidende* published the interview with me. It aroused great excitement. A West Berlin State Attorney thereupon subpoenaed Bonde-Henriksen for interrogation on his conversation with me. Bonde-Henriksen cited the journalist's obligation to professional discretion and refused to give evidence. He lodged a protest against the subpoena with the Federal Minister of Justice both in his own name and in that of the West Berlin Association of Foreign Journalists which he represented. Strauss, State Secretary in the Federal Ministry of Justice, came to Berlin to put matters right with Bonde-Henriksen; Vockel, the Federal Plenipotentiary, was also present. On this occasion Strauss stated that I could return to the Federal Republic at any time. Bonde-Henriksen told me all this when we next met in the East Berlin Press Club. Since our previous meeting had created such a stir I was doubtful whether I could speak to him openly. I sensed that our contacts in the Press Club were being closely observed, an impression confirmed by a question from the Danish communist journalist, Helge Larsen. He said: 'You are seeing a lot of that fellow Bonde-Henriksen here. What does he want from you?' I was unhappy about this since Larsen was a close friend of Wollweber whom he would certainly tell about my meetings with Bonde-Henriksen.

For some time Bonde-Henriksen was not to be seen in the Club. He returned in late August after a prolonged stay in West Germany. He told me that he had visited Prince Louis Ferdinand who had awarded him the private Order of the House of Hohenzollern. He showed me the medal and ribbon as proof that he had the Prince's confidence. This decided me to discuss my plans for escape quite openly with him, but I could not do so at the time since Gabriel Brügel joined our table. Bonde-Henriksen went on to another subject and said that his interview with me had been of great interest to Danish students; they wished to invite me to lecture in Copenhagen. I would think about that, I replied, although I knew very well that I would never be allowed to go to Copenhagen. Bonde-Henriksen then generously invited Brügel to come to Copenhagen as well, adding: 'Naturally Dr John must not slope off in Copenhagen or my career as a journalist would be at an end.' I did not know what to make of this. Bonde-Henriksen then departed.

After this I did not see Bonde-Henriksen for several weeks; he was reporting the electoral campaign in the Saar. In the last week of October he appeared in the Press Club again and told me that he had been invited to Prince Louis Ferdinand's birthday celebration on 9 November and would I like to give him a letter? I wrote a three-line note saying that I had not changed and was 'always the same.' The Prince sent me back a message through Bonde-Henriksen saying that he had been happy to get my note 'and' Bonde-Henriksen whispered, 'he said: "Help Otto." ' This he was ready to do, Bonde-Henriksen said under his breath. So the bridge was there. I told Bonde-Henriksen of my plan to escape during a performance at the Opera.

I had already been to the Opera once and so I asked Bonde-Henriksen to contact the British secret service officer already mentioned and ask him to leave me a car with British markings among the numerous other Western cars in the Opera car-park, first sending me the key via Bonde-Henriksen. The Englishman refused, however, saying that this might lead to diplomatic repercussions and that I should 'simply' take the underground to West Berlin!

From the few words which I was able to whisper to him in the Press Club, interjected into innocent conversation, Bonde-Henriksen had appreciated my situation. 'I'll get you out,' he said. I had a substitute plan for escape. On various occasions I had to go to the University; I had already addressed the students there and had always used a back entrance. My guards were accustomed to seeing me enter the University that way. I hoped that, once among the students in the unfamiliar atmosphere of the University, I could shake off my guards, emerge on the other side of the building and climb into a waiting car.

I explained the plan to Bonde-Henriksen with the aid of a sketch drawn on a cigarette packet. He discussed it in West Berlin with my colleague Wichmann. To avoid the Press Club, I met Bonde once more in the Neva Restaurant. We agreed on 12 December at 4.50 p.m. as the date and time for the attempt. I chose this date because, according to the guard rota, two young fellows would be on duty that day and I thought that they would be the easiest to shake off.

The day before, which was a Sunday, I invited Helge Larsen home with me and gave him too much to drink, hoping to find out whether his friend Wollweber had any suspicions about me. Larsen said that 'the S.S.D. people' could not make head or tail of me but respected me as a protégé of the Russians.

The next morning I drove to my office as usual and then to lunch in the Press Club where Larsen was dousing his hang-over in Pilsen. We sat together. I then drove back to my office. Shortly after four o'clock I told my guards that I had an appointment with Professor Daniel in the University. We drove to the back entrance and I said: 'I'll leave my briefcase in the car and be straight back.' The bluff worked. In the briefcase were 8000 marks which I had drawn from Voigt that morning ostensibly to buy a large yacht. I drew the attention of my two young guards to this money and they thought it more important to guard that than follow me. So they allowed me to go into the University alone!

I quickly left the building on the opposite side but Bonde and the car were not there. It was now dark. Driving past at midday I had noticed that Unter den Linden was closed on the Opera side because of the Christmas market. I went up to the barrier to intercept Bonde there. He did not arrive and I gave our plan up for lost. To avoid attracting attention by standing around, I went round the block adjoining the Opera. As I crossed the square next the Opera I saw Bonde-Henriksen's Ford in the car-park between the Opera and the University. I ambled up to it from behind and got in.

Bonde-Henriksen was surprised that I had not come from in front, out of the University gate. I asked him how he had dealt with the barriers. 'I simply drove straight through,' he said. We had no time to talk further. As agreed, I wound a thick muffler round my neck, put on a pair of spectacles and stuffed a pipe into my mouth. We drove off. At the Friedrichstrasse crossing the lights went green and we now had only a few hundred yards to the Brandenburg Gate.

Bonde-Henriksen had decked his car out with a 'Press' plate and a Danish flag to distinguish it as a foreign vehicle. 'If the Vopos [East German police] at the Brandenburg Gate fire,' he said, 'I'll just step on it. There are police and frontier guards on the other side to shoot us out of it, if necessary.' He approached the check-point at the regulation speed of 2 m.p.h. and stopped. I puffed thick clouds of smoke from my pipe. The Vopo looked at the Danish insignia. 'The boot behind is open, officer, if you want to look,' Bonde-Henriksen said. The Vopo waved us on and we glided slowly through the Brandenburg Gate.

My colleague Wichmann was waiting at the airport and had reserved seats for us under assumed names on the plane for Cologne-Wahn. As I left the aircraft I was received by Dr Brückner, Chief of Security in Bonn, with one or two of his officials. I took this to be a precaution for my safety, as also the fact that I was initially accommodated in Security Headquarters. In fact, as I was told next day by Wichmann – senior Federal Attorney and not to be confused with my Berlin colleague of the same name – I had been arrested.

29
The Trial

M Y wife was living in London where she had fled from Germany for the second time – first from the Nazis in 1936 and then nearly twenty years later because, once I had appeared in East Berlin, she had no means of livelihood; my salary no longer came in and she was not allowed to continue to teach singing – a modern version of the Nazis' 'kith and kin' arrest. Pupils and old friends had rallied round her in London and she was once more teaching singing there, living with Gisela, her daughter by her first marriage.

Since my disappearance from West Berlin my wife had analysed every one of my letters in consultation with German and Allied experts in order to extract every possible clue from them. She had discussed with one of my British colleagues the wording of every sentence in her letters to me. Since her departure for London and my return from Moscow to East Berlin she used to phone me almost every Sunday evening, primarily to reassure herself that I was still alive. My letters were no guarantee of this, a British secret service expert having warned her that my handwriting could well be forged. She had been given my telephone number by one of our friends, Erich Kleiber, the conductor, to whom I had given it when he was conducting in East Berlin. We could not say much to each other over the telephone since we knew that our conversations were tapped by every Eastern and Western secret service. For this reason I invariably ended with the words 'may all go well with you, my love'.

When my wife called on the Sunday evening before my escape, just after I had said goodbye to Helge Larsen, she asked, as she always did before Christmas, what I would like from her. She wanted to know whether she could not send me something of practical use. 'No,' I said, and then 'Auf Wiedersehen' – words which I had never used before to end a telephone conversation. She realised the implication at once, called her daughter and said: 'Otto's coming back.' She was completely astonished, however, when I called her from Bonn on the very next evening to say that I was once more in West Germany.

Dr Brückner put the call through for me from his office in Security Headquarters and I felt myself safer under his protection than anywhere else in the 'free' West. This impression was confirmed when he received me in most friendly fashion and offered me a guest-room in his office for the night. In fact, he had been instructed by Dr Wichmann, the Federal State Attorney, to keep me under detention.

Meanwhile in Karlsruhe Dr Wichmann had obtained an arrest warrant from the Federal High Court and with this in his pocket he came to Bonn next day. Some time before, my wife and her daughter had arrived on the first plane from London. I was surprised that, as we met once more, Dr Brückner remained on our heels all the time; as I was to learn years later, he wrote a report for Dr Wichmann about our reunion.

Before Dr Wichmann's arrival I saw Henrik Bonde-Henriksen once more. The previous evening Dr Brückner had parted us at the airport and Bonde had ridden in one of the Security Service escort vehicles. He had then driven on to Cologne to discuss with my staff in the office the article on my escape which he intended to transmit to his newspaper that very evening. Before leaving for East Berlin to fetch me he had warned his newspaper by letter not to take seriously anything which he might be compelled – like me – to say over the East Berlin radio, should he be arrested with me during my escape. I was only able to say a few words to him and could hardly thank him properly for having risked so much on my behalf, since Dr Wichmann was already at the door.

Having sent Dr Brückner out of the room, Wichmann asked whether I had any information for him demanding rapid action on his part. I replied that I would set down everything which had happened to me in East Berlin and Moscow in a detailed report and that emergency measures were not necessary. He gazed at his fingernails in thoughtful silence and said: 'You are free – and you are not free. You will be interrogated judicially.' Before I could say a word he added: 'I must warn you to make no attempt to escape back to the Eastern zone.'

This remark was incomprehensible to me. I only realised later that, in Karlsruhe, sentence had already been pronounced on me because I had been labelled by the Press as a defector. All the articles on my case disregarded the fact that, although agents often returned from behind the Iron Curtain, no important defector had ever done so. I said to Dr Wichmann that morning that further conversation with him seemed to me superfluous but that I was, of course, at his disposal for a judicial interrogation. He concealed from me the fact that he had an arrest warrant in his pocket. Without a further word I withdrew to the room in which I had spent the night.

Heinz Stöckert, the ex-Wehrmacht captain who was at this time still working for the Soviet secret service in East Berlin, later told me that on this same morning the Soviet secret service officers supervising the East Berlin Ministry of State Security had carried out feverish inquiries. A Soviet colonel had said: 'Every good thing we do is wrecked by the Germans. One just can't rely on the Germans.' Soviet officers, however, were apparently left completely speechless when they heard next day that I had been arrested in Bonn. Shortly afterwards Wollweber, the East Berlin Minister of State Security, was relieved of his post and General Pitovranov was transferred to the Soviet Embassy in Peking.

The Russians, moreover, never understood why I had returned to Bonn when, through Henrik Bonde-Henriksen, I had the opportunity to ask for asylum in one of the Scandinavian countries. This I learnt seven years later from a senior Russian diplomat whom I met socially in the house of a German industrialist. I then attempted, through this Russian, to persuade Khrushchev to clear up my case, arguing that I had been a victim of Stalinism. When I met the Russian diplomat a couple of weeks later at lunch in a smart Cologne hotel, he said: 'There is no answer for you from Moscow.' He had only one question for me which he asked, undoubtedly on instructions from Moscow: 'When did you actually begin to plan your escape to Bonn?' With a certain sense of satisfaction I replied: 'From the moment my head was clear after waking up among your Stalinists in Karlshorst.'

It had never entered my head that it was not my duty to return to Bonn and there justify my actions in public. After the press campaign against me it was clear that this would be no simple matter. But I never imagined that I would have to defend myself before the High Court on a charge of treason; instead I had wished to give evidence before the Bundestag Commission of Enquiry which had been set up to deal with my case.

Nothing could have made a permanent existence behind the Iron Curtain worth while for me. It could never have been compatible either with my liberal political views or with the ethical concepts and principles for which I had fought against the Hitler régime in the resistance. There was no plausible reason and certainly no proof why I should have defected to the East of my own free will.

In my case I cannot blame the man in the street for being prejudiced against me since his opinion was coloured by the popular press, and that was badly informed. Dr Wichmann, the Federal Attorney, and the judges who ultimately sentenced me, had every opportunity to know better. In a case like this, forensic erudition alone is not enough. Jean Bodin, one of the most famous lawyers of the epoch of witches' trials whose doctrines are still quoted in universities today, regarded it as incontrovertible fact that witches stole, roasted and ate little children. The trial to which I was subjected was, in my view, a modern version of the witch's trial, a recrudescence of political superstition.

The first step was an interrogation in Special Branch headquarters in Wiesbaden lasting nine days and conducted by an investigating judge from the Federal High Court, the highest court dealing with political crime. This judge considered me unfit for interrogation since I was still exhausted from the exertions of the preceding days. I insisted on being interrogated, however, since I wished to get this stage behind me as quickly as possible. Once I had signed the record, which covered over one hundred pages, the judge issued an arrest warrant at the request of Dr Wichmann, the Federal Attorney, on the grounds that 'it was not yet established whether I had gone voluntarily to East Berlin that night' and that 'I could be suspected of a desire to leave the country since I had good connections abroad, particularly in Britain'.

This took place on Christmas Eve, our wedding anniversary. I was allowed to ring my wife once more. For her this was the beginning of a long period of anxiety and agitation. She urged me to engage a defence counsel at once and, to pacify her, I authorised her to brief Dr Dix, a Cologne barrister. I was quite clear, however, that a defence counsel could not help me and that my fate depended solely on whether the judges would believe me. I thought that there was hope of this seeing that, as he left, the investigating judge had given me to understand that he did not regard my account as incredible and that the issue of the arrest warrant was based solely on the suspicion that I had defected; as if to excuse himself, he had said: 'You must admit that, in your case, the risk of defection is an obvious inference. During the war you escaped to England from the Gestapo after 20 July 1944, and now the Russians. You must accept detention while under investigation.'

The next morning two Criminal Police officers, whom I had known in my official capacity, arrived from Bonn with a police car to take me to Pforzheim prison, no cell being available in Karlsruhe. A Federal Judge, Kurt Weber, was nominated as investigating judge in my case. He was a man of my generation and I knew him slightly as one of the judges responsible for the blunders over the arrests in the notorious 'Vulkan affair'. Without even interrogating me he allowed me to languish for three months in Mannheim prison, to which I had been transferred after Christmas 1955. On the orders of Loesdau, a Federal attorney, I was isolated from all other prisoners and was only allowed an exercise period after dark in the prison courtyard; I was not permitted to attend any of the entertainments organised for the prisoners or even a religious service.

When Weber eventually appeared in the prison to open my interrogation, he summoned me into the ornate prison meeting hall, where I found him alone with no recording official. He apologised for such a remarkably long failure to appear, saying that he had first had to study the files in the Federal Attorney's office which contained statements from over 800 witnesses dating from the time of my disappearance from West Berlin. In a confidential tone he then said: 'If everything happened as you have said, then your case is a real tragedy.' I thought that I could trust him, but he was bent on making a career for himself out of my case. This he failed to do and he finally retired in January 1966, not having achieved promotion to President of his Bench.

Weber delayed my interrogation for so long that I eventually threatened to go on hunger strike. Only then did he appear and open his investigation. We spoke of my wife's first letter to East Berlin in which she had urged me to keep alive and 'look after my health'. I emphasised how painful the memory of this was to me and Weber assured me that he could well understand my feelings since his young Jewish wife had been gassed by the Nazis. This remark reinforced my confidence in him. I answered all his questions as best I could and left it to him to draft the record. Only after the con- clusion of the investigation and when I had already briefed Dr Caemmerer, Sen., a Karlsruhe barrister, as my defence counsel, did I learn from him what Weber's attitude towards me had really been.

Five months after my arrest came a remand date. The judges gave me no opportunity to defend myself; the word was already going round in Bonn that the President of the Bench had said in the mess that 'he was glad to be able to conduct the case against me'. He was an ex-military judge advocate who hardly allowed me to speak and interrupted me continuously. His remarks were a clear foretaste of what his judgement was to be and he did not even trouble to conceal his prejudice against me.

Again and again he reproached me, saying that there could be no possible justification for my appearance on behalf of the Eastern propagandists, even had the Russians used pressure or force on me; once I had awoken in Karlshorst, I ought simply to have refused to do anything. I had not shown the courage in face of the Russians demanded of any common soldier in war; in wartime a soldier must not be afraid. It must suddenly have occurred to him that comparison with soldiers fighting at the front was not entirely apt, since he switched to a somewhat less military argument: 'A fireman must not be afraid either. Any fireman is required to risk his life every day. No less could be expected of Dr John!'

The Bench decided to extend my detention and ordered that I be housed in the Psychiatric Clinic of Heidelberg University, allegedly so that I might have a chance to recover. I had meanwhile lost nearly three stone in weight and was suffering more than when a prisoner of the Russians. My wife had besought me to seize this chance to recover in the Heidelberg clinic and so I did not object. I was accommodated in the restricted section of the clinic, admittedly in a single room, but next to a large ward for serious mental cases.

My 'convalescence' was limited by law to six weeks. Professor von Baeyer, the head of the clinic, had me medically examined, and then I had to recount my entire life's history to him with special emphasis on events preceding my kidnapping and my experiences behind the Iron Curtain. He is supposed to have said in private that he regarded me as sincere. In his submission to the court, however, he confined himself to his medical responsibilities, merely stating that neurological examination had detected no mental disturbance in my case.

Meanwhile Weber had been travelling round the country inter-rogating witnesses, all of whom had already been questioned immediately after my disappearance from West Berlin. He appeared once or twice in the clinic to complete my own interrogation; he was primarily interested in my statement that I had once been in Adenauer's private house in Rhöndorf with State Secretary Globke when the Chancellor suspected Jakob Kaiser, the Minister for All-German Questions, of maintaining illegal relationships with East Berlin. Dr Adenauer had stated categorically that I had never been in his house, and Globke, the only other witness, 'could no longer remember'. I was able to describe the rooms and furniture which I had seen in Adenauer's house and Weber finally admitted that 'the old gentleman's memory is perhaps no longer so good as yours'.

Shortly before my release from the clinic Weber appeared once more and attempted to intimidate me and force a confession from me. For the first time I realised his true character. He told me that for some time he had been exchanging letters with Dr Wohlgemuth in East Berlin and he plied me with the stories which Wohlgemuth had been serving up in his own defence. Weber actually believed Wohlgemuth's tale: that I had gone to the Russian zone with him for an East–West talk arranged by him and had decided to remain there. I asked Weber how he could take such fairy-stories from the East with any seriousness. He hesitated but said with a chuckle: 'I shall bring Dr Wohlgemuth to the main hearing. He will expose you in public.'

He was furious at his failure to make any impression on me. 'No one believes that you were kidnapped,' he blurted out, 'not even your wife.' The exact opposite could be proved. After my disappearance my wife's reactions had been closely observed by both my German and Allied colleagues, as the files of the case showed clearly. The senior officials of my late Internal Security Office and my Allied colleagues had warned my wife to give no hint outside her immediate circle of friends that I might have been kidnapped, for fear that my escape might be made more difficult. Weber could easily have checked up on this. He attempted, however, to play my wife off against me as a witness and this I found particularly hard to bear.

This final interrogation by the investigating judge brought me to the end of my powers of physical resistance. Signs of jaundice became visible in my eyes. I was transferred to the prison hospital at Ludwigsburg, an old fortress known as the 'democrats' hump' in Swabia because, in absolutist days, the first Swabian democrats had been incarcerated there. I was following their tradition. My clinical examination on admittance showed a high bile content in my blood which the doctors diagnosed as due to the presence of three gallstones. I had carried these around with me for years, however, without trouble. I realised at once that the acidity in my blood was due to an influx of bile caused by continuous suppression of impotent rage. As an old popular saying goes, the bile runs over when a man cannot give vent to his wrath in some other way.

By temperament I am incapable of behaving like an irascible man. Dr Wichmann completely misread my attitude and took the fact that I remained so unmoved as proof of my guilt. Shortly after my arrest, for instance, as I heard later from Dr Dix, my defence counsel, he had been saying to all and sundry: 'That fellow John would carry on quite differently if he felt himself innocent.' He tried to interrogate me via Dr Dix and coolly suggested to him that he should visit me in my cell late in the evening when I was tired. While I was in the Heidelberg clinic he suggested that Dr Dix should visit me, give me too much to drink and extract a confession from me that way.

Dr Dix, my defence counsel, was a further vexation to me. He had been chosen by my wife in consultation with Ritter von Lex, the State Secretary. I had realised all along that there was little he could do for me since, to judge from the attitude of the judges during the remand proceedings, my sentence was a foregone conclusion. I could no longer tolerate him, however, when, shortly after my admittance to the prison hospital at Hohenasperg, he produced the astounding information that he could not cite Dr Globke, Adenauer's State Secretary, as a witness for the defence since he was a friend of his and he did not wish to involve him in perjury! I took the case away from him, but he told the Press that he had relinquished it. Next day the newspapers reported that he had relinquished the case since he no longer believed in my innocence.

This was only one of many hostile press reports fed to the public during my detention while under investigation. They originated from Dr Loesdau, the Federal Attorney in charge of the prosecution, and Weber, the Federal Judge, who had always denied to me giving any information whatsoever to the Press. I was at my wits' end. What was the point of briefing another defence counsel? But my wife was not prepared to accept this. She went to Karlsruhe to find a defence counsel there. Her hopes were rising because Dr Wichmann, the senior Federal Attorney, had recently reached the age limit and had been replaced by his deputy, Dr Güde, with the title Federal Attorney-General.

My wife asked for an interview with Dr Güde in the Federal

High Court. He received her in the presence of Dr Loesdau as the expert in charge of the case; he listened to what she had to say but stressed that he personally had nothing to do with my case. Finally he recommended to her as defence counsel a Karlsruhe barrister, Dr Caemmerer, Sen.; he had proved himself a staunch anti-Nazi, was a few years older than me and, after a talk with me, emerged determined to leave no stone unturned to obtain my acquittal. He was reinforced in this by a conversation on my case which he had had with Dr Güde shortly before his talk with me. Dr Güde had said that he did not really understand what Dr Wichmann had been after; apart from the statements which I had myself made, Wichmann possessed nothing which could disprove them or lead to a sentence.

During my first conversation with Dr Caemmerer he was accompanied by his son whom I had already met when lecturing to prisoners of war in England eight or nine years previously and whom I knew to be a firm supporter of the principles of democracy, social justice and the rule of law. He encouraged me by saying that Dr Güde was basically on my side; he and his father, he said, could speak quite frankly to Dr Güde since they knew him well. Dr Caemmerer, Sen., was a Catholic and a member of the Catholic Students Union; he was also a member of the Socialist Party and he therefore had the best of contacts.

I began to regain hope and to think that all might be well with my case in the end, particularly when Herr von Perbandt, head of the Personnel Department in the Ministry of the Interior, visited me accompanied by one of my former staff to bring me greetings from all those in Bonn who believed in my innocence. It was a gesture of affection and civil courage, the sole moral support I received from official quarters. It could only have come from a man like Perbandt who had proved his worth as an evangelical Christian in the resistance to the Nazi régime. I was also encouraged by the touching pertinacity of my wife who had installed herself in a hotel in nearby Bietigheim so as to be near me and be able to visit me as often as allowed. In this respect Dr Schmidt, the prison governor, was especially helpful; he placed his office at our disposal for my wife's visits and invariably encouraged me in the hope that the case would finally go well for me.

My slowly reviving confidence soon disappeared once more. Wilhelm Bentele, a Stuttgart industrialist, and his wife showed interest in my fate because I had supported him when he had been arrested on insufficient grounds for alleged illegal relationships with the East during the notorious 'Vulkan affair'. Herr Bentele sent his lawyer, Dr Ruisinger, to Dr Güde to find out whether I needed a defence counsel, the Press having reported that Dr Dix had relinquished the case. Dr Güde told Dr Ruisinger that I had meanwhile engaged Dr Caemmerer and was therefore in the best of hands. Dr Güde said that he was anxious, however, because my wife was jeopardising my defence; she was 'gossiping everywhere' that Dr Wohlgemuth had hypnotised her husband with the aid of drugs and had abducted him while in a state of trance. If Frau John continued to talk in this way, it might have the worst possible effect on the trial.

The theory that I had been kidnapped while hypnotised did not originate from my wife. She had heard that Dr Wohlgemuth had experimented with hypnosis to anaesthetise patients and, in order to throw some light on my abduction, she had accordingly visited Professor I. H. Schulz, the well-known Berlin psychiatrist and specialist in hypnosis. Schulz had previously cleared up the case of a young German who had been abducted into the French Foreign Legion by means of hypnosis and, on this basis, he had expounded to my wife the theory that I had been kidnapped with the aid of drugs and hypnosis. My wife had in no sense 'gossiped everywhere'; in her statements for the record, however, to Dr Güde and to her immediate friends and advisers she had described this as the probable method by which I had been abducted by Dr Wohlgemuth.

Herr and Frau Bentele felt that they must arrange for my wife to be told by Dr Ruisinger himself about his talk with Dr Güde and so they invited them both to tea. Before Dr Ruisinger arrived, however, Frau Bentele came out with this, to her, most important piece of information and told my wife of Dr Güde's warning that her statements could only endanger my position. My wife was so horrified that she rushed out into the garden, stumbled over two flagstones and broke her left arm.

Meanwhile Dr Loesdau had assembled the case for the prosecution based on Weber's summary of evidence. It was labelled 'secret' and served upon me in August 1956, nearly nine months after my arrest. I was accused of treason and engaging in propaganda for the overthrow of the Federal government. Dr Güde, so I was told by Dr Caemmerer, had described the prosecution's case as 'a botched-up piece of work' and had not even therefore signed it personally.

The prosecution's case bore clear marks of massive collaboration by Weber, the investigating judge – though legally an investigating judge should not seek to influence a case. Though his investigations had lasted eight months, he had brought to light nothing which was not already on the files. In my case I believe that the records of the investigations were of less importance to the prosecution than the fact that Weber had spread the word among Federal attorneys, judges and generally in Bonn that Dr Wohlgemuth would be present for the main hearing, would disprove my statements by evidence on oath and so publicly expose me.

Dr Caemmerer, Sen., my defence counsel, naturally found all this most disturbing. He came to me in great agitation and besought me to tell him the entire truth. He tried to extract from me anything which might show that Wohlgemuth could conclusively disprove me at the main trial; I still had friends who would stand by me, he said, but I would be committing moral suicide if I were exposed as a liar before the world press. After a talk lasting more than two hours Dr Caemmerer shook me by the hand and, as he left, said: 'I believe you. But we shall be confronted by judges who are under pressure from many quarters. You have always stood in the way of the ex-Nazis and the generals who are now up to their tricks again. They have no wish to see you rehabilitated.'

Dr Caemmerer went to Bonn to discuss my case with my former Minister, his State Secretary and other senior officials who were unprejudiced. He found much goodwill and a desire to help in my defence, 'also because of the political significance of this sinister trial', as he put it. None of them, however, had any practical advice to give. The Minister held the view that my defence could not succeed because public opinion had been prejudiced against me through the Press! In the Bonn ministries people were whispering that the Bench proposed to sentence me to seven or eight years' hard labour. This was confirmed to Dr Caemmerer even by Dr Güde. Dr Caemmerer tried to break this to me gently. I could do no more than wonder and say: 'My poor wife!'

Under the pressure of news like this the bile content of my blood rose to such an extent that the doctors pronounced my condition serious. Dr Caemmerer had meanwhile been indefatigable in unearthing from the records evidence which exposed Dr Wohlgemuth as an agent of the East. He also discovered a whole series of incontrovertible facts tending to show that I had actually been kidnapped. None of this mitigating evidence appeared in the case for the prosecution. Finally Dr Caemmerer told me that Güde had assured him that he personally would favour acquittal provided that Wohlgemuth did not appear at the main hearing and disprove me by some credible piece of evidence.

On this point I was confident and said so to Dr Caemmerer. I was firmly convinced that Wohlgemuth could not and would not dare to appear as a witness against me before the court.

Then, however, a further source of anxiety arose. At the request of the prison doctor, who was no longer willing to carry sole responsibility for me, I was examined by a panel of doctors. They pronounced that I should have my gall bladder removed at once; the operation was apparently essential to avoid cirrhosis of the liver which sooner or later would inevitably lead to death. 'You would like to live at least another twenty years,' the head surgeon said to me. Dr Caemmerer obtained agreement from the Court, confirmed by Dr Güde, that if I were willing to undergo the operation, my arrest should be suspended and I should be released forthwith; I would also be permitted to go abroad for the operation – to America, for instance, where Anthony Eden had recently had his gall bladder removed by a well-known specialist. Many people wanted me to avoid trial by this method, my friends because they feared that I would be sentenced to eight years' imprisonment, others possibly because, by evasion, I should brand myself as a guilty traitor.

I thought only of the possibility that I might not survive the operation and might thus depart this life as a 'traitor'. Moreover I still felt strong enough to stand trial, particularly since I now placed great hopes in Dr Güde. I told the doctors that I would only undergo the operation after the trial, if in fact it was necessary at all. My condition was simply the result of all the hardships which I had had to endure ever since July 1954. As soon as I was free, I said, I would quickly get well again. Of this I was confident and in fact, despite all that I have had to undergo, I still have my gall bladder today.

The main hearing before the Third Bench of the Federal High Court opened on 12 November 1956, almost a year after my escape from East Berlin. The day before Dr Caemmerer urged me to 'stick it out' and, moreover, to leave the defence entirely to him, since he had so agreed with Dr Güde. He regarded it as a good omen that at the last moment Dr Jagusch had been nominated as additional member of the Bench; in an authoritative memorandum to the Court he had interpreted the punishment code for political offences in a sense favourable to me. During the trial, which lasted nearly five weeks, I was accommodated in Karlsruhe prison. Although at this time the world was in turmoil as a result of the Suez crisis and the rising in Hungary, all Western newspapers of international significance sent reporters to the trial.

After I had given my own evidence fresh witnesses were heard every day until mid-December. Under pressure from both the Caemmerers (Sen. and Jr.) I had declared myself ready to forgo the interrogation of, and confrontation with, Dr Adenauer. The witnesses could produce no firm evidence why or how I had disappeared from West into East Berlin. Some of them said that they could not believe that I had gone over to the East voluntarily. Then came the day on which Dr Wohlgemuth was to be heard. He did not appear, despite the fact that the Court had guaranteed him safe conduct including the opportunity to proceed to another Western country outside the Federal Republic; he could easily have earned a lot of money by writing a series of articles in the West – an American agency had already offered me 10,000 dollars for four articles. My wife had turned this down on the advice of my Minister to avoid any suggestion of influencing the course of the trial.

Wohlgemuth sent the Bench a letter, couched in arrogant terms, refusing to appear as a witness in Karlsruhe. The last part of the letter was contemptuous, not only of me but also of the Court – so much so that the President did not read that passage. Urged by Weber, however, the Bench was set on obtaining some statement from Wohlgemuth and authorised a judge to take his evidence on the sector boundary in Berlin, a procedure he had declared himself ready to accept. When Dr Manzen, the judge concerned, appeared with Dr Loesdau representing the Federal Attorney and Dr Caemmerer, Jr, representing me, they were challenged by Dr Wohlgemuth to come across the sector boundary to him; he was standing there on the sector boundary ready to give evidence as agreed, he said. This ludicrous judicial scene, which nevertheless formed part of the case against me, was not taken into account either by the Court or the Press in forming their opinion on Wohlgemuth.

The hearing of evidence ended and Dr Güde rose to make his speech for the prosecution. He opened with general psychological considerations and then proceeded to attack me as a weakling and to do so in a manner which I had hitherto thought characteristic only of judges in totalitarian countries. Schallies, the Karlsruhe law reporter, aptly described Güde's performance as 'a public moral castigation'. When I protested indignantly to Dr Caemmerer during a pause in the proceedings, he comforted me, saying that Güde thought this procedure to be the only way of saving me from a long term of imprisonment.

There followed a summary of the evidence for the prosecution by Dr Loesdau. Then Drs Caemmerer, father and son, made their pleas. No other counsel could have defended me with greater conviction, honesty and eloquence than Dr Caemmerer, Sen. Next morning he told me that he had spent the evening drinking wine with Dr Güde, but had been unable to dissuade him from applying for a two–year sentence. This I must accept, he said, particularly seeing that, taking into account my period in detention, I should only have a few months to do.

On 22 December 1956 sentence was pronounced – four years' hard labour. Grounds for the verdict: The Bench had to admit that none of the accusations raised against me in public were justified. There was also no proof that I had betrayed State secrets. It was, however, proved that 'on 20 July 1954 I had driven into East Berlin with Dr Wohlgemuth, that I had entered into discussion with Eastern agencies there and had thereupon decided to remain there and occupy myself politically'. This was almost word for word what Wohlgemuth had said in his letter from East Berlin to the investigating judge.

What was the proof? My description of my awakening from my stupor in Karlshorst was not considered plausible since it was 'full of clichés' and I had expressed no indignation against Dr Wohlgemuth or the Russians; the authorities in the Soviet zone would not have dared to produce me in front of the world press after 'only' three weeks, if I had not gone over to them of my own free will; at an 'earlier' period, in other words the resistance period, I had secretly and on my own initiative made contacts with the object of playing politics; I had not confided in anybody in the East nor had I informed authoritative quarters in the Federal Republic of my position; if Wohlgemuth had really kidnapped me, he would not have returned to his apartment that night as it was proved that he did; in my letters to my wife I had attempted to make my voluntary defection comprehensible to her (ten passages were cited out of some 150 letters).

The legal grounds given for the verdict were that I had betrayed fictitious state secrets in that, while in East Berlin, I had broadcast certain statements which, had they been true, would necessarily have been rated as genuine state secrets. In simple language this meant that I was guilty because, although I had betrayed neither persons nor secrets to the East, I had served up for public consumption lies which, had they been true, would have amounted to secrets, the disclosure of which would have been punishable. This form of legal logic is incomprehensible outside the Federal Republic, as reputable lawyers from all over the world have since confirmed to me. Equally incomprehensible are the other grounds for the verdict: that my intention was proved to undermine the constitutional order of the Federal Republic and to overthrow the Federal government – into whose jurisdiction I had escaped!

The increase of the sentence from the two years demanded by Dr Güde, the Attorney-General, to four years was a unique and totally incomprehensible augmentation of my punishment. The Bench justified it as necessary in order to prevent the public saying: 'The little fish are hanged, the big fish go scot free' – a form of rough popular justice reminiscent of the Nazi era. The *Manchester Guardian*'s comment was: 'Curious grounds for a Sentence'.

There was no appeal against my sentence. The verdict was given by a court both of first and final instance. My judges had all been trained under the Nazi régime. The President had been a military judge advocate. The verdict against me proved that in cases of political offences the law was used in as authoritarian and reactionary a manner as under the Weimar Republic. My martyred friends and I had once fought in the resistance to set up a state based on the rule of law. My sentence showed that this had been mere illusion.

30
The Mystery Solved

AFTER hearing my sentence I was taken back to my cell in Karlsruhe prison. Shortly after, precisely at midday, I heard the news broadcast for the prisoners over the courtyard loudspeaker and my sentence was the first item. Spontaneously there arose from the cells loud catcalls and whistles, the first demonstration against the verdict on me. There soon followed severe criticism from authoritative lawyers both at home and abroad. Six months after the Karlsruhe verdict the Bundestag Commission charged with examining my case pronounced that its 'own investigations' had shown that my case was 'not yet unequivocally clear', an unmistakable and unusual criticism of the administration of justice by the highest political court in the Federal Republic. This was an expression of the increasing disquiet in political and legal circles over the working of the judicial system, personified by Dr Jagusch who had been President of the highest German court for many years and had been a 'guardian of the law' under the Nazis (he was meanwhile retired for falsification of his personal papers); the end result was a fundamental change in the code for political offences under a law of 25 June 1968. The change annulled those parts of the code under which I had been sentenced as an 'enemy of the State'. Today I could not even have been indicted. I had no right of appeal, however, and so I served my sentence in the prison in Münster, Westphalia.

In the prison garb that I wore not a button was my own property. As during my period of detention, I was kept isolated from all other prisoners. I therefore spent a total of three years and eight months in solitary confinement after having already been seventeen months in the hands of the Soviet secret service. For my first six months in prison I had no information of any sort from outside; I had only a bible to read; I was not even allowed to work.

My heaviest burden was my permanent anxiety for my wife particularly when, in May 1957, her broken arm was expected to be amputated. One of my fellow-prisoners, a doctor who acted as assistant to the prison medical officer, helped me with friendly advice and a secret supply of pills.

About this time (summer 1957) I was allowed to read and do some literary work. Karl Gerold, editor of the *Frankfurter Rundschau*, sent me his newspaper every day. In the prison library I found a wide choice of classical and contemporary literature. My days were now filled with reading and drafting plays and a trilogy of novels. Every six weeks I wrote to my wife and received letters from her. At Christmas 1957, a year after my sentence, she was allowed to visit me.

My wife was earning her livelihood in London as a singing teacher. Dr Caemmerer, my defence counsel, together with colleagues, journalists and politicians who were incensed over the unjust verdict on me, were working for a pardon from the Federal President and my wife was full of hope that they would succeed. The President had been a friend both of her and her father in the past.

So once more I was waiting in prison and hoping for the day of liberation – as I had done in Lisbon, in the London internment camp and while a prisoner of the Soviets behind the Iron Curtain. Each time that I had succeeded in escaping to the freedom of the West I had ended in prison.

My only exercise consisted of cleaning a lavatory and polishing the little passage which separated me from the main block of cells. For this daily performance the warder opened my cell door each morning. Yet such trifles made my prison life more tolerable. The warders treated me as if I were a respected visitor. Once a week Otto Kröhnert, the prison chaplain and a pastor of the Confessional Church, held a bible study hour and on Sundays a church service. He increased my faith; he was completely selfless in his devotion to the prisoners and helped wherever he could.

There were nearly 2000 criminals in the prison and I met all kinds – thieves, murderers, sexual offenders and the whole gamut of greater or smaller wrong-doers. Though I came in personal contact only with very few – during daily exercise, the bible study hour or the church service – the inmates did their best to ease my imprisonment. Since I earned nothing and was only allowed three marks a month for the purchase of supplementary food or tobacco, one or other of my fellow-prisoners was always passing me a piece of chocolate, a slab of margarine or a cigarette. One of them rigged me up a little receiver hidden in a matchbox, so that I could listen to the radio at night. Unfortunately it did not work very well.

To keep my mental processes in order in the loneliness of my cell I adopted the Jesuit method, making an active effort to assemble my thoughts. I found it difficult – I did not know that Jesuits are never in principle left alone for long periods lest they fall victim to introspection. Over and over again I asked myself: What has my life amounted to? In retrospect one's errors are recognisable. Nevertheless I stand by the principles which have guided my life, even though they entailed the rejection of much good advice and have brought me more misery than joy. Now, looking back over sixty years, the balance sheet of my life looks like this:

I grew up in the country, under the authority of the monarchy and the church; my childhood was governed by their standards. In my mind, therefore, the upheaval of 1918 represented a crime against the people. Only when we moved during the 1920s to the cosmopolitan spa of Wiesbaden did my picture of the world and of men change. Under the influence of contemporary progressive German and foreign literature I veered towards more liberal ideas. Ever since my student days Albert Schweitzer had been my model. My plan to make a career for myself in the foreign service was wrecked by Hitler's 'seizure of power'. From the time of the 30 June 1934 murders I was convinced that Hitler's policy would lead to war. I wanted to leave Germany to avoid having to fight for Hitler. I had, however, rejected the opportunity offered me by the German Lufthansa in order to join the Resistance – out of moral indignation, not for political reasons. I wished to make some contribution to the overthrow of this criminal régime. But it was all in vain and an illusion. I barely escaped the gallows and reached London.

I never intended to remain in London. This became clear to me during the years when I was an exile there. With my specialist qualifications I could perfectly well have occupied myself in London as adviser on International Law, but that was no solution. When I returned to Germany and took over the Federal Internal Security Office, I was confident that the Republic was headed for a Christian democratic future. I continued to believe in this despite the fact that, with his highly authoritarian methods of leadership, Dr Adenauer had already given the green light for rearmament and was using for this purpose much of the old Nazi administrative machine. Consequently, as a symbolic resistance figure and an alleged agent of the British, I stood in many people's way. Nevertheless, I would never have relinquished my post voluntarily. Then I was kidnapped and to this day I do not know how it was done. I was unconscious until I awoke as a prisoner of the Soviet secret service. With what object had the Russians kidnapped me? I mulled over this question continuously in my prison.

I had certainly not been abducted into East Berlin to be used for propaganda purposes. The Russians were not to know how I would behave as their prisoner. Their interrogation of me in Gagra, particularly Michailov's cross-examination, was not specially directed towards my office or my knowledge of official matters. They had remarked sarcastically that they were better informed about my Office than I was myself and had concentrated on my connections with the British secret service, in particular on my knowledge of alleged secret agreements between the British government and the German Resistance in the event of a successful *coup d'état* against Hitler. Once I had been returned to East Berlin, no one made any attempt to interrogate me on intelligence matters. There remained only one explanation: that they believed that I had been infiltrated into the West German secret service by the British.

Fresh light was thrown on this subject only in late-1961 when Anatol Golytsin, a Soviet secret service officer, defected to the Americans. He indicated that the K.G.B. had used my appearance in East Berlin as cover for the mass arrests of Gehlen agents in the Eastern zone betrayed by Heinz Felfe, their agent in the Gehlen organisation. They presented me as a defector to East Germany who had given them the necessary information and so diverted suspicion from their real informant, Felfe. This enabled Felfe to continue to work for a further seven years as a Soviet agent inside the Federal intelligence service. Golytsin's information provided some form of explanation for my abduction. It had in any case been a paying proposition for the Soviets, after their arrest of a whole series of Gehlen agents, to be able to present the story of 'the traitor John'. On their return to the Federal Republic, however, several of the captured agents said that, once in prison in the Eastern zone, they had quickly realised that I was not their real betrayer but that it must have been someone inside the Federal intelligence service.

I continued to believe in this explanation for years after my release. Nevertheless, at times I had my doubts. From the Russian point of view, my possible suicide, which they took such pains to prevent, would have led to a world-wide scandal and it seemed to me that this was too great a risk to run if all they wanted was to interrogate me about the British secret service and use me as cover for a mass arrest of Western agents. I had no illusions however about the brutal methods of interrogation employed under Stalinism. And Stalinism had not yet faded into history at the time when I was kidnapped.

The true background to my abduction only emerged gradually. In 1967 British journalists in London questioned me about my relationship with Kim Philby, the notorious Soviet agent inside the British secret service who had fled to Moscow in 1963. They wanted to publicise Philby's activity as an agent working for the Soviets. As a result they discovered that at the time when I had been in Lisbon during the war probing the possibilities of negotiating with the British government on behalf of the German resistance, Philby had occupied the 'Iberian desk', in other words had been the senior SIS official dealing with Spain and Portugal. These clues made me prick up my ears. I finally became certain of the reasons for my abduction when I read Philby's book, *My Silent War*, written in Moscow and published in 1968, also Hugh Trevor-Roper's comments on it in his book, *The Philby Affair*.

During the war Trevor-Roper had been working with Philby in SIS. In his book he sets out all he knew, but had hitherto kept secret, about Philby's activity as an agent. According to Trevor-Roper, when the Anglo-Russian alliance was operative Philby was in no position to betray any important secrets since these were anyway exchanged between the Allies on the highest political level. At this time Philby's only real possibility of 'serving the vital interests of Russia' lay in opposing any attempt by the German resistance to use the British government as an intermediary for the conclusion of a pact with the Western Powers directed against the Soviet Union in the event of a successful *coup* in Germany. At this time, so Philby says in his own book, 'the air was opaque with mutual suspicions of separate peace feelers'. On the British side Philby stopped any 'dickering with the Germans', as he calls it in his book. As Trevor-Roper records, for instance, he described one of my reports, in which I sought to inform the British government about the anti-Hitler resistance and its political aims, as 'unreliable'. Philby forbade further dissemination of my report in the office and resolutely refused even to discuss it. 'In a matter so important'

Trevor-Roper and his colleagues found this totally inexplicable. When I was released from prison in Lisbon in October 1944 Rita Winsor had confided to me that up to the very last moment someone in London had been resisting my entry into England – it was Philby.

When Guy Burgess and Donald Maclean fled to Moscow in May 1951 Philby, as a close friend of Burgess, became an object of suspicion to the British government. In fact it was he who had given the two Soviet agents timely warning to escape to Moscow before they were discovered. Philby was closely interrogated and cross-examined but contrived to argue his way out of his predicament. There were no conclusive proofs against him. He remained a 'security risk', however, and in 1952 was accordingly dismissed from the British secret service with compensation of £4000. This generous treatment by the British government made Philby an object of suspicion to his Soviet friends and masters. They kept him in London for a further two years. It was obviously of vital importance for the Soviet secret service to know whether this agent of theirs, who had been working in the highest British quarters, was reliable or whether he had been a double agent playing it both ways. Philby could only be tested against me, one of his sole surviving opponents from the German resistance. This was why the K.G.B. took action and abducted me when Wohlgemuth offered himself for the purpose. This is the only explanation I can give for the fact that my interrogations in Gagra concentrated upon my connections with the British secret service and upon potential promises by the British government in the event of a successful *coup d'état* against Hitler.

At this time one of Stalin's nightmares had been some secret agreement between the Western Powers and the German resistance. Philby undoubtedly informed the Soviets that, on behalf of Dr Goerdeler, I had told the British government that 'they simply could not allow the Russians into Europe and so make the world-wide antagonisms between Britain and the Soviet Union insoluble for all time'. Had the British followed up these peace feelers, I would undoubtedly have made Philby's acquaintance since he was the senior SIS official responsible for Spain and Portugal. I told the Russians the truth: that all our peace feelers had failed in face of 'steadfast British loyalty to their treaties with the Russians'. Ever since the end of 1943 I had been telling Graf Stauffenberg that the Western Powers would persist in their demand for unconditional surrender. Throughout Michailov's questioning about names and contacts in the British secret service I had never mentioned Philby, since I never suspected that he had been my anonymous opponent. Michailov had finally convinced himself that Philby had not been a 'double-crosser', had not been going behind the Russians' backs and that they could rely on him. I am sure that in this way Philby was rehabilitated in Russian eyes without my ever knowing anything about it. This took place in Gagra in October 1954. Shortly thereafter, as he says in his book, Philby received a letter from a Soviet friend urging him to 'be of good cheer and presaging an early resumption of relations'. Philby, with his outstanding connections, was therefore once more able to work as a Soviet agent in Britain. From 1956 he was again working for SIS, camouflaged as a reporter for the *Observer* and the *Economist* in Beirut. Thence, in January 1963, he fled to Moscow where he now lives, covered in glory, on a state pension.

Unsuspectingly I had done the Russians an inestimable service with my statements. I now, therefore, understand why after my interrogations in Gagra I was no longer in Soviet custody and never saw Michailov again. After my return to East Berlin, although under strict guard by the East German Security Service, I was more or less left to myself. Without Philby's and Trevor-Roper's books I could never have discovered these underlying implications. While I was being interrogated in Gagra and frequently thereafter, however logically I thought over the matter, I could never make out what the ultimate purpose in abducting me had been. Now that I can see it all clearly it is somewhat easier for me to bear my fate, though not the obvious injustice of the Karlsruhe sentence. Nevertheless, at no time, not even in my moments of deepest depression during my detention, have I regretted returning to the Federal Republic and refusing to avail myself of Henrik Bonde-Henriksen's offer to take refuge in some Scandinavian country and ask for asylum there. I have accepted my sentence as something decreed by destiny in the sense of Goethe's Orphean dictum which stands as the motto to this book.

On 28 July 1958 I was released after three years and eight months in solitary confinement. I felt both strong and healthy enough to start a new life on the very next day in any activity open to me. Dr Hans Caemmerer, who had assisted his father in my defence, gave me real proof of his friendship in that he came in his car to fetch me from Münster prison. On the drive back to Cologne we lunched in the restaurant of a little town and there heard the radio announcement that I had been pardoned by the President and had been released from Münster prison an hour before. In fact, President Heuss had merely granted me the pardon to which I was entitled by law and usage; every major or minor criminal, if a first offender, has one-third of his sentence remitted for good behaviour – and I served thirty-two months out of a sentence of forty-eight. I did not receive even a week's remittance. With this so-called pardon came a ban, contrary both to the constitution and to the law, forbidding me to make any statement in public about my trial. After four years of isolation I returned to a new and totally strange world, the sovereign welfare state of the West German Federal Republic.

At the door of our house in Cologne photographers were assembled – but no friends. My wife had flown in from London and was waiting for me alone in the apartment which she had arranged. 'Now we will forget it all and live once more,' she said. But I do not wish to die a traitor and with all my strength I shall continue to strive for my rehabilitation.

Report for Graf Stauffenberg – March 1944

THE political and military decision to carry out an invasion has been irrevocably taken. The invasion may be expected between mid-June and the end of the month in two major assaults on the Continent between Bordeaux and Hamburg, alternatively between Brest and Antwerp and in Holland and/or West Germany.

To the vital question whether and to what extent further delay in the invasion may be counted upon, I must, in so far as my information goes, reply in the negative. It has been reported to me from a reliable source that, with the nomination of Eisenhower, all influence by political quarters upon the execution of the operation has been eliminated. The planning and execution of the operation will now be governed solely by purely military decisions which Eisenhower, in his capacity as Supreme Commander, will be responsible for taking. An authoritative American, said to be in close touch both with Eisenhower's headquarters and with Washington, expressed himself somewhat as follows: 'Nothing can now change the decision to carry out the invasion, even should the President die. And it is better this way since the American lack of a sense of political direction might jeopardise military operations, were not a firm decision about the invasion taken now. Previously people in America were as much at sea and in doubt about the invasion as they are now about the forthcoming elections; people at home do not think clearly and cannot make up their minds what policy to follow in order to solve the problem of the war.' This statement, guaranteed to come from a reliable source, must, in my view, be taken as an indication that even the leading American politicians can no longer influence the progress of preparations for and execution of the invasion. A statement by a representative of the American Embassy recently recalled from Madrid appears relevant in this connection: The United States had started total mobilisation in June 1940 on a plan visualising a four-year mobilisation period. This plan has been fully adhered to and implemented. By June 1944 this total mobilisation has produced an army fully prepared and equipped for invasion.

In various conversations I attempted to elucidate whether the intentions of the British leaders, referred to in my previous report, to direct the main invasion operations against the Balkans, might lead to a further delay in the invasion. It was stressed that the basic political decision to invade the Continent had been taken and that these British proposals would be considered, and if necessary carried out, as a purely military problem concerned with the execution of the invasion. As previously reported, these views of the British military leaders have not prevailed and, though less keen on the invasion, they have accepted that it will take place on the west European coastline. The result has been a certain scepticism on the part of the British leaders regarding the success of the invasion; they are also disappointed because, as a result, a total commitment is required from Britain contrary to the British, and in particular Churchill's, principle not to put all the eggs into one basket. There can, however, be no doubt that the British leaders have accepted the plan for invasion on the west coast and are now pursuing it with all energy; nevertheless, even today, negotiations are in progress in Britain with representatives of Tito visualising an invasion operation in the Balkans. There can, however, be no justification for the assumption that the British leaders could now change decisions taken under Eisenhower's command concerning invasion operations against the west coast of Europe or even delay their implementation. The determination of the British leaders to co-operate fully in invasion in the West now that it has been decided, is also shown in their attitude towards any tendency to come to an understanding with Germany. There is said to be only one viewpoint – unconditional surrender must be imposed by military means. On this they are absolutely at one with the Americans. Stettinius' conversations in Britain gave complete satisfaction to both sides, although one-hundred-per cent agreement was not reached on all questions. On the other hand, deliberately and designedly, all sorts of rumours about dissension between Britain and America are spread around the Continent by British and American representatives; their purpose is to mislead German leaders about the invasion.

Little was to be learnt about the influence exerted by Russia upon the planning and progress of the invasion. It was pointed out, however, that the Russian leaders planned and acted entirely independently of Allied invasion plans. Stalin's primary object, which he pursues unswervingly, is the destruction of the German Wehrmacht. Everything done with the German Liberation Committee in Moscow is mere deception and political trickery. According to Stalin himself the object of Russian propaganda is to instil into the people hatred of the Nazis, although he himself harbours a certain sour admiration for what Hitler has done in Germany and Germany in occupied Russia. Stalin has a healthy respect for the training of the German army and in particular for its officers. He, like Churchill, does not hold the view that 'Hitler is merely a tool in the hands of more capable men'. No one should count upon an internal collapse in Germany – and Stalin does not do so. Victory over Germany can only be achieved by total destruction of the Wehrmacht. For this reason invasion is essential. In Stalin's view the air war can, nevertheless, contribute to destruction of the faith in Hitler's invincibility. Stalin, with his 'cold realistic way of thinking', is said to have proposed to the Americans that they should merely occupy strongpoints of importance, the property of those nations which have not unequivocally co-operated with the Allies and are not strong enough to defend themselves. This should be taken primarily as a reference to Spain, where the Allies could easily obtain a foothold with the aid of the Republicans (see my report before last on the possibilities of Allied military intervention in Spain as a diversionary operation to the invasion).

To summarise: No store should be set on the possibility that Allied plans and preparations for the invasion or their implementation will undergo any change or delay as a result of political influences from the Allied side.

II

The British Ambassador left Madrid about a fortnight ago, telling his friends that, *if* he returned, he would be back in four weeks time. He said that he hoped to take over an appointment in England. The British government's regulations for the isolation of the British Isles are being strictly enforced. It is therefore all the more important to keep an eye on the few people who come to the Continent from Britain. As far as I could tell, aircraft on the England–Lisbon run are as full as ever in both directions. The destination of the majority of passengers, however, who come and go through Lisbon is Africa or the East. Since the imposition of the restrictions only two persons have arrived in Madrid. One of them is a director of the B.B.C. and son-in-law to a well-known Spanish doctor whose family is friendly with Hoare. Lisbon is the best place for keeping an eye on traffic between Britain and the Continent since the airline can be observed from there. An attempt should be made to gain contact with the Dutch crews who pass through there.

It is an interesting fact that the British who come to the Continent now make large-scale personal purchases – a good indication of the supply situation in Britain.

At the moment British secret service activity in the Iberian peninsula consists almost exclusively of the detection of German agents and pressure to have them expelled from Spain and Portugal. A favourite and profitable subject for the start of a conversation is the alleged tension between Russia and the Allies. Practically all German agents fall into this trap.

In view of the enormous efforts required for the invasion, problems connected therewith are being given priority in England at the moment. The British political leaders, and particularly Churchill's entourage, however, are continually seeing fresh problems emerge which neither the invasion nor indeed any military methods will solve. Churchill's object is said to be the maintenance of the Empire. He is supposed to have said: 'Our intention is to hold what we have. I did not become His Majesty's Prime Minister in order to preside over the liquidation of the British Empire.'

III

The previous American Chargé d'Affaires in Madrid has been recalled. The reason is said to be his cautious handling of the Spaniards. This means the loss of a useful contact. Instead, however, it has been possible to establish a fresh direct contact to the American Embassy and something may be expected from this. It has produced the following information regarding the relationship between America and Russia: The fundamental error in American policy has been lack of a clear line of foreign policy for over fifty years; the low point was reached in 1939 with the rupture of trade relations with Japan and refusal of arms deliveries to Britain and France. Facts have opened the Americans' eyes. Recognition of the necessity for a basic change in foreign policy is of particular significance for future relationships with Russia and is the main governing factor in America's attitude to Russia in this war. Russia is and will be in the future one of the greatest political powers in the world and, after victory over Japan, the most powerful force in the Pacific after the United States. The problem is whether Russia intends to extend her power so far westwards in Europe that it will affect British and American interests which consist of achieving an unequivocal settlement of European relations. America is interested in a European settlement which will relieve her of the necessity for constant military intervention in Europe, whether in purely European affairs or to maintain against Russian pretensions the new European order to be created after the war. America is now supporting Russia in this war with all her resources and there are at present no grounds for the assumption that a split will develop between America and Russia in this war against Germany and Japan. Whether this co-operation between America and Russia can continue after the war depends upon the settlement reached regarding the buffer states between Russia and Europe – Finland, Sweden, Poland, the Danube states, the Balkan states and Turkey – whether, in fact, it can be a settlement governed by considerations other than military. It cannot be foreseen today which of the above states may or must become satellites of Russia.

In any case it is clear that the buffer states cannot be re-established as outposts of a 'Western coalition' against Russia by means of agreements with the Western Powers. Moreover American and Russian interests in Europe only affect each other indirectly, whereas in the Pacific they do so directly. Accordingly American policy is entirely directed towards the support of Russia in the war against Germany with all available forces and it is now quite certain that neither America nor Russia will make peace with Germany without the agreement of the other.

Final Report for London from Madrid – 26 June 1944

THE opposition in Germany has consolidated itself into a shadow government in which the former Social Democrats and representatives of the Centre Party exert the main influence. As before the shadow government's object is to bring about an internal political change before the total collapse of Germany in order to end the war as rapidly as possible; for lack of adequate resources, however, it is not in a position to do this alone. All hopes of a *coup d'état* by the generals have proved illusory. The shadow government, however, has found active support among staff officers in the headquarters and General Staff of the Wehrmacht who are both determined and able to combine with the shadow government in liquidating the Nazi war adventure and the Nazi system as quickly as possible.

This project stems from the conviction that it is in the interests of the Allies, of the states of Europe and of Germany herself to prevent further destruction in Europe and the complete collapse of Germany as a result of continuation of the war. After the liquidation of the Nazi régime and the war which it has instigated, the reconstruction of Europe would be undertaken in concert between the Allies and the forces of law and order in Germany. Only the latter, by virtue of their attitude and their struggle against Nazism, can be authorised or in a position to create new conditions throughout Germany.

Only the attitude of the Allies constitutes the real obstacle to realisation of this project today. All contact with the opposition in Germany has so far been refused and no attempt has been made to convince it that the Allies are prepared to co-operate with it either now or in the future or to differentiate between the Nazis and the rest of Germany. So long as this situation persists, no action against the Nazis can be initiated in Germany. The Hitler régime will never capitulate. But the elimination of the system and a rapid liquidation of the war can be prepared and carried through by the opposition in concert with the Allies, provided that conditions and the *modus procedendi* are established in concert.

Bibliography

Abshagen, K. H., *Canaris. Patriot und Weltbürger* (Deutsche Verlags-gesellschaft, Stuttgart, 1949). Translated by Alan Brodrick as *Canaris* (Hutchinson, 1956).

Alsop, St., and Braden, Th., *Sub Rosa. The O.S.S. and American Espionage* (New York, 1946).

Barth, K., *Theologische Existenz heute* (Kaiser Verlag, Munich, 1933).

Bell, G. K. A., 'The Background of the Hitler Plot', in *Contemporary Review,* no. 168 (1945) pp. 203-8 (also in Dietrich Bonhoeffer, *Letters and Papers from Prison,* vol. 1).

Bethge, E., 'The Challenge of Dietrich Bonhoeffer's Life and Theology', the Alden-Tuthill Lectures in the *Chicago Theological Seminary Register,* vol. LI (Feb 1961) no. 2, pp. 1-38.

—, 'Adam von Trott und der deutsche Widerstand', in *Vierteljahrshefte für Zeitgeschichte,* no. 11 (1963) pp. 213-23.

Böhm, F., 'Revolutionär wider Willen? Zu der Auseinandersetzung über Carl Goerdeler und den 20 Juli', in *Die Gegenwart,* no. 10 (1955) pp. 262-7.

Bonhoeffer, D., *Widerstand und Ergebung* (Kaiser Verlag, Munich, 1951).

—, *Gesammelte Werke* (Kaiser Verlag, Munich, 1958). Translated by Reginald Fuller as *Letters and Papers from Prison* (Macmillan, 1967).

Boveri, M., *Der Verrat im 20 Jahrhundert* (Rowohlt, Hamburg, 1957).

Buchheim, H., and Schmithenner, W. (eds), *Der deutsche Widerstand gegen Hitler* (Kiepenheuer & Witsch, Cologne, 1966).

Budde, E., and Lütsches, P., *Die Wahrheit über den 20 Juli* (Raven, Düsseldorf, 1953).

Bullock, A., *Hitler. A Study in Tyranny* (Harper & Row, 1964).

Bundeszentrale für Heimatdienst, *20 Juli 1944,* reproduced from a special number of *Das Parlament* of 20 July 1952, 1st and 2nd editions by Hans Royce, 3rd edition (1960) by Erich Zimmermann and Hans-Adolf Jacobsen (Berto-Verlag, Bonn).

Colvin, I., *Master Spy* (McGraw-Hill, 1951).

Delmer, S., *Trail Sinister* (Secker & Warburg, 1961).

Delp, A., *Im Angesicht des Todes* (Knecht-Carolus Druckerei, Frankfurt, 1947).

Diels, R., *Lucifer ante portas* (Deutsche Verlagsanstalt, Stuttgart, 1950).

—, *Der Fall Otto John* (Göttinger Verlag, Göttingen, 1954).

Dille, J., 'A Tip Berlin's Police Ignored', in *Life* (International ed.), vol. 17 (1954), no. 6, pp. 30-2.

Dulles, A. W., *Germany's Underground* (Macmillan, 1947).

Ehlers, D., *Technik und Moral einer Verschwörung. Der Aufstand am 20 Juli 1944* (Bundeszentrale für politische Bildung, Bonn, 1964).

Eyck, E., *Geschichte der Weimarer Republik* (Eugen Rentsch Verlag, Erlenbach, Zurich and Stuttgart, 1954-6).

Fechter, P., *Menschen und Zeiten: Begegnungen aus fünf Jahrzehnten* (Deutsche Buchgemeinschaft, Gütersloh, 1950).

Fitzgibbon, C., *The Shirt of Nessus* (Norton, 1956).

Foerster, W., *Ein General kämpft gegen den Krieg* (Dom Verlag, Munich, 1949).

Forsthoff, E., *Der totale Staat* (Hanseatische Verlagsanstalt, Hamburg, 1933).

Friedensburg, F., *Die Weimarer Republik* (Norddeutscher Verlagsanstalt, Hanover and Frankfurt, 1957).

Frischauer, W., *The Man Who Came Back. The Story of Otto John* (Muller, 1958).

Galen, Cardinal Graf von, 'Rechtsbewusstsein und Rechtsunsicherheit', speech in Rome, March 1956, distributed as MS.

Gerken, R., *Spione unter uns. Methoden und Praktiken der Roten Geheimdienste nach amtlichen Quellen* (Auer-Cassianeum, Donauwörth, 1965).

Gisevius, H.-B., *Bis zum bitteren Ende* (Fretz und Wasmuth Verlag, Zurich, 1946). Translated by Richard and Clara Winstone as *To the Bitter End* (Houghton Mifflin, 1947).

Goebbels, J., *Diaries 1942-1943,* ed. and trans. Louis P. Lochner (Doubleday, 1948).

Gollwitzer, H., Kuhn, K. and Schneider, R., *Du hast mich heimgesucht bei Nacht. Abscheidsbriefe und Aufzeichnungen des Widerstandes 1933-1945* (Kaiser Verlag, Munich, 1954).

Görlitz, W., *Der deutsche Generalstab* (Verlag Frankfurter Hefte, 1950). Translated by Brian Battershaw as *A History of the German General Staff* (Praeger, 1953).

Guderian, H., *Erinnerungen eines Soldaten* (Kurt Vowinckel, Heidelberg, 1951). Translated by Constantine Fitzgibbon as *Panzer Leader,* with a foreword by Sir Basil Liddell Hart (Michael Joseph, 1952).

Haffner, S., '"Beinahe". Die Geschichte des 20 Juli 1944', in *Neue Auslese,* 2nd year, no. 8.

Hagen, H. W., *Zwischen Eid und Befehl. Tatzeugen-Bericht von den Ereignissen am 20 Juli 1944 und 'Wolfsschanze'* (Munich, 1958).

Hagen, L., *The Secret War for Europe* (Macdonald, London, 1968).

Hagen, W. (*alias* Hoettl), *Die geheime Front. Organisation, Personen und Aktionen des deutschen Geheimdienstes* (Nibelungen Verlag, Linz, 1950).

Halder, F., *Kriegstagebuch* [War Diary], vol. 1, *Vom Polenfeldzug bis zum Ende der Westoffensive (14 August 1939-30 June 1940),* eds. H. -A. Jacobsen and A. Philippi (Kohlhammer Verlag, Stuttgart, 1952).

—, *Hitler als Feldherr* (Dom Verlag, Munich, 1950)

Hansard, 19 March 1959.

Hassel, J. D., *Verräter? Patrioten! Der 20 Juli 1944* (Cologne, 1946).

Hassell, Ulrich von, *Vom anderen Deutschland* (Fischer Bücherei, Frankfurt and Hamburg, 1964). Translated as *Diaries 1938-1944* (Doubleday, 1947).

Henderson, J. L., *Adolf Reichwein, Eine politische-pädagogische Biographie,* ed. H. Lindemann (Deutsche Verlagsanstalt, Stuttgart, 1958).

Henk, E., *Die Tragödie des 20 Juli 1944. Ein Beitrag zur politischen Vorgeschichte* (Rausch, Heidelberg, 1946).

Herrschaft, H., 'Die Versuchung der Zeit (Affäre Dr John)', in *Militärpolitisches Forum,* no. 9 (1954) pp. 27-32.

Heusinger, A., *Befehl im Widerstreit* (Rainer Wunderlich, Hermann Leinz, Tübingen and Stuttgart, 1950).

Heuss, T., 'Bekenntnis und Verpflichtung': speeches on 10th anniversary of 20 July 1944 (Wunderlich Verlag, Stuttgart, 1955).

—, *Hitlers Weg. Eine historisch-politische Studie über den Nationalsozialismus* (Rainer Wunderlich, Hermann Leinz, Stuttgart, Berlin and Leipzig, 1952).

Hildebrandt, R., *Wir sind die letzten. Aus dem Leben des Widerstandskämpfers Albrecht Haushofer und seine Freunde* (Michael Verlag, Berlin-Neuwied, 1949).

Hitler, A., *Mein Kampf.* Various editions; first published, 1925, by Zentralverlag der N.S.D.A.P., Munich. Translated by Ralph Mannheim (latest edition, Hutchinson, 1970).

Hochhuth, R., *Der Stellvertreter* (Rowohlt, Reinbek, 1963).

Horne, A., 'Otto John Goes East', in *Return to Power* (Praeger, 1956).

Hossbach, F., *Zwischen Wehrmacht und Hitler* (Wolfenbütteler Verlagsanstalt, Wolfenbüttel and Hanover, 1949).

International Military Tribunal (I.M.T.), *Record of the Nuremberg Trials 14 November 1945- 1 October 1946.* 42 vols (H.M.S.O., 1947-9).

Joesten, J., 'The Otto John Story', in *They Call It Intelligence* (Abelard-Schumann, 1963).

John, O., *Ich wählte Deutschland* (Ausschuss für deutsche Einheit, Berlin, 1954).

—, 'Dr John's Foggy Trail', in *Newsweek* (European ed.), vol. 44 (1954) no. 6, p. 20; no. 7, p. 20; no. 8, p. 22.

—, 'West Germany. End of a Nightmare? (Otto John's Return)', in *Newsweek* (European ed.), vol. 46 (1955) no. 26, p. 22.

—, 'The Man with 100 Secrets', in *Time* (Atlantic ed.), vol. 64 (1954) no. 5, pp. 24-5; no. 7, pp. 21-2; no. 8, p. 25.

—, 'The Returncoat', in *Time* (Atlantic ed.), vol. 66 (1955) no. 26, p. 16.

—, 'Ist Otto John unschuldig?' in *Aktuell,* no. 1 (1962) pp. 12-18.

—, 'John-Ausschuss. Die Referenz-Kartei', in *Der Spiegel* (1955), no. 8, pp. 9-10; no. 12, pp. 9-10; no. 17, pp. 9-10.

—, 'Otto-John-Prozess. Kein übergrosser Fall', in *Der Spiegel,* no. 46 (1956) pp. 18-20.

John, O., "Berichte über Harnack, Leuschner, Moltke, Mierendorff, Haubach, Reichwein, Dohnanyi', in *Blick in die Welt,* nos 6-12 (1946-7).

Kelsen, H., *Allgemeine Staatslehre* (Berlin, 1925).

Kielmansegg, Graf J. A. von, *Der Fritschprozess 1938* (Hoffmann und Campe, Hamburg, 1949).

Kiesel, G., 'S.S-Bericht über den 20 Juli. Aus den Papieren des S.S.-Obersturmbannführers Dr Georg Kiesel', in *Nordwestdeutsche Hefte,* no. 2 (Feb 1947) pp. 77-79.

Kordt, E., *Nicht aus den Akten. Die Wilhemstrasse in Frieden und Kreig* (Union Deutsche Verlagsgesellschaft, Stuttgart, 1950).

Laqueur, W. Z., *Young Germany. A History of the German Youth Movement,* with an introduction by R. H. S. Crossman (Basic Books, New York, 1962).

Leber, A., 'Sozialdemokraten um den 20 Juli. Den toten immer lebendigen Freunden', in *Telegraf,* 20 July 1946.

—, *Das Gewissen steht auf. 64 Lebensbilder aus dem deutschen Widerstand 1933-1945* (Mosaik Verlag, Berlin and Frankfurt, 1954).

Leber, J., *Ein Mann geht seinen Weg* (Mosaik Verlag, Berlin and Frankfurt, 1952).

Lilje, H., *Im finstern Tal* (Lätare Verlag, Nuremberg, 1947).

Lochner, L., *What about Germany* (Dodd, Mead, 1942).

Louis Ferdinand von Hohenzollern, *Als Kaiserenkel durch die Welt* (Argon Verlag, Berlin, 1952).

McCloy II, J. J., *Conspiracy against Hitler* (Stuttgart, 1963).

Mann, G., *Deutsche Geschichte des 19 und 20 Jahrhunderts* (Büchergilde Gutenberg, Frankfurt, 1958).

Manstein, E. von, *Verlorene Siege* (Athenäum Verlag, Bonn, 1955). Translated by A. G. Powell as *Lost Victories* (Regnery, 1958).

Manvell, R., and Fraenkel, H., *The July Plot* (Simon & Schuster, 1962).

Meinecke, F., *Die deutsche Katastrophe. Betrachtungen und Erinnerungen* (Brockhaus, Wiesbaden, 1947).

Namier, Sir L., *In the Nazi Era* (St. Martin's, 1952).

Neuhäusler, J., *Kreuz und Hakenkreuz* (Verlag der katholischen Kirche Bayerns, Munich, 1946).

Niemöller, W., *Die evangelische Kirche im Dritten Reich* (Bechauf, Bielefeld, 1956).

O'Donnell, J. P., 'The Case of the Amazing Turncoat', in *Saturday Evening Post,* vol. 227 (1955) pp. 17-18, 50-9.

Pechel, R., *Deutscher Widerstand* (Eugen Rentsch Verlag, Erlenbach and Zurich, 1947).

Peter, K. H. (ed.), *Spiegelbild einer Verschwörung*—the Kaltenbrunner report to Hitler and Bormann on the *coup* of 20 July 1944. Secret documents from the former R.S.H.A. edited by Archiv Peter für historische und zeitgeschichtliche Dokumentation (Seewald Verlag, Stuttgart, 1961).

Philby, H., *My Silent War* (MacGibbon & Kee, 1968).

Picard, M., *Hitler in uns selbst* (Rentsch Verlag, Zurich, 1946).

Pölchau, H., *Die letzten Stunden* (Verlag Volk und Welt, Berlin, 1949).

Prittie, T., *Germans against Hitler* (Hutchinson, 1964).

Rathenau, W., *Gesammelte Schriften* (Fischer Verlag, Berlin, 1918-29).

Rauschning, H., *Gespräche mit Hitler* (Europa Verlag, Zurich, 1939). Translated by J. Murphy as *Voice of Destruction* (Putnam, 1940).

Reck-Malleczewen, F. P., *Tagebuch eines Verzweifelten* (Lorch, Stuttgart, 1947).

Ritter, G., *Carl Goerdeler und die deutsche Widerstandsbewegung* (Deutsche Verlagsanstalt, Stuttgart, 1956).

Rothfels, H., *Die deutsche Opposition gegen Hitler* (Fischer Bücherei, Frankfurt, 1958).

Rudel, H. U., *Dolchstoss oder Legende?* (Rottach-Egern, n.d.).

Salomon, E. von, *Die Geächteten* (Deutsche Buchgemeinschaft, Gütersloh, 1961).

Sauerbruch, F., *Das war mein Leben* (Kindler und Schiermayer, Bad Wörishofen, 1951).

Schacht, H., *Abrechnung mit Hitler* (Rowohlt, Hamburg, 1948). Translated by Edward Fitzgerald as *Account Settled* (Weidenfeld & Nicolson, 1949).

Schellenberg, W., *Memoiren* (Verlag für Politik und Wirtschaft, Cologne, 1956). Translated by Louis Hagen as *The Schellenberg Memoirs,* with an introduction by Alan Bullock (André Deutsch, 1961).

Scheurig, B., *Freies Deutschland. Das Nationalkomitee und der Bund der deutschen Offiziere in der Sowjetunion 1943-1945* (Nymphenburger Verlag, Munich, 1960).

Schlabrendorff, Fabian von, *Offiziere gegen Hitler,* ed. Gero von Gaevernitz (Europa Verlag, Zurich, 1946). *Revolt against Hitler* (Eyre & Spottiswoode, 1948).

Schlange-Schöningen, H., *Am, Tage danach* (Hammerich und Lesser, Hamburg, 1946).

Schoeps, H. J., *Das war Preussen* (Haude und Spener, Berlin, 1964).

Shulman, M., *Defeat in the West* (Secker & Warburg, 1954).

Steltzer, Th., *Von deutscher Politik* (Knecht-Carolusdruckerei, Frankfurt, 1949).

Strölin, K., *Verräter oder Patrioten? Der 20 Juli 1944 und das Recht auf Widerstand* (Vorwerk, Stuttgart, 1952).

Taylor, A. J. P., *The Origins of the Second World War* (Atheneum, 1961).

Trevor-Roper, H. R., *The Last Days of Hitler,* 3rd ed. (Macmillan, 1967).

—, *The Philby Affair* (William Kimber, 1968).

Tschoeltsch, E., 'Zum Fall John', in *Der Notweg*, no. 8 (1954) pp. 6-7.

Vansittart, Lord R., *Black Record. Germans Past and Present* (Hamish Hamilton, 1941).

Weisenborn, G., *Der lautlose Aufstand. Bericht über die Widerstandsbewegung des deutschen Volkes* (Rowohlt, Hamburg, 1953).

Wheeler-Bennett, Sir J., *The Nemesis of Power* (St. Martin's, 1954).

Winnig, A., *Aus 20 Jahren* (Wittig, Hamburg, 1948).

Zeller, E., *Geist der Freiheit. Der zwanzigste Juli* (Müller, Munich, 1963).

Zuckmayer, C., *Carlo Mierendorff. Porträt eines deutschen Sozialisten*, (Suhrkamp Verlag, Berlin, 1949).

Index

Soedermann, Dr Harry, 262, 263
'Soldatensender Calais' (Forces Network Calais), 171–5, 178, 224, 251
Solf, Frau, 132, 135
Sonderegger, Kommissar, 112
Soustelle, 156
Spain, 99; Civil War, 81, 82, 155, 161; Foreign Ministry, 155; Air Force, 158
Specht, General, 148
Speer, Albert, 78
Speidel, 216
Spengler, Oswald, 65, 67
Spreewald, 101
Stalin, Joseph, 49, 50, 84, 86, 139, 209, 243, 248, 256, 287, 314
Stalingrad: German defeat at, 53, 67, 90, 92, 93, 100, 101, 104, 108, 260
Stauffenberg, Berthold, 148
Stauffenberg, Claus von, 77, 92, 125, 126–7, 134, 141, 142, 143, 144, 145, 153–4, 164, 165, 270, 314. *See also* 20 July Plot
Stern, 266
Stettin, 126, 129–30, 137
Stevens, 61, 62
Stieff, General, 107
Stöckert, Heinz, 258, 296
Stockholm, 85, 111, 122, 139
Strauss, Colonel-General, 191–2
Strauss, State Secretary, 290–1
Strong, General, 182
Stülpnagel, General Karl Heinrich von, 35
Sudetenland, 30, 31, 33, 34, 37, 49, 65
Suez crisis, 306
Sulzbach, Captain Herbert (*Zwei lebende Mauern*), 187
Swabia, 300
Sweden, 262–3
Switzerland, 58, 71, 110, 112, 121, 184, 206
Sylt, 136

Taubert, Dr, 207
Taylor, General Telford, 28, 188
Tegel, 114
Tejo, 167
Tempelhof, 84, 145, 146
Terrasa, Juan, 82–3, 85, 96, 97, 98, 99, 122, 127, 134, 136, 145, 155, 157, 158
Teusch, Christine, 208
Thediek, 225
Thomas, General, 58, 59, 63
Thomas, Georg, 36
Thüringer Wald, 258
Tiebel, Erwin, 210

Times Literary Supplement, 31
Tirpitz, Grand Admiral von, 105
Tobruk, 90
Tony, *see* Graham-Meingott, Tony
Tramm, Oskar, 233
Tresckow, Colonel Henning von, 87, 88, 90, 92, 105–6, 107, 120, 123, 125, 209–10
Trettner, Heinz, 187
Trevelyan, Humphrey, 288
Trevor-Roper, Hugh, 248; *Philby Affair*, 313–15
Trott zu Solz, Adam von, 46–7, 55, 58, 101–3, 104, 105, 125, 136, 138, 140, 143, 152, 153
Truelle, M., 145, 156
Truscott, General, 203, 214
Tunis, 108
Turkey, 272
20 July Plot, 20, 52, 53, 131, 133, 136, 138, 146–52, 183, 185, 197, 205

Udet, Ernst, 75–6
Ulanova, 265
Ulbricht, Walter, 225, 226, 257
Union of Soviet Socialist Republics: Red Army, 93, 118, 211, 270, 273, 280; KGB, 104–5, 111, 210, 231, 234, 236, 242, 257, 262, 271, 272, 278, 296, 309, 311, 314
United Europe movement, 191
United Kingdom: House of Commons, 23, 136, 141, 156–7; pre-war policy, 27; Royal Air Force, 54, 99, 134, 159, 163; Secret Service, 58, 61, 62, 81, 158, 159, 166, 271, 272, 276, 292, 294, 313, 314, 315; British Broadcasting Corporation, 85, 97, 119, 133, 155, 159, 172, 176, 177, 178, 183, 271; prisoners of war, 122; Intelligence Corps, 169; Foreign Office, 178, 180, 224, 272; general election (1945), 178; Ministry of Information, 179; German prisoners in, 182–7; War Office, 185, 186; Admiralty, 186; Institute for International Relations, 195; Royal Navy, 271
United Nations, 74
United States of America: Army, 28, 180, 210–11, 215; Navy, 71; Secret Service, 81, 83, 210–11; Air Force, 229
Unruh, Professor Adalbert von, 22
Urals, 74
Uranium Association, 124

'V' weapons, 124; V1, 144, 158; V2, 168